BASEMENT

THIS DAY IN
African-American
Music

TED HOLLAND

POMEGRANATE ARTBOOKS • *San Francisco*

To my mother, Mrs. Erline D. Holland

1010096249

Photographs courtesy Michael Ochs Archives

Page 40, Otis Spann, © 1993 Val Wilmer/Michael Ochs Archives/Venice, CA
Page 47, Marvin Gaye, © 1993 Don Paulsen/Michael Ochs Archives/Venice, CA
Page 72, Prince, © 1992 Sherry Rayn Barnett/Michael Ochs Archives/Venice, CA
Page 77, Eric Dolphy, BMI Photo Archives/Michael Ochs Archives/Venice, CA
Page 78, Clifton Chenier, © 1991 Jon Sievert/Michael Ochs Archives/Venice, CA
Page 89, Buddy Guy, Dick Waterman/Michael Ochs Archives/Venice, CA
Page 91, Robert Cray, © Jon Sievert/Michael Ochs Archives/Venice, CA
Page 99, John Lee Hooker, © 1993 David Corio/Michael Ochs Archives/Venice, CA
Page 110, B. B. King, © 1993 Jon Sievert/Michael Ochs Archives/Venice, CA
Page 116, Miles Davis, BMI Photo Archives/Michael Ochs Archives/Venice, CA
Page 118, Albert Collins, © 1990 Jon Sievert/Michael Ochs Archives/Venice, CA
Page 124, Chuck Berry, © 1991 Alice Ochs/Michael Ochs Archives/Venice, CA
Page 136, W. C. Handy, photographer Hooks Brothers, © 1992 Michael Ochs Archives/Memphis Music & Blues Museum
Page 139, Tina Turner, © 1991 Sherry Rayn Barnett/Michael Ochs Archives/Venice, CA
Page 140, Jimi Hendrix, © 1993 Michael Montfort/Michael Ochs Archives/Venice, CA
Page 149, Eddie "Cleanhead" Vinson, © 1993 Val Wilmer/Michael Ochs Archives/Venice, CA
Page 150, Anita Baker, © 1986 Raymond Boyd/Michael Ochs Archives/Venice, CA

Published by Pomegranate Artbooks
Box 6099, Rohnert Park, California 94927

Library of Congress Cataloging-in-Publication Data
Holland, Ted, 1945–
    This day in African-American music / Ted Holland.
        p.   cm.
    Includes bibliographical references and index.
    ISBN 1-56640-571-8
    1. Afro-Americans — Music — Chronology. 2. Music — United States
— Chronology. I. Title.
    ML3479.H64 1993
    780'.89'96073 — dc20   93-5840
                                                           CIP
                                                           MN

Designed by Bonnie Smetts Design

Printed in Korea

I'd like to thank God; Tom Burke, Katie Burke and Jill Anderson at Pomegranate Artbooks; my wife, Gerri; Cheryle Kinley, Wendy Faucette, Jane Starnes and Wanda Williams, for turning stacks and stacks of stuff into a viable manuscript; Angela Kent, for riding herd on about a million index cards; my mother and dad, for financing my teenage record-store safaris; Stephen Klepka, for teaching me the value of history; John Spencer, for turning me on to Ernie's Record Mart in the tenth grade; Maynard G. Krebs, for being the only cat on prime-time TV in 1959 who dug Diz and Miles; Rick O'Brien, Herb Gidney and the Mystics Revue, for some unbelievable road adventures; Bob Ramsey, for stealing me some time; Lisa and the crew at the Little Professor Bookstore; everybody at IT'S Printing; Gil Caldwell; the public libraries of Charlotte and Cornelius, North Carolina, New Orleans, Atlanta, New York, Chicago and Memphis, as well as the library at Central Piedmont Community College; the staffs of the Delta Blues Museum, the Rhythm and Blues Foundation, Roots and Rhythm, Rhino Records, Don Cornelius Productions and the Wax Museum; the media-relations departments of Antilles, Flying Fish, Shanachie, Blind Pig, Black Top, Alligator, Arista, RCA, Warner, Capitol, Blue Note, Malaco, GRP, Sparrow, Mercury, Columbia and MCA record companies; and, most of all, our cat, Nicky, for never once jumping up onto the middle of my desk throughout this whole operation.

Perhaps our history is the most important thing we have. History is a guide that shows us where and what we were yesterday and how we got to be where and what we are today. It may give us a heady inkling or an ominous warning of what we may become a tomorrow from now.

Musically, it is important to know that before Bobby Brown there was James Brown, and before James Brown there was Louis Jordan; before Boyz II Men there were the Temptations, and before the Temptations there were the Five Royales, and before the Five Royales there were the Inkspots; before Wynton there was Miles, and before Miles there was Diz, and before Diz there was Satchmo; before Aretha wailed, Ruth Brown wailed; before Hammer rapped, Joe Tex rapped; before the Reverend James Cleveland and Shirley Caesar shouted the gospel, Brother Joe May and Mahalia Jackson shouted the gospel; before B. B. King and Lucille played "Austin City Limits," Robert Johnson journeyed down to the Crossroads and met the devil and his hellhound face to face.

Maybe if we remember our musical history, we will remember other things that have shaped our lives: before Bill Clinton there was JFK, and before JFK there was FDR, and before FDR there was Abraham Lincoln; before Saddam Hussein there was Adolph Hitler; before Kuwait there was Vietnam, and before Vietnam there was World War II, and before that there was the American Civil War; before integration there was segregation, and before segregation there was slavery, and before slavery there was freedom....

Ted Holland
Cornelius, North Carolina
September 1993

This Day in
African-American Music

JANUARY 1

1923: Jazz legend Milt Jackson is born in Detroit.

Milt Jackson is considered the premier vibraphonist of the modern jazz era. In the 1940s, along with Dizzy Gillespie, Charlie Parker, Kenny Clarke and Thelonious Monk, Jackson was a pioneer of the revolutionary jazz genre known as bebop. He played his first professional gig at the age of 16. Jackson studied music at Michigan State University and played with several local bands before being discovered by Dizzy Gillespie in 1945.

Milt Jackson's first showcase was as a featured performer with Gillespie's big band, in 1946. In 1952 Milt Jackson cofounded the famous Modern Jazz Quartet, with pianist John Lewis, bassist Percy Heath and drummer Kenny Clarke.

MILT JACKSON

1958: Rapper Grandmaster Flash is born Joseph Saddler in Barbados.

One of the first commercially successful entertainers in the field of rap music, Flash, with his crew, the Furious Five, was responsible for one of the most socially conscious recordings in pop music history: "The Message" (1982), a rhyming funk litany of the evils and desperation of ghetto life. "The Message" hit the pop Top 40 and is seen as a major factor in rap music's becoming a popular platform for reflections on black life, social inequality and politics.

Flash was raised in The Bronx. He and the Furious Five, consisting of rappers Kid Creole, Rahiem, Cowboy, Scorpio and Melle Mel, were signed by the premier rap label, Sugar Hill Records, in 1980. Later that year, they first hit the charts with a song called "Freedom." Follow-ups included "The Birthday Party" (1981), "The Adventures of Grand Faster Flash" and "The Wheels of Steel" (1981) and "It's Nasty" (1982).

In 1984 the crew broke up. Flash continued to record solo, charting with such raps as "Sign of the Time" (1985), "Style" (1986) and "U Know What Time It Is" (1987).

JANUARY 2

1929: Velvet-voiced Arthur Prysock is born in Spartanburg, South Carolina.

In 1944 Prysock joined the Buddy Johnson Orchestra and performed the vocals on the Johnson R&B hits "They All Say I'm the Biggest Fool" (1946) and "Because" (1950). In the early '50s Arthur Prysock went solo.

Prysock had a succession of R&B and pop chart hits, including "I Didn't Sleep a Wink Last Night" (1952), "The Very Thought of You" (1960) and "When Love Is New" (1976). Although he was never accepted as either a mainstream R&B singer or a jazz singer, his lush vocal style made him one of the most noted romantic ballad singers in the history of black music. His brother, Red Prysock, was a noted R&B saxman.

1977: Jazz pianist Erroll Garner dies.

JANUARY 3

1902: Jazz trombonist Preston Jackson is born in New Orleans.

Jackson played with Louis Armstrong and the famed Preservation Hall Jazz Band.

1947: Singer Zulema is born Zulema Cusseaux in Tampa, Florida. Zulema founded the pop singing group Faith, Hope & Charity, with Brenda Hilliard and Albert Bailey. The group hit the black charts in 1970 with "So Much Love" and "Baby Don't Take Your Love." In 1971 Zulema became a solo performer. Her biggest hits were "Wanna Be Where You Are" (1975) and "Change" (1978).

1957: Fats Domino records "I'm Walkin'." Released in mid-March, "I'm Walkin'" soared to number 1 on the R&B charts and number 4 on the pop music charts.

Antoine "Fats" Domino's popular blend of rock 'n' roll, jump blues and quasi-Dixieland jazz was dubbed the New Orleans Sound in the '50s and '60s. One secret of the Fatman's success was that he recorded most of his hits in that city, using the same crew of outstanding session musicians. Between 1950 and 1964, Fats Domino placed 60 songs on the national R&B and pop record charts—songs like "Blue Monday," "Blueberry Hill," "Ain't That a Shame" and "I'm in Love Again."

Along with Domino, trumpeter Dave Bartholomew, who served as arranger and session leader, wrote most of the hit songs. Also on board were drummer Earl Palmer; sax players Red Tyler, Lee Allen and Herb Hardesty; bass player Frank Fields and guitarists Walter Nelson and Ernest McLean.

JANUARY 4

1916: Jazzman and jiveologist Bulee "Slim" Gaillard is born in Detroit.

An accomplished singer, songwriter and composer, and a musician fluent on piano, guitar, vibraphone and tenor sax, Slim Gaillard is best remembered as one of the architects of jive, the rhythmic, nonsensical jazz talk of the '30s and '40s. In fact, Gaillard created his own genre of jive, called "vout." He even wrote a dictionary of vout, just to hip the squares in a hurry. Vout was part poetry, part song lyric and part scat singing with phrases like "Hit me some jive, Jack/Put it in your pocket till I git back/Woah nocky socky/Jing, jing."

In the late '30s, Gaillard teamed with bassist Slam Stewart. Slim and Slam produced the hit record "Flat Foot Floogie with the Floy Floy." By the mid-40's Slim Gaillard was a top nightclub attraction, backed by a wild musi-comedy trio made up of bassist Bam Brown, pianist Dodo Marmarosa and drummer Zutty Singleton. As a solo performer, Gaillard had such hits as "Cement Mixer," "Laughing in Rhythm" and "Down by the Station."

1946: Singer Arthur Conley is born in Atlanta.

"Do you like good music/Sweet soul music?" was the burning question that Conley rode to fame in 1967, the opening line of "Sweet Soul Music," an anthem and tribute to the popular black music of the day. Conley's rendition of the song became one of the best-selling singles of 1967 and is one of today's most-played "oldies."

Conley was fronting his own group, Arthur and the Corvettes, when he was discovered by Otis Redding, who was co-writer and producer of "Sweet Soul Music." Among Arthur Conley's other chart hits are "Funky Street" and "People Sure Act Funny When They Git a Little Money."

JANUARY 5

1931: Award-winning dancer and choreographer Alvin Ailey is born in Rogers, Texas.

Alvin Ailey was largely responsible for the mass appeal that modern dance now enjoys. He basically revolutionized modern dance by taking classical dance and fusing it with African rhythms,

blues, funk and jazz. In 1958 he created the Alvin Ailey Dance Theater, considered one of the most prestigious and creative dance repertory companies in the world today.

Ailey studied at UCLA and joined the Lester Horton Dance Company in 1950. When Horton died, in 1953, Ailey took over the company and became its creative director. In 1954 he went to New York as a featured Broadway dancer. His creative genius came to light in 1958, when he created and choreographed a piece called *Blues Suite*. In 1960 he presented *Revelations*, which mixed modern dance with black gospel music. Other famous pieces created by Ailey include *Cry*, *Night Creatures* and *Solo for Mingus*. Alvin Ailey choreographed works for television specials, motion pictures, Broadway musicals and operas. He also created works for such renowned dance companies as the Joffrey Ballet, the Harkness Ballet, the Paris Opera Ballet and American Ballet Theatre. Alvin Ailey appeared in the films *Showboat*, *Jamaica* and *Sing, Man, Sing*. He died on December 1, 1989.

1932: Vocalist Johnny Adams is born Lathan John Adams in New Orleans.

Many critics and pop music experts consider Adams the quintessential modern R&B singer. He is also one of the true treasures in the rich vault of R&B, blues and jazz talent from the New Orleans area. Johnny Adams has been dubbed the Tan Canary because of his smooth but bluesy style, which incorporates vocalizations ranging from scat to screams. Adams began his singing career with gospel groups—the Soul Revivers, and Bessie Griffin and the Soul Consolators. He began recording in 1959 and has released over 100 singles and many albums but hit the mainstream pop charts only a few times. His best-known hit was "Reconsider Me," which went Top 40 in 1969.

1979: Jazz bassist Charles Mingus dies in Cuernavaca, Mexico.

JANUARY 6

1929: Wilbert Harrison is born in Charlotte, North Carolina.

Harrison recorded one of rock 'n' roll's all-time classic hits, "Kansas City."

One of 23 children, Harrison joined the Navy at age 17. Upon completion of his hitch he settled in Miami, where he won several amateur talent contests by singing a rocking version of Frankie Laine's pop hit "Mule Train." This led to his getting a recording contract with a small label in 1951. His first record was a rocker called "This Woman of Mine," which never made the national charts.

Harrison was basically a one-man band, playing guitar, harmonica, piano and drums. He also performed in a wide variety of musical styles, ranging from blues to gospel to country to calypso. In 1957 he moved to New Jersey and began playing in Newark-area clubs. In his club act he conceived the song that eventually would become "Kansas City." He took the beat and rhythm riffs from "This Woman of Mine" and combined them with the lyrics of a song written by Jerry Leiber and Mike Stoller, "KC Lovin'," which had been recorded by bluesman Little Willie Littlefield in 1952. "Kansas City" was released on Fury Records in April 1959 and soared to number 1 on both the R&B and pop charts.

Wilbert Harrison did not return to the charts for a decade. In 1969 he reappeared, with "Let's Work Together," a blues-rock piece that never placed on the black charts but made Top 40 in the pop polls.

1937: Doris Troy is born Doris Payne in New York City.

Troy's one Top 10 record, "Just One Look," was a monster million-seller in the summer of 1963. (The funky piano riffs were performed by Horace Ott.) "Just One Look" remained near the top of both the pop and soul charts for 14 weeks.

Doris Troy's father was a preacher, and she began singing in church and with assorted gospel music groups, one of which included another future recording star, Dionne Warwick. Troy then joined a jazz trio called the Halos.

In 1959 Doris Troy wrote a song called "How About That?" It became a Top 40 hit for Dee Clark. Troy began singing on demo tapes for other songwriters and doing background vocals for such artists as Chuck Jackson, Solomon Burke and Maxine Brown. She supplemented her income by doing various odd jobs—for example, working as an usherette at the Apollo Theater, where she met James Brown. With Brown's help, she began recording as half of a duo called Jay & Dee.

After the success of 1963's "Just One Look," Doris Troy moved to England and signed with the Beatles' newly formed Apple Records. Over the next few years she continued to do background vocals on such projects as Pink Floyd's *Dark Side of the Moon* LP. Later she returned to New York and became involved in writing and producing gospel music.

1944: Vocalist, pianist, songwriter, producer and arranger Van McCoy is born in Washington, D.C.

McCoy hit the number 1 spot on the pop, soul and disco charts in 1975 with his instrumental single "The Hustle."

Van McCoy produced records for such well-known artists as the Shirelles, Chuck Jackson, Maxine Brown, Gladys Knight and the Pips, the Drifters, the Presidents, Brenda and the Tabulations, Aretha Franklin, David Ruffin, Jackie Wilson, the Stylistics and Peaches & Herb. Among the many songs he wrote were "Baby, I'm Yours," for Barbara Lewis; "When You're Young and in Love," for the Marvelettes; and "Right on the Tip of My Tongue," for Brenda and the Tabulations. Van McCoy died of a heart attack on July 6, 1979.

1947: Singer Shirley Brown is born in West Memphis, Arkansas.

Brown was raised in East St. Louis and worked with bluesman Albert King before signing with Stax Records. She had the 1974 hit "Woman to Woman."

1908: Jazz trumpeter Henry "Red" Allen is born in New Orleans.

Allen, along with Louis Armstrong and Roy Eldridge, was considered a top trumpet stylist of the '30s. Late in his career, Red Allen was described by one jazz critic as "the most creative and avant-garde trumpet player in New York."

Allen's father had led a brass band in New Orleans. Allen joined the famed King Oliver Jazz Band in 1927. He also worked in the big bands of Luis Russell, Fletcher Henderson and Lucky Millinder. He began recording in the late '20s and was best known for jivey pieces like "Ride, Red, Ride," "Yeah, Man," "Queer Notions" and "Nagasaki." In 1940 he formed his own combo and toured the country for the next 14 years. In 1954 he became a regular at a New York bar, the Metropole. His Metropole lineup included legendary saxman Coleman Hawkins, with whom he had played 20 years earlier in Henderson's band. During this period, Allen became something of a cult figure, a musician other musicians came to see and hear. He drew much attention because his stylings were so intricate and out of the ordinary.

Red Allen died of cancer on April 17, 1967, in New York City.

1955: Contralto Marian Anderson debuts with the Metropolitan Opera Company in New York City.

Anderson was the first black singer to join the Met.

1967: Clarence Carter makes his chart debut with a song called "Tell Daddy." Later that year, as "Tell Mama," the song is a hit for Etta James.

Carter, nicknamed "Doctor CC," was born in 1936 in Montgomery, Alabama, and was blind by the age of one. He attended Taladega School for the Blind and learned to play guitar and piano.

He teamed up with vocalist and pianist Calvin Scott, and the pair recorded as Clarence and Calvin for the Fairlane, Duke and Fame labels. In 1966 Scott was injured in an auto accident, and he retired.

Carter began his recording career as a solo artist. His first major hit came in 1968, with the song "Slip Away," which went Top 10 on both the soul and pop charts. He followed it up with smashes like "Too Weak to Fight" (1968), "Snatching It Back" (1969), "The Feeling Is Right" (1969), "Doin' Our Thing" (1969), "I Can't Leave Your Love Alone" (1970) and his million-selling classic "Patches" (1970).

Carter continued to record throughout the '70s and early '80s, but without much success on the charts. Then, in the mid-1980s, he signed with the independent Atlanta-based Ichiban label and released a song called "Strokin'." It caught on with beach-music fans in the Southeast and helped revive Carter's career. Carter is now one of the top attractions on the beach-music club and concert circuit. He was married for a while to pop and gospel vocalist Candi Staton.

1937: British vocalist and pop star Shirley Bassey is born in Cardiff, Wales.

Bassey's first hit in Britain was a cover of Harry Belafonte's "The Banana Boat Song," in 1956.

She is best known to American record buyers for singing the themes of two James Bond thrillers: "Goldfinger" (1965) and "Diamonds Are Forever" (1972). In England, Shirley Bassey's forte has been show tunes. Her booming voice has been heard in "Climb Every Mountain," from *The Sound of Music*, and "As Long As He Needs Me," from *Oliver*.

1940: Little Anthony Gourdine is born in Brooklyn, New York.

As lead singer of the legendary group Little Anthony and the Imperials, he can be heard on "Tears on My Pillow" (1958), "Shimmy, Shimmy KoKo Bop" (1960), "I'm on the Outside Looking In" (1964), "Goin' Out of My Head" (1965), "Hurt So Bad" (1965) and "Take Me Back" (1965).

Little Anthony and the Imperials racked up a total of 19 chart hits

LITTLE ANTHONY

between 1958 and 1975. The group developed a reputation for tight vocal work and was one of the most dynamic stage acts in black music history.

Little Anthony's first group was the Duponts, which he joined in 1955. He left the Duponts to form the Chesters, with Tracy Lord, Ernest Wright, Clarence Collins and Glouster Rogers. In 1958 producer Richard Barrett signed the Chesters to End Records and changed the group's name to Little Anthony and the Imperials.

Little Anthony and the Imperials was one of a very few black groups and entertainers who placed more hits on the pop charts than on the R&B charts.

JANUARY 9

1914: Jazz drummer Kenny Clarke is born in Pittsburgh, Pennsylvania.

In the 1940s Clarke was one of the founders of bebop. In the 1950s he became the original drummer for the famed Modern Jazz Quartet.

In 1935 Clarke began playing with trumpeter Roy Eldridge, and in 1937 he joined Edgar Hayes's band and toured Europe. After short stints with Claude Hopkins and Teddy Hill, Clarke became leader of the house band at Minton's in New York City, where he began his association with what was to become the emerging style of bebop. There, he encouraged and welcomed young musicians like Charlie Parker and Dizzy Gillespie to sit in for jam sessions.

Clarke worked with Louis Armstrong, Ella Fitzgerald, Benny Carter, Red Allen, Coleman Hawkins and Dizzy Gillespie's big band during the 1940s. Toward the end of that decade he moved to France.

In 1951 he returned to the U.S. to work with Billy Eckstine, and in the same year he teamed up with pianist John Lewis and vibist Milt Jackson to back Charlie Parker. This collaboration led to the formation of the Modern Jazz Quartet, with bassist Percy Heath as the fourth member.

Clarke later quit the Modern Jazz Quartet and returned to France. In Europe he became one of the most in-demand jazzmen, both for recording sessions and for live concerts, and worked with jazz greats Miles Davis, Bud Powell, Dexter Gordon, Dizzy Gillespie and Thelonious Monk.

Clarke was an all-around jazz drummer, equally at home in highly improvisational small combo settings or in the straight-ahead mode of the big bands. Unique cymbal work and rimshots punctuated his style.

Kenny Clarke died on January 26, 1985.

1940: Country singer, songwriter and pianist Big Al Downing is born in Lenapah, Oklahoma.

Downing got his start in country music as a session musician on records by honky-tonk queen Wanda Jackson in the '50s. In 1958 he recorded some country tunes for the small White Rock record label.

In the early '60s Downing gave up country to try his hand at R&B. He made a couple of records with Little Esther Phillips, and in the early '70s he signed with Chess Records.

In 1974 and 1975 he hit the black charts with "Baby Let's Talk It Over" and "I'll Be Holding On." In 1978 Al Downing returned to country, signing with the country division of Warner Brothers Records. His first release for Warner, "Mr. Jones," went to number 20 on the national country charts. Over the next nine years, Al Downing placed 14 singles on the country and western charts. His biggest hits were "Touch Me" and "I'll Be Your Fool Once More" (1979).

He never achieved the success of Charley Pride, but Big Al Downing still ranks as one of the few black entertainers to make inroads into country music.

JANUARY 10

1915: Bandleader Woodrow Wilson "Buddy" Johnson is born in Darlington, South Carolina.

Vocalist, composer, arranger and pianist, Buddy Johnson was one of the most unheralded figures in American pop music: he maintained an 18-piece orchestra from 1941 to the mid-1960s, but you won't find his name in the big band almanacs, and even though he placed over 30 hits on the black music charts from 1940 to 1957, most of the R&B books have also overlooked him.

Johnson began playing the piano at the age of four. In 1938 he moved to New York, where he played in small clubs around Harlem. In 1939 he toured Europe with the Cotton Club Revue, which was expelled from Germany during the Nazi "cultural purge."

Johnson started recording in 1940, for Decca Records. His first hit was "Stop Pretending (So Hip You See)." In 1941 he had a super R&B and jukebox smash with "Please Mr. Johnson," which featured his sister Ella Johnson on vocals. Throughout the '40s he remained at the top of the R&B charts, with such hits as "Let's Beat Out Some Love" (1943), "When My Man Comes Home" (1944), "That's the Stuff You Gotta Watch" (1945), "They All Say I'm the Biggest Fool" (1946, with the vocals of a youthful Arthur Prysock), "Fine Brown Frame" (1946) and "Did You See Jackie Robinson Hit the Ball?" (1949). Around New York, Johnson's big band became a fixture at such venues as the Savoy Ballroom, from which Johnson broadcast his own radio show, and the Apollo Theater.

In the '50s Buddy Johnson cranked out the R&B hits "Because, Parts 1 & 2" (1950), "Hittin' on Me" (1953) and "I'm Just Your Fool" (1954). With his string of hits and one of the tightest bands around, Johnson was in demand on the R&B package tours (14 acts plus the Buddy Johnson Big Band) that performed all over the country. In 1952 black dance and show promoters dubbed Johnson King of the One-Nighters.

In the '60s Buddy Johnson reduced his big band to a small combo. As a songwriter, he wrote such well-known tunes as "Since I Fell for You" and "Fine Brown Frame." Johnson died of a brain tumor on February 9, 1977.

1925: Drummer Max Roach is born in Brooklyn, New York.

When it comes to speed and precision jazz drumming, Max Roach is king. Roach first became noted as a major force in modern jazz when he served as Charlie "Bird" Parker's drummer, from

1946 to 1948. During the bebop era, he recorded and played with Thelonious Monk and Dizzy Gillespie.

In 1954 Max Roach assembled one of the most creative and innovative quintets in jazz history. The outfit consisted of Roach on drums, Clifford Brown on trumpet, Sonny Rollins on tenor sax, Richie Powell on piano and George Morrow on bass. In 1956 Brown and Powell were killed in an auto crash.

In the late '50s Max Roach turned his attention to the civil rights movement and collaborated, in 1960, with songwriter Oscar Brown, Jr., and vocalist Abbey Lincoln on the album *We Insist: Freedom Now Suite*. The project's stinging statements prompted the major recording studios and record labels to blacklist Roach for over 20 years. During this period Roach released some of his finest albums, including *Percussion Bitter Sweet*, with Abbey Lincoln and Eric Dolphy, and *Speak, Brother, Speak*, with Clifford Jordan.

MAX ROACH

1935: Bluesman Eddy Clearwater is born in Macon, Mississippi.

A self-taught guitarist, Clearwater has been a stalwart on the Chicago blues scene since the end of the 1950s. His music shows influences of country and western and gospel. In fact, he began his career in gospel music, as both a solo performer and a member of various gospel groups. According to the blues grapevine, when he switched from gospel to blues he was given the name Clearwater by a booking agent who

thought it would be a nice takeoff on singer Muddy Waters's monicker.

1948: Jimmy Ricks & the Ravens debut on the national R&B charts with the Top 10 hit "Write Me a Letter."

The Ravens were formed in New York City in 1945 and first recorded in 1946. They were the first of the successful "bird" doo-wop groups. They were also one of the first black groups to cross over and attract a major following among white audiences. The Ravens were unique in being the first pop group to feature contrasting lead vocalists— deep-voiced bass Jimmy Ricks and high-tenor Maithe Marshall. The other Ravens were tenor Leonard Puzey and baritone Warren Suttles.

"Write Me a Letter" began a string of chart hits for the Ravens. They followed up with "Ol' Man River," "Send for Me If You Need Me," "Bye Bye Baby Blues," "Be On Your Merry Way," "Rick's Blues," "Don't Have to Ride No More," "Rock Me All Night Long," "September Song," "Silent Night"/ "White Christmas" in 1948 and in 1955 their classic "Green Eyes."

In 1956 Jimmy Ricks went solo, and the classic Ravens era ended.

1976: Master bluesman Howlin' Wolf dies of cancer. He is buried in Oakbridge Cemetery, Hillside, Illinois.

JANUARY 11

1904: Bluesman Clarence "Pinetop" Smith is born in Troy, Alabama.
He got his nickname as a child because of his affinity for climbing pine trees.

Pinetop Smith was one of the greatest boogie and blues pianists of the '20s. Self-taught, he began playing parties and clubs in Birmingham, Alabama, in 1918. He moved to Pittsburgh, Pennsylvania, in 1920. In the mid-1920s he joined the vaudeville circuit and often toured with top box-office draws of the day, such as Butter Beans and Susie. When not touring, Pinetop played anywhere he could—at rent parties, in brothels and other settings. At a dance at the Masonic Lodge Hall in Chicago, Pinetop Smith was shot and killed in a fight on March 15, 1929.

1924: Bluesman Slim Harpo is born James Moore in Lobell, Louisiana.

Slim Harpo was one of the few true gutbucket bluesmen to crack the pop music Top 40 charts. In 1961 he placed "Rainin' in My Heart" at number 34, and in 1966 his very danceable "Baby Scratch My Back" was number 16.

Harpo taught himself to play the harmonica. Under the name Harmonica Slim, he began playing juke joints and street corners around Lafayette, Louisiana, in the '40s.

In the '50s he got a job backing up blues guitarist Lightnin' Slim, who recorded for the Louisiana-based Excello label. Excello signed Harpo, too, and for the next several years the team of Lightnin' Slim and Slim Harpo played one-nighters across the country, mostly in small clubs in the South.

After the success of "Baby Scratch My Back," Slim Harpo curtailed his constant touring. He went into the trucking business in Baton Rouge, working only larger venues, such as the Whiskey à Go Go, in Los Angeles, and the Fillmore East, in New York City. He died of a heart attack on January 31, 1970.

JANUARY 12

1904: Blues legend Mississippi Fred McDowell, guitarist and vocalist, is born in Fayette County, Tennessee.

McDowell began playing and singing the blues while earning a living as a farmhand, about 1926. Like most bluesmen of the era, he adopted the hobo life-style, drifting around the South playing everything from Saturday night fish fries to Sunday afternoon church socials. In the late '30s he settled down around Como, Mississippi. McDowell continued to play the blues, and he cut several records, but he was never able to make a living solely from the blues.

In the '60s, widespread interest in folk music and protest songs also rejuvenated interest in the blues, especially acoustic country blues, which was McDowell's forte. Suddenly McDowell, as well as others who had most recently been playing small clubs and church picnics, found themselves playing at the Newport Jazz Festival and the Philadelphia Folk Festival and on the campuses of major colleges and universities. During this time McDowell recorded for the Arhoolie and Vanguard labels, toured Europe, made appearances on PBS and was the subject of film documentaries. He also found himself in the position of guru to a whole new generation of guitar players who wanted to study his licks, among them a young Bonnie Raitt.

The blues revival renewed interest in records that McDowell had cut years earlier. Among Mississippi Fred McDowell's best-known blues recordings are "Kokomo Blues," "Mortgage on My Soul" and "I Ain't Gonna Be Bad No More."

McDowell continued to tour and perform until 1971, when he became ill. He died of cancer on July 3, 1972, in Memphis.

MISSISSIPPI FRED McDOWELL

1909: Vocalist, pianist and bandleader Jay McShann is born James Columbus McShann (nicknamed "Hootie") in Muskogee, Oklahoma.

Jay McShann is an integral figure in the rich history of jazz and R&B from the Kansas City area. He began playing the piano at the age of twelve. After a short stint in college, he worked as an itinerant musician throughout the West before settling in Kansas City, in the early '30s. His first band featured a young sax player named Charlie Parker.

In 1941 McShann was leading a blues 12-piece swing band when he was signed to Decca Records. He had hits with "Confessin' the Blues" and "Hootie Blues" in 1941. In 1943 he scored a huge R&B hit with "Get Me on Your Mind," which featured Al Hibbler on vocals.

McShann's musical career was interrupted by World War II. After a hitch in the Army he regrouped his band, in 1945. It took a while, but McShann found his way back to the top of the R&B charts in 1949, with a song called "Hot Biscuits." His biggest hit was the 1955 tune "Hands Off," with Priscilla Bowman on vocals.

1946: Singer, songwriter, keyboardist, percussionist and record producer George Duke is born in San Rafael, California.

George Duke has been a prolific contributor to the worlds of rock, soul and jazz music. He got his degree in music composition from the San Francisco Music Conservatory in 1967 and formed a jazz trio. After the trio broke up, Duke worked in widely varied musical atmospheres—with the Don Ellis Big Band, jazz violinist Jean-Luc Ponty, Frank Zappa's Mothers of Invention and jazz legend Cannonball Adderley. He was also in demand as a session musician.

In the late 1970s George Duke became an important part of the electronic jazz-funk fusion movement. In 1977 he released the album *Reach for It*. The title cut soared to number 2 on the soul music singles chart and was followed by another hit, "Dukey Stick," in 1978.

In 1981 Duke performed the first of many collaborations with bassist Stanley Clarke. The results were the best-selling LP *The Clarke/Duke Project* and another top-of-the-chart single, "Sweet Baby." Duke also began working as a producer, turning out hit records for Smokey Robinson, Al Jarreau, Deneice Williams and Philip Bailey.

George Duke continued to record top-selling records in his own right throughout the '80s, scoring with the LPs *The Clarke/Duke Project II* (1983), *I Love the Blues* (1984), *Thief in the Night* (1985) and *The Clarke/Duke Project III* (1988) and with the singles "Heroes" (1983) and "Broken Glass" (1986).

1962: The Ikettes' "I'm Blue" debuts on national record charts.

Next to Gladys Knight's Pips and Ray Charles's Raelettes, Ike and Tina Turner's Ikettes are probably the best-known backup singers in the history of rhythm and blues music.

The Ikettes were not just cutie-pies; like Tina Turner, they were nitty-gritty funky and sensual. Their dancing and background vocals were an important part of the famed Ike and Tina Turner Revue, one of the most fiery R&B packages ever to do a string of one-nighters.

Like most other road groups, the Ikettes had numerous turnovers in personnel, sometimes from one night to the next. The first Ikettes were Robbie Montgomery, Sandra Harding and Frances Hodges. Until 1960 they were called the Artettes because they backed a singer named Art Lassiter. Ike Turner had written the song "A Fool in Love" for Lassiter, who was supposed to record it with the Artettes on background vocals. On the day of the recording session, however, Lassiter and Turner had a falling out over money. Lassiter never showed up for the session, and producer Ike Turner got Tina, a vocalist with his Kings of Rhythm, to record the song instead, with the Artettes on backgrounds.

By late 1961 the group consisted of Delores Johnson, Eloise Hester and Jo Armstead. In 1962 Ike Turner produced "I'm Blue," with Johnson on lead vocals and Tina Turner singing background with the Ikettes. The song was leased to Atco Records, and it topped the R&B charts at number 3, landing in the Top 20 on the *Billboard* pop charts.

The most famous trio of Ikettes was the mid-1960s combo of Robbie Montgomery (one of the originals), Vanetta Fields and Jessie Smith. This crew recorded the song "Peaches and Cream," which hit the charts in 1965. Over the years the Ikettes included such now-familiar figures as P. P. Arnold, Bonnie Bramlett and Claudia Linnear.

1979: Donny Hathaway commits suicide in New York City.

Hathaway was a singer, songwriter and keyboardist who topped the charts with hits like "The Ghetto" and such soulful duets with Roberta Flack as "You've Got a Friend," "Where Is the Love" and "The Closer I Get to You." He leapt to his death from the 15th floor of New York's Essex Hotel. He was 33 years old.

JANUARY 14

1916: Tenor saxophonist Thomas Maxwell Davis is born.

Davis was an important figure in the emerging R&B scene during the late '40s and early '50s. Aside from being a top-notch tenor sax "honker," Davis was a songwriter, arranger and record producer.

His best-known hits as a performer were "Popsicle" (1952), and "Slow Walk" (1956). He wrote the song "Bad Bad Whiskey," which became a number 1 R&B hit for Amos Milburn in 1950, and his chilling sax can be heard on most of Milburn's records of that era.

As an arranger, producer and session man, Davis worked with a virtual who's who of R&B, including B. B. King, Amos Milburn, Clarence "Gatemouth" Brown, Sid Austin, Lowell Fulson, Red Prysock, Pee Wee Crayton and Percy Mayfield. He was also the staff arranger and bandleader for the legendary R&B company Aladdin Records.

1938: Songwriter Allen Toussaint is born in New Orleans.

To chronicle the works of Toussaint is basically to chronicle the history of New Orleans R&B of the 1960s. Most top hits of the day from the Crescent City had Toussaint's stamp of excellence on them, since he was a writer, arranger, producer and piano player.

Toussaint formed his first band at the age of 13 and appeared in talent shows at the famed Dew Drop Inn in New Orleans. In the 10th grade he quit school to become a professional musician, playing in the bands of Earl King and Shirley & Lee. He also served as a session musician on some Fats Domino records.

Toussaint didn't have much luck as an artist. Most of the record companies he auditioned for turned him down. When he did record, his work didn't sell very well.

In 1957 he arranged and played on Lee Allen's instrumental hit "Walking with Mister Lee." In 1960 he was hired as staff writer, arranger, producer and session leader for the newly formed Minit Records. It was here that Toussaint came to prominence as a hit-record crafter. He worked with the tops in New Orleans R&B talent, including Irma Thomas, Jessie Hill, Ernie K-Doe, Chris Kenner and Aaron Neville.

Among the songs that Toussaint wrote are "Holy Cow," "Working in a Coal Mine" and "Get Out of My Life Woman," for Lee Dorsey; "Lipstick Traces," for Benny Spellman; "Java," for Al Hirt; "All These Things," for Art Neville and Joe Stampley & the Uniques; "Mother-in-Law" and "A Certain Girl," for Ernie K-Doe; and "Southern Nights," for Glen Campbell. As an arranger, he put together Lee Dorsey's "Ya Ya" and Jessie Hill's unforgettable funk piece "Ooh Poo Pah Doo."

1944: Vocalist Linda Jones is born in Newark, New Jersey.

Jones is best remembered for her 1967 hits "Hypnotized" and "What've I Done to Make You Mad?" Between 1967 and 1972 she placed nine singles on the soul charts. On March 24, 1972, at age 26, she died of diabetes.

1968: Rap star L. L. Cool J. is born James Todd Smith in Queens, New York.

"L. L. Cool J." means "Ladies Love Cool James." He is one of the most commercially successful rappers around.

He first hit the charts in 1985, with the smash "I Can't Live Without My Radio." He followed his initial success with "I'm Bad" (1989), "I Need Love" (1987), "Going Back to Cali" (1988) and "Mama Said Knock You Out" (1990). His best-selling albums include *Bigger & Deffer*, *Walking with a Panther* and *Mama Said Knock You Out*.

JANUARY 15

1930: Blues guitarist Earl Hooker is born in Clarksdale, Mississippi.

Earl Hooker was never a blues superstar. He was most noted as a superb and highly skilled backup musician who lent his talents to the bands of such performers as Otis Rush, Muddy Waters, Joe Hunter, Junior Wells and Junior Parker.

Like most Delta bluesmasters, Hooker was basically a self-taught musician. He had mastered the guitar by the age of 10 and became proficient on harmonica, banjo, drums, mandolin, organ and piano.

After moving to Chicago, in the early '40s, Hooker began playing street-corners and neighborhood gigs with the likes of BoDiddley and Robert Nighthawk. His first professional job came in 1945, as a member of the Nighthawks, a backup band. He later worked with Ike Turner and backed up Sonny Boy Williamson on the famed King Biscuit radio broadcasts on KFFA in Helena, Arkansas.

In 1952, Earl Hooker signed with the King label. He never had a major hit, but he formed his own group and toured throughout the U.S. until the mid-1950s. Later in his career he recorded some sides for Checker Records.

Earl Hooker had a cousin who also made a name for himself in the blues world: John Lee Hooker.

Earl Hooker died of tuberculosis on April 21, 1970, in Chicago.

JANUARY 16

1942: Singer and guitarist Barbara Lynn is born Barbara Lynn Ozen in Beaumont, Texas.

Barbara Lynn is best known for her 1962 Top 10 R&B and pop hit, "You'll Lose a Good Thing." She began her career in the late 1950s, playing boogie and blues in Texas juke joints. She was discovered by producer Huey P. Meaux while fronting her own all-woman group, Bobbie Lynn & the Idols, in a club called Lou Ann's.

Barbara Lynn was unique in the early '60s, as a female guitar player and a left-handed one at that. Today Barbara Lynn continues to play on the thriving R&B club circuit in her native Texas.

1959: Singer Sade (pronounced shah-DAY) is born Helen Folasade Adu in Ibadan, Nigeria.

Sade moved to England at the age of four. In 1980 she joined a musical group while studying fashion design at St. Martin's School of Art, in London. She was signed by Epic Records in 1983. In

1984 she had her first British Top 10 hit, "Your Love Is King."

Her Top 10 hit "Smooth Operator" was one of the most-played songs of 1985, as was its follow-up, "The Sweetest Taboo." Sade's best-selling LPs are *Diamond Life* (1984), *Promise* (1985) and *Stronger Than Pride* (1988).

1973: Gospel legend Clara Ward dies.

Clara Ward was given two lush, extravagant funerals filled with gospel music and celebrities. They were as spectacular as the electrifying concerts that she and her famed Clara Ward Singers were noted for. The first funeral was held in her hometown of Philadelphia, in the Metropolitan Opera House. Among those who sang were gospel great Alex Bradford and superstar Aretha Franklin. The second funeral, the "Going-home service of praise and thanksgiving," was held in Los Angeles.

JANUARY 17

1934: Jazz pianist Cedar Walton is born in Dallas.

Walton is best known for his performances with J. J. Johnson, from 1958 to 1960; Art Farmer, in 1960 and 1961; and drummer Art Blakey, from 1961 to 1964. Walton can also be heard on many of the classic Blue Note and Prestige recordings of the '60s.

1945: Delphonics lead singer William Hart is born in Washington, D.C.

The Delphonics were the group that cemented what came to be known as the Philadelphia Sound in the '60s and '70s. The sound combined a wailing falsetto lead, tight streetcorner-style background harmonies and mellow but dynamic string accompaniment.

The Delphonics were William Hart, his brother Wilbert and Randy Cain. The group had begun in 1965 as the Four Gents, with a fourth member, Ritchie Daniels. The Four Gents cut their first record in 1967, for a small local label called Moonshot. Soon they moved up to the bigger Cameo-Parkway label. While racking up a couple of Philly-area hits at Cameo-Parkway, they

met record producer Stan Watson and writer-producer-arranger Thom Bell.

In 1968 Stan Watson formed his own Philly Groove label. He signed the group to record, with Thom Bell handling their sessions. That year, Ritchie Daniels went into the service, and the trio became the Delphonics.

The Delphonics hit the major record charts in February 1968, with "La La Means I Love You," written by Thom Bell and William Hart. The song remained on the charts for 15 weeks, peaking at number 2 on the soul charts and number 8 on the pop lists. The group quickly followed with a string of Hart-Bell compositions, including "I'm Sorry," "Break Your Promise," "Ready or Not," "You Got Yours and I'll Get Mine," "Didn't I Blow Your Mind This Time" and "Trying to Make a Fool of Me."

In 1971 changes took place for the group, in both personnel and production. Randy Cain left and was replaced by Major Harris. Thom Bell left Philly Groove to begin his own operation.

William Hart took over production, and between 1971 and 1974 the Delphonics charted with "Over and Over," "Walk Right Up to the Sun" and "Tell Me This Is a Dream."

In 1974 Major Harris went solo.

1970: Billy Stewart dies.

Soul music's beloved "Fat Boy" fell victim to the rigors of the road and the one-nighter lifestyle. In the days before glamorous rock tours, even the most successful black singers earned their bread and butter by playing endless strings of one-night stands in small clubs, at arena shows and dances and on college campuses. By the late '60s Billy Stewart was at the top of the charts. He and his band traveled the country in a pair of Cadillacs, hauling their equipment in trailers. Stewart's fee was between $1,200 and $2,000 a night, from which he had to pay the band and all his road expenses.

Stewart and three members of his band—Norman Rich, William Cathey and Rico Hightower—were killed when the car in which they were riding plunged off Interstate 95 into the Neuse River, a mile south of Smithfield, North Carolina. Billy Stewart was 32 years old.

JANUARY 18

1941: Temptations lead singer David Ruffin is born in Meridian, Mississippi.

David Ruffin began singing gospel music as a child, with his family group. Later he was a member of the Dixie Nightingales. He began recording as a solo performer in 1960 and joined the Temptations in 1963.

As a member of the Temptations, Ruffin supplied lead vocals on some of their best-known and best-selling hits, including "My Girl" and "Ain't Too Proud to Beg." In 1968, citing creative differences, Ruffin left the group but remained with Motown Records, resuming his solo career.

David Ruffin scored his first Top 10 hit in 1969, with "My Whole World Ended (the Moment You Left Me)." Follow-ups included "I've Lost Everything I Ever Loved" and "Stand By Me," a duet with his brother, Jimmy Ruffin. In 1975 Ruffin hit number 1 on the soul charts with "Walk Away from Love" and followed it up with the Top 10 soul hits "Heavy Love" and "Everything's Coming Up Love."

In 1982 he participated in the Temptations' Reunion Tour. In the mid-1980s Ruffin teamed up with former Temptation Eddie Kendricks for two midchart hits: "I Couldn't Believe It" and "One More for the Lonely Hearts Club." Ruffin and Kendricks were also featured on the video *Daryll Hall and John Oates Live at the Apollo Theater.*

DAVID RUFFIN

David Ruffin died of a drug overdose on June 1, 1991.

1969: Gospel singer Roberta Martin dies in Chicago.

Roberta Martin was born in Helena, Arkansas, in 1907. In 1931 she joined Chicago's famous Ebenezer Baptist Church choir as a pianist. In 1933 she formed a gospel quartet, the Roberta Martin Singers.

Roberta Martin learned the gospel-music business from the ground up, as a pupil of the Reverend Thomas Dorsey and Sallie Martin. She joined Dorsey and Martin in gospel-music publishing ventures and was instrumental in developing a national concert circuit of churches and arenas. But even though she treated gospel music as a business, Martin was a fiercely religious woman.

By 1945 the Roberta Martin Singers were among the highest-grossing of all gospel performers, earning as much as $3,000 a week, even without recording. They began recording in the late '40s and had hits with "Only a Look" (1948), "Where Can I Go" (in the mid-1950s) and "Certainly Lord" (1958).

Not only was Roberta Martin a powerful singer and an accomplished pianist, she is also rated one of the all-time great arrangers of black gospel music. As she lay in state in Chicago's Mount Pisgah Baptist Church, more than 50,000 fans passed by to pay their last respects.

JANUARY 19

1959: The Platters' "Smoke Gets in Your Eyes" hits the number 1 spot on the pop charts.

Between 1955 and 1959 Tony Williams and the Platters hit number 1 on the pop charts four times. Their first number 1 pop hit was "The Great Pretender," in 1955, followed by "My Prayer" (1956), "Twilight Time" (1958) and "Smoke Gets in Your Eyes."

The song was written in 1933 by the famed songwriting duo of Jerome Kern and Otto Harbach, for the Broadway show *Roberta*. It also hit the number 1 spot on the charts when it was recorded by the Paul Whiteman Orchestra, in 1934.

JANUARY 20

1889: Leadbelly is born Huddie William Ledbetter in Mooringsport, Louisiana, on the Jeter plantation in Caddo parish.

Part black and part Cherokee, he was raised in Leigh, Texas, and got his first musical training as a child from his uncle, Terrell Ledbetter. He learned guitar and harmonica and began playing dives in the Leigh area.

Around 1906 he became a singing hobo, working across the South and playing wherever he could for whatever people would pay. About 1910 he teamed up with another blues legend, Blind Lemon Jefferson, and the two played together off and on for the next four years.

Much of Leadbelly's legend stems from his battles with the law. In 1914 he was arrested for assault in Harrison County, Texas, but escaped from the work farm where he had been sentenced. In 1916 he landed in a Texas prison again, for murder this time. He also spent four years in Louisiana State Prison for attempted murder. Leadbelly's luck began to change in 1930, when he recorded some tunes for the Library of Congress record label. In 1933 he met folklorist John A. Lomax, who was touring southern plantations and prisons, looking for and recording folk music and blues. Through Lomax, Leadbelly cut more records and began to play concerts on college campuses. He moved to New York City in 1937. At the height of his success, he once again found himself in trouble with the law. He spent most of 1939 in Rikers Island Prison, for assault.

In 1940 he was recording for the Bluebird and Biograph labels and had his own weekly radio show. During the early '40s he headlined hootenannies (folk-music concerts) with Woody Guthrie and with Sonny Terry and Brownie McGhee. In 1944 he moved to Los Angeles. He had another radio show there and made a film short: *Three Songs by Leadbelly*. In the late '40s he recorded for the Folkways label, had a series on NBC radio and headlined concerts in the U.S. and Europe.

Leadbelly was a true legend in American folk music. He was called king of the 12-string. The most colorful explanation of his name holds that he carried a load of buckshot in his abdomen from one of his many battles. His playing and his music influenced everyone from Woody Guthrie to Janis Joplin. Separating the myths from the realities of his life has been the work of many books and films.

Leadbelly died of amyotrophic lateral sclerosis (Lou Gehrig's disease) on December 6, 1949, in New York City's Bellevue Hospital. His best-known recordings include "The Bo Weevil," "Old Cotton Fields at Home," "Goodnight, Irene," "Scottsboro Blues" and "Midnight Special."

1936: Bluesman Luther Tucker is born in Memphis.

As a guitarist, Tucker accompanied virtually every well-known bluesman since the early '50s, including Muddy Waters, Otis Rush, Junior Wells, Little Walter, Sunnyland Slim, James Cotton, John Lee Hooker and Charlie Musselwhite. He was also a familiar face on the Chicago blues scene and on the national blues festival circuit.

Luther Tucker died of a heart attack on June 18, 1993.

JANUARY 21

1936: Blues guitarist Snooks Eaglin is born in New Orleans.

Glaucoma had blinded Eaglin by the age of nineteen months. By the age of six he was a self-taught guitarist. He began singing in local churches and played with a local band called the Flamingos, whose pianist was thirteen-year-old Allen Toussaint.

Eaglin signed with Imperial Records in 1960. By the mid-1960s he was a featured performer at the New Orleans Playboy Club. Throughout the '70s, Snooks Eaglin was the main accompanist of the legendary New Orleans music guru Professor Longhair.

1941: Richie Havens is born in Brooklyn, New York.

Havens formed a gospel group at the age of 14. He taught himself to play guitar while working as a portrait artist in

Greenwich Village. He was one of a few black singers who came to prominence in the folk- and protest-song movement of the 1960s. In the early part of that decade he was a regular performer on New York's coffeehouse circuit, playing at the Cafe Wha and the Fat Black Pussy Cat.

In 1963 Havens signed with Venue-Folkways Records and toured with Nina Simone. Later on in the '60s he appeared at the "hippie culture capital," the Fillmore West, in San Francisco. He was featured in the 1967 film *Monterey Jazz* and appeared on "The Tonight Show," "The Ed Sullivan Show" and "The Mike Douglas Show." Richie Havens's dynamic, soul-stirring rendition of "Sometimes I Feel Like a Motherless Child" is one of the highlights of the 1969 concert film *Woodstock*, but his only Top 40 hit came in 1971, with his cover of the Beatles' "Here Comes the Sun."

1942: Edwin Starr is born Charles Hatcher in Nashville.

Starr was raised in Cleveland, Ohio, and began his musical career with a group called the Futuretimes. From 1963 to 1965 he worked with Bill Doggett. In 1965 he was signed to a small Detroit label, Ric-Tic, on which his first hits were released. When Ric-Tic was purchased by Berry Gordy's Motown conglomerate, Starr was signed to Motown's Gordy label, where he remained until the mid-1970s.

Edwin Starr had one of the great "gospelesque" voices of the "soul singers" era. He topped the pop and soul charts with "Agent Double O'Soul" (1965), "Stop Her on Sight (SOS)" (1966), "Twenty-five Miles" (1969), "War" (1970) and "Funky Music Sho Nuff Turns Me On."

1950: Billy Ocean is born Leslie Sebastian Charles in Trinidad.

His story is one of perseverance. When he was nine his family moved to England, and in the early '70s he began performing. Ocean recorded his first single in 1974. Throughout the '70s he continued to make records that hardly sold at all. But in 1977 he had a number 2 single in England, "Red Light Spells Danger." After that, there was little or

nothing until he signed with Jive Records, in 1984.

From the summer of 1984 through 1988, Billy Ocean had a string of Top 10 reggae-tinged pop hits, beginning with "Caribbean Queen," which hit number 1. "Lover Boy" and "Suddenly" followed, reaching number 2 and number 4, respectively. In late 1985 he hit number 2 again, with "When the Going Gets Tough, the Tough Get Going," the theme from the film *The Jewel of the Nile*. "There'll Be No Sad Songs" was number 1 in 1986, and Ocean charted again later that year, with "Love Zone" and "Love Is Forever." His third number 1 hit came in 1988, with "Get Outta My Dreams (and Into My Car)."

1984: Jackie Wilson dies of a stroke suffered onstage at the Latin Casino in Camden, New Jersey, on September 25, 1975. The stroke left him in a coma for over eight years.

Wilson had over 50 singles on the Top 100 charts between 1957 and 1972, but he was broke when he died.

JANUARY 22

1908: Bluesman Hammie Nixon is born in Brownsville, Tennessee.

Nixon began working with Sleepy John Estes in the '20s, and their concert and recording collaboration lasted well into the '60s. Hammie Nixon was one of the most influential early blues harmonica players. Country blues was his specialty, but he also played guitar, jugs, kazoo, Jew's harp, washboard and tub string bass.

He died at home in Brownsville on August 17, 1984.

1915: The Reverend C. L. Franklin is born in Sunflower County, Mississippi.

Clarence Le Vaughn Franklin heard the call from God at the age of 14. He earned his B.A. degree from LeMoyne College. After earning his divinity degree, he was a pastor in Tennessee, Mississippi and New York and became minister of Detroit's New Bethel Baptist Church in 1946.

Franklin was famous for his fiery, inspirational sermons, which he began recording for Chess Records in 1953. His

first recorded sermon was *The 23rd Psalm*. His best-known album is *The Eagle Stirreth Her Nest*, which sold over a million copies. In all, Reverend Franklin recorded over 60 albums of sermons.

Franklin was the father of superstar Aretha Franklin. He died on July 27, 1984.

1924: Jazzman James Louis "J. J." Johnson is born in Indianapolis.

In 1942, at the age of 18, Johnson, who invented the art of bebop trombone and is considered the dominant jazz trombonist of the '40s and '50s, joined Benny Carter's big band. After four years with Carter, he joined the Count Basie band in 1945, where he remained for two years. Johnson then moved on to his own small group and began recording. From 1947 to 1949 he played with Illinois Jacquet's group, recording the hit singles "Jet Propulsion" and "Riffin' at 24th Street" for Bluebird Records. He also played with Dizzy Gillespie in 1949 and 1951. In the early '50s he recorded with Miles Davis.

In 1954 he teamed up with fellow trombonist Kai Winding for two years. In 1961 and 1962 he was once again with Miles Davis, and he played with Sonny Stitt in the mid-1960s.

In 1970 J. J. Johnson moved to Los Angeles, to concentrate on scoring films and TV shows. His most definitive bebop LP is *The Eminent J. J. Johnson*, which features trumpeter Clifford Brown.

1935: Sam Cooke is born in Chicago.

Cooke was one of eight children. His father was a Baptist minister, and young Sam began singing in the church choir at the age of six. As a teenager he joined a gospel group, the Highway Q.C.s. In 1950 Cooke joined the famed Soul Stirrers gospel group. He sang lead on some of the Soul Stirrers' biggest hits, including the classics "Touch the Hem of His Garment" and "Pilgrim of Sorrow." With his sensual vocals and boyish good looks, he became a gospel-music heartthrob.

The Soul Stirrers were recording for Art Rupe's Specialty Records, which also recorded hard-core rock 'n' rollers like Little Richard and Larry Williams.

SAM COOKE

Fearful of backlash from fiercely devout gospel-music buyers, Specialty had never mixed the two musical styles. But in the mid-1950s Cooke became interested in popular music. Cooke expressed this interest to Bumps Blackwell, head of Specialty's A&R (artist and repertoire) department, and Blackwell had Cooke cut a couple of pop tunes, released under the pseudonym Dale Cook.

When Cooke recorded more pop material, he and Blackwell approached Art Rupe about releasing it under Sam Cooke's real name. Rupe refused, on two counts: gospel singers did not sing rock, and Rupe just plain didn't like the new record. He even told Cooke that if he could sell it to another label, he could be released from his gospel contract. Cooke and Blackwell found a buyer in the small Keen label. In October 1957 Keen decided to release Cooke's recording "You Send Me," a song written by Sam's brother, L. C. Cooke. "You Send Me" went to number 1 and remained on the charts more than six months.

As a gospel singer, Sam Cooke was an almost sanctified wailer. But as a pop artist he sang in a voice that was syrupy and mellow. His gospel roots showed in his concert performances.

Between 1957 and 1965 Sam Cooke placed over 40 records on the Top 100 singles charts. His string of hits on the Keen label included "I Love You for Sentimental Reasons," "Everybody Loves to Cha Cha Cha," "Only Sixteen" and "Wonderful World." In 1960 Cooke switched to the bigger RCA label and in August of that year hit the number 2 spot, with "Chain Gang." His RCA Top 10 hits included "Twistin' the Night Away," "Bring It on Home to Me" (with Lou Rawls doing backup) and "Another Saturday Night."

On December 11, 1964, Sam Cooke was shot and killed at a Los Angeles motel. The following month RCA released a double-sided hit, "Shake," which became Cooke's last Top 10 record, and "A Change Is Gonna Come." Many people feel that he recorded the latter because he had a premonition of death.

JANUARY 23

1927: "Professor" Alex Bradford is born in Bessemer, Alabama.

Alex Bradford began his showbiz career at the age of four, as a vaudeville dancer. He was steadily influenced by the sacred and secular music that surrounded him. He joined the Holiness Church at the age of six and founded his first group, the Bronx Gospelaires, as a youngster living in New York City.

After finishing school, Bradford returned to Alabama, where he taught school for a while and acquired the nickname "Professor." With World War II came a stint in the service. Bradford performed at camp shows and moonlighted as a lay preacher at a church near his base.

After the war he moved to Chicago, then the black gospel-music capital of the world, but he made few inroads into gospel music until he met Sallie Martin. With Martin's help, Bradford began writing, performing and recording. He wrote "Since I Met Jesus" for the Roberta Martin Singers and formed his own group, the Bradford Specials.

In the early 1950s, as a gospel singer, organist, pianist, arranger and composer, Professor Alex Bradford came to be known as "the singing rage of the gospel age." His showmanship in the world of gospel music was unmatched; some critics have even suggested that Little Richard stole much of his flamboyance from Alex Bradford.

In June 1953 Bradford recorded his greatest hit, "Too Close to Heaven," which sold over a million copies and made Bradford a household name among gospel-music fans.

Bradford's records were electrifying, but they couldn't hold a candle to his live shows. Most churchfolk had never seen the likes of the Bradford Specials. They wore long, flowing robes of every imaginable color. They not only sang, they danced—smooth, well-choreographed routines to hard music that rocked the roof.

In the '60s things slowed for Professor Bradford, as far as church-based gospel music was concerned. He joined the touring company of a gospel musical, *The Black Nativity*, and traveled across the U.S. and Europe. He also toured in two Vinette Carroll musicals, *Don't Bother Me, I Can't Cope* and *Your Arms Too Short to Box with God*.

Professor Bradford died on February 15, 1978.

1948: Anita Pointer of the Pointer Sisters is born in East Oakland, California.

Both Pointer parents were Church of God ministers, and all four sisters began singing in the church choir. In the late '60s the three oldest—Anita, Ruth and Bonnie—formed a singing group, and June, the youngest, joined a short time later. While performing in local clubs, they came to the attention of legendary rock promoter Bill Graham, who became their manager. They also were hired by record producer Dave Rubinson to do background vocals on records by Boz Scaggs, Taj Mahal, Elvin Bishop and Cold Blood.

The group's first record contract, with Atlantic, failed to produce anything worthwhile, and they also parted company with Graham. Then Rubinson signed the Pointer Sisters to Blue Thumb Records. Their first LP was released in 1973, yielding a Top 20 single, "Yes We Can Can," in the early fall of '73. In 1974 their song "Fairy Tale" went Top 20 on the pop charts and landed on the country charts as well.

In 1978 the Pointer Sisters signed with Planet Records. In the same year Bonnie Pointer left to pursue a solo career, signing with Motown Records. The label switch was just what the Pointer Sisters needed. At Blue Thumb the sisters had performed in a variety of music styles; Planet producer Richard Perry channeled their efforts in one direction: pop, danceable tunes, with appeal to mixed audiences. "Fire" (written by Bruce Springsteen) hit the number 2 spot on the pop charts in late '78. The Pointer Sisters racked up a rapid succession of pop Top 10 records, including "He's So Shy" (1980), "Slow Hand" (1981), "Automatic" (1984), "Jump for My Love" and "Neutron Dance" (1984).

1961: Maxine Brown debuts on the R&B charts with her own composition, "All in My Mind."

The record peaked at number 2 and went Top 20 on the pop charts. Brown followed up with a Top 10 soul hit, "Funny," later in the year. In 1964 Maxine Brown hit the charts again, with "Oh No Not My Baby," and between 1965 and 1967 she charted several times, with a series of duets with Chuck Jackson.

Lilting-voiced Maxine Brown was born in Kingstree, South Carolina, and worked as a model and gospel singer in New York City before embarking on her pop recording career.

1961: Actor and singer Paul Robeson dies of a stroke in Philadelphia.

Star of such films as *Sanders of the River* (1935), *Showboat* (1936), *King Solomon's Mines* (1937) and *The Emperor Jones* (1953), Robeson was sympathetic with the Communist Party–U.S.A. during the '30s. In the '50s, with the atmosphere created by Senator Joseph McCarthy's House Un-American Activities Committee, Robeson was forced to seek work in Europe.

JANUARY 24

1934: Vocalist Ann Cole is born Cynthia Coleman in Newark, New Jersey.

Ann Cole's father was a member of the Coleman Brothers gospel group. In 1949 Cole formed her own gospel group, the Colemanaires. In the '50s she switched to R&B (and changed her name).

Ann Cole's biggest hit was "Are You Satisfied" (1956). She also charted with "Got My Mojo Workin' (But It Just Won't Work on You)" in 1957. (Incidentally, it was Cole, not Muddy Waters, who first recorded that song.) Other hits were "In the Chapel" (1957), "The Love in My Heart " (1958) and "Have Fun" (1962).

As a result of injuries suffered in an auto accident in the '60s, Ann Cole was left an invalid.

1941: Aaron Neville is born in New Orleans.

Neville first made his mark on the world of music in 1966, with his number 1 hit "Tell It Like It Is." In 1977, with his brothers Art, Charles and Cyrille, he founded the Neville Brothers band. The Neville Brothers released their self-titled debut LP in 1978, and in 1981 they released their best-selling *Fiyo on the Bayou*, followed in 1984 by *Neville-A-Zation* and in 1990 by *Legacy: A History of The Neville Brothers*. The music of the Neville Brothers contains elements from every part of the black music experience—funk, blues, gospel, rock and jazz—ranging from spine-tingling ballads to rowdy street rock.

In the '90s Aaron Neville hit the pop charts again, in a series of duets with Linda Ronstadt. One, "All My Life," won the 1990 Grammy for best pop duo.

1953: The Five Royales make their chart debut with "Baby Don't Do It."

One of the greatest R&B groups of all time, the Five Royales—consisting of leader and songwriter Lowman Pauling, Clarence Pauling, Johnny Tanner, Obediah Carter and Johnny Moore—began in Winston-Salem, North Carolina, in 1942, as a gospel group called the Royal Sons. They began recording in the late '40s. In 1951, Lowman Pauling talked the group into switching to R&B. The group's label, Apollo Records, agreed.

The Five Royales' harmonies are a combination of doo-wop and rock-hard jubilee quartet gospel. "Baby Don't Do It" hit number 1 on the R&B charts, as did its follow-up, "Help Me Somebody." Subsequent hits on Apollo included "Crazy, Crazy, Crazy," "Too Much Lovin'," "I Do" and "Laundromat Blues." In the mid-1950s they switched to the King label and kept rolling out the hits, with songs like "Tears of Joy," "Think," "Dedicated to the One I Love" and "The Real Thing."

1970: James "Shep" Sheppard, lead singer and songwriter for Shep & the Limelites, is found murdered in his automobile on the Long Island Expressway in New York. He also had been robbed.

Sheppard's first group, the Heartbeats, was founded in New York in 1954. The other members were Wally Roker, Walter Crump, Robbie Adams and Vernon Walker. Their biggest hit was "A Thousand Miles Away" (1956). When the group broke up, in 1960, Sheppard worked for a while in the restaurant business.

In 1961 he formed Shep & the Limelites, with Clarence Bassett and Charles Baskerville. Success came immediately. Their song "Daddy's Home" hit number 2 on the charts and is one of the most romantic "makeout" and "slow drag" ballads ever recorded. Follow-up ballads included "Ready for Your Love," "Three Steps from the Altar" and "Our Anniversary." Shep & the Limelites and the Heartbeats were two of pop music's all-time best-selling doo-wop groups.

JANUARY 25

1899: Guitarist and singer Sleepy John Estes is born in Ripley, Tennessee.

Estes got his nickname as a child because he suffered from a chronic blood-pressure disorder: easily fatigued, he was forced to do an unusual amount of napping. At the age of six he was blinded in his right eye while playing baseball. By 1950 Estes was completely blind.

He began playing house parties around 1916. In the late '20s he recorded for Victor Records and moved to Chicago in 1930.

The '60s blues revival found Estes playing the Newport Folk Festival and touring Europe, where there was more of a market for his records than in the U.S. In the early '70s he developed a following in Japan, and he toured there in 1974.

Over the years he recorded for a number of labels, including Champion, Decca, Bluebird and Vanguard. Among his best-known songs are "Milk Cow Blues," "Married Woman Blues," "Jailhouse Blues," "Drop Down Mama," "I'm Going Home" and "Rats in My Kitchen."

Sleepy John Estes died of a stroke on June 5, 1977.

1929: Jazz saxophonist Benny Golson is born in Philadelphia.

Benny Golson played a wide variety of jazz and R&B during his career. The artists he appeared with ranged from R&B shouter Bullmoose Jackson and his Bearcats to Lionel Hampton, from Earl Bostic to Art Blakey. In the mid-1950s Jackson sat in and did arrangements for Dizzy Gillespie's Revival Big Band. In 1959 he teamed up with Art Farmer to form the Art Farmer/Benny Golson Jazztet.

1939: Etta James is born Jamesetta Hawkins in Los Angeles.

Etta James was only a teenager, singing with a group called the Peaches, when she was discovered by Johnny Otis, who game James her nickname, "Miss Peaches." After a stint at Otis's Los Angeles nightclub, she was signed by Modern Records.

Her first number 1 R&B hit came in 1955, with "The Wallflower." The record was an "answer" to Hank Ballard's "Work with Me Annie." Originally it had been titled "Roll with Me Henry," but that title was considered too risqué for radio. Another Top 10 R&B hit followed: "Good Rockin' Daddy."

In 1960 James signed with Chess Records' subsidiary, Argo. She compiled a huge list of R&B and Top 40 hits, including "All I Could Do Was Cry," "If I Can't Have You" (1960), "My Dearest Darling" (1960), "At Last" (1961), "Trust in Me" (1961), "Stop the Wedding" (1962), "Pushover" (1963) and "Tell Mama" (1967).

Throughout the '60s and '70s James had a constant battle with drugs, finally licking the problem in the late '70s. Etta James continues to record today, making nightclub, concert and festival appearances. Her recent LPs include *The Seven Year Itch* (1988), *Sticking to My Guns* (1990) and *The Right Time* (1992).

JANUARY 26

1928: Actress and singer Eartha Kitt is born in South Carolina. Kitt recorded several blues and jazz albums but is better known for her film, television, stage and nightclub appearances. The sultry singer's films include *New Faces* (1954), *St. Louis Blues* (1958), *Anna Lucasta* (1958) and *Saint of Devil's Island* (1961). In the mid-1960s she appeared as Catwoman on the campy "Batman" TV series. Later she was blacklisted by the American entertainment industry for expressing her anti–Vietnam War sentiments.

EARTHA KITT

1934: The Apollo Theater presents its first live stage show, *Jazz à la Carte*, featuring Benny Carter and his big band, the Palmer Brothers, Troy Brown, Mabel Scott, Morton & Margot, Aida Ward, the Three Rhythm Kings, 16 female dancers and emcee Ralph Cooper. The feature film of the day was *Criminal-at-Large*. All proceeds went to the Harlem Children's Fresh-Air Fund.

1934: Huey "Piano" Smith, one of the most underrated of the early black rock 'n' rollers, is born in New Orleans.

Smith got his professional start as a teenager, with Guitar Slim's band, and became a well-known session player around the New Orleans area. He was discovered and signed by Johnny Vincent of Ace Records while playing in the band of guitarist Earl King.

Smith and his own group, the Clowns, with lead singer Bobby Marchan and Willie Nettles, James Rivers, Raymond Lewis, Curley Smith, Gerri Hall, John Williams, Jessie Hill and Robert Parker, first hit the pop and R&B charts in 1957, with the rock classic "Rocking Pneumonia and the Boogie- Woogie Flu." They had their biggest hit the following year, with a lyrically nonsensical hodgepodge called "Don't You Just Know It (Daaaayo, Gooba Gooba Gooba, Ah, Ha, Ha, Ha)." The string of hits ended in 1959, when lead singer Marchan left to start a solo career.

Smith's piano work is a boogie-woogie rocker style that is easily distinguishable from the styles of his contemporaries Fats Domino and Little Richard.

1946: The Delta Rhythm Boys make their R&B debut with their biggest hit, "Just a-Sittin' and a-Rockin'."

Like the Mills Brothers and the Ink Spots, the Delta Rhythm Boys were a very successful black vocal group of the '40s. They appeared in musical revues, nightclubs, Broadway shows, films and jukebox "soundies." At the height of its popularity, the group consisted of Carl Jones, Traverse Crawford, Kelsey Pharr, Otha Lee Gaines and arranger and accompanist Rene DeKnight.

Given their success in other venues, the Delta Rhythm Boys didn't concentrate on cutting records until the early '40s. Some of their best-known records are "Dry Bones" (1941), "Gee Ain't I Good to You" (1945) and "If You See Tears in My Eyes" (1950). With personnel changes, the Delta Rhythm Boys continued to perform until the 1980s.

JANUARY 27

1908: Trumpeter and vocalist Oran Thaddeus "Hot Lips" Page is born in Dallas.

Page began his musical career in blues singer Ma Rainey's backup band. He also played behind Bessie Smith and Ida Cox. In the '20s he was with Walter Page's Blue Devils, and in the '30s he was in Bennie Moten's band and Count Basie's Kansas City band.

In 1937 Page moved to New York and formed his own big band, playing lead trumpet and singing lead vocals. Page's voice and choices of material were much more blues-oriented than was true of most other big-band singers of the era.

In 1941 and 1942 he was with Artie Shaw's band and played trumpet in the band's recording of "St. James Infirmary." Page then reassembled his own big band for a while but soon switched to working with a smaller combo. During the '40s he also worked with the bands of Don Redman, Sidney Bechet, Pearl Bailey and Ethel Waters. In 1949 he made his first European tour.

Hot Lips Page died on November 5, 1954, in New York City.

1914: Texas blues guitarist, pianist and vocalist Andrew "Smoky" Hogg is born in West Connie, Texas.

Hogg, the cousin of fellow bluesman Lightnin' Hopkins, began recording for Decca Records in the late 1930s.

He served a stint in the Army and after being discharged, in the mid-1940s, built up a following as a club performer in the Houston area and in Los Angeles. He signed with Modern Records and in 1948 had a Top 10 R&B hit, "Long Tall Mama." He had another one two years later, "Little School Girl."

Smoky Hogg died of a hemorrhaging ulcer on May 1, 1960, in McKinney, Texas.

1918: Blues guitarist Elmore James is born on a farm near Richland, Mississippi.

Legend has it that James learned his craft as a teenager, playing on homemade guitars built from such homely items as brooms. Early on he met and played with bluesman Robert Johnson.

By 1939 James had settled in Belizoni, Mississippi, and was playing with a band that included a trumpet, a sax, a couple of guitars and a drummer.

He served in the Navy during World War II and saw action on Guam. When he came out he played with blues artists Sonny Boy Williamson and Homesick James. Williamson managed to get his own radio show and brought James along as a featured performer. By this time Elmore James had mastered the electric guitar, too.

In 1951 James recorded "Dust My Broom" for Trumpet Records. It was an R&B Top 10 hit. His success prompted James to leave the South for Chicago, where he signed with Meteor Records. His biggest hit on Meteor was "I Believe" (1953). Throughout the '50s and early '60s James was a mainstay on the Chicago blues scene, recording for the Chief, Fire and Chess labels.

Elmore James was one of the most influential guitarists in the history of popular music. He is still revered by slide guitarists, who consider the riffs he used on "Dust My Broom" to be groundbreaking, in terms of sound and artistry. His bottleneck renderings had an unusual "scream" about them, almost as if his amplifier were exploding through the strings. The reverence paid to James as a pioneer guitarist came to light in the '60s when Jimi Hendrix, B. B. King and Johnny Winter named him as a major influence on their own guitar stylings.

James suffered a heart attack and died in Chicago on May 24, 1963.

1930: Singer Bobby "Blue" Bland is born Robert Calvin Bland in Rosemark, Tennessee.

Bland began singing gospel in Memphis in the late '40s. He joined the Beale Streeters, which included B. B. King, Johnny Ace and Roscoe Gordon. When King began making it as a solo performer, Bland served as his chauffeur and valet. He also sang with the Johnny Ace Revue.

Bland first recorded in 1952. In the mid-1950s he signed with Don Robey's Duke label. Bland had his first number 1 hit in 1957, with "Farther Up the Road." From 1957 until about 1967 he found a groove in the pop-hit bluesy tunes usually written by Don Robey, Joe Scott or Joe Medwick. The arrangements were blues rhythm, punctuated by stinging horn interjections arranged by Joe Scott, who also led Bland's road band. With his rich voice, Bland made "blues shouting" acceptable on white pop radio. His biggest hits include "Little Boy Blue" (1958), "I'll Take Care of You" (1959), "I Pity the Fool" (1961), "Turn on Your Love Light" (1961), "Stormy Monday Blues" (1962), "That's the Way Love Is" (1963), "Call on Me" (1963), "These Hands (Small But Mighty)" (1965), "I'm Too Far Gone" (1966), "I Wouldn't Treat a Dog the Way You Treated Me" (1974) and "Members Only" (1985).

In the '70s and '80s Bland teamed up with his old Beale Streeter partner, B. B. King, for a series of recordings and concerts. In a career that continues in the present, Bobby "Blue" Bland has been one of the most commercially successful blues artists in pop music history. He has placed more than 60 singles on the R&B, soul, and black music charts, and almost 40 have crossed over to the Hot 100 pop charts.

BOBBY "BLUE" BLAND

1972: Queen of gospel Mahalia Jackson dies.

Mahalia Jackson's funeral was held in Chicago's Aerie Crown Theater and was more of a gospel-music celebration. It made national headlines and the network news. Celebrities included Mayor Richard Daley, Sammy Davis, Jr., Aretha

Franklin, Ella Fitzgerald, Clara Ward and the Reverend Thomas Dorsey. The climax was Aretha Franklin's singing of "Precious Lord." Several days later a second funeral was held in Jackson's hometown of New Orleans.

JANUARY 28

1950: Larry Darnell's "For You My Love" is the number 1 R&B single.

Darnell, along with Fats Domino and Roy Brown, was an early formulator of the New Orleans R&B sound. In 1949 and 1950 he hit the Top 10 on the R&B charts with such tunes as "I'll Get Along Somehow," "Lost My Baby," "I Love My Baby" and "Oh Babe."

Darnell was born Leo Edward Donald in Columbus, Ohio, in 1929. He settled in New Orleans and was a top attraction at the famed Dew Drop Inn. Larry Darnell died of cancer on July 3, 1983.

JANUARY 29

1920: Bandleader Paul Gayten is born in Kentwood, Louisiana.

A jack-of-all-trades in the R&B music business of the '50s, Gayten was also a vocalist, pianist, session musician, songwriter and arranger and was a Chess Records A&R man in the New Orleans area. He had chart hits with "Since I Fell for You" (1947) and "I'll Never Be Free" (1950). His arrangements and his Paul Gayten Orchestra can be heard on recordings by Clarence "Frogman" Henry and vocalist Arnie Laurie.

1952: Bluesman Willie Dixon dies of a heart attack in Burbank, California.

The best-known blues songwriter in pop music history, Dixon wrote such classics as "Hoochie Coochie Man," "Wang Dang Doodle," "Spoonful" and "Little Red Rooster."

JANUARY 30

1911: Jazz trumpeter Roy Eldridge is born in Pittsburgh, Pennsylvania.

Eldridge learned to play the trumpet from his brother. In the '20s he played with an assortment of bands, including Horace Henderson's Dixie Stompers and Speed Webb's band. In the early '30s he was with McKinney's Cotton Pickers and with the big bands of Teddy Hill, Elmer Snowden and Charlie Johnson. For a while he had his own band, too. In 1935 he joined Fletcher Henderson's orchestra.

Eldridge really came to prominence when he was hired by Gene Krupa, in 1941. One centerpiece of the Krupa band was the hits performed by Eldridge and singer Anita O'Day. When Krupa's band broke up, in 1943, Eldridge joined the CBS radio network band.

Eldridge was a featured soloist with Artie Shaw's big band in 1944 and 1945, but repeated encounters with racism while on tour with the mainly white band prompted him to leave. He soon formed his own band, but the venture was short-lived. In the early '50s he headed for Europe.

Like Miles Davis, Louis Armstrong and Dizzy Gillespie, Roy Eldridge is considered one of jazz's most influential and important trumpet players. Throughout the '50s, '60s and '70s Eldridge played with the likes of Count Basie, Ella Fitzgerald, Gillespie, Oscar Peterson and Benny Goodman. In 1980 he suffered a stroke and was forced into all but total retirement.

1928: Singer Ruth Brown is born Ruth Weston in Portsmouth, Virginia.

Ruth Brown, dubbed "Miss Rhythm," was truly one of the pioneers of R&B music. She began her professional career in 1946, as a vocalist with the Lucky Millinder Band. In 1949 she signed with Atlantic Records and had her first hit, "So Long." She was Atlantic's best-selling artist of the 1950s, placing two dozen singles on the R&B charts between 1949 and 1960. Her greatest hits include "Tear Drops from My Eyes" (1950), "I'll Wait for You" (1951), "5-10-15 Hours" (1952), "Mama He Treat Your Daughter Mean" (1953), "Oh, What a Dream" (1954), "Mambo Baby" (1954), "It's Love Baby (24 Hours a Day)" (1955) and "Lucky Lips" (1957).

By the early 1960s hard-driving R&B records like Ruth Brown's had given way to smoother, less blues-oriented soul music. Strings and mellowness were in; honking and shouting were out. In 1962 Ruth Brown left Atlantic Records.

For most of the period between 1962 and the mid-1970s Brown was out of the music scene. She brought up her children and worked at an assortment of jobs, ranging from domestic help to school bus driver. In the late '70s she began making appearances as an actress on TV sitcoms. She also revived her musical career and appeared in *Hairspray* (1988), a film by John Waters. In 1989 she won a Tony award for her work on Broadway in the play *Black and Blue*.

1946: Singer Jackie Ross is born in St. Louis.

Ross began singing at the age of three on her parents' gospel radio program. She moved to Chicago at the age of eight. When she was signed by Chess Records, she was a vocalist with blues singer Syl Johnson's band. Jackie Ross struck chart gold in the fall of 1964, with her Chess hit "Selfish One."

1959: Singer and dancer Jody Watley is born in Chicago.

In 1974 Watley moved to Los Angeles, where she danced on the popular TV show "Soul Train." In 1977 a record producer hired her as a member of the group Shalamar, along with Jeffrey Daniels and Howard Hewitt. During Watley's tenure, Shalamar had such disco-flavored hits as "Up-Town Festival" (1977), "The Second Time Around" (1979), "Make That Move" (1981), "A Night to Remember" (1982) and "Dead Giveaway" (1983). In 1984 Watley left to pursue a solo career.

Watley came to wide notice in 1987, when her self-titled debut LP landed at number 4 on the *Billboard* charts and produced a string of hit singles, including "Looking for a New Love, "Still a Thrill," "Don't You Want Me" and "Some Kind of Love." The accompanying music video was one of the best of that year's crop and got much play on MTV. Jody Watley had made the transition from "Soul Train" to rock stardom.

1965: The Manhattans make their chart debut.

The Manhattans hailed from Jersey City, New Jersey, and consisted of lead singer George Smith, bass Winifred

Lovett, tenors Sonny Bivens and Wally Kelly and baritone Richard Taylor.

Their first chart record was more rock 'n' roll than soul: "I Wanna Be (Your Everything)." It went to number 12 on the R&B charts and cracked the pop Hot 100. The Manhattans were charting into the 1980s, with releases like "Follow Your Heart" (1965), "One Life to Live" (1972), "There's No Me Without You" (1973), "Don't Take Your Love" (1974), "Hurt" (1975), "I Kinda Miss You" (1976), "It Feels So Good to Be Loved So Bad" (1977), "Am I Loving You" (1978), "Shining Star" and "Crazy" (1983). They had a number 1 soul and pop hit in 1976, with "Kiss and Say Goodbye."

In 1970 George Smith died of spinal meningitis and was replaced by Gerald Alston, who remained until 1988.

THE MANHATTANS

JANUARY 31

1906: Bluesman Roosevelt Sykes is born in Elmar, Arkansas.

Sykes was an accomplished guitarist, organist and pianist and began by playing in churches around Helena, Arkansas. At the age of 12 he ran away from home. He survived by playing piano in gambling houses and joints.

In the late '20s he was recording for the pioneering blues record label Okeh and playing in New York and Chicago. In the '30s he recorded for the Bluebird and Victor labels and acted as a talent scout for Victor and Decca Records.

In the early '40s Sykes settled in Chicago. He formed his own band, the Honeydrippers, and played clubs throughout the South and the Midwest.

Sykes was a prolific recording artist. He had a string of R&B chart hits in 1945 and 1946 for Victor and Bluebird. These included "I Wonder," "Honeydripper" and "Sunny Road." In the '50s he recorded for Imperial and United; in the '60s for Decca and Prestige.

He was constantly on the road, playing clubs, blues and folk festivals and concerts around the U.S. and in Europe.

Called the Honeydripper because of his always dapper appearance, and because of his 1945 hit record by that name, Roosevelt Sykes is considered one of the most important of the Delta bluesmen. Many bluesologists feel that it was Sykes who fueled the transition and helped bridge the gap between acoustic country blues and electric urban blues.

Roosevelt Sykes remained active until his death, on July 11, 1983, in New Orleans.

1928: Flamboyant R&B performer Chuck Willis is born in Atlanta.

Willis was working as a house painter when he began singing with Red McAllister's band. He first recorded in 1951, for the Columbia R&B subsidiary Okeh Records. His first chart hit was "My Story" (1952).

His major career move came in 1956, when he signed with Atlantic Records. His first record for Atlantic, "It's Too Late" (1956), went to number 3 on the black charts. Willis also struck gold with other hits, such as "What Am I Living For" (1958) and "Hang Up My Rock & Roll Shoes" (1958). His biggest hit was his 1957 recording of blues singer Ma Rainey's "C. C. Rider," with which Willis had a number 1 black music chart hit and Top 20 pop chart hit. The song was popular with teenagers, but Willis's wording ("C. C. Rider See What You Has Done") drew the ire of parents and educators for its abominable grammar.

Known as King of the Stroll (after the 1957 dance craze he popularized) and as the Sheik of the Shake (because of his trademark turban), Willis was also a master songwriter. He crafted "The Door Is Still Open" for the Cardinals, "Close Your Eyes" (recorded by the Five Keys and Peaches & Herb) and "Oh, What a Dream" (recorded by Ruth Brown and Patti Page).

Chuck Willis's music was generally accepted by the new rock 'n' roll generation. Willis became both a pop and an R&B star, as well as a top concert performer.

When his career was in full swing, Chuck Willis was injured in a car accident and died of complications on April 10, 1958, in Atlanta.

FEBRUARY 1

1894: Pianist James P. Johnson, known as the father of stride piano, is born in New Brunswick, New Jersey.

Johnson was classically trained, but about 1912 he started playing around New York City—on Coney Island, in tough dives like Dave's Dance Hall, and at rent parties.

Stride piano, an early '20s style that encompassed ragtime, blues, boogie and classical, basically was rent-party piano playing: if you wanted to throw a good rent party, the main ingredient was a good stride pianist. Stride pianists were usually big-handed, big-wristed guys who didn't bother tickling the piano keys; they banged them barrelhouse style—loud, and all night long. Perhaps the best-known of all stride pianists was Fats Waller, who took his lessons from Johnson.

Johnson's reputation grew so much that in 1916 he was hired by the Aeolian Company to cut rolls for player pianos. In 1921 he began recording. One of his first big records was "Carolina Shout."

In 1923 Johnson wrote a theatrical musical, *Runnin' Wild*, which was responsible for introducing the dance craze of the '20s, the Charleston. He also collaborated with poet Langston Hughes on several works, and he wrote such extended musical pieces as *Yamecrow* and *Symphony Harlem*.

During the '20s Johnson wrote hit songs like "If I Could Be with You One Hour Tonight," "Weeping Blues" and "Worried and Lonesome Blues." On piano, he backed Bessie Smith on "Preachin' the Blues." Throughout the '30s and '40s he composed symphonies, toured Europe in musical revues, recorded and played nightclubs.

In 1951 Johnson suffered a disabling stroke. He died on November 17, 1955, in New York.

1939: Jazz pianist Joe Sample is born in Houston.

In 1960 Joe Sample, along with trombonist Wayne Henderson, saxman and bassist Wilton Felder and drummer Nesbert "Stix" Hooper, formed the Jazz Crusaders. The band had originated in 1956 as the Modern Jazz Sextet and included, among others, saxophonist Hubert Laws. In 1972 the group became the Crusaders.

The Jazz Crusaders released their LP *Freedom Sound* in 1961. Their music was called "the Gulf Coast sound" because it was a combination of jazz and the Texas R&B horn sound.

In the '70s the pop-jazz sound of the Crusaders found its way onto the R&B and pop singles charts. "Put It Where You Want It," "Keep That Same Ole Feeling" and "Street Life" gave the Crusaders a younger, more varied audience.

Some of their top LPs were *Old Socks, New Shoes...New Socks, Old Shoes* (1970), *Crusaders I* (1972), *Those Southern Nights* (1976) and *Images* (1978).

In 1978 Wayne Henderson left, and guitarist Larry Carlton came on board. In the same year Joe Sample released his first solo LP, *Rainbow Seeker*. Others followed: *Carmel,* (1979) *Voices in the Rain* (1981), *The Hunter* (1983), *Oasis* (1985) and *Ashes* (1990). Stix Hooper left the group in 1983.

As composer, producer and musician, Joe Sample has worked with B. B. King, Minnie Riperton, Randy Crawford, Bobby "Blue" Bland, Joe Cocker, Steve Winwood and Quincy Jones.

1959: The king of punk funk, Rick James, is born James Johnson in Buffalo.

James got into music after he joined the Navy, then deserted and headed for Canada. In Toronto he joined a band with Neil Young, called the Minah Birds. Later, in England, he joined a group called Main Line. He then moved to Detroit and started the Stone City Band

and was signed by Motown in 1977. His first LP, *Come Get It*, was released in 1978.

From 1978 to 1988 Rick James was a superstar of black pop music. His hard-driving blend of electronic rock, dance music and basic nitty-gritty funk produced two dozen chart singles, including "You and I" (1978), "Mary Jane" (1978), "Bustin' Out" (1979), "Give It to Me Baby" (1981), "Super Freak" (1981), "Standing on the Top" (1982), "Cold Blooded" (1983), "Glow" (1985) and "Loosey's Rap" (1988).

In 1985, however, James's luck had begun to turn. He got into legal difficulties with Motown. His contract was up, but Motown claimed that he still owed an album, and that most of the tracks recorded for what would have been his last Motown LP were unacceptable.

In 1987 he signed with Reprise Records. In the early '90s he found himself in trouble with the law for a variety of drug- and sex-related offenses.

Rick James has also composed for and produced the Mary Jane Girls, comedian Eddie Murphy and Teena Marie.

FEBRUARY 2

1924: Jazz saxophonist Sonny Stitt is born in Boston.

Both of Stitt's parents were music teachers, and so he learned piano, clarinet and sax as a child. As a teenager, he went on the road with Tiny Bradshaw's R&B band. He also played in the bands of Billy Eckstine and Dizzy Gillespie.

One of Stitt's fortes is that he is proficient on alto, tenor and baritone sax.

Stitt began his recording career in 1945, while with Gillespie, and was recognized as the first saxman able to play styles and riffs akin to those of Charlie Parker. (In fact, jazz critics say that because their styles were so similar, Stitt was forced to live in the great Parker's shadow.)

Stitt came into his own around 1949, with a series of recordings on the Prestige label. In 1950 he formed a band with Gene Ammons. By the early '50s Stitt was fronting his own group and recording prolifically. Later in the '50s he played with Gillespie and Art Blakey. In the '60s he worked with Miles Davis; in the '70s, with Blakey, Gillespie and Thelonious Monk. Some of his best LPs are *Night Work*, *POW* and *Moonlight in Vermont*.

Sonny Stitt died of cancer on July 22, 1982.

1956: Sam Cooke and the Soul Stirrers record "Touch the Hem of His Garment," their biggest and best-known single.

The Soul Stirrers were founded in 1934 in Trinity, Texas, by Robert H. Harris, who served as lead singer. Other members of the group were Silas Roy Crain, bassman Jesse Farley, T. L. Bruster and R. B. Robinson. In the late '30s the Soul Stirrers had their own radio show and began recording around 1945 for Aladdin Records. In 1950 they had one of their biggest hits, "By and By." Harris quit the group in the same year: he could no longer handle the constant traveling and the rigors of life on the road. Crain took over initially as lead singer, but in 1951 Sam Cooke, then a teenager, was recruited from the Highway Q.C.s.

With the handsome, vibrant Cooke as lead, the Soul Stirrers enjoyed their greatest success, especially with women gospel-music fans. The group packed churches and arenas to the rafters and recorded such hits as "Jesus, Wash Away My Troubles" and "Nearer to Thee."

Sam Cooke left the group in 1957, to pursue a solo career in pop music. His replacement was Johnnie ("Who's Making Love to Your Old Lady?") Taylor. Over the years, other leads for the Soul Stirrers have been James Medlock, Paul Foster, Leroy Taylor and Willie Rogers.

FEBRUARY 3

1898: Pianist and vocalist Lil Hardin Armstrong is born in Memphis.

Lil Hardin was classically trained. She worked around Chicago as a piano demonstrator for a local department store and played with such bands as Sugar Johnny's Creole Orchestra and Freddie Keppard's Original Creole Orchestra.

She met trumpeter Louis Armstrong when both were playing in King Olwin's Creole Jazz Band. They were married on February 5, 1924. Soon she formed her own band, with Louis out front.

According to many jazz sources, Lil Hardin Armstrong was the driving force behind the early success of her husband. She coaxed and encouraged him and often suggested bits that would make his stylings more distinctive. But the marriage didn't work out. They separated in the early 1930s and were divorced in 1938. There was also a messy court battle over royalties for the music that they had written.

At one point, she billed herself as "Mrs. Louis Armstrong."

For the last 30 years of her life, Lil Hardin Armstrong was a cabaret and club pianist around Chicago. She also led her own all-woman band and was a house musician for Decca records. She died of a heart attack on August 27, 1971, in Chicago.

1933: Varetta Dillard, one of the great R&B singers of the '50s, is born in New York.

Dillard was raised in the Bronx. She was working as a secretary when she was discovered singing in an Apollo Theater amateur-night contest and signed by Savoy Records. She chalked up hits like "Easy, Easy, Baby" (1952), "Them There Eyes" (1952), "Mercy Mr. Percy" (1953), "You're the Answer to My Prayers" (1955) and "Promise Mr. Thomas" (1955).

1935: Johnny "Guitar" Watson, a commercially successful bluesman since the early '50s, is born in Houston.

Watson moved to Los Angeles and, after playing in amateur contests, found work in the bands of Big Jay McNeely and Joe Houston, under the name Young John Watson. He began recording in 1952. He had his first R&B hit in 1955, with "Those Lonely, Lonely

Nights," and another in 1962, with "Cuttin' In." In between hits, he worked with rock 'n' roller Larry Williams. In the late '60s Okeh Records teamed Watson and Williams for a series of recordings.

Watson's most commercially successful records came in the 1970s, when he released a series of singles and LPs best described as funk-backed blues. His biggest hit of the period was "A Real Mother for Ya," which went to number 5 on the soul charts in 1977. Another hit for Watson during this period was "Ain't That a Bitch."

1943: Singer Dennis Edwards is born in Birmingham, Alabama.

When David Ruffin left the Temptations, in 1968, Dennis Edwards, formerly of the Contours, took his place as lead singer. Edwards sang on "Cloud Nine," "Psychedelic Shack," "Runaway Child Running Wild" and "Papa Was a Rolling Stone."

In 1978 Edwards left the Temptations, to try a solo career, but he returned to the group in 1980. In 1984 he tried again and finally got his solo career in gear, with a number 2 hit on the black charts, "Don't Look Any Further." He followed up with "You're My Aphrodisiac" and "Coolin' Out."

In 1987 Dennis Edwards returned once more to the Temptations.

1928: Chicago's famed Regal Theater opens.

The Regal, the Apollo in New York, the Howard in Washington, D.C., the Uptown in Philadelphia and the Royal in Baltimore were the leading venues for black stage shows in the '30s, '40s, '50s and '60s. They presented the stars of jazz, gospel, blues and R&B, often featuring seven shows a day, along with a feature film. At one point these were the crown jewels of the Theater Owners' Booking Association (TOBA), a network across the U.S. Many performers said that TOBA stood for "tough on black asses" because of the rigorous show and travel schedules.

The Regal opened at high noon on a Saturday. It seated 3,500. An adult ticket cost 50 cents; kids got in for 15 cents. The theater closed in the '70s.

1956: James Brown records "Please, Please, Please" and launches his fantastic recording career.

The song, by Brown and Johnny Terry, was recorded at the King Records studios in Cincinnati and released on Federal Records in March. Background vocals were supplied by the Famous Flames: Bobby Byrd, Johnny Terry, Sylvester Keels and Nash Knox. The musicians in the session were Nafloyd Scott on guitar, Wilbert Smith and Ray Felder on tenor sax, Fats Gonder on piano, Clarence Nash on bass and Edwison Gore on drums.

Brown and the Flames had built a reputation in Georgia, where they were discovered by Ralph Bass, who signed them to a contract and gave them a $200 advance. Brown and the Flames drove up from Augusta, Georgia, to Cincinnati for their first recording session. In three hours they recorded four sides: "Please, Please, Please," "I Feel That Old Feeling Coming On," "I Don't Know" and "Why Do You Do Me."

"Please, Please, Please" was almost not released. Bass took the record to his boss, King owner Syd Nathan, and Nathan hated it. He threatened not to release it and to fire Bass, too. But, upon its release, "Please, Please, Please" peaked at number 5 on the R&B charts and remained on the charts for 19 weeks.

JAMES BROWN

FEBRUARY 4

1970: The Jackson Five's "I Want You Back" is the number 1 pop song.

The song was their debut single and the first of four consecutive number 1 pop hits for the Jacksons in 1970. Michael, Jackie, Tito, Jermaine and Marlon Jackson followed up with "ABC," "The Love You Save" and "I'll Be There."

FEBRUARY 5

1941: Singer and songwriter Barrett Strong is born in Mississippi.

Strong was introduced to Berry Gordy, Jr., in 1957 by Jackie Wilson. Gordy and Strong worked together on several projects. Barrett Strong had the first hit for Motown. In early 1960 his recording of "Money (That's What I Want)" landed at number 2 on the R&B charts and in the Top 40 on the pop charts.

Strong later teamed up with Norman Whitfield, and the two became one of Motown's best and most prolific writer-producer pairs. They were responsible for such Temptations hits as "Just My Imagination," "Papa Was a Rolling Stone," "Ball of Confusion," "Cloud Nine," "I Wish It Would Rain" and "I Can't Get Next to You." Whitfield and Strong also collaborated on recordings for other Motown artists, including "War," for Edwin Starr, and "Smiling Faces," for the Undisputed Truth.

1969: Singer and dancer Bobby Brown, a superstar of the '80s and '90s, is born in Boston.

With Ralph Tresvant, Ronald DeVoe, Michael Bivins and Ricky Bell, Brown formed the highly successful New Edition in the early '80s. New Edition posted hits like "Candy Girl" (1983), "Is This The End" (1983), "Cool It Now" (1984), "Mr. Telephone Man (1984), "Lost in Love" (1985), "Count Me Out" (1985), "A Little Bit of Love" (1986) and "With You All the Way" (1986).

In 1986 Brown went solo and scored that year with a number 1 black chart hit, "Girlfriend." Brown reached megastardom with the release of his 1988 LP *Don't Be Cruel*. With its accompanying videos, it yielded a pair of dynamite Top 10 singles, "My Prerogative" and "Every Little Step."

Bobby Brown is noted for his fiery, well-choreographed hip-hop dance routines, and his live stage show has made him a top box-office draw. He is married to singer Whitney Houston.

FEBRUARY 6

1944: Singer Willie Tee is born Wilson Turbenton in New Orleans.

Tee is best known for his "pimp songs" "Teasin' You" (Top 10 R&B in 1965) and "Thank You, John."

1945: Singer Bob Marley, who consolidated the style of Jamaican music known today as reggae, is born in Kingston, Jamaica.

While in school, Marley met Peter Tosh and Bunny Wailer. Together they formed a group called the Wailers, in 1964, and the group recorded what was considered to be the first reggae music, combining Latin, gospel, calypso, jazz and ska influences with a Jamaican musical style called "rock steady." The most important ingredient in reggae is the lyrics.

The group had a best-seller on Jamaica with a song called "Summer Dawn." In 1966 the Wailers broke up, and Marley moved to the U.S. with his mother, but he returned to Jamaica to avoid U.S. military service. He, Tosh and Wailer reorganized the Wailers and had an international hit with the single "Small Axe."

Marley began to study the teachings of black-rights advocate Marcus Garvey and became a devout Rastafarian. He and Bunny Wailer were arrested for marijuana possession in 1968.

Marley first became known to most Americans in 1973, for writing the number 1 hit "Stir It Up," recorded by Johnny Nash. The following year, rock guitarist Eric Clapton took Marley's "I Shot the Sheriff" to number 1. Marley used the royalties from these songs to set up his own small label and was later signed to Island Records.

Bob Marley and the Wailers toured Europe and the U.S. before Wailer and Tosh, unhappy with the financial arrangements, quit the group. To replace Wailer and Tosh, Marley recruited a female backup group to do vocals. It was called the I-Threes and consisted of Marley's wife, Rita; Judy Mowatt; and Marcia Griffiths.

In 1975 Marley record the LP *Natty Dread*, considered a classic by music critics. It was also a best-seller. Some of his other well-known albums are *Jah Live* (1975), *Exodus* (1977), *Babylon by Bus* (1978) and *Uprising* (1980).

Marley's highly political lyrics made him enemies at home. In December 1976 he was shot four times by members of a political gang. He moved to Miami, where he remained for 18 months, but later he returned triumphant to Jamaica.

During a 1980 world tour Marley developed brain cancer. He died in Miami on May 11, 1981. He left no will, but he did leave millions of dollars in royalties, as well as scores of heirs. Today the legal fight for his estate rages on.

1950: Natalie Cole, daughter of Nat "King" Cole, is born in Los Angeles.

Cole made her singing debut with her father, at the age of 11. After graduating from the University of Massachusetts, in 1972, she embarked on a career as a club performer.

While appearing in Chicago, Cole was approached by record producers Marvin Yancy (whom she later married) and Chuck Jackson about cutting an album. Once the LP was finished, it took a while to find a buyer for it. Finally it was bought and released by Capitol Records. It was titled *Inseparable* and provided Cole in 1975 with a pair of single hits, "This Will Be" and the title cut. It also won her Grammy awards as best new artist and best R&B vocalist.

Her second album produced another hit single, "Sophisticated Lady," and netted another Grammy for Cole, this time as best R&B vocalist. In the late '70s she had pop and R&B hits with "Mr. Melody" (1976), "I've Got Love on My Mind" (1977) and "Over Love" (1978). Her albums of the era included *Unpredictable*, *Thankful*, *I've Got Love on My Mind* and *Natalie—Live*.

For the next few years Natalie Cole's career was shelved by drug and personal problems. She returned to recording in the mid-1980s. Her 1986 album *Everlasting* gave her several hits, including "Jump Start" and the Top 10 recording "Pink Cadillac."

In 1989 she hit number 3 with the single "Miss You Like Crazy." In 1991 Natalie Cole recorded and released her masterpiece LP, *Unforgettable*, a tribute to the music of her father. In terms of both music and production, *Unforgettable* is one of the best LPs ever recorded.

1988: Public Enemy, one of rap music's most successful and controversial groups, makes its chart debut with "Bring the Noise."

Public Enemy's stated mission is to champion the cause of the so-called black underclass, which the group has done with a series of best-selling LPs, including *Yo: Bum Rush the Show*, *It Takes a Nation of Millions to Hold Us Back* and *Fear of a Black Planet*. Public Enemy's hard-hitting lyrics dwell on political and social ills. But the group has also been accused of being anti-white, anti-gay, anti-Semitic and anti-American.

Some rappers come across as gangsters; Public Enemy presents itself as a paramilitary outfit, complete with a private, uniformed security force. Group members are rappers Chuck D (Carlton Ridenhour) and Flavor-Flav (William Drayton) and deejay Terminator X (Norman Rogers). Their best-selling single raps include "Don't Believe the Hype" and "Fight the Powers That Be."

FEBRUARY 7

1883: Ragtime pianist Eubie Blake is born James Herbert Blake in Baltimore.

Eubie Blake learned to play ragtime piano by listening to the music played in gambling dens and whorehouses. As a child, he would sneak off from his devoutly religious mother, go to the risky side of town and dig the music. By the time he was 15 he was playing in an establishment called Aggie Sheldon's. At the age of 16 he wrote his first piano rag, "The Charleston Rag." In 1914 he wrote "Fizz Water Rag" and "The Chevy Chase Rag." In 1915, while playing with Joe Porter's Serenaders, he met Noble Sissle. Blake and Sissle began writing together and wrote a hit song, "It's All Your Fault," for Sophie Tucker.

Sissle and Blake were also a top nightclub act. In 1921 they landed on Broadway with a show they had written, *Shuffle Along*, the first all-black Broadway musical.

They wrote other musicals and revues, including *Plantation Review*, *Revue Nègre*, *Rhapsody in Black* and *Bamville Review*. In collaboration with Andy Razaf, Blake also wrote the musical *Blackbirds of 1930*, which yielded a hit rag, "Memories of You."

Throughout the '30s Blake continued to score musicals. In the '40s, during the war, he and Sissle teamed up again to form their own USO show. After the war, Blake went to college for a degree in music.

In 1959 he recorded the album *Wizard of the Ragtime Piano*. In 1965 he appeared at the Newport Jazz Festival, and in 1974 he recorded a "live" album at the Montreux Jazz Festival.

Eubie Blake performed until he died, on February 12, 1983, five days after celebrating his 100th birthday.

1934: Earl King, one of the best R&B and blues guitarists to come out of New Orleans, is born Earl Johnson. In the '50s and early '60s he had such hits as "Trick Bag" and "Those Lonely, Lonely Nights."

1934: King Curtis, the number 1 soul saxophonist of the '60s, is born Curtis Ously in Fort Worth, Texas.

Curtis began his career in 1950 and was soon touring in Lionel Hampton's band. He also played in Alan Freed's rock 'n' roll show band after moving to New York.

Curtis played a blend of jazz, soul and R&B honk. Besides having the chart hits "Soul Twist" (1962), "Soul Serenade" (1964), "Memphis Soul Stew" (1967) and "Ode to Billy Joe" (1967), he was one of the most in-demand session musicians of the era. His work supported Aretha Franklin, Bobby Darin, Brook Benton, Nat "King" Cole, the Coasters, Andy Williams and the Shirelles.

King Curtis was stabbed to death outside his New York apartment house on August 14, 1971.

KING CURTIS

FEBRUARY 8

1889: Bluesman Lonnie Johnson is born Alonzo Johnson in New Orleans.

Johnson's dad was a musician, and Johnson learned guitar and violin as a child. By the age of 13 he was already a working musician in the Storyville red-light district of New Orleans. From 1910 to 1917 he worked on riverboats, in tent shows and on various theater circuits.

In 1925 he joined the pioneering Okeh Records label, not only as a recording artist but also as a staff musician. During this period he recorded with Louis Armstrong's Hot Five, and these recordings are considered some of Johnson's best work. In 1927 he recorded with Duke Ellington. In 1929 he had his own radio show in New York City.

During the '30s Johnson recorded for the Columbia, Decca and Blue Bird labels. Some of his blues records had unique titles, like "Got the Blues for Murder Only and She's Making Whoopee in Hell Tonight."

In 1947 he signed with King Records and had a string of R&B chart hits, including "Tomorrow Night," which went to number 1 in 1948, "Pleasing You As Long As I Live" (1948), "So Tired" (1949) and "Confused" (1950).

Lonnie Johnson should be required listening for anyone who is serious about picking a guitar. His key was his versatility. He was equally at home playing a lyrical, intricate jazz riff or banging out a down-home blues stomp. He was also an accomplished pianist and violinist. At one time he was billed as the world's greatest blues singer. What really brings his talent and stature to light, however, is the long and widely varied list of guitar players who name Johnson as a major influence on their own styles. The list includes jazzmen like the great Charlie Christian, as well as bluesmen like B. B. King and Albert King, T-Bone Walker, Robert Johnson, Lowell Fulson, Lightnin' Hopkins and even country picker Cal Smith.

Lonnie Johnson remained a working musician until he suffered a fatal stroke, on June 16, 1970, in Toronto.

1929: Vocalist and pianist Floyd Dixon is born in Marshall, Texas.

Floyd Dixon moved to Los Angeles when he was 13. He decided he wanted to be a singer when he heard records by Charles Brown and Amos Milburn. He taught himself to play piano. He began entering amateur contests and won first prize at both the Million Dollar Theater and the Barrelhouse nightclub.

Dixon came to be regarded as one of the top R&B keyboardists on the West Coast and began recording in 1949 with groups like Johnny Moore's Three Blazers and Eddie Williams and the Brown Buddies.

He hit the charts in '49, with a song called "Dallas Blues." He also did the vocals on an Eddie Williams hit of the same year, "Broken Hearted." Other best-selling singles by Floyd Dixon are "Mississippi Blues" (1949), "Sad Journey Blues" (1950), "Walking and Talking" (1950), "Telephone Blues" (1951), "Call Operator 210" (1952), "Red Cherries" (1952), "The River" (1952) and "Tired, Broke and Busted" (1952).

Floyd Dixon continues to perform and record today. His latest LP is *Boogie Bear Woman*.

1938: Singer and guitarist Ray Sharpe is born in Fort Worth, Texas.

Sharpe hit the Top 20 in 1959, with a catchy rocker called "Linda Lu." In the early '80s he had a top-selling beach-music LP, *The Texas Boogie Blues*.

1941: Chicago-based singer, songwriter and producer Otis Leaville is born in Atlanta.

Leaville got into music because of his association with a boyhood chum, Major Lance, and he hit the soul Top 10 in 1965, with "I Love You."

1969: The Chi-Lites make their chart debut with "Give It Away," which reached number 10 on the soul charts.

Lead singer and chief songwriter Eugene Record, Robert Lester, Marshall Thompson and Creadel Jones made up the Chi-Lites. In 1972 they had a number 1 pop hit with their ballad "Oh Girl." A previous ballad of theirs, "Have You Seen Her," had reached number 3. Other best-sellers by the Chi-Lites include "Are You My Woman" (1970), "Give More Power to the People" (1971), "The Coldest Days of My Life" (1972), "A Letter to Myself" (1973), "Stoned Out of My Mind" (1973), "Toby" (1973) and "There Will Never Be Any Pearl" (1974).

Eugene Record went solo in 1976. In the same year, the Chi-Lites were prosecuted for income-tax evasion.

The Chi-Lites regrouped in 1980. In 1983 they had a Top 10 black chart hit, "Bottoms Up."

FEBRUARY 9

1937: West Coast singer, guitarist and pianist Johnny Heartsman is born in San Francisco.

Heartsman had his biggest hit in 1957, with "Johnny's House Party."

1943: Singer Barbara Lewis is born in South Lyon, Michigan.

Barbara Lewis was discovered by producer Ollie McLaughlin. Her first Top 10 pop and soul hit came in 1963, with "Hello Stranger." She followed up with "Puppy Love" (1964), "Baby, I'm Yours" (1965) and "Make Me Your Baby" (1965).

In the late '60s Barbara Lewis retired from the music business.

FEBRUARY 10

1927: Opera singer Leontyne Price is born in Laurel, Mississippi.

Price studied at Central State College and at the Juilliard School of Music. She began her career in the early 1950s, as a soloist and recitalist with symphony orchestras throughout the U.S., Canada and Europe.

In 1957 she made her debut with the San Francisco Opera, playing Mme. Ledoine in *Prologues des Carmelites*. She also frequently appeared on the NBC television network.

Price has performed in the opera capitals of the world—Vienna in 1958, Berlin in 1964 and Rome in 1966—and gave a recital at the Brussels World's Fair in 1968. She also made several appearances at Milan's famed La Scala and at the Metropolitan Opera in New York. She has made many tours for the U.S. State Department and has won more than 20 Grammy awards for her classical recordings. One of Leontyne Price's most famous roles is as Bess in the opera *Porgy and Bess*.

1932: Zydeco performer Rockin' Dopsie (pronounced DOOP-see) is born Alton Jay Rubin in Carencro, Louisiana.

Dopsie is recognized as one of the world's best accordion players. He learned how to play the instrument from his father at 14.

When zydeco music's king, Clifton Chenier, died, Rockin' Dopsie became the foremost exponent of this Louisiana-based musical style, which incorporates cajun, country and blues.

Rockin' Dopsie is often called "the hardest-working man in zydeco land." Among his best-selling albums are *Big Bad Zydeco*, *Good Rockin'* and *Hold On*.

1939: Singer Roberta Flack, one of the best-selling pop music artists of the '70s and early '80s, is born in Asheville, North Carolina.

Roberta Flack learned to play the piano as a youngster, and she attended Howard University on a music scholarship. After graduation she took a job teaching school.

In 1968 she began performing in clubs around Washington, D.C., and was spotted by jazzman Les McCann, who arranged an audition with Atlantic Records.

Her debut LP, *First Take*, went to number 1. Her other best-selling LPs include *Chapter 3*, *Killing Me Softly with His Song*, *I'm the One* and *Quiet Fire*.

In 1972 Flack and Donny Hathaway had a number 1 soul single, "Where Is the Love." In the early '80s she recorded several duets with Peabo Bryson. Other hits by Roberta Flack are "You've Got a Friend (1971), "The First Time Ever I Saw Your Face" (1972), "Killing Me Softly with His Song" (1973), "Feel Like Makin' Love (1974), "The Closer I Get to You" (1978), "You Are My Heaven" (1980) and "Tonight I Celebrate My Love" (1983).

FEBRUARY 11

1908: Bluesman and folk singer Josh White is born in Greenville, South Carolina.

Eric Burdon and the Animals had the biggest hit record of the blues song "House of the Rising Sun," but it was Josh White who first brought the song to notice.

Josh White began singing in choirs at the Church of God, where his father was a preacher. He got interested in the blues when he was hired as a guide for a street-corner bluesman named Blind John Henry Arnold. White then dropped out of school and worked as a combination guide and accompanist for Arnold and several other singers, including Blind Blake and Blind Joe Taggart.

In the early '20s he went to Chicago with Arnold. White first recorded with Blind Joe Taggart around 1928. In 1929 he returned home to finish high school.

In the '30s White moved to New York City and formed the Josh White Singers. The group performed in a variety of musical styles, from blues to gospel, working with such artists as Paul Robeson and Leadbelly in venues that ranged from churches to cafe society.

In 1940 White debuted on the CBS radio show "Back Where I Come From," which featured down-home music and such artists as Woody Guthrie and Sonny Terry and Brownie McGhee. Throughout the '40s White continued to appear in musical revues, clubs and films, including *The Crimson Canary*.

He entertained President Franklin D. Roosevelt at the White House in 1941. In 1942 he appeared with Paul Robeson in the Langston Hughes operetta *The Man Who Went to War*. In 1944 he appeared at Carnegie Hall.

With the coming of TV, White was a guest on "The Arthur Godfrey Show." During the folk-music craze of the early '60s he appeared on the TV show "Hootenanny." He also recorded for the Electra and ABC-Paramount labels and published the best-selling *Josh White Song Book* and the *Josh White Guitar Method* instruction books. His son, Josh White, Jr., also began making a name for himself as a folk singer.

Josh White died during open-heart surgery on September 5, 1969.

JOSH WHITE

1937: Phillip Walker, one of the best of the current crop of electric bluesmen, is born in Welsh, Louisiana.

He began his career as a 13-year-old, sitting in with blues players around Port Arthur, Texas. He cut his teeth in the backup bands of such artists as Roscoe Gordon, Lonesome Sundown, Clifton Chenier, Lloyd Price, Etta James, Jimmy Reed, Lowell Fulson, Little Richard and Fats Domino.

His best LPs are *Blues: The Bottom of the Top* and *As Tough as I Want to Be*.

1941: Singer Earl Lewis is born in New York City.

Lewis and his group, the Channels (Larry Hampden, Bill Morris, Edward Doulphin and Clifford Wright), had their biggest hit during the summer of 1956, with "The Closer You Are." They followed up with "The Gleam in Your Eyes" (1957), "That's My Desire" (1957), "Altar of Love" (1958), "My Love Will Never Die" (1959) and "Bye, Bye, Baby" (1959).

Earl Lewis's ringing falsetto voice may have been the most distinctive of the doo-wop era. Lewis had an unmatchable wail then, and he is still wailing today as one of the top draws on the doo-wop nostalgia circuit.

1942: Singer and keyboardist Leon Haywood is born in Houston.

In the early '60s Leon Haywood played with Big Jay McNeely and Sam Cooke. He first hit the soul charts in the fall of 1965, with "She's with Her Other Love." Some of his other chart successes are "It's Got to Be Mellow" (1967), "Believe Half of What You See" (1974), "I Want to Do Something Freaky to You" (1975) and his biggest hit, "Don't Push It, Don't Force It" (1980).

1942: Singer Otis Clay, one of Chicago's best-known and most successful club performers, is born in Waxhaw, Mississippi.

Clay began his career as a gospel singer with his family group, the Morning Glories. He also sang with the Voices of Hope, the Christian Travelers, the Golden Jubilaires and the Pilgrim Harmonizers. In the early '60s he was leader of the Gospel Songbirds, who recorded for Nashboro Records. He spent 1964 and 1965 with the Sensational Nightingales.

Clay switched to R&B in 1965. His first record was a local Chicago hit, "Tired of Falling In and Out of Love." In 1967 he hit the national charts, with "That's How It Is" and "Lasting Love."

1943: Singer Little Johnny Taylor —often confused with Johnnie ("Who's Making Love to Your Old Lady") Taylor — is born John Young in Memphis.

Taylor grew up in Los Angeles. He sang with blues and gospel groups, such as the Mighty Clouds of Joy and the Stars of Bethel.

He had a number 1 R&B hit in 1963, "Part-Time Love." His other best-known

singles are "You'll Need Another Favor" (1963), "Everybody Knows About My Good Thing" (1971) and "Open House at My House" (1972).

FEBRUARY 12

1935: Singer Gene McDaniels is born in Kansas City, Kansas.

McDaniels had several Top 40 pop hits in 1961 and 1962, including "A Hundred Pounds of Clay," "Tower of Strength," "Point of No Return" and "Chip, Chip." He then turned his attention to songwriting and record producing. Gene McDaniels wrote Roberta Flack's hit "Feel Like Makin' Love."

1945: Singer King Floyd is born in New Orleans.

King Floyd exploded onto the charts in 1970, with his funky hit "Groove Me." It went to number 1 on the soul and Top 10 pop charts. Other hits include "Baby, Let Me Kiss You" (1971) and "Woman, Don't Go Astray" (1972).

1965: Junior Walker and the All Stars make their chart debut with "Shotgun."

The song sparked a dance craze called the Shotgun, in which partners pantomimed breaking open a shotgun, loading it up and firing on each other. The record reached number 1 on the soul charts and peaked at number 4 on the pop charts.

This group—with Walker on sax, Willie Wood on guitar, Vic Thomas on organ and James Graves on drums—was the most distinctive act in the Motown Records stable. Most Motown acts were well-polished combos; Walker and company were a kick-butt, gut-bucket bar band. The band originally recorded for Harvey Fuqua's label, Harvey Records, which was bought out by Motown.

Junior Walker himself was born Autry Dewalt II in 1942 in Blytheville, Arkansas. He supposedly got the tag "Junior Walker" as a child because his feet were his only mode of transportation. Walker grew up in South Bend, Indiana, where the group was formed.

Junior Walker and the All Stars went on to place more than two dozen singles on the charts between 1965 and 1979. The best of the lot are "Do the

Boomerang" (1965), "Shake and Finger-pop" (1965), "Cleo's Back" (1965), "I'm a Roadrunner" (1966), "How Sweet It Is" (1966), "Come See About Me" (1967), "Hip City" (1968), "What Does It Take" (1969), "These Eyes" (1969), "Gotta Hold On to This Feeling" (1970), "Do You See My Love" (1970) and "Walk in the Night" (1972).

FEBRUARY 13

1988: Keith Sweat's "I Want Her" is the number 1 black chart single.

Singer and songwriter Keith Sweat grew up in Harlem. He attended City College of New York and worked as a supervisor on the floor of the New York Stock Exchange. In 1987 he released his debut LP, *Make It Last Forever*, which sold over two million copies. "I Want Her" came from that album and also reached the pop Top 10.

FEBRUARY 14

1893: John Henry Perry Bradford—pianist, songwriter, composer, song hustler and talent scout—is born in Montgomery, Alabama.

Bradford spent the early 1900s playing vaudeville shows, saloons, rent parties and what have you, mostly in the South and New York. He was called "Mule" because of his persistence and stubbornness, which led to the '20s blues-record craze.

Bradford had been managing a blues-singing vaudevillian, Mamie Smith. He had also written a song called "Crazy Blues." Okeh Records had scheduled the great Sophie Tucker to record the song, but Bradford wanted it cut by Mamie Smith. He pestered officials at Okeh until they agreed to let Mamie Smith record "Crazy Blues."

The song was a huge success, selling well beyond Okeh's expectations and making Mamie Smith an overnight star. There was a tremendous demand for more blues records, and so Okeh became the first record company to sign a roster of black artists and launch a "race record" series.

Bradford also wrote a series of dance songs and peddled them to anyone who would buy. In 1912 he got Ethel Waters to include one of his tunes, "Messin' Around," in her theater act. Some of his other compositions are "Stewin' the Rice," "The Possum Trot," "The Bullfrog Hop," "The Baltimore Buzz," "Scratchin' the Gravel," "That Thing Called Love" and "You Can't Keep a Good Man Down."

In 1922 he conceived his biggest hit song, the sexually suggestive "The Original Black Bottom Dance." By the mid-1920s the risqué Black Bottom was the rage—wherever it wasn't banned, that is. On Christmas night of 1926 Chicago police raided several night spots and arrested over 500 people for doing the Black Bottom.

Perry Bradford died on April 20, 1970, in Queens, New York.

1937: Bluesman Magic Sam is born Samuel Maghett in Grenada, Mississippi.

At the age of 10 he taught himself to play a homemade guitar. In 1950 he moved to Chicago, where his first job was with a gospel group. He worked in the band of Homesick James before forming his own band, in 1955. In 1957 he began recording for the Cobra label.

He spent a short time in the Army and then recorded for Chief Records. In 1966 he recorded for Delmark. Up to this point, most of Magic Sam's live gigs had been on the Chicago blues club circuit, but in 1968 he started to get international bookings. Besides playing at the Ann Arbor Blues Festival, the Shrine Auditorium in Los Angeles and Winterland in San Francisco, he appeared at London's Albert Hall.

Several good collections exist of Magic Sam's recorded works. Among the best are *Easy Baby*, *West Side Soul* and *The Magic Sam Legacy*.

Magic Sam is something of a cult figure among musicians and blues aficionados. His renderings are revered and his guitar technique is studied. One reason is that just as his career was taking off, he died. He was only 32 years old when he suffered a fatal heart attack, on December 1, 1969.

1942: Actor, singer and dancer Gregory Hines, one of the world's

best-known and most highly versatile performers, is born in New York City.**

Gregory Hines got his professional start at the age of five, when he and his brother Maurice danced as the Hines Brothers. From 1963 to 1973 they teamed up with their father as the highly successful dance trio of Hines, Hines and Dad, often featured on "The Ed Sullivan Show."

Hines is literally a star of stage, screen, television and recordings. He has appeared in such Broadway musicals as *Eubie*, *Comin' Uptown* and *Sophisticated Ladies*. His film credits include *Wolfen* (1981), *The History of the World, Part I* (1981), *The Deal of the Century* (1983), *The Cotton Club* (1984), *White Nights* (1985), *Running Scared* (1986) and *Tap* (1988).

In the mid-1980s Hines recorded a successful LP, which yielded a number 1 black chart hit, "There's Nothing Better Than Love," a duet with Luther Vandross.

1943: Jazz saxman Maceo Parker is born in Kingston, North Carolina.

Parker grew up in a musical environment. By the time he was a teenager, he and his brothers Melvin and Kellis were playing in their uncle's band, Bobby Butler and the Mighty Blue Notes. Maceo and Melvin Parker attended North Carolina A&T University and majored in music.

When the godfather of soul, James Brown, issued his famous call "Maceo, brother, put it where it's at," Maceo Parker answered the call. Brown had hired Melvin Parker as a drummer in 1964, and Melvin brought along Maceo, whom Brown also hired. Maceo Parker became the main tenor saxman and centerpiece of the James Brown Orchestra in the '60s, contributing pieces to Brown's recordings like his classic solo on "Cold Sweat." (The drummer who "got some" on "Cold Sweat" was Clyde Stubblefield, and the bassman was Bernard Odum.)

In 1970 what was essentially still the James Brown Orchestra was recording under the name Maceo and All the King's Men. Throughout the '70s Parker worked with funksters Bootsy Collins and George

Clinton. In the late '80s Maceo Parker made a move into the world of jazz, with the release of his *Roots Revisited* LP, which landed at number 1 on the *Billboard* jazz chart and stayed there for seven weeks. It got Parker named R&B/soul artist of the year in the *Down Beat* magazine critics' poll. Parker followed up with *Mo' Roots* in 1991 and *Life on Planet Groove* in late 1992.

1945: Singer Clarence "Blowfly" Reid is born in Cochran, Georgia.

Clarence Reid's best-known hit was 1969's "Nobody But You Babe." Since then Reid has been heard and seen mostly as his masked, triple-x-rated alter ego, "Blowfly."

FEBRUARY 15

1901: Bluesman James "Kokomo" Arnold is born in Lovejoy, Georgia.

Arnold took up guitar at the age of 10. By the time he settled in Chicago, in 1925, he was a well-respected slide guitarist. In Chicago, Arnold reportedly made a living as a bootlegger, writing songs and playing blues on the side.

In 1930 he began recording for Decca Records. He cut songs like "Paddlin' Madeline Blues," "Cold Winter Blues" and "Chain Gang Blues." His nickname comes from his 1934 hit "Old Original Kokomo Blues," named after a popular brand of coffee at the time. He also wrote "Milk Cow Blues," which was an early hit for Elvis Presley. Arnold often recorded under the name Gitfiddle Jim and frequently recorded with fellow bluesman Peetie Wheatstraw.

Kokomo Arnold died of a heart attack on November 8, 1968.

1941: The Duke Ellington Orchestra records "Take the A Train," one of Ellington's classic pieces, in Hollywood.

The Ellington orchestra was one of the finest ever assembled. A gig with Duke Ellington was a job that most black musicians of the period cherished. There were no boarding houses or bus trips; the Ellington crew traveled in style by rail, in private Pullman cars.

The band lineup for the "A Train" session was Duke Ellington, piano and director; Wardell Jones, trumpet; Ray

Nance, trumpet and violin; Rex Stewart, cornet; Joe Nanton and Lawrence Brown, trombones; Juan Tizol, valve trombone; Barney Bigard, clarinet; Johnny Hodges, clarinet and soprano and alto sax; Harry Carney, clarinet and alto and baritone sax; Otto Hardwick, alto and bass sax; Ben Webster, tenor sax; Fred Guy, guitar; Jimmy Blanton, string bass; and Sonny Greer, drums. "Take the A Train" was arranged by Billy Strayhorn.

1965: Singer Nat "King" Cole dies.

One of the great Nat "King" Cole's trademarks was his cigarette holder and lighted cigarette. In December 1964 Nat Cole began a losing battle with lung cancer. He was forced to cancel engagements and enter a hospital in Santa Monica, California, on January 25, 1965, where doctors removed his left lung.

NAT "KING" COLE

FEBRUARY 16

1916: Rock 'n' roll instrumentalist William Ballard "Bill" Doggett is born in Philadelphia.

Doggett came up through the big-band system of the '30s and '40s, working with Lucky Millinder and Jimmy Mundy. He was at home on either piano or organ and was also a competent arranger. He arranged for the Ink Spots and did charts for the bands of Louis Armstrong, Lionel Hampton and Count Basie.

In the mid-1940s Doggett moved toward R&B, playing in the bands of Johnny Otis, Illinois Jacquet and Louis Jordan.

In 1952 Bill Doggett formed his own combo and had one of the rock 'n' roll era's earliest and biggest instrumental hits, "Honky Tonk, Parts I and II." In 1956 the song went to number 1 on the R&B charts and number 2 on the pop charts. It remained on the charts for seven months. He followed "Honky Tonk" with hits like "Slow Walk" and "Ram-Bunk-Shush."

1937: Singer Ted Taylor is born in Farm Town, Oklahoma.

Before becoming a solo act, in 1955, Taylor sang with a variety of gospel and doo-wop groups. He turned out good records and was exciting to watch in person, but he never managed to achieve star status. From the mid-1960s until the mid-1970s Taylor's records were in the middle of the R&B charts and on the "bubbling underlist" of the pop charts. His biggest hit was "Stay Away From Me, Baby" (1965). Other singles were "It's Too Late" (1969), "How's Your Love Life, Baby" (1971) and "Something Strange Is Going On in My House" (1970).

Ted Taylor died in an auto accident on October 22, 1987.

FEBRUARY 17

1902: Contralto Marian Anderson, one of the most beloved performers in modern music history, is born in Philadelphia.

Anderson's early musical training came in church choirs. Later on she studied voice with Giuseppe Boghetti.

In 1925 Marian Anderson won a contest, outperforming over 300 other singers. Her prize was an appearance with the New York Philharmonic Orchestra. She also was awarded a Rosenwald Fellowship to study and perform in Europe.

Marian Anderson made her European concert debut in Berlin in 1930 and spent most of the next five years touring Europe. She returned to the U.S. in 1935. Her triumphant return tour included appearances at

New York City's Town Hall and at Carnegie Hall. In 1936 she sang at the White House.

In 1939 Marian Anderson was scheduled to give a concert at Constitution Hall in Washington, D.C. The concert was blocked by the Daughters of the American Revolution, who refused to let Anderson appear there because she was black. When the incident came to the attention of Eleanor Roosevelt, the first lady intervened. With the aid of Mrs. Roosevelt, Marian Anderson's concert was held on Easter Sunday at the Lincoln Memorial and attended by over 75,000 people.

In 1942 Anderson established the Marian Anderson Award for young singers. In 1955 she became the first black singer to join New York's Metropolitan Opera Company. She appeared in Verdi's *Un ballo in maschera*. Marian Anderson's autobiography, *My Lord, What a Morning*, was published in 1956.

In 1957 and 1958 Anderson toured throughout Asia, and in 1958 President Dwight D. Eisenhower appointed her a delegate to the United Nations General Assembly. In 1960 she sang at John F. Kennedy's presidential inauguration.

Marian Anderson died on April 7, 1992.

1922: Singer Tommy Edwards is born in Richmond, Virginia.

Edwards began performing as a child. In the '40s he had a radio show in Richmond. In 1946 he wrote Louis Jordan's hit "That Chick's Too Young to Fry." In 1950 he moved to New York, took a job making demos and was signed to a recording contract by MGM Records. Among his early recordings were Perry Comoesque versions of "The Morning Side of the Mountain" and "Please, Mr. Sun."

Tommy Edwards's shining moment in pop music history came with his 1958 monster hit, "It's All in the Game," a song he had first recorded in 1951. It hit number 1 and stayed on the charts for 22 weeks, but Edwards never again managed to hit the Top 10.

1933: Singer Bobby Lewis is born in Indianapolis.

Pop musicologists put Bobby Lewis in the category of "one-hit wonder," but he actually had two Top 10 hits in the spring and summer of 1961. The big one was the million-selling "Tossin' and Turnin'." His follow-up, "One-Track Mind," peaked at number 9.

1982: Jazz genius Thelonious Monk dies in Englewood, New Jersey.

One of the jazz world's most eccentric figures, Monk had suffered a variety of health problems and gone into seclusion. He had not played publicly in six years when he succumbed to a stroke, at the age of 64.

FEBRUARY 18

1941: Irma Thomas, soul queen of New Orleans and considered by many to be the best female R&B singer today, is born in Ponchatoula, Louisiana.

Irma Thomas has been singing professionally since the late 1950s, when she swapped a 50-cent-per-hour dishwashing job for a gig as singer with Tommy Ridgely's band, the Untouchables.

In the 1960s she had a string of R&B chart hits while recording for the Ron, Minit, Imperial and Chess labels. Her first hit was "Don't Mess with My Man" (1960). Her biggest was "Wish Someone Would Care" (1964). She also recorded a song called "Time Is on My Side," which became a hit for the Rolling Stones.

In the 1970s Thomas moved to Los Angeles and got out of the music business. She returned periodically to New Orleans, however, and performed at the New Orleans Jazz Festival. In 1974 she went back to stay and reestablished her recording career.

In 1979 Thomas released her landmark LP, *The Soul Queen of New Orleans*. In the 1980s she signed with independent Rounder Records, noted for cultivating R&B, folk and blues artists without commercializing them. Irma Thomas also became a top draw on the national club circuit, recording several fine LPs recently, including *Simply the Best—Live* and *True Believer*.

1956: The Flamingos make their chart debut, with "I'll Be Home."

Formed in Chicago in 1952, the Flamingos first recorded in 1953. Originally the group consisted of lead singer Solly McElroy, Zeke and Jake Carey, Paul Wilson and John Carter. McElroy left in 1954, and lead vocals were taken over by Nate Nelson. In 1956 Zeke Carey and John Carter were drafted into the Army and replaced by Tommy Hunt and Terry Johnson.

"I'll Be Home" put the Flamingos on the charts, peaking at number 5 on the R&B lists. Follow-ups included "A Kiss from Your Lips" and "Lovers Never Say Goodbye."

John Carter returned to the group in 1958, and the Flamingos signed with End Records. In 1959 they had their biggest record, "I Only Have Eyes for You," a Top 10 hit on both the R&B and pop charts.

FEBRUARY 19

1940: Singer, songwriter and producer William "Smokey" Robinson is born in Detroit.

Smokey Robinson began writing songs in the first grade. While attending Northern High School in Detroit, he formed a group called the Matadors, later the Miracles, with Ronnie White, Pete Moore, Bobby Rogers and Claudette Rogers.

The Miracles recorded a song called "Got a Job," an answer to the Silhouettes' hit "Get a Job." Berry Gordy, Jr., produced their song "Bad Girl" and leased it to Chess Records. When Motown was formed, the Miracles were signed to the new label.

Perhaps no one besides Gordy is more synonymous with Motown Records than Robinson is; his story essentially *is* the story of Motown Records.

In January of 1961 the Miracles' recording of "Shop Around" became the first Motown single to hit number 1 on the R&B charts. It also hit number 2 on the pop charts. Over the next decade Smokey Robinson and the Miracles became a household name, placing more than three dozen singles on the national record charts. Their biggest hits were "What's So Good About Goodbye" (1962), "I'll Try

Something New (1962), "Mickey's Monkey" (1963), "Ooh Baby Baby" (1965), "The Tracks of My Tears" (1965), "My Girl Has Gone" (1965), "Going to a GoGo" (1966), "I'm the One You Need" (1966), "I Second That Emotion" (1967), "If You Can Want" (1968), "Special Occasion" (1968), "Baby, Baby Don't Cry" (1969), "Point It Out" (1969), "The Tears of a Clown" (1970) and "We've Come Too Far to End It Now" (1972).

Robinson, besides writing all the Miracles' biggest hits, wrote for other Motown artists. He wrote "You Beat Me to the Punch," "Two Lovers" and "Get Ready" for the Temptations; "When I'm Gone" for Brenda Holloway; and "The Hunter Gets Captured by the Game" for the Marvelettes.

In January 1972 Smokey Robinson left the Miracles to become a solo performer. His string of hit records continued, with "Baby Come Close" (1973), "I Am I Am" (1974), "Baby That's Backatcha" (1975), "There Will Come a Day" (1977), "Cruisin'" (1979), "Let Me Be the Clock" (1980), "Being with You" (1981), "Tell Me Tomorrow" (1982), "Just to See Her" (1987) and "One Heartbeat" (1990).

FEBRUARY 20

1937: Jazz singer Nancy Wilson, one of the world's best-known stylists, is born in Chillicothe, Ohio.

Wilson began her career singing in clubs around Ohio. She joined Rusty Bryant's band as vocalist and began recording in 1956.

In the early 1960s she recorded with jazz man Cannonball Adderley. The result was a best-selling jazz LP and a hot R&B single, "Save Your Love for Me."

Wilson is equally at home in the worlds of jazz, R&B and pop. She has made over 50 albums and has collected several Grammy awards, including best R&B vocalist in 1964. And, while albums are her strong suit, she has also placed over a dozen singles on the R&B and pop music charts. Her best-known singles are "You're As Right As Rain," "You Don't Know How Glad I Am" and "Face It, Girl, It's Over."

In 1974-75 she starred in an Emmy Award-winning TV series, "The Nancy Wilson Show."

Nancy Wilson is noted as one of the music industry's great humanitarians. Over the years she has donated her time and energy to the NAACP, Operation PUSH and the United Negro College Fund. At one time she was a member of the Presidential Council on Minority Business Affairs.

NANCY WILSON

1954: The Spiders make their chart debut with "I Didn't Want to Do It."

Formed in 1947 as the Zion City Harmonizers and based in New Orleans, the Spiders were made up of lead singer Chuck Carbo, Joe Maxan, Matthew West, Oliver Howard and Chick Carbo.

"I Didn't Want to Do It" was released on Imperial Records and hit number 3 on the R&B charts. The Spiders quickly ran up a string of hits in 1954 and 1955, including "You're the One," "I'm Slippin' In," "Twenty-One" and "Witchcraft."

The Spiders broke up in 1956, when Chuck Carbo went solo.

FEBRUARY 21

1903: Bluesman Scrapper Blackwell is born Francis Hillman Blackwell, in either North Carolina or South Carolina, one of 16 children in a Cherokee Indian family.

The family moved to Indianapolis when Blackwell was three. He taught himself to play guitar and started playing at parties in Indianapolis and Chicago as a teenager.

Blackwell is best known for his work with vocalist and pianist Leroy Carr. He teamed up with Carr in 1928, and they recorded the hit record "How Long How Long Blues." What Carr and Blackwell played was a forerunner of the popular style of jazzy R&B that the Nat "King" Cole Trio performed in the 1940s: piano rhythms with vocal lines and intricate guitar fills and arpeggios. In fact, even though Blackwell is called a blues player, his guitar stylings were actually jazz. He and Carr toured and recorded together until Carr's death, in 1935.

Blackwell then retired from music for a while, making only a few club appearances. In 1959 he began to record again and to make more frequent personal appearances. In 1961 he recorded a superb album, *Mr. Scrapper's Blues*.

On October 7, 1962, Scrapper Blackwell was shot to death in Indianapolis.

1933: Vocalist and pianist Nina Simone is born Eunice Kathleen Waymon in Tryon, N.C.

Nina Simone learned to play piano as a youngster. Considered a child prodigy, she was given a scholarship to the Juilliard School of Music in New York. She had planned a career as a classical concert pianist but found it was easier to make a living playing and singing in nightclubs.

In 1959 she recorded "I Loves You, Porgy," from the opera *Porgy and Bess*, for the small Bethlehem Records company. Unexpectedly, the record soared up the charts, ending up at number 2 on the R&B charts and in the Top 20 on the pops. Nina Simone signed with Columbia Pictures–owned Colpix Records and had hits with "Nobody Loves You When You're Down and Out" and "Trouble in Mind."

In the 1960s Nina Simone was one of the first black artists to bring subjects like racism, bigotry, civil rights and political activism to popular music. Her best-known and most popular song of this genre was 1969's "To Be Young, Gifted and Black," which made the Top 10 on the R&B charts. Other songs in the same vein included "Old Jim Crow," "Backlash Blues," "Why? (The King of Love Is Dead)" and the unforgettable "Mississippi God Damn."

FEBRUARY 22

1936: Singer Ernie K-Doe is born Ernest Kador, Jr., in New Orleans.

Ernie K-Doe had one of the biggest-selling singles of 1961, "Mother-in-Law." It was written by Allen Toussaint and went to number 1 on both the pop and soul charts. (The bass voice on "Mother-in-Law" belongs to Benny Spellman, who himself had a couple of R&B hits, with "Lipstick Traces" and "Fortune Teller.") K-Doe's other chart hits include "Certain Girl" and "Te-Ta-Te-Ta-Ta."

FEBRUARY 23

1946: Johnny Moore's Three Blazers, a vocal and instrumental group formed in Los Angeles in 1944, make their chart debut with "Drifting Blues." It peaked at number 2.

The group had a dozen R&B Top 10 hits between 1946 and 1955. Original members were Johnny Moore on guitar, Charles Brown on vocals and piano and Eddie Williams on bass. They were later joined by Moore's brother Oscar, who had previously been with the Nat "King" Cole Trio.

In 1948 Charles Brown left for a successful solo career, and in 1949 Eddie Williams began recording with his own group, the Brown Buddies. After Brown's departure, the group had a series of vocalists, including Billy Valentine and Frankie Ervin. The group's hits include "Sunny Road" (1946), "So Long" (1946), "New Orleans Blues" (1947), "Changeable Woman Blues" (1947), "Groovy Music Blues" (1948), "Merry Christmas Baby" (1948), "Where Can I Find My Baby" (1949), "Walkin' Blues" (1949) and "Dragnet Blues" (1953).

FEBRUARY 24

1968: The Ohio Players make their chart debut with "Trespassin'" on the small Compass label.

"Trespassin'" only made it to number 50 on the soul charts. The Ohio Players had boarded the "funk music" train in the late 1960s. In 1971 they signed with Detroit-based Westbound Records, and their hit string began.

Their first Westbound single, "Pain," reached number 35. In early 1973 the Ohio Players struck gold, with a number 1 million-seller called "The Funky Worm." The band then signed with the larger Mercury Records label and had three more million-sellers: "Skin Tight" (1974), "Fire" (1974) and "Love Roller Coaster" (1975). The last two went to number 1 on the pop charts.

The group was formed in Dayton, Ohio, in 1959 and was originally called the Ohio Untouchables. The Players performed behind the Wilson Pickett–led Falcons on the record "I Found a Love" and became the house band for a couple of small record labels, including Lupine, for which they recorded in 1962.

Like most struggling bands, the Ohio Players underwent a number of personnel changes. By the time they hit their stride, the band consisted of Leroy "Sugarfoot" Bonner on guitar and vocals, Billy Beck on keyboards, Clarence "Satch" Satchell on sax, Marvin Pierce on trumpet, Pee Wee Middlebrooks on trumpet, Marshall Jones on bass and Jimmy Williams on drums.

The Ohio Players were one of the best-selling recording acts of the 1970s. Other hits were "Jive Turkey" (1974), "I Want to Be Free" (1975), "Sweet Sticky Thing" (1975), "FOPP" (1976), "Who's She Coo" (1976) and "O-H-I-O" (1977).

FEBRUARY 25

1896: Blueswoman Ida Cox, a contemporary of the great Bessie Smith, is born in Cedartown, Georgia.

In her heyday, she was called "the uncrowned queen of the blues" and "the sepia Mae West."

Ida Cox's career began when she ran away from home to join a minstrel show. She worked with outfits like the Rabbit Foot Minstrels and the White and Clark Black and Tan Minstrels. In 1920 she worked with Jelly Roll Morton. In 1923 she signed with Paramount Records. Her most prolific recording years were from 1923 to 1929.

Cox was one of Paramount's best-selling "race" artists. Her hits included "Monkey Man Blues," "Death Letter Blues," "Black Crepe Blues," "Coffin Blues," "Graveyard Dream Blues," "Give Me a Break Blues," "Moaning Groaning Blues," "Mean Papa Turn Your Key" and "You Stole My Man."

Throughout the 1930s Ida Cox was a major box-office draw on the theater circuit, headlining her own *Darktown Scandals Revue*. In 1939 she went to New York City and played the Cafe Society and Carnegie Hall.

She was still touring in 1944, when she suffered a stroke and retired. In 1961 she came out of retirement to record the album *Wildwomen Don't Have the Blues* with the Coleman Hawkins Quintet and Roy Eldridge.

Ida Cox died of cancer on November 10, 1967.

FEBRUARY 26

1928: Antoine "Fats" Domino is born in New Orleans; some sources list his birthdate as May 10, 1929.

Domino was one of nine children. His dad played violin, and his uncle had played in Kid Ory's Dixieland band. By the age of 10 Domino was already playing local honky-tonks. He got the "Fats" nickname from a fellow musician.

In the mid-1940s he joined Dave Bartholomew's dance band. Domino then injured his hands while working at a factory and was out of the music business for two years. When his hands healed, he returned to Bartholomew's outfit.

Playing and singing with Bartholomew's band got Domino a huge following around New Orleans. In 1949, with the band backing him, he cut his first record, "The Fat Man." It was an instant local hit and quickly got national play. "The Fat Man" landed at number 2 on the R&B charts, and Domino became a star. This song was the first hit for Imperial Records.

Between 1950 and 1964 Fats Domino placed over 60 singles on the R&B charts, including nine at number 1. They were "Goin' Home" (1952), "Ain't That a Shame" (1955), "All By Myself" (1955), "Poor Me" (1955), "I'm In Love Again"

(1956), "Blueberry Hill" (1956), "Blue Monday" (1956), "I'm Walkin'" (1957), and "I Want To Walk You Home" (1959). "Ain't That a Shame" was also discovered by white rock 'n' roll audiences. The song became his first Top 10 pop hit.

Fats Domino is considered one of the most influential artists of the rock 'n' roll era, on several counts. Apart from the music he recorded, he represented one of the earliest examples of the rock 'n' roll lifestyle. He presented a world-class stage show, with a well-rehearsed, tight backup orchestra. The Fat Man's appearance was extravagant. He wore tuxedos, played white baby-grand pianos, and on every one of his fingers was a huge diamond ring. Fats Domino also appeared in such 1950s rock 'n' roll movies as *Shake, Rattle and Rock*, *The Big Beat* and *The Girl Can't Help It*.

FATS DOMINO

FEBRUARY 27

1923: Tenor saxophonist Dexter Keith Gordon is born in Los Angeles.

At the age of 17 Gordon joined Lionel Hampton's band. Hampton's main tenor man was the famed Illinois Jacquet. Early sax duels between Jacquet and the youthful Gordon set up what was to become a hallmark of Gordon's career: fast and frenetic jazz "chases," rapid-fire exchanges between two saxmen.

After a short stint with the Lee Young Sextet, Gordon joined Fletcher Henderson's orchestra. He was also in the orchestras of Louis Armstrong, in 1944, and Billy Eckstine, in 1944 and 1945.

Gordon and Gene Ammons recorded the sax duel "Blowin' Away the Blues" in 1945. That year Gordon also recorded "Blow, Mr. Dexter" for Savoy Records.

In 1946 he teamed up with Wardell Gray to record "The Chase." In the late 1940s and early 1950s he worked with Gray, Tadd Dameron, Fats Navarro and Helen Humes.

In 1952 Dexter Gordon was arrested for narcotics possession and spent most of 1953 and 1954 in prison. In 1956 he was arrested again for the same offense.

Gordon took up acting in 1960, playing a junkie in the play *The Connection*. He also began recording again.

In the fall of 1962 he moved to Europe and settled in Copenhagen. He returned briefly to the U.S. in 1965, 1969 and 1970. Gordon had basically retired when, in 1986, he took the lead in *Round Midnight*, a film about a jazz player who leaves America and takes up residence in Europe. The success of the film and its soundtrack recording renewed interest in Dexter Gordon's music.

Some of his best LPs are *The Chase; Long, Tall Dexter: The Savoy Recordings; Our Man in Paris;* and *Round Midnight.*

1926: Okeh Records presents its first "Race Records Artists Night" at the Chicago Coliseum.

In the 1920s, on the strength of the success of singers like Bessie Smith and Mamie Smith, record companies decided that there was a strong and viable market for recordings in the black community. Music especially made and marketed for blacks was called "race music." (Like everything else at that time, record companies' rosters were segregated.)

Okeh Records led the way in signing black blues artists. Thousands of fans turned out for Okeh's concerts to see the likes of Louis Armstrong, Bennie Moten and his orchestra, Sara Martin, Chippie Hill, Blanche Calloway, Clarence Williams and Sippie Wallace.

FEBRUARY 28

1934: Percussionist Willie Bobo is born in New York City.

The son of a Puerto Rican immigrant, Willie Bobo taught himself to play bongos at the age of 14. His first job in the music business was as a bandboy (gofer) for Machito's Latin Orchestra.

In the 1950s and 1960s Bobo was recognized as one of the top Latin-jazz percussionists in the world. He worked in the bands of such varied artists as Tito Puente, Cal Tjader, Herbie Mann, Miles Davis, Les McCann and Cannonball Adderley. He also had his own group, which included a young keyboardist named Chick Corea.

Willie Bobo died on September 11, 1983.

1944: Singer and songwriter Barbara Acklin is born in Chicago.

Acklin got her start doing backup vocals at Chess Records in the mid-1960s. Then, using the name Barbara Allen, she cut her first solo sides for an independent label, Special Agent, in 1966.

Barbara Acklin's big break came in 1967, when producer Carl Davis hired her as a staff songwriter for Brunswick Records. She was also paired up with the Duke of Earl, Gene Chandler, for a couple of duet hits, "Show Me the Way to Go Home" and "From the Teacher to the Preacher," in 1968. In that year she also had her best-known hit, "Love Makes a Woman."

In all, Barbara Acklin had a dozen records on the soul charts between 1968 and 1975. As a songwriter, she co-wrote the Chi-Lites' 1971 hit "Have You Seen Her?"

FEBRUARY 29

1990: Paula Abdul's "Opposites Attract" is the number 1 pop single.

The song was Abdul's fourth number 1 pop single and her fourth million-seller. The video clip for the piece was innovative. It paired Abdul with an animated dance partner, M. C. Skat Kat, whose vocal rap was provided by Derrick Delite.

MARCH 1

1927: Actor and singer Harry Belafonte is born in Harlem.

In 1957 Belafonte was dubbed the King of Calypso on the strength of his hit record "The Banana Boat Song," which reached number 5 on the charts and stayed around for 20 weeks. Belafonte had begun his island-craze cruise up the pop music charts in 1956, when he hit the Top 20 with "Jamaica Farewell."

Before hitting with "The Banana Boat Song," Harry Belafonte was a successful actor. He was a member of the American Negro Theater Company and had appeared in such Broadway shows as *Almanac* (for which he won a Tony in 1953) and *Three for Tonight* (1955). He has also appeared in films: *Bright Road* (1952), *Carmen Jones* (1954), *Island in the Sun* (1957), *The World, the Flesh and the Devil* (1957), *The Odds Against Tomorrow* (1959), *The Angel Levine* (1969), *Buck and the Preacher* (1971) and *Uptown Saturday Night* (1974).

Harry Belafonte then branched out into producing. His productions included the play *To Be Young, Gifted and Black*, TV specials such as "Harry" (Belafonte) and "Lena" (Horne) and the hip-hop film *Beat Street*.

In 1987 Harry Belafonte replaced Danny Kaye as the goodwill ambassador for UNICEF.

1948: Norman Connors is born in Philadelphia.

As a jazz drummer, Connors has worked with John Coltrane, Archie Shepp and Pharaoh Sanders. In the early 1970s he formed his own pop group and began to record. Vocalists on those recordings included Jean Carn, Michael Henderson, Phyllis Hyman and Prince Philip Mitchell.

As a vocalist, he began hitting the soul charts in 1975, with songs like "Valentine Love" (1975), "You Are My Starship" (1976), "Once I've Been There" (1977) and "Take It to the Limit" (1980).

Norman Connors has also produced Henderson, Carn and Hyman, as well as Dee Dee Bridgewater and Aquarian Dream.

MARCH 2

1921: Tenor saxman Eddie "Lockjaw" Davis is born in New York City.

Davis's musical experience had come in the 1940s big bands of Cootie Williams, Andy Kirk, Lucky Millinder and Louis Armstrong. In 1952 he joined Count Basie's band.

In 1955 Davis and organist Shirley Scott recorded an album called *The Cookbook*. Its success resulted in both the formation and the popularity of the jazz-pop small organ/sax combos of the late 1950s.

In 1960 Davis formed a two-tenor quintet with Johnny Griffin. He also worked as a road manager and booking agent.

Eddie "Lockjaw" Davis died in 1986.

1957: The doo-wop Jive Bombers make their chart debut with "Bad Boy," their one and only hit.

The song was written and originally recorded by Lil Hardin Armstrong, in 1936.

The Jive Bombers were based in New York City. The members were Earl Jackson, Al Tinney, William "Pee Wee" Tinney and Clarence Palmer.

MARCH 3

1947: Louis Jordan's "Ain't Nobody Here But Us Chickens" is the number 1 R&B single.

Arkansas-born Jordan was the man who made R&B a viable entity in the world of American pop music. Beginning with "What's the Use of Getting Sober," Jordan racked up 18 number 1 R&B singles between 1942 and 1950.

Louis Jordan was a top nightclub performer with both black and white audiences. He also made feature-length films and jukebox "soundies" (the 1940s cousin of music videos). Jordan's tunes were mostly humor-filled jump-blues ditties, with titles like "The Chicks I Pick Are Slender, Tender and Tall," "Is You Is or Is You Ain't My Baby," "Salt Pork, West Virginia," "Stone Cold Dead in the Market," "Reet, Petite and Gone" and "Saturday Night Fish Fry."

MARCH 4

1944: Singer, songwriter and guitarist Bobby Womack is born in Cleveland.

Bobby Womack began his musical career singing with his family gospel group. In the early 1960s he and his brothers—Cecil, Curtis, Harris and Friendly—formed a group called the Valentinos, which was signed to Sam Cooke's SAR record label.

The Valentinos recorded two classic singles, "Lookin' for a Love" (1962) and "It's All Over Now" (1964). When Sam Cooke was killed, SAR died with him.

Bobby Womack went on to work as a session guitarist in Muscle Shoals, Alabama, playing on records by Wilson Pickett, Joe Tex, Aretha Franklin and many others.

As a solo artist, Womack first hit the soul Top 20 in 1968, with his version of "Fly Me to the Moon." He also charted with versions of "California Dreamin' " (1968) and "I Left My Heart in San Francisco" (1969).

In 1971 Bobby Womack began a run of solid chart hits, with "That's the Way I Feel About Cha." He scored number 1 soul hits with "Woman's Gotta Have It," in 1972, and a remake of the Valentinos' "Lookin' for a Love" in 1974, a million-seller, as was "Harry Hippie" (1972). Among his other best-selling singles are "Nobody Wants You When You're Down and Out" (1973), "You're Welcome, Stop On By" (1974), "Check It Out" (1975), "Daylight" (1976), "If You Think You're Lonely Now" (1981) and "I Wish He Didn't Trust Me So Much" (1985).

Bobby Womack provided the film score for the 1973 film *Across 110th Street* and had a best-selling duet with Patti Labelle, "Love Has Finally Come at Last," in 1984.

He was married for a time to the widow of Sam Cooke. His brother Cecil is married to Sam Cooke's daughter Linda, and they record under the name Womack and Womack.

BOBBY WOMACK

MARCH 5

1922: Egbert Austin "Bert" Williams, one of the greatest black vaudeville performers, dies of pneumonia in New York City.

Williams was born in the British West Indies in 1874 or 1877. His family moved to California when he was 11. He went to Stanford University but quit after one semester and began performing in saloons on the Barbary Coast.

In 1893 he teamed up with George Walker to play theaters, saloons and tent shows. Williams and Walker toured throughout the Midwest, billed as "Two Real Coons" and working in blackface. In 1896 they opened in New York City, to rave reviews. They began to play only the finest music halls. In the late 1890s Williams and Walker helped popularize

the dance known as the Cakewalk. In 1899 they had a hit show called *A Lucky Coon* and followed it up with two hit revues, *The Policy Players* and *Sons of Ham*.

They scored their biggest success in 1903, in the Broadway show *Dahomey*. It was such a hit that Williams and Walker took it to England after its Broadway run and presented a command performance at Buckingham Palace. Follow-up shows included *Abyssinia*, in 1906, and *Banana Land*, in 1907. In 1909 George Walker suffered a stroke, and he died in 1911.

Bert Williams then became a successful solo performer. He appeared in *The Follies of 1910*, *Midnight Follies*, *Follies of 1919* and *Broadway Brevities*. He also appeared in the silent films *Darktown Jubilee* (1914) and *A Natural-Born Gambler* (1916). In February 1922 he was starring in the stage comedy *Under the Bamboo Tree* when he collapsed onstage.

Bert Williams often appeared in shows in which he was the only black performer. Most photos of Williams show him nattily attired in top hat and tails.

1929: Singer, songwriter, guitarist and harmonica player J. B. Lenore (Lenoir) is born in Monticello, Mississippi.

In the 1940s he backed up the likes of Elmore James and Sonny Boy Williamson. He moved to Chicago in 1949 and played behind Muddy Waters, Big Bill Broonzy, Memphis Minnie and Big Maceo. That year he also formed his own group, the Bayou Boys. Over the years he recorded for the Chess, Checker and Parrot labels. He was noted for his distinctive high-pitched voice. His biggest single hit was "Mama, Talk to Your Daughter" (1955).

Lenore continued to be based in Chicago, but in the mid-1960s he toured England and Europe. He developed a loyal following overseas. Nevertheless, he was often overshadowed by the reputations of his contemporaries Muddy Waters and Howlin' Wolf.

In 1966 he was injured in a car crash. On April 29, 1967, J. B. Lenore suffered a fatal heart attack in Urbana, Illinois.

1933: Singer Tommy Tucker is born in Springfield, Ohio. Some sources list his birth year as 1934 or 1939.

Tommy Tucker was the funky alter ego of jazz musician Robert Higgenbotham, who played organ, piano, drums, bass and clarinet behind such performers as Rahsaan Roland Kirk and Eddie "Cleanhead" Vinson in the 1950s. Higginbotham unleashed Tommy Tucker around 1959, playing in small clubs.

Tommy Tucker is best known for his 1964 recording of "High Heel Sneakers." He died of food poisoning on January 22, 1982.

1948: Singer and songwriter Eddy Grant is born in Plaisance, Guyana.

Grant had a string of Top 40 reggae-rock hits in 1983-84. His biggest was "Electric Avenue," which reached number 2.

MARCH 6

1893: Walter "Furry" Lewis, one of Bluesdom's best slide guitarists and singers, is born in Greenwood, Mississippi.

Lewis learned to play a homemade guitar at the age of six. He ran away from home to join a medicine show and, in the early 1900s, played with W. C. Handy's orchestra. Around 1916, while hoboing across the South, he lost a leg in a train accident.

In the 1920s he played everything from fish fries to riverboats with the likes of Memphis Minnie and Blind Lemon Jefferson. In the late '20s he began recording for the Victor and Vocalion labels. Some of his best-known records from that period are "Rock Island Blues," "Good Looking Girl Blues," "Mean Old Bedbug Blues," "Furry's Blues," "Mistreatin' Mama," "I Will Turn Your Money Green" and "Cannonball Blues."

Furry Lewis was another of the old-time bluesmen whose careers were revived in the '60s and '70s. He recorded for the Rounder and Adelphi labels, played the folk and blues festival circuit, made television appearances and was in several films, including *The Roots of American Music*, *Blues Under the*

Skin, *Out of the Blacks and Into the Blues*, and the Burt Reynolds movie *W. W. and the Dixie Dance Kings*.

Furry Lewis died on September 14, 1981, in Memphis.

1925: Jazz guitarist Wes Montgomery is born in Indianapolis.

Wes Montgomery didn't take up the guitar until well into his teens. From 1948 until 1950 he toured with Lionel Hampton's band. He then returned home to Indianapolis, where he worked a day job and played small local clubs at night.

In the late '50s he and his brothers, bassist Monk Montgomery and vibraharpist Buddy Montgomery, formed a group called the Mastersounds. Wes Montgomery remained in Indiana while the rest of the group moved to the West Coast.

In 1959 he was "discovered" by Cannonball Adderley and began recording with a trio. In 1960 and 1961 he worked on the West Coast with his brothers and John Coltrane. In the early '60s he worked with pianist Wynton Kelly's trio.

The big break in Wes Montgomery's career came in 1965, when he signed with Verve Records. His best-selling and best-known recordings came during his Verve years. He released several albums, light jazzy renderings of such pop hits as "California Dreamin' " and "The Shadow of Your Smile." The albums were highly orchestrated (usually arranged by Oliver Nelson) and brought Montgomery a new crop of fans from among Top 40 listeners and college students. His best LPs from that period were *Bumpin'* (1967) and *Movin' Wes* (1965).

There is no mistaking the guitar stylings of Wes Montgomery. Like Miles Davis's trumpet and Thelonious Monk's piano, Montgomery's guitar doesn't just emit notes, it speaks. Montgomery's method was quite unusual: he played with a thumb pick. Critics say that he took up where Charlie Christian left off.

Wes Montgomery died of a heart attack on June 15, 1968, in Indianapolis.

MARCH 7

1942: Musician, songwriter, arranger and producer Hamilton

Bohannon is born in Newman, Georgia.

Bohannon graduated from Clark College, in Atlanta. He worked as a drummer for Stevie Wonder in the late 1960s and as bandleader and arranger for the Temptations' backup group before beginning his solo career in the mid-1970s. Hamilton Bohannon's list of black chart hits includes "Foot Stompin' Music" (1975), "Let's Start the Dance" (1978) and "The Party Train" (1982).

MARCH 8

1958: The Silhouettes' "Get a Job" is the number 1 pop single.

With its "sha-na-na-na, sha-na-na-na-na" opening, "Get a Job" is one of the most famous hits of the doo-wop era. The Silhouettes, a Philadelphia-based group, were lead singer William Horton, tenor Richard Lewis, baritone Earl Beal and bass Raymond Edwards. "Get a Job" was their only hit.

MARCH 9

1933: Lloyd Price is born in Kenner, Louisiana.

Lloyd Price was one of 11 children. His parents taught him to play guitar and piano.

In 1949 he formed his own band and performed on the radio in New Orleans. In 1952 he had a number 1 R&B hit with "Lawdy, Miss Clawdy," as well as the Top 10 follow-ups "Oooh, Oooh, Oooh," "Restless Heart," "Tell Me, Pretty Baby" and "Ain't It a Shame."

In 1953, in the midst of his hot streak, Lloyd Price was drafted into the Army and spent the next two years entertaining U.S. forces. Upon his discharge, in 1956, he resumed his recording career, signing with ABC-Paramount Records.

His first hit on that label was "Just Because," in 1957. The record hit number 3 on the R&B and pop Top 40 charts. In late 1958 Lloyd Price hit the top of all the charts with the rock 'n' roll classic "Stagger Lee." He racked up more number 1 and Top 10 hits over the next two years, including "Where Were You (On Our Wedding Day)" (1959), "Personality" (1959), "I'm Gonna Get Married" (1959), "Come Into My Heart"

(1959), "Won't Cha Come Home" (1959), "Lady Luck" (1960) and "Question" (1960).

Lloyd Price's last Top 20 hit came in 1963, a cover of Erroll Garner's "Misty" on Price's own Double L label.

LLOYD PRICE

1945: Singer Laura Lee is born in Chicago.

Laura Lee was raised in Detroit and sang with the Meditation Gospel Singers. In 1967 she signed with Chess Records and in the same year had her first hit, "Dirty Man," one of the most soulful records ever. Her other hits include "Uptight, Good Man" (1967), "Women's Love Rights" (1971) and "Rip Off" (1972).

In the mid-1970s Laura Lee returned to gospel singing.

1948: Singer Jeffrey Osborne is born in Providence, Rhode Island.

Osborne first made the charts as lead singer of the 10-piece R&B funk outfit LTD (Love, Togetherness and Devotion). LTD hit the R&B and pop charts with "Love Ballad" (1976), "Back in Love Again" (1977), "Never Get Enough of Your Love" (1978) and "Holding On" (1978).

In 1980 Osborne left LTD to become a solo act. His debut chart single was "I Really Don't Need No Light," in 1982. He quickly followed up with such smashes as "On the Wings of Love"

(1982), "Don't You Get So Mad" (1983), "Stay with Me Tonight" (1983), "Plane Love" (1984), "Don't Stop" (1984) and "You Should Be Mine" (1986).

With his rich romantic voice, Osborne also hit the charts with a pair of duets: with Joyce Kennedy, "The Last Time I Made Love" in 1984, and "Love Power," with Dionne Warwick, in 1987.

MARCH 10

1983: Michael Jackson's "Billie Jean" is the number 1 pop single and the first single from Jackson's *Thriller* LP, released in 1982, the best-selling album ever. "Billie Jean," written by Jackson and produced by Quincy Jones, sold over two million copies and remained at the number 1 spot on the pop singles chart for seven weeks.

MARCH 11

1919: Bandleader, composer and arranger Mercer Ellington, son of the legendary Duke Ellington, is born in Washington, D.C.

In the late 1930s and early 1940s he had his own band. During the '50s and '60s he had a variety of music-related jobs, ranging from disc jockey to road manager for the Cootie Williams band to musical director for Della Reese.

Over the years, he also worked with his dad's band in a variety of capacities, including player, composer and road manager. Upon the elder Ellington's death, he took over the reins of the Duke Ellington Orchestra. He also conducted the score for the Ellington-based Broadway musical *Sophisticated Ladies*.

1950: Singer Bobby McFerrin is born in New York City.

McFerrin's father was a member of the Metropolitan Opera Company, and his mother was a soloist and vocal coach. In 1958 the McFerrin family moved to Los Angeles, where McFerrin's father dubbed the vocal parts for Sidney Poitier in the film *Porgy and Bess*.

McFerrin studied music theory and composition at Sacramento State and got a job as keyboardist for the Ice Follies touring company band.

In the mid-1970s he began singing. He settled in New Orleans and fronted a group called the Astral Project. Later he moved to the San Francisco Bay area. Eventually he became a solo act, working in piano bars and the like.

In 1980 McFerrin provided some of the vocals for Weather Report's *Sportin' Life* LP. On the strength of that performance, he obtained a recording contract.

By the mid-1980s McFerrin and his one-of-a-kind vocalizings were racking up recognition and awards. In 1986 he won two Grammy awards: best male jazz vocal, for his work on the soundtrack of the Dexter Gordon film *Round Midnight*, and best vocal arranger, for his work with Manhattan Transfer on the album *Another Night in Tunisia*. He won three more in 1988: best male jazz vocal, best children's record (for *The Elephant's Child*), and best performance in a long-form video (for *Spontaneous Inventions*, a concert video that captures Bobby McFerrin at his best).

Bobby McFerrin once said that his ambition was to be an instrument for improvising spontaneous music. He has achieved that goal, and more. McFerrin's vocal acrobatics make him a super scat-jazz singer, a human synthesizer and a one-man doo-wop group.

McFerrin also provided the theme music for NBC's top-rated "The Cosby Show."

1957: Singer Cheryl Lynn is born in Los Angeles.

Cheryl Lynn was discovered on TV's "The Gong Show." She went on to the pop, soul and disco charts in 1978, with "Got to Be Real."

MARCH 12

1940: Jazz and pop vocalist Al Jarreau is born in Milwaukee.

Jarreau started singing when he was four. After college and graduate school at the University of Iowa, where he received a master's degree in psychology, Jarreau landed a job with the State of California as a rehabilitation counselor based in San Francisco.

He began singing with a trio headed by George Duke. In 1968 he turned his full attention to singing and moved to Los Angeles, where for the next several years he played such clubs as Dino's, the Troubador and the Bitter End West.

In 1975 Jarreau signed a contract with Warner Brothers Records and released his debut LP, *We Got By*. Jarreau's earliest success came in Europe. His debut album won him the German equivalent of a Grammy award, for best new international soloist, and his second LP, *Glow*, won him a second German award in 1976.

In 1977, on the strength of his double live-concert album, *Look at the Rainbow*, success came Jarreau's way in the U.S., too. He was declared best male vocalist and best new jazz artist by *Performance* magazine, and he won a Grammy for best jazz vocal performance.

In 1978 he won both the *Down Beat* critics' and readers' polls for best jazz vocalist and best male vocalist. In 1979 he received a Grammy for best jazz vocalist and a silver medal at the Tokyo Music Festival.

Jarreau's first LP for the '80s was *This Time*, released in the spring of 1980. In 1982 he recorded the album *Breaking Away*, which netted him Grammies for both best male pop vocal and best male jazz vocal. The LP also went platinum. That year Jarreau also won best jazz vocalist in the *Playboy* magazine music poll, as well as NAACP Image awards for both album of the year and male artist of the year.

Throughout the 1980s Jarreau continued to record best-selling LPs: *Jarreau*, *Al Jarreau Live in London*, *L is for Lover* and *Hearts Horizon*. He also provided the theme music for the hit TV series "Moonlighting."

1977: The Gap Band, a trio of brothers from Tulsa, makes its chart debut with "Out of the Blue," the first of over two dozen singles that the band placed on the charts.

Ronnie, Charles and Robert Wilson combined rock, funk, R&B and disco beats to rack up a decade's worth of chart hits, including three at number 1: "Burn Rubber" (1980), "Early in the Morning" (1982) and "Outstanding" (1982). Other best-sellers include "Shake" (1979), "Steppin' Out" (1979), "I Don't Believe You Want to Get Up and Dance (Oops Up Side Your Head)" (1980), "Yearning for Your Love" (1981), "You Dropped a Bomb on Me" (1982), "Party Train" (1983), "Beep a Freak" (1984), "Going in Circles" (1984) and "Big Fun" (1986).

MARCH 13

1913: Blues singer and guitarist Otis "Lightnin' Slim" Hicks is born in St. Louis.

Lightnin' Slim played down-home blues with a Bayou funk. He is known for his collaboration with fellow blues-man and brother-in-law Slim Harpo and for his 1959 recording of "Rooster Blues." Other recordings include "My Starter Won't Work," "Bedbug Blues," "Long, Lean Mama" and "G.I. Slim."

Lightnin' Slim died of cancer on July 27, 1974, in Detroit.

1926: Jazz drummer Roy Haynes is born in Roxbury, Massachusetts.

Haynes started out in the early 1940s, around Boston. In 1945 he joined Luis Russell's band and was with Lester Young from 1947 to 1949. In 1949 he joined the Charlie Parker Quintet. In the 1950s he worked with the likes of Sarah Vaughan, Miles Davis and Thelonious Monk and, in the '60s, with George Shearing, Kenny Burrell, Stan Getz, John Coltrane and Gary Burton.

1961: The Vibrations make their chart debut with "The Watusi."

Originally known as the Jayhawks, the Vibrations were formed in Los Angeles in 1955 and consisted of lead singer James Johnson, Carl Fisher, Richard Owens, Dave Govan and Don Bradley.

In 1956 the Jayhawks hit the Top 10 on the R&B charts, with a novelty doo-wop tune called "Stranded in the Jungle." In 1960 they changed their name to the Vibrations and signed with Checker Records. "The Watusi" was their first chart hit for Checker; it hit the Top 20 on the R&B and Top 40 pop charts.

The Vibrations decided to do a little work on the side. Under the name of the Marathons, they signed with Arvee Records and, in the summer of 1961, had a hit record called "Peanut Butter." Naturally, Checker Records sued them.

The Vibrations next appeared on the charts in 1964, with the song "My Girl Sloopy," which became a big hit one year later as "Hang On, Sloopy," recorded by the McCoys. The Vibrations also had a mid-size hit in 1965, with their rendition of "Misty."

1962: Jazz trumpeter Terence Blanchard is born in New Orleans.

Terence Blanchard is one of the brightest stars on the jazz horizon. Blanchard first came to notice in 1982, when he replaced Wynton Marsalis in Art Blakey's Jazz Messengers.

In 1987 he and saxman Donald Harrison formed the Harrison Blanchard Quintet. Their 1988 LP, *Black Pearl*, was critically acclaimed. Terence Blanchard quit playing in 1989, saying that he was burned out, but a year later he released a self-titled solo LP that hit the Top 5 on *Billboard*'s jazz charts.

Blanchard also has an ongoing collaborative relationship with film director Spike Lee. He worked on soundtracks for Lee's *School Daze* (1988) and *Do the Right Thing* (1989). In 1990 he served as technical director (he taught Denzel Washington how to act like a trumpet player) and composed the score for Lee's *Mo' Better Blues*. He also scored Lee's 1991 *Jungle Fever* and his 1992 *Malcolm X*.

MARCH 14

1931: Vocalist Phil Phillips is born John Phillip Baptiste in Lake Charles, Louisiana.

Phil Phillips is one of the charter members of rock 'n' roll's One-Hit-Wonder Club. His one hit was "Sea of Love" (1959), which landed at number 2 on the pop charts and stayed around for over four months. There was renewed interest in the song in 1989, when it served as the centerpiece of the Al Pacino film of the same title.

1934: Composer, arranger, producer and entrepreneur Quincy Jones is born in Chicago.

Quincy Delight Jones, Jr., was raised in Seattle. He received a scholarship to the Berklee College of Music, in Boston. In 1950 he joined Lionel Hampton's band as arranger and trumpet player. He also worked in Paris, as musical director for Barclay Records.

He began recording in 1956. His first LP, *This Is How I Feel About Jazz*, included such notable players as Charles Mingus and Milt Jackson. Jones also wrote arrangements for such artists as Count Basie, Ray Charles, Dinah Washington and Sarah Vaughan.

In the early 1960s Quincy Jones was named musical director for Mercury Records. In this capacity, he produced Lesley Gore's 1963 number 1 pop hit "It's My Party." In 1964 he was made vice president of Mercury, and he began scoring films in the mid-1960s.

In 1974 aneurisms forced Quincy Jones to undergo brain surgery, and this event kept him out of the music business for two years. But in 1979 he began producing LPs for Michael Jackson. The first was *Off the Wall*, which began Jackson's incredible success as a solo performer.

One of the keys to Quincy Jones's musical career is that he is at home with all types of music, from opera to rap, and is able to relate to performers ranging from rappers to Frank Sinatra. His best-selling singles include "Is It Love That We're Missing" (1975), "One Hundred Ways" (with James Ingram, 1981), "I'll Be Good to You" (with Ray Charles and Chaka Khan, 1989) and "The Secret Garden" (1990).

Quincy Jones is the most nominated performer in the history of the Grammies. As of 1991 he had 76 nominations and 25 wins. His composing,

QUINCY JONES

arranging and producing talents have enhanced such best-selling and critically acclaimed LPs as *Birth of a Band*, *The Great Wide World of Quincy Jones*, *Smackwater Jack*, *Body Heat*, *Mellow Madness*, *The Dude*, *L.A. Is My Lady* and *Back on the Block*.

His work for the movies includes composing and arranging musical scores for *In the Heat of the Night*, *For Love of Ivy*, *The Heist* and *The Wiz*. He also produced *The Color Purple*.

For television, he composed the score for the hit miniseries "Roots" and is the executive producer of "The Fresh Prince of Belair."

In 1985 Quincy Jones produced the best-selling "We Are the World" on behalf of USA for Africa.

1934: Jazz organist Shirley Scott is born in Philadelphia. A mainstay since the mid-1950s, Scott was married at one time to sax player Stanley Turrentine. She also served as musical director for Bill Cosby's quiz show, "You Bet Your Life."

MARCH 15

1905: Big-voiced blues singer Bertha "Chippie" Hill is born in Charleston, South Carolina.

Bertha Hill ran away from home to became a dancer in a minstrel show. She was a singer and dancer on the theater circuit in the early 1920s and worked with Ethel Waters, Louis Armstrong and King Oliver.

Hill is best remembered for her 1920s recording of "Trouble in Mind." In the '30s and '40s she was a noted club performer.

Bertha Hill suffered multiple injuries in a hit-and-run car accident and died on May 7, 1950, in New York City.

1912: Blues guitarist Lightnin' Sam Hopkins is born in Centerville, Texas.

Hopkins began playing the blues in the 1920s. His early influences were Blind Lemon Jefferson and Lonnie Johnson. Throughout the '20s and '30s he was teamed with fellow bluesman Texas Alexander, playing the usual gamut of clubs, socials and rent parties.

Lightnin' Hopkins did not record

until 1946. His first sides were for Aladdin Records and featured pianist "Thunder" Smith. In 1949 Hopkins cracked the Top 20 on the R&B chart, with a song called "Tim Moore's Farm." His other best-sellers of the period were "T-Model Blues" (1949), "Shotgun Blues" (1950), "Give Me Central 209" (1952) and "Coffee Blues" (1952). His string of hit singles ended in the early '50s, but Lightnin' Hopkins was recording prolifically into the '70s.

He became a legend, especially in Texas. In a long line of rough-edged Texas boogie 'n' blues guitar players, Lightnin' Hopkins was granddaddy of them all. His licks were fast and hard, and his voice was untinged by any shade of commercialism. He played clubs and festivals throughout the U.S. and Europe. In 1964 he played Carnegie Hall. He was the subject of several European-made blues documentary films, and in 1971 he recorded the soundtrack for the movie *Sounder*.

Lightnin' Hopkins played the blues right up until his death, on January 30, 1982.

1933: Pianist and composer Cecil Taylor is born in New York City.

Taylor began playing the piano at the age of five. He attended the New York College of Music and then spent three years at the New England Conservatory of Music, studying composition and theory.

His professional career began in the early 1950s, in small groups led by Hot Lips Page and Johnny Hodges. In the mid-1950s he formed his own group, which featured soprano saxophonist Steve Lacy and became a fixture at New York's Five Spot Cafe. In 1957 Taylor was well into his "abstract" groove and was one of the highlights of that year's Newport Jazz Festival. By the end of the decade, though, Taylor's prominence in avant-garde jazz had been overshadowed by that of Ornette Coleman.

In 1962 Taylor went to Europe to perform and record, but by the mid-1960s he was rarely performing anymore. In 1968, however, he was featured soloist with the Jazz Composers Orchestra, and he began

performing again in solo concerts and with a group.

In the early 1970s Taylor turned his attention to teaching. He taught at the University of Wisconsin, Glassboro State College (New Jersey) and Tulane University (New Orleans), all the while prolifically composing.

Many critics and students of jazz consider Cecil Taylor to be the pioneering force in the movement of abstract or avant-garde jazz. Some of his best-known LPs are *Jazz Advance* (1956), *Conquistador* (1966) and *Winged Serpent*.

1944: Sly Stone is born Sylvester Stewart in Dallas.

In the mid-1960s Sly Stone was a successful radio deejay, until he decided that he would be better at making hit records than at playing them. He formed a funk-rock band called the Family Stone in 1967. It featured himself on lead vocals and keyboards and included his brother Freddie on guitar, his sister Rosie on piano, Larry Graham on bass, Gregg Errico on drums, trumpeter Cynthia Robinson and saxophonist Jerry Martini. Sly Stone was also the group's principal songwriter and producer.

Sly and the Family Stone debuted on the music charts in February of 1968, with the tune "Dance to the Music," which made it to the Top 10. Over the next several years they racked up three million-selling number 1 singles: "Everyday People" (1968), "Thank You" (1970) and "Family Affair" (1971). They also had hit singles with "I Want to Take You Higher" (1969), "Everybody Is a Star" (1970) and "If You Want Me to Stay" (1973). They appeared in the concert film *Woodstock*, and Sly Stone produced such acts as Bobby Freeman, the Beau Brummels and the Mojo Men.

Larry Graham left in 1973 to form Graham Central Station. Sly Stone became embroiled in personal and drug-related problems, and by the mid-1970s Sly and the Family Stone were no more. They are remembered as one of the first groups to make funk commercially successful.

1910: Bluesman James "Yank" Rachell is born in Brownwell, Tennessee.

Yank Rachell, although proficient on guitar, harmonica and fiddle, is usually though of as the best blues mandolin player around. He is known for his work with Sleepy John Estes and Sonny Boy Williamson. Some of his best recordings are "Blues Mandolin Man," "Mandolin Blues" and "Chicago Style."

Rachell is also an underrated blues songwriter, having written several best-selling tunes recorded by other artists: "Hobo Blues" (John Lee Hooker), "Army Man Blues" (Big Joe Williams) and "LuDella" (Jimmy Rogers).

1957: The Dell Vikings debut on the R&B charts with "Come Go with Me," considered a treasure of the doo-wop era. It hit the Top 10 on both the R&B and pop charts.

The Dell Vikings were formed in 1955, when all the members were in the Air Force and stationed in Pittsburgh. The group was unique in being integrated. It consisted of Norman Wright, Kripp Johnson, Gus Bachus, David Lerchey and Clarence Quick.

The Dell Vikings recorded "Come Go with Me" for Fee Bee Records, a small label, and when the song took off it was purchased and distributed nationally by Dot Records.

After that, things got really interesting. Mercury Records offered the Dell Vikings a bonus to leave Dot and sign with Mercury. When they signed with Dot, only Kripp Johnson had been of legal age, and he was the only one bound to the contract. He stayed at Dot. The other four went to Mercury, and by mid-1957 there were two groups of Dell Vikings recording for two different labels. The Mercury group hit the Top 20 with "Cool Shake" in the summer of 1957.

1970: Singer Tammi Terrell dies of a brain tumor, first diagnosed in 1967 after she collapsed onstage.

Tammi Terrell was born Tammy Montgomery in Philadelphia in 1947. In the mid-1960s she was part of the James Brown show before signing with Motown.

She and Marvin Gaye sang some of pop music's most successful duets. Their hits included "Ain't No Mountain High Enough" (1967), "Your Precious Love" (1967), "If I Could Build My World Around You" (1967), "If This World Were Mine" (1968), "Ain't Nothing Like the Real Thing" (1968) and "You're All I Need to Get By" (1968).

1917: Nat "King" Cole is born Nathaniel Adam Coles in Montgomery, Alabama.

Cole was raised in Chicago and formed his first band, the Royal Dukes, at the age of 17 with his brother, Eddie. In the summer of 1936 the band was called Eddie Cole's Solid Swingers and recorded for the Decca label. When the records didn't sell, Cole joined the Chicago troupe of the musical revue *Shuffle Along*. In 1937 he went West with the show. After it closed, he formed a trio with bassist Wesley Prince and guitarist Oscar Moore and called it the the King Cole Trio.

The group recorded first for a small Los Angeles label, in 1939. In 1940 the trio signed with Decca Records and had a hit in 1941, with "Sweet Lorraine," as well as a best-seller the following year, with "That Ain't Right."

In 1943 Johnny Miller replaced Wesley Prince, and the King Cole Trio performed in the motion pictures *Pistol Packin' Mama* and *Here Comes Elmer*. The same year saw the King Cole Trio sign with Capitol Records. Early in 1944 the group hit the number 1 spot on the R&B charts, with "Straighten Up and Fly Right." Other hits quickly followed: "I Can't See for Lookin'," "Gee Baby, Ain't I Good to You," "It's Only a Paper Moon" and "Get Your Kicks on Route 66."

In 1946 Nat "King" Cole recorded one of his classics, the million-selling "The Christmas Song." During this period he also appeared in several more films, including *Pin-Up Girl, Stars on Parade, Swing in the Saddle, See My Lawyer* and *Breakfast in Hollywood*. In 1947 Cole hit number 1 on the pop charts, with "I Love You for Sentimental Reasons," and in 1948 his "Nature Boy"

was the year's best-selling single record. He officially went solo in 1950.

Nat "King" Cole struck gold with such hits as "Exactly Like You" (1949), "My Mother Told Me" (1950), "Mona Lisa" (1950), "Too Young" (1951), "Pretend" (1953), "Send for Me" (1957) and "Looking Back" (1958).

In 1958 Cole starred as W. C. Handy in the film *St. Louis Blues*. He appeared in other films as well, such as *Small-Town Girl, The Blue Gardenia, China Gate, Night of the Quarter Moon* and *Cat Ballou*. He also had his own TV variety show.

In 1962 Nat "King" Cole captured the attention of the "American Bandstand" generation, landing at number 2 on the pop charts with "Ramblin' Rose" and following up with Top 20 hits like "Dear Lonely Hearts" and "Those Lazy, Hazy, Crazy Days of Summer."

In 1964 ill health forced him to stop performing. He died of lung cancer on February 15, 1965.

1937: Singer, actor and TV game-show host Adam Wade is born in Pittsburgh.

Wade hit the pop Top 10 three times in 1961, with the ballads "Take Good Care of Her," "The Writing on the Wall" and "As If I Didn't Know." He hosted the game show "Musical Chairs" in the mid-1970s and had his own West Coast–based talk show in the 1980s.

1938: Country Charley Pride, undoubtedly the most successful black performer in the annals of country music, is born in Sledge, Mississippi.

Charley Pride initially set his heart on a career as a professional baseball player. He played with the Memphis Red Sox of the Negro American League, in the early 1950s, and in the minor Pioneer League after getting out of the service, in 1958.

Pride was discovered in 1963 by country singer Red Sovine and was signed by the country division of RCA Records. One secret of Pride's success was to be a black man with a pure country sound. Early in his career his recording company and his booking agent never sent out pictures of him. When he walked onstage in a club or arena a few fans would be rattled, but they usually calmed down once they heard him sing.

Starting in 1966, Charley Pride placed over 60 singles on the country charts, more than two dozen of which hit number 1. The roster of his number 1 hits includes "All I Have to Offer You Is Me" (1969), "Is Anybody Goin' to San Antone" (1970), "Kiss an Angel Good Mornin' " (1971), "Don't Fight the Feelings of Love" (1973), "She's Just an Old Love Turned Memory" (1977), "Honky Tonk Blues" (1980), "Mountain of Love" (1981) and "Why, Baby, Why" (1982).

In 1971 Charley Pride was named the Country Music Association's Entertainer of the Year.

1941: "Wicked" Wilson Pickett is born in Prattville, Alabama.

Pickett moved to Detroit in 1955 and began his career singing with gospel groups. In 1960 he joined the Falcons and sang lead on their 1962 hit "I Found a Love." Soon afterward Wilson Pickett embarked on a solo career, signing with Lloyd Price's Double L label. In 1963 his recording of "It's Too Late" landed Pickett in the Top 10 on the soul charts.

In 1965 he moved to Atlantic Records. When his first two singles on Atlantic flopped, the company sent him to Memphis to record at the Stax Records complex. The Stax-Pickett merger provided instant results in the the form of a number 1 R&B single, "In the Midnight Hour."

During the "soul music" era of the mid-1960s to the mid-1970s there was no performer more dynamic than Wilson Pickett. He was a wailer, a screamer and a shouter who made intensely gospel-flavored records and had an electrifying stage presence. He racked up such soul and pop hits as "Don't Fight It" (1965), "634-5789" (1966), "99 and a Half Won't Do" (1966), "Land of 1,000 Dances" (1966), "Mustang Sally" (1966), "Soul Dance #3" (1967), "Funky Broadway" (1967), "I'm in Love" (1967), "I'm a Midnight Mover" (1968) and "Hey Jude" (1969).

In 1970 Wilson Pickett switched from recording in the Deep South and began working with the Philadelphia-based production team of Kenny Gamble and Leon Huff. He continued his chart success, with records like "Engine Number 9" (1970); a pair of 1971 million-sellers, "Don't Let the Green Grass Fool You" and "Don't Knock My Love"; and "Fire and Water" (1972).

WILSON PICKETT

1959: Singer, actress and dancer Irene Cara is born in New York City.

Irene Cara starred in the 1980 hit musical film *Fame.* She also took its theme song of the same title to the number 4 spot on the pop charts.

In 1983 she had a million-selling single with "Flashdance (What a Feeling)," the theme from the film *Flashdance.* As an actress, Cara also appeared on TV in such miniseries as "Roots Two" and in films like *D.C. Cab* and *The Cotton Club.*

MARCH 19

1894: Comedienne Jackie "Moms" Mabley is born Loretta Mary Aiken in Brevard, North Carolina.

Moms Mabley, a pioneer among women standup comics, was billed as the funniest woman in the world. She is best remembered for her "old man" jokes: "The only thing an old man can do for me is give me a young man's telephone number." Moms always appeared

onstage toothless, wearing a frumpy old hat, coat and dress and big brogans.

Moms Mabley began her career in the 1920s in vaudeville, often appearing with Butter Beans and Susie. She was a major draw on the black theater circuit in the '40s, '50s and '60s. She sold out the Apollo in New York and the Howard in Washington countless times.

She recorded a score of "party" comedy LPs for Chess and Mercury Records, 13 of which made the *Billboard* pop album charts. They included *Moms Mabley Onstage, Moms Mabley at the UN, The Funny Sides of Moms Mabley, Moms Mabley at the Playboy Club* and *Moms Mabley Breaks It Up.* She also appeared in such films as *Boarding House Blues, The Emperor Jones* and *Amazing Grace.*

In 1969 she hit the pop Top 40 singles charts singing her tribute to Abraham Lincoln, Martin Luther King, Jr., and John F. Kennedy. Moms Mabley died on May 23, 1975.

1930: Jazz saxophonist Ornette Coleman is born in Fort Worth, Texas.

Coleman started playing alto sax at the age of 14. His first professional gigs were in R&B bands, backing up people like Big Joe Turner and Pee Wee Crayton. In the early 1950s he played briefly with Paul Bley.

Ornette Coleman is master of a genre known as free jazz, which is more radical and has even fewer musical boundaries than the abstract or avant-garde jazz of Cecil Taylor. Before it was accepted as an art form within an art form, free jazz provoked the hostility of the mainstream jazz community—aficionados, critics and even fellow musicians. In 1956 Coleman met trumpeter Don Cherry. Coleman and Cherry shared theories about improvisation, and in 1958 they recorded their first LP, *Something Else.*

Coleman then signed with Atlantic Records. In the fall of 1959 he brought his free-jazz stylings to New York's Five Spot Cafe. Free jazz became established and accepted over the next five years. Coleman recorded seven LPs for Atlantic and made appearances at top jazz venues, including the Newport Jazz Festival.

But Ornette Coleman was not happy about the money he was making or about dealing with club owners and the like. In 1962 he quit, but he returned in 1965, playing top clubs in New York and touring Europe. In 1971 he opened his own venue, Artist House, in New York City. In 1975 he formed a group called the Prime Time Band.

His most critically acclaimed LPs include *The Shape of Jazz to Come* (1959), *Free Jazz* (1960), *Of Human Feelings* (1979) and *Song X* (with Pat Metheny, 1985).

1939: Singer Clarence "Frogman" Henry is born in Algiers, Louisiana.

Henry got his nickname because his range ran from deep bass to a high falsetto. He first hit the Top 10 on both the R&B and pop charts in 1956, with "Ain't Got No Home." His other chart hits include "But I Do" (1961), "You Always Hurt the One You Love" (1961) and "Lonely Street" (1961).

1938: Singer Walter Jackson is born in Pensacola, Florida.

Jackson was raised in Detroit. He was crippled by polio as a child and performed onstage with the aid of crutches. In the late 1950s he recorded with a group called the Velvetones.

Of all the singers of the Chicago Sound era, which included Jerry Butler and Curtis Mayfield, none had a fuller, richer voice than Jackson did. Jackson began recording solo in 1962. He signed with Okeh Records and hit the soul charts in 1964, with a Curtis Mayfield composition, "It's All Over." Jackson's forte was ballads, and in 1965 he hit the soul Top 20, with "Suddenly I'm All Alone." Other hits from his Okeh period are "Lee Cross," "Welcome Home," "It's an Uphill Climb to the Bottom," "Speak Her Name" and "My Ship Is Coming In." His biggest chart hit was "Feelings," in 1976.

Walter Jackson died of a cerebral hemorrhage on June 20, 1983.

MARCH 20

1915: Vocalist and guitarist Sister Rosetta Tharpe is born Rosetta Nubin in Cotton Plant, Arkansas.

Tharpe's mother was an outstanding gospel singer named Katie Bell Nubin. By the age of six Tharpe had mastered the guitar and was traveling with her mother to churches and conventions.

In 1938 she joined Lucky Millinder's band as a vocalist. That year she also recorded her first gospel side for Decca Records and had an immediate hit, with "This Train." She also appeared with Cab Calloway and took her brand of gospel music into top nightclubs like Cafe Society.

By the 1940s she was at the top of the R&B charts, with such songs as "Trouble in Mind" (1942), "Strange Things Happen Every Day" (1945), "Didn't It Rain" (1948), "Precious Memories" (1948) and "Up Above My Head I Hear Music in the Air" (1948). In late 1949 her version of "Silent Night" hit number 6 on the R&B charts.

In the late 1940s she also recorded under the name Sister Katy Marie, and in 1947 she teamed up with Marie Knight for a series of thrilling gospel duet recordings. The duo split up in the early '50s, after cutting some blues records with which Tharpe was very unhappy. She quickly returned to gospel music.

Sister Rosetta Tharpe was one of very few artists to have successfully juggled a career in both gospel and R&B. In both styles she was an unabashed rocker. During the late '50s and the '60s she performed and recorded in Europe.

Sister Rosetta Tharpe suffered a stroke and died in Philadelphia on October 9, 1973.

MARCH 21

1893: Blues vocalist and guitarist Bo Carter is born Armenter Chatman in Bolton, Mississippi.

Carter is best remembered for his bawdy recordings and double-entendre lyrics. From the late 1920s until 1940 Carter released records like "Corrine, Corrine," "Mean Feeling Blues," "Please Warm My Wiener," "Ride My Mule," "I Love That Thing," "My Pencil Don't Write," "Ramrod Daddy" and "Howling Tomcat Blues."

In the mid-1939s Carter went blind, and by the early 1940s he had left the music business.

Bo Carter suffered a cerebral hemorrhage and died on September 21, 1964.

1902: Bluesman Eddie "Son" House is born in Riverton, Mississippi.

As a teenager, he became a preacher around Mississippi and Louisiana and continued his ministry until the early 1920s. Around 1923 he took up guitar and began playing and singing the blues. He recorded for the Paramount label and, in 1930, issued two classics, "Preachin' Blues" and "Death Letter."

From 1930 to 1942 he recorded for the Library of Congress. In 1942 he moved to Rochester, New York, and retired from music.

Son House began to record again in 1948. In the 1960s he appeared at the Newport Folk Festival and recorded for Columbia Records. Throughout the late '60s and early '70s he worked blues and folk festivals in the U.S. and Europe. He is remembered for his gruff voice and his bottleneck guitar stylings.

Son House died on October 19, 1988, in Detroit.

1930: Otis Spann, king of the modern blues piano players, is born in Jackson, Mississippi.

Spann's mother had worked with Bessie Smith and Memphis Minnie, and by the age of seven Spann was playing piano in his father's church. In the late

OTIS SPANN

1930s he won an amateur contest at the Alamo Theater in Jackson. He attended Campbell Junior College and was a Golden Gloves boxer and a semipro football player. He also served in the U.S. Army.

In the late 1940s he moved to Chicago and began playing clubs with Muddy Waters, Memphis Slim and Roosevelt Sykes. In the early 1950s he recorded with Waters and throughout that decade was a featured member of his backup band, noticed by record companies because of his work on Waters's 1960 LP *Muddy Waters at Newport*.

In 1960 Spann recorded his classic LP *Otis Spann Is the Blues*. Throughout the 1960s he continued to play with Waters and recorded several albums: *Half Ain't Been Told*, *The Blues Never Die* and *Nobody Knows Chicago Like I Do*.

Otis Spann died of cancer on April 24, 1970, in Chicago.

1951: Stylistics lead singer Russell Thompkins, Jr., is born in Philadelphia.

In the Philadelphia-based mellow romantic-ballad groove, the Stylistics took up where the Delphonics left off. They had the same writer, arranger and producer—Thom Bell. Besides Russell Thompkins, the Stylistics consisted of Airron Love, James Smith, James Dunn and Herbie Murrell.

Thompkins's wailing falsetto can be heard on such early Stylistics hits as "Stop, Look, Listen to Your Heart" (1971), "You Are Everything" (1971), "Betcha By Golly Wow" (1972), "I'm Stone in Love with You" (1972), "Break Up to Make Up" (1973) and "You Make Me Feel Brand New" (1974). Most of these were million-sellers.

1987: Rappers Salt-N-Pepa—Cheryl "Salt" James, Sandy "Pepa" Denton and their deejay, Spinderella (Dee Dee Roper)—make their chart debut with "My Mike Sounds Nice."

The group has had a pair of platinum-selling singles, "Push It" (1987) and "Expression" (1990). Salt-N-Pepa is the best-selling female rap group working today.

The women were working in a Sears department store when they met a fellow employee by the name of Herby Luv Bug, who moonlighted as a rap record producer. Their collaboration has led not only to best-selling singles but to a trio of hot LPs: *Hot, Cool and Vicious* (1987), *A Salt with a Deadly Pepa* (1988) and *Blacks Magic* (1990).

MARCH 22

1943: Vocalist and guitarist George Benson is born in Pittsburgh.

George Benson began playing the guitar at the age of eight. As a teenager playing in a rock 'n' roll band, he listened to and studied a wide variety of guitar players, from Wes Montgomery to Charlie Christian to country picker Hank Garland. Benson's playing has been most influenced by Montgomery.

In 1961 Benson joined the quartet of jazz organist Brother Jack McDuff. In 1965 he formed his own group. In the late 1960s he signed with Verve Records and recorded a series of Wes Montgomery–like LPs.

In the early 1970s Benson was a staff musician and recording artist for Creed Taylor's CTI label. He recorded several LPs for CTI, including *Bad Benson*, *Back Talk* and *Good King Bad*.

In 1975 George Benson signed with Warner Brothers Records and released the LP *Breezin'*, which sold over two million copies. One of its vocal tracks, "This Masquerade," hit the Top 10 on the pop music charts. In 1976 he received a Grammy for best new artist.

Benson's vocals are pleasingly pop but also jazzy, and he has won attention for his ability to scat in unison with his guitar licks. He has compiled a list of hit singles that includes "The Greatest Love of All" (1977), "On Broadway" (1978), "Give Me the Night" (1980) and "Turn Your Love Around" (1981). His best-selling LPS include *In Flight*, *Livin' Inside Your Love* and *Give Me the Night*.

MARCH 23

1918: Vocalist Granville H. "Stick" McGhee, younger brother of well-known bluesman Brownie

McGhee, is born in Knoxville, Tennessee.

In 1949 McGhee recorded the song that put Atlantic Records on the map: the R&B classic "Drinking Wine, Spo-Dee-O-Dee, Drinking Wine." Stick McGhee died of cancer on August 15, 1961.

1953: Singer Chaka Khan is born Yvette Marie Stevens in Great Lakes, Illinois.

Khan fronted the pop-rock band Rufus in the 1970s and charted with such hits as "Tell Me Something Good" (1974), "You Got the Love" (1974) and "Sweet Thing" (1976).

In the late '70s she began recording solo, hitting the Top 40 with "I'm Every Woman" (1978). Her biggest hit was "I Feel for You" (1984). Chaka Khan's other hit singles include "Own the Night" (1985), "Love of a Lifetime" (1986) and "I'll Be Good to You" (1989).

MARCH 24

1904: Boogie-woogie piano player Pete Johnson is born in Kansas City, Missouri.

Johnson was raised in an orphanage. He became an attraction in clubs around Kansas City in the mid-1920s.

In the 1930s he met blues shouter Big Joe Turner, when both worked in Piney Brown's club in Kansas City. They collaborated on such hits as "Piney Brown's Blues" (1941), "Roll 'em Pete" (1941), "S. K. Blues" (1945) and "Johnson and Turner Blues" (1945).

Johnson is recognized as one of the leading forces in the boogie-woogie revival of the late 1930s. In 1954 he was paralyzed by a stroke. Pete Johnson died of a heart attack on March 23, 1967.

1937: Singer Larry "Billy" Stewart, known as the Fat Boy because of his 300-pound frame and his 1962 hit record of that name, is born in Washington, D.C.

Stewart was a unique vocalist. He employed techniques of scatting—doubling and quadrupling the syllables of words and singing in a high-pitched, almost falsetto voice. In recording sessions and live concerts, Stewart often utilized an ahead-of-its-time sound system that employed such features as tape echo, which made his sound all the more unique.

Stewart grew up singing in church. He entered talent contests at the Howard Theater and sang with his uncle "Houn' Dog" Ruffin's combo. In 1955 he joined a singing group called the Rainbows. Two of the other Rainbows were Don Covay and Marvin Gaye. Later Stewart played piano in BoDiddley's backup band.

In 1956 he signed with Chess Records but had no hits. He left Chess in 1962 and went on to record several hits for other labels, including Eric, Okeh and United Artists. Besides "Fat Boy," "Reap What You Sow" was a hit for Stewart in 1962. Other pop and soul hits were "Strange Feeling" (1963), "I Do Love You" (1965), "Sitting in the Park" (1965), "Summertime" (1966), "Secret Love" (1966) and "Cross My Heart" (1968).

Billy Stewart died in a car accident on January 17, 1970.

MARCH 25

1942: The queen of soul, Aretha Franklin, is born in Memphis.

Aretha Franklin cut her musical teeth by singing gospel music at New Bethel Baptist Church, in Detroit, whose pastor was her father, legendary gospel great C. L. Franklin. In her teens, Aretha Franklin recorded her first album, *The Gospel Sound of Aretha Franklin*, for Chess Records.

In the early 1960s she was signed to Columbia Records. In six years with that label she recorded 10 albums.

In 1966 Franklin signed with Atlantic. Her first release for that label was a gold record, "I Never Loved a Man (the Way I Love You)." The LP of the same name yielded her first gold album and produced her best-known hit, a cover of Otis Redding's "Respect." Hit after hit followed: "Baby, I Love You," "A Natural Woman," "Chain of Fools," "Since You've Been Gone" and the LPs *Aretha Arrives* and *Lady Soul*. In her first year at Atlantic she earned five gold records and was awarded the first of eight consecutive Grammy awards for best female R&B vocal performance.

She continued to score in the 1970s, with hits like "Think," "I Say a Little Prayer," "See-Saw," "Spanish Harlem," "Bridge Over Troubled Water," "Rock Steady" and "You're All I Need to Get By." Franklin also wrote and coproduced many of her own hits.

Franklin started off the 1980s by switching labels. She signed with Clive Davis's Arista Records, and her initial release for that label, the LP *Aretha*, yielded a hit, "United Together," and earned her a 14th grammy. In 1980 she also made her film debut, in *The Blues Brothers*. Franklin had her 24th gold record in 1982, with the album *Jump to It*.

In 1985 came the LP *Who's Zoomin' Who*, Franklin's most successful effort ever. It went platinum and gave her such Top 10 hits as "Freeway of Love" and the title cut. "Freeway of Love" gained Franklin another Grammy for best female R&B vocal performance, and she scored a nomination with the Eurythmics for "Sisters Are Doin' It for Themselves." She also won two American Music Awards.

In 1987 Aretha Franklin returned to her roots and recorded *One Lord, One Faith, One Baptism*, a gospel album that landed on *Billboard*'s Top 200.

ARETHA FRANKLIN

MARCH 26

1917: Singer Rufus Thomas is born in Cayce, Mississippi.

Thomas began his career by working in minstrel shows. He did some recording in the late 1940s and early 1950s. In 1953 he took a job as a disc jockey at a Memphis radio station, WDIA. That year he also hit the R&B charts for the first time, with "Bearcat," an "answer" song to Big Mama Thornton's "Hound Dog."

Rufus Thomas signed with Stax Records in 1960, after approaching the company about signing his daughter, Carla ("Gee Whiz") Thomas. He had a string of quasi-comic, funky, dance-oriented hits in the 1960s and 1970s. His biggest hits include "The Dog" (1963), "Walking the Dog" (1963), "Can Your Monkey Do the Dog" (1964), "Do the Funky Chicken" (1970), "Push and Pull" (1970), "The Breakdown" (1971) and "Do the Funky Penguin" (1971). He also created dance steps to accompany his recordings. One dance, the Dog, was deemed obscene and was banned on several TV dance-party shows.

1925: Jazzman James Moody, master of the flute and of tenor and alto saxophone, is born in Savannah, Georgia.

Moody was raised in Newark, New Jersey, and took up alto sax at the age of 16. After serving in the U.S. Air Force, he joined the bebop big band of Dizzy Gillespie, in 1947. That year he also made his first recordings as a band leader, under the name James Moody and His Bebop Men, employing players from Gillespie's band.

In 1949 he moved to Europe. There he recorded the improvisational masterpiece "I'm in the Mood for Love." In 1951 he returned to the U.S. and worked with Dinah Washington and Eddie Jefferson. In the early 1960s he rejoined Gillespie's band.

In 1985 James Moody received a Grammy nomination for best jazz instrumental performance, for his playing on Manhattan Transfer's *Vocalese* LP. Moody's best-known LPs include *Moody's Moods* (1956), *The Blues and Other Colors* (1967) and *Sweet and Lovely* (1989).

1950: Vocalist Teddy Pendergrass is born in Philadelphia.

Pendergrass first came to notice in the early 1970s, as lead singer of Harold Melvin and the Blue Notes. With his rich, full baritone and romantic lyrics, he sang lead on such Top 20 hits as "If You Don't Know Me By Now" (1972), "The Love I Lost" (1976), "Bad Luck" (1975) and "Wake Up, Everybody" (1976).

Pendergrass embarked on a solo career in 1977. He released a series of albums containing mostly love ballads, with sensual, almost graphic lyrics, and toured the world with his "For Ladies Only" concerts. By the early 1980s he was easily the world's top black male sex symbol.

At the height of his career, on March 26, 1982, Teddy Pendergrass suffered massive internal and spinal-cord injuries in a car accident that left him a quadripelegic. But he went on, in the mid-1980s, to record a pair of moderately successful LPs. He returned to the top of the charts in 1988, with the LP *Joy*.

Teddy Pendergrass's best-selling singles include "I Don't Love You Anymore," "Close the Door" (1978), "Turn Off the Lights" (1979), "Can We Try" (1980), "Love T.K.O." (1980), "You're My Latest, My Greatest Inspiration" (1981), "Hold Me" (1984), "Love 4/2" (1986) and "Joy" (1988).

1944: Diana Ross is born Diane Earle in Detroit.

Led by Ross's sultry vocals, the Supremes were and remain the top-selling female vocal group of all time. In 1967 the Supremes were renamed Diana Ross and the Supremes.

In 1970 Diana Ross ventured out as a solo artist. She achieved immediate success with classics like "Reach Out and Touch Somebody's Hand," "Ain't No Mountain High Enough" and "Touch Me in the Morning."

The '70s also saw Ross turn to films. She made her debut in *Lady Sings the Blues* and earned an Academy Award nomination and a Golden Globe award for her portrayal of legendary blues singer Billie Holiday. She also appeared in *Mahogany* (1975) and *The Wiz* (1978).

In the 1980s came other hit records: "Upside Down," "I'm Coming Out," "It's My Turn" and the smash "Endless Love," a duet with Lionel Richie.

Ross was also active in TV in the 1980s. In 1981 she starred in the CBS TV special "Diana." That was followed by "Standing Room Only: Diana Ross," an HBO special, and "For One and For All," her 1983 Central Park concert beamed around the world live via satellite.

With the most number 1 hits as a female solo artist in music history, as well as over 50 albums in her quarter-century career, Diana Ross is one of the all-time recording greats. From her 1963 debut with the Supremes to 1987, not a year passed without Diana Ross placing material on the charts.

MARCH 27

1905: Vocalist and pianist Leroy Carr is born in Nashville.

Carr was raised in Indianapolis and taught himself to play piano. As a teenager, he dropped out of school and joined a traveling circus. He then served in the U.S. Army and began singing and playing in Paris, in the early 1920s.

Carr's recordings were made between 1928 and 1935. His best-known song is "How Long, How Long Blues." Other great recordings by Carr (with guitarist Scrapper Blackwell) include "Suicide Blues," "You Left Me Crying," "Low Down Out Blues," "Hard Times Done Drove Me to Drink," "No Good Woman Blues," "Alhi Blues" and "Rocks in My Bed."

Though he is classified as a blues singer, Carr's best-known work reveals him to be more of a "smoothie" than a shouter. His famed collaborations with Blackwell are essentially precursors of the musical style that made the King Cole Trio so popular in the 1940s.

Leroy Carr died of nephritis due to acute alcoholism on April 29, 1935.

1915: Bluesman Robert "Junior" Lockwood is born in Marvell, Arkansas.

Lockwood learned his Delta blues from the master—his stepfather, Robert Johnson.

In the 1930s Lockwood worked with Sonny Boy Williamson and Howlin' Wolf. He moved to Chicago in 1940 and has been based there ever since.

As well as recording on his own, Lockwood has been a much sought-after session guitarist and can be heard on records by Williamson and such other blues greats as Little Walter and Otis Spann.

Lockwood is still active on the blues club circuit. His best LPs include *Robert Lockwood and Johnny Shines*, *Steady Rolling Man* and *Hangin' On*.

1924: Vocalist Sarah Vaughan— one of the jazz world's most famous song stylists, with her gutsy, unmistakable soprano voice—is born in Newark, New Jersey.

Vaughan began studying the piano at the age of seven and was soon playing organ and singing in her church choir. In October 1942 she won an amateur talent contest at Harlem's Apollo Theater, with a rendition of "Body and Soul."

She joined Earl "Fatha" Hines's band as vocalist and second pianist. In 1944 she joined Billy Eckstine's band and first recorded in 1944, for Continental Records. After the breakup of Eckstine's band, in 1945, she became a solo artist.

By the mid-1950s Sarah Vaughan, known also as "Sassy" and "the divine one," had acquired a following among jazz fans and had also begun to hit the R&B and pop charts, with such records as "Make Yourself Comfortable" (1954) and "Whatever Lola Wants" (1955). In 1959 she scored a huge success with "Broken-Hearted Melody." Over the years Sarah Vaughan recorded many critically acclaimed LPs, including *Sarah Vaughan*, *Sarah Vaughan and Billy Eckstine Sing the Irving Berlin Songbook*, *Sarah Vaughan Sings Gershwin*, *Sassy*, *Send in the Clowns* (with the Count Basie Orchestra), *The Divine* and *Crazy and Mixed Up*.

Sarah Vaughan was married several times—to her manager, George Treadwell, musician Waymon Reed and pro footballer Clyde Atkins. In 1989 she received a lifetime-achievement Grammy. She died of lung cancer on April 3, 1990.

1932: Vocalist and harmonica player Herman "Little Junior" Parker is born in Clarksdale, Mississippi. Some sources list his birthday as March 3, 1927, and his birthplace as West Memphis, Arkansas.

In the late 1940s Parker was leader of Howlin' Wolf's backup band. In 1951 he was with the famed Memphis band the Beale Streeters before forming his own band, the Blue Flames. In the 1953–54 period he was part of the Johnny Ace Revue.

Parker was one of the most commercially successful bluesmen of the 1950s and 1960s. His string of R&B chart singles includes "Feelin' Good" (1953), "Next Time You See Me" (1957), "Driving Wheel" (1961) and "In the Dark" and "Annie Get Your Yo Yo" (1962). His biggest hits were on the Houston-based Duke label.

Little Junior Parker died of a brain tumor on November 18, 1971.

1937: Guitarist and vocalist Johnny Clyde Copeland, one of the most popular of the current crop of Texas bluesmen, is born in Haynesville, Louisiana.

Copeland was raised in Magnolia, Arkansas, and began his musical career as a sideman, backing up the likes of Bobby "Blue" Bland, T-Bone Walker, Big Mama Thornton, Otis Redding and Eddie Floyd.

Copeland recorded throughout the late 1950s and the 1960s but didn't really catch on until he moved to New York and began recording for the small Rounder label.

His best-selling LPs are *Texas Twister*, *Bringing It All Back Home*, *Copeland Special* and *Make My Home Where I Hang My Hat*.

MARCH 28

1923: Jazzman Thaddeus Joseph "Thad" Jones is born in Pontiac, Michigan.

Jones, along with being a composer and arranger, was a master of trumpet, cornet and valve trombone. He worked as player, composer and arranger with Count Basie's band from 1954 to 1963. From 1965 to 1978 he co-led the Thad Jones–Mel Lewis Jazz Orchestra.

In 1978 Jones moved to Denmark and formed his own jazz band, Eclipse. Among his best recordings are *Thad Jones and Charles Mingus*, *Thad Jones/Mel Lewis: At the Village Gate* and *The Fabulous Thad Jones*.

Thad Jones died in Copenhagen on August 21, 1986.

MARCH 29

1918: Singer, actress and comedienne Pearl Bailey is born in Newport News, Virginia.

Bailey began her career as a dancer in Philadelphia. Between 1933 and 1945 she sang with a variety of bands. In 1946 she scored an R&B hit with the song "Fifteen Years (and I'm Still Serving Time)." That same year she made her New York stage debut, in *St. Louis Woman*. She also appeared in such shows as *Arms and the Girl*, *House of Flowers*, *Bless You All* and *Hurry Up, America*. In the 1960s she won a Tony award for her performance in the Broadway musical *Hello, Dolly*.

Pearl Bailey's film credits include *Variety Girl*; *Carmen Jones*; *St. Louis Blues*; *Porgy and Bess*; *Norman, Is That You?*; *That Certain Feeling*; and *All the Fine Young Cannibals*.

She also starred in her own television variety show, as well as in several television specials.

In 1952 Pearl Bailey married jazz drummer Louis Bellson. She died on August 17, 1990.

PEARL BAILEY

MARCH 30

1914: Blues harmonica player Sonny Boy Williamson number 1 is born in Jackson, Tennessee. (Sonny Boy Williamson number 2 was Alex "Rice" Miller, who had the 1955 hit "Don't Start Me Talking.")

Sonny Boy Williamson number 1 was born John Lee Williamson. He worked with John Estes and Sunnyland Slim

around Tennessee and Arkansas before moving to Chicago, in 1934. He was considered one of the shapers of the style that we know today as modern Chicago blues. He first recorded for Blue Bird Records in 1937.

Throughout the 1940s he worked as a club performer and as a member of Muddy Waters's band. In 1947 and 1948 he had R&B chart hits with "Shake the Boogie" and "Better Cut That Out."

One June 1, 1948, upon leaving a nightclub, Sonny Boy Williamson was mugged, beaten and murdered.

1963: Rapper M. C. Hammer is born Stanley Kirk Burrell in Oakland.

In the 1970s Burrell was a batboy for the Oakland A's baseball team. He got the nickname Hammer because folks around the ballpark thought he resembled Hammerin' Hank Aaron, baseball's home-run king.

When Hammer began his career as an entertainer, he borrowed money from several A's players to start his own record company. Hammer first burst upon the scene in 1990, with the hit single "U Can't Touch This." He followed up with such million-selling singles as "Have You Seen Her," "Pray," and "Too Legit to Quit."

M. C. Hammer's top selling LPs include *Let's Get It Started*; *Please Hammer, Don't Hurt 'Em*; and *Too Legit to Quit*. He recorded the theme for the movie *The Addams Family*, as well as a series of TV commercials for Kentucky Fried Chicken.

M. C. Hammer is a top box-office attraction at concert venues. He is the most commercially successful artist in rap today. His stage show features legions of uniquely costumed dancers who perform nonstop for two to three hours per show. Aside from being a rapper, Hammer is also a dancer, songwriter, record producer, record-company owner and owner of a stable of top-flight thoroughbred race horses.

MARCH 31

1905: Vocalist and pianist Big Maceo is born Major Merriweather in Atlanta.

During the 1940s Big Maceo was one of the most prominent session musicians in Chicago. In 1946 he suffered a stroke and lost the use of his left hand, but he continued to play and perform. His best-remembered R&B hits are "Worried Life Blues" (1941), "Things Have Changed" (1945) and "Chicago Breakdown" (1946).

Big Maceo died of a heart attack on February 26, 1953.

1911: Freddie Green, solo guitarist for over forty years in the rhythm section of Count Basie's orchestra, is born in Charleston, South Carolina.

1921: Singer and guitarist Lowell Fulson (often called Fulsom) is born in Tulsa, Oklahoma.

Fulson's grandfather was a country fiddler. His mother was a singer and guitarist. Fulson's first professional musician's job was with a group called Dan Wright's String Band, in Ada, Oklahoma.

In 1939 he joined bluesman Texas Alexander as a guitar player and moved to Texas. From 1943 to 1945 he served in the U.S. Navy. After the war he moved to California.

Lowell Fulson first recorded in 1946, teaming up with pianist Lloyd Glenn. Fulson first hit the R&B charts in 1948, with "Three O'Clock Blues." In 1950 and 1951 he had a string of Top 10 R&B hits, including "Every Day I Have the Blues," "Blue Shadows," "Lonesome Christmas," "Low Society Blues" and "I'm a Night Owl." When not leading his own band, Fulson worked with such top R&B stars as Ivory Joe Hunter, Big Joe Turner, Pee Wee Crayton, Bullmoose Jackson and Hot Lips Page. (Early in their musical careers, Ray Charles and jazz saxophonist Stanley Turrentine were members of Lowell Fulson's backup band.)

In 1954 he signed with Checker Records and recorded the blues classic "Reconsider, Baby." In 1967 he wrote and recorded "Tramp," which became a big hit for Otis Redding and Carla Thomas.

Fulson is one of the most underrated of the modern bluesmen. He is associated with the two styles of modern blues: Texas blues and West Coast blues.

1956: The Coasters make their chart debut, with "Down in Mexico."

The Coasters were formed in Los Angeles in 1955. Originally they consisted of lead singer Carl Gardner, Leon Hughes, Billy Guy, Bobby Nunn and Adolph Jacob.

Gardner and Nunn had been members of the Robins, a group that charted with "If It's So, Baby" (1950) and "Smokey Joe's Cafe" (1955). In 1958 Will "Dub" Jones, formerly of the Cadets, replaced Nunn as bass singer, and in 1961 former Cadillacs lead singer Earl "Speedo" Carroll joined the group.

In the '50s and '60s the Coasters were the clown princes of rock 'n' roll. They mixed humor with doo-wop and rock. Their style and routines were hilarious. They racked up over two dozen R&B and pop chart hits, including "Searchin'" (1957), "Youngblood" (1957), "Yakety Yak" (1958), "Charlie Brown" (1959), "Poison Ivy" (1959) and "Little Egypt" (1961).

Most of the Coasters' hits were written and produced by the team of Jerry Leiber and Mike Stoller.

APRIL 1

1895: Blues singer Alberta Hunter is born in Memphis.

Hunter sang as a child in school and began doing club work around 1912 in Chicago. In 1918 she worked with the legendary King Oliver.

She began her recording career in 1921. On her earliest records she was accompanied by Fats Waller, Fletcher Henderson, Eubie Blake and Louis Armstrong.

In 1922 she took over Bessie Smith's role in the musical comedy *How Come* and was a consistent box-office draw on the theater and club circuits throughout the '20s. In 1927 she embarked on her first European tour and remained abroad for two years.

In the early 1930s Alberta Hunter starred in such musical variety shows as *Change Your Luck*, *The Cherry Lane Follies* and *Struttin' Time*. In 1933 she toured Europe a second time and made films in England. In 1939 she appeared with Ethel Waters in the show *Mamba's Daughter*. She spent most of the late 1930s abroad.

In the early '40s Hunter recorded for the Decca label. Throughout World War II she worked USO shows in Europe and Asia.

In the '50s she recorded with such groups as Buster Bailey's Blues Busters and Lovie Austin's Blues Serenaders. She then retired as a performer and pursued a second career as a practical nurse, receiving her license from a nursing program sponsored by the YWCA.

In the '70s she reemerged as a performer and appeared on such TV shows as "Today," "The Mike Douglas Show," "Camera Three," "The Dick Cavett Show" and "To Tell the Truth." In 1978 she appeared at the Newport Jazz Festival.

Alberta Hunter died on October 17, 1984.

1897: Singer Lucille Bogan, a 1920s blueswoman who recorded for Okeh, is born in Amory, Mississippi.

Bogan's biggest hit was "Sweet Petunia" (1927). She also recorded under the name Bessie Jackson.

Lucille Bogan stopped recording around 1934. She died on August 10, 1948, in Los Angeles.

1927: Singer and pianist Amos Milburn is born in Houston.

Milburn graduated from high school at the age of 15. He lied about his age and joined the U.S. Navy. Milburn earned 13 battle stars during the war. At the end of the war he returned to Houston and formed a six-piece combo.

In 1964 he met Ann McCullum, who became his manager and got him a contract with Aladdin Records. Milburn recorded 75 sides before finally hitting the charts in 1948, with "Chicken Shack Boogie," an R&B number 1 song. He followed up with such smashes as "It Took a Long Long Time" (1948), "Bewildered" (1948), "A & M Blues" (1949), "Hold Me, Baby" (1949), "In the Middle of the Night" (1949), "Roomin' House Boogie" (1949), "Empty Arms Blues" (1949), "Lets Make Christmas Merry, Baby" (1949), "Real Pretty Mama Blues" (1949), "Walking Blues" (1950) and "Sax Shack Boogie" (1950). The record labels read "Amos Milburn and His Aladdin Chickenshackers." Amos Milburn was the top R&B artist of 1949 in both juke-box play and retail sales.

Milburn was called the king of rhythm and booze because most of his biggest R&B hits were associated with whiskey. At the top of the R&B charts in the early fifties, he placed such titles as "Bad, Bad Whiskey" (1950), "Just One More Drink" (1951), "Thinking and Drinking" (1952), "Let Me Go Home Whiskey" (1953), "One Scotch, One Bourbon, One Beer" (1953) and "Good,

Good Whiskey" (1954). His recording career declined in the mid-1950s.

Amos Milburn died on January 3, 1980.

1949: Keyboardist, author, poet and composer Gil Scott-Heron is born in Chicago.

Scott-Heron attended Lincoln University. He earned a master's degree in creative writing and taught at Columbia University. In 1968 he published his first novel.

He formed a jazz partnership with bassist Brian Jackson. In the late '70s and early '80s Scott-Heron hit the charts with such compositions as "Johannesburg" (1975), "The Bottle" (1977), "Angel Dust" (1978), "Legend in His Own Mind" (1981) and his song about Ronald Reagan, "Re-Ron" (1984).

Gil Scott-Heron's music and poetry deal with such issues as drugs, racism and apartheid.

APRIL 2

1939: Marvin Gaye is born Marvin Pentz Gaye, Jr., in Washington, D.C.

Gaye grew up in D.C., where he began singing in his father's church. He also sang in local groups like the Rainbows and the Marquees, and he was a member of Harvey Fuqua's reorganized Moonglows.

Gaye moved to Detroit in 1960 and found work at Motown Records as a session drummer. He later married Anna Gordy, the sister of Berry Gordy, Jr.

Gaye was Motown's most successful male solo act. Between 1962 and 1982 he placed more than 60 singles on the pop and soul charts. He racked up 13 number 1 soul hits and a trio of number 1 pop hits: "Stubborn Kind of Fellow" (1962), "Pride and Joy" (1963), "How Sweet It Is" (1965), "I'll Be Doggone" (1965), "Ain't That Peculiar" (1965), "I Heard It Through the Grapevine" (1968), "Too Busy Thinking About My

Baby" (1969), "What's Going On" (1971), "Mercy Mercy Me (the Ecology)" (1971), "Inner City Blues" (1971), "Let's Get It On" (1973), "Got to Give It Up" (1977) and his only million-seller, "Sexual Healing," recorded in Europe in 1982.

Marvin Gaye also sang duets. The most popular were with the late Tammi Terrell. From 1967 to 1970 Marvin and Tammi charted with such songs as "Ain't No Mountain High Enough," "Your Precious Love," "If I Could Build My World Around You," "Ain't Nothing Like the Real Thing" and "You're All I Need to Get By." Other Gaye duets include 1964's "What's the Matter, Baby," with Mary Wells, 1967's "It Takes Two," with Kim Weston, and 1974's "Don't Knock My Love," with Diana Ross.

Gaye suffered a variety of problems in the '70s. He went into seclusion after the death of Tammi Terrell. He went through a messy divorce, had tax and drug problems and left Motown. He moved to Europe and signed with Columbia Records in 1982.

On April 1, 1984, Marvin Gaye was fatally shot by his father during an argument. Gaye was posthumously inducted into the Rock 'n' Roll Hall of Fame in 1987.

MARVIN GAYE

1977: Frankie Beverly and Maze make their chart debut with "When I'm Alone."

Frankie Beverly and Maze create a superb blend of harmony and funk heavily influenced by the sounds of Motown and Philly. The heart of the group is lead singer Frankie Beverly, heavily influenced by Marvin Gaye. Over the years, group members have included Wayne Thomas, Sam Porter, Robin Duke, Roame Lowry, McKinley Williams, Joe Provost, Billy Johnson, Phillip Woo and Ron Smith. They had a number 1 soul hit in 1985, with "Back in Stride." Other hits include "Workin' Together" (1978), "Feel That You're Feelin'" (1979), "Running Away" (1981), "Love Is the Key" (1983) and "Too Many Games" (1985).

APRIL 3

1894: Actor and bandleader Dooley Wilson is born in Tyler, Texas.

Wilson made his screen debut in *Casablanca*, as the guy sitting at the piano warbling "As Time Goes By," but he had already enjoyed a long career in show business. Wilson had worked in vaudeville and radio. From 1919 to 1930 he was one of Europe's most popular bandleaders. His other films include *My Favorite Blonde*, *Stormy Weather* and *Passage West*.

Dooley Wilson died on May 30, 1953, in Los Angeles.

1936: Jazz organist Jimmy McGriff is born in Philadelphia.

McGriff had a series of soul and jazz hits in the early 1960s—records like "I've Got a Woman" (1962), "All About My Girl" (1963) and "The Worm" (1968). After some pop experiments, McGriff returned to mainstream jazz. Some of his most popular LPs are *Blues for Mr. Jimmy*, *State of the Art* and *The Starting Five*.

1941: Spinners lead singer Philippe Wynne is born in Cincinnati. Though he didn't join the group until 1971, Wynne sang lead on the Spinners' biggest hit.

The Spinners were formed in Detroit at Ferndale High School. They originally consisted of Bobby Smith, Billy Henderson, Henry Fambrough and Pervis Jackson. In 1961 they hit the charts, with "That's What Girls Are Made For." Later they signed with Motown and charted with "I'll Always Love You" (1965) and "Truly Yours" (1966).

G. C. Cameron took over lead vocals in 1968. The Spinners scored with "It's a Shame," in 1970. Philippe Wynne, who had worked with the Bootsy Collins band in the late '60s, took over from Cameron.

When the Spinners signed with Atlantic Records, in 1972, their most successful chart run began. Their million-sellers included "I'll Be Around" (1972), "Could It Be I'm Falling in Love" (1972), "One of a Kind Love Affair" (1973), "Then Came You," with Dionne Warwick (1974), "They Just Can't Stop It (the Games People Play)" (1975) and "Rubber Band Man" (1976).

In 1977 Philippe Wynne went solo. His biggest hit was "Hats Off to Mama" (1977). He was also part of the Parliament/Funkadelic crew.

On July 13, 1984, while performing at Ivey's Nightclub in Oakland, California, Philippe Wynne suffered a heart attack and died.

APRIL 4

1913: Vocalist and pianist Cecil Gant is born in Nashville.

During the latter part of World War II and shortly thereafter, Cecil Gant was billed as "Private Cecil Gant, the G.I. Sing-sation." Gant worked war-bond rallies and had a number 1 R&B hit in 1944, with "I Wonder." His other hits included "Cecil's Boogie" (1945), "Grass Is Getting Greener Every Day" (1945), "I'm Tired" (1945), "Another Day, Another Dollar" (1948), "Special Delivery" (1948) and "I'm a Good Man but a Poor Man" (1948). Cecil Gant also recorded under the name Gunter Lee Carr.

Gant died of pneumonia on February 4, 1952.

1915: Muddy Waters is born McKinley Morganfield in Rolling Fork, Mississippi.

Muddy Waters was one of 10 children, the son of a sharecropper. He taught himself to play the harmonica at the age of nine. He didn't learn guitar until he was around 15. He began singing in church choirs and made a living as a farmer.

In the 1930s Waters began playing the blues in juke joints and other such venues around Clarksdale, Mississippi. In 1940 he joined a carnival, and in 1941 he recorded for the Library of Congress.

To music fans around the world, Muddy Waters *is* the blues. He was the biggest mover and shaker in what has become known as Chicago blues. He moved to that city in 1943, playing small clubs, street corners and rent parties. In 1947 he formed a trio with guitarist Jimmy Rogers and harmonica master Little Walter. He soon enlarged the band and played clubs like the Zanzibar, Boogie Woogie Inn and Romeo's Place. In 1948 he hit the R&B charts, with "I Feel Like Going Home."

Muddy Waters signed with Chess Records in 1950. His first big hit for Chess was "Louisiana Blues," in early 1951. He recorded blues classic after blues classic over the next several years: "Long Distance Call" (1951), "Honey Bee" (1951), "Still a Fool" (1951), "She Moves Me" (1952), "Mad Love" (1953), "I'm Your Hoochie Coochie Man" (1954), "Just Make Love to Me " (1954), "I'm Ready" (1954), "Manish Boy" (1955), "Forty Days and Forty Nights" (1956), "Don't Go No Farther" (1956) and "Got My Mojo Working" (1957).

Muddy Waters recorded such classic blues LPs as *The Real Folk Blues*, *Muddy Waters Live at Newport* and *The Best of Muddy Waters* (the original is Chess number 1427).

Throughout the '60s and '70s Muddy Waters continued to record and make concert and festival appearances. He appeared on TV shows like "Soundstage," "The Mike Douglas Show" and "Don Kirshner's Rock Concert."

Muddy Waters died on April 30, 1983.

1934: Record producer and songwriter Carl Davis is born in Chicago.

Davis had been a successful songwriter, arranger, producer and A&R (artist and repertoire) man with independent labels around Chicago. In 1963 Columbia Records revived its Okeh label and put Davis in charge. The label's roster included Major Lance (for whom Davis produced), Billy Butler and the Chanters, Walter Jackson, the Artistics and Ted Taylor. Curtis Mayfield also worked as songwriter and staff musician. Carl Davis was one of the major molders of what became known in the 1960s as the Chicago sound.

Okeh folded, and Davis became head of A&R at Brunswick Records, whose biggest star was Jackie Wilson. Davis crafted Wilson's later hits, such as "Higher and Higher" and "I Get the Sweetest Feeling." He also produced such other Brunswick acts as Barbara Acklin, Gene Chandler and the Chi-Lites.

1939: Trumpeter Hugh Masakela is born in Witbank, South Africa.

Masakela began playing the trumpet at the age of 14. In 1959 he moved to England and moved again a year later to New York City. He was married to singer Miriam Makeba from 1964 to 1966. Hugh Masakela is best known for his million-selling 1968 instrumental hit "Grazing in the Grass." In 1972 he released a top-selling jazz LP, *Home Is Where the Music Is*.

In 1980 Hugh Masakela returned to Africa and now mostly plays there and in Europe.

1944: Singer Major Lance, one of the best-known pop and soul stars of the early and mid-1960s, is born in Chicago.

Lance had been an amateur boxer and a dancer on local TV shows, as well as a member of a group called the Five Gospel Harmonaires.

He began recording in 1959. His biggest hits were "The Monkey Time" (1963), "Um, Um, Um, Um Um, Um" (1964), "The Matador" (1964), "Rhythm" (1964), "Sometimes I Wonder" (1965), "Come See" (1965) and "Ain't It a Shame" (1965). Most of these were written by Curtis Mayfield.

In the mid-1970s Major Lance

formed his own label. In the late '70s he served time in prison for drug-law violations.

1928: Platters lead singer Tony Williams is born in Elizabeth, New Jersey.

The classic rock 'n' roll/R&B group the Platters was formed by songwriter and manager Buck Ram in Los Angeles in 1953. The original members, apart from Williams, were David Lynch, Paul Robi, Herb Reed and Zola Taylor.

The group first recorded "Only You" for Federal Records, in 1954, but Federal didn't like the song and wouldn't promote it. In 1955 the Platters signed with Mercury Records. They rerecorded "Only You," and the song went to number 1 on the R&B charts and number 5 on the pop charts.

The Platters followed up "Only You" with a series of romantic ballads: "The Great Pretender" (1955), "The Magic Touch" (1956), "My Prayer" (1956), "You'll Never, Never Know" (1956), "Twilight Time" (1958), "Smoke Gets In Your Eyes" (1958) and "Harbor Lights" (1960).

In 1961 Tony Williams went solo, after which he performed primarily in nightclubs. Williams died on August 14, 1992, of diabetes and emphysema.

1932: Singer Billy Bland is born in Washington, North Carolina. Bland's claim to fame is the 1960 Top 10 hit "Let the Little Girl Dance."

1917: Blues harmonica player Big Walter "Shakey" Horton is born in Horn Lake, Mississippi.

Horton learned to play harmonica in Memphis from Hammie Nixon and worked with Memphis Minnie. He moved to Chicago in 1953 and worked as a session musician.

Horton was one of Chicago's best-known blues harp players. He recorded with such well-known bluesmen as Muddy Waters, Howlin' Wolf, Johnny Shines, Otis Rush, Sonny Boy Williamson (John Lee Williamson), Willie Dixon and Johnny Winter.

Though he recorded several albums, none was a big hit.

Walter Horton died on December 8, 1981.

1961: Actor, comedian and singer Eddie Murphy is born in Hempstead, New York.

Murphy is best known for his hit films *48 Hours, Beverly Hills Cop I* and *II, Trading Places* and *Coming to America*. His biggest venture into the world of music came in 1985, when he had a million-selling single, "Party All the Time," written, produced and arranged by punk-funk king Rick James.

APRIL 7

1915: Eleanora "Billie" Holiday is born in Baltimore. She took her name from her favorite actress, silent-screen star Billie Dove. The world called her Lady Day.

Billie Holiday was a victim of rape in her childhood. In her early teens she became a prostitute. She began singing in her late teens and was discovered by John Hammond.

In 1933 Hammond had her record two numbers with Benny Goodman, "Your Mother's Son-in-Law" and "Riffin' the Scotch." In 1935 Holiday began recording with the Teddy Wilson Orchestra. The musicians on these historic sessions included Johnny Hodges, Harry Carney, Ben Webster, Lester Young, Artie Shaw and Bunny Berrigan.

In 1937 Holiday had a stint with Count Basie's band, and in 1938 she had one with Artie Shaw's band. In 1938 she became featured performer at the newly opened Cafe Society. By 1944 her recordings included full string sections. Billie Holiday's recordings from this period include such classics as "Strange Fruit," "I Cover the Waterfront," "Billie's Blues," "He's Funny That Way," "I Got a Right to Sing the Blues," "This Year's Kisses," "Fine and Mellow," "Yesterdays" and "I'll Get By." In 1946 she appeared in the film *New Orleans* with Louis Armstrong.

In May of 1947 Billie Holiday was arrested on drug charges. She served time in jail until February of 1948. The press, both jazz and mainstream, was filled with stories about Holiday's drug- and alcohol-related and sexual escapades.

In 1952, after several attempts at drug rehabilitation, Holiday signed with Verve Records. She toured Europe in 1954. In 1956 her autobiography, *Lady Sings the Blues*, was published.

Many of her LPs and collections are available. Some of the best include *Fine and Mellow: 1939 and 1944, The Legend of Billie Holiday, The Billie Holiday Songbook* and *The Silver Collection*. There are also several boxed sets.

By 1958 Billie Holiday was basically living in seclusion in New York City. In May of 1959 she collapsed and was taken to a hospital, where she was arrested for drug possession. She died on July 17, 1959.

BILLIE HOLIDAY

1922: Bandleader and Latin percussionist Ramón "Mongo" Santamaria is born in Havana.

Santamaria hit the pop music Top 10 in 1963, with his version of Herbie Hancock's "Watermelon Man." Santamaria had worked in the bands of Perez Prado, Tito Puente and Cal Tjader before forming his own group, in 1961.

1938: Jazz trumpeter Freddie Hubbard is born in Indianapolis.

His earliest professional gigs were around Indianapolis, with Wes and Monk Montgomery. In 1959 he joined Sonny Rollins's band. In 1960 he was a member of J. J. Johnson's quintet and toured Europe with Quincy Jones's big band. In 1961 he joined Art Blakey's Jazz Messengers. Throughout the '60s he worked with the likes of Herbie Hancock, Dexter Gordon and Max Roach. Hubbard's horn is heard on the soundtrack of the 1965 film *The Pawnbroker*. He also recorded for Blue Note and Atlantic Records.

In the '70s Hubbard recorded for CTI and Columbia. In 1977, with Hancock, Wayne Shorter, Ron Carter and Tony Williams, he formed the band VSOP.

Freddie Hubbard is one of the fastest-fingered trumpet players in jazz. Among his most acclaimed LPs are *First Light, Hub-Tones, Sky Dive, Born to Be Blue* and *Sweet Return*.

APRIL 8

1922: Jazz singer Carmen McRae is born in New York City.

At the age of 16 McRae wrote "Dream of Life," which was recorded by Billie Holiday. During the 1940s she sang with the bands of Benny Carter, Count Basie and Mercer Ellington. In the late '40s she worked as a solo pianist and vocalist in clubs around New York.

McRae began recording in 1953. Her best LPs include *Any Old Time, Fine and Mellow, You're Looking at Me* and *Setting Standards*.

1964: Rapper Biz Markie is born Marcel Hall in Harlem.

Markie's work includes a lot of humor. In the mid-1980s he scored with such singles as "Make the Music with Your Mouth," "Pickin' Boogers" and "Vapors." In 1990 he had a platinum record (two million copies) with "Just a Friend."

APRIL 9

1895: Bluesman Mance Lipscomb is born in Navasota, Texas.

Lipscomb began playing the blues around 1909 but didn't record until around 1958. He recorded for Arhoolie.

In the early 1960s he was "discovered" and made the folk and blues festival rounds.

Lipscomb's best recordings are from the 1960–64 period, songs like "Going Down," "Shake, Mama, Shake," "Joe Turner Killed a Man" and "Cocaine Done Killed My Baby." His most highly recommended LPs are *Texas Songster*, *Sharecropper*, *Texas Songster II* and *You'll Never Find Another Man Like Mance*.

Mance Lipscomb died on January 30, 1976.

1898: Singer and actor Paul Robeson is born in Princeton, New Jersey, the son of a minister.

Robeson was an excellent student and athlete. He was a two-time All-American football player at Rutgers University, where he was also elected to Phi Beta Kappa, was a champion debater and sang in the glee club. Robeson then attended Columbia University Law School and paid his way by playing pro football.

In the early 1920s, while in law school, Paul Robeson developed an interest in drama. He appeared in the plays *Simon the Cyrenian* and *Voodoo*. As the lead in *Voodoo*, he toured England in 1922.

Robeson graduated from law school in 1923 but continued to work in the theater and perform in nightclubs, such as Harlem's Cotton Club. He also had a role in the highly successful black musical *Shuffle Along*.

He joined a prestigious white law firm, but racism drove him out. He quit when a white secretary refused to take dictation from him.

Robeson then played the lead in Eugene O'Neill's *All God's Chillun Got Wings*. One of his most famous roles was in *The Emperor Jones*. He also appeared in the 1924 silent film *Body and Soul*. In 1925 Robeson went to London to star in the British production of *The Emperor Jones*. In 1928 he starred in *Showboat*, which was highlighted by Robeson's rich bass rendering of "Ole Man River."

Robeson eventually moved to England, where he felt less affected by racism. While there he starred in such

films as *The Emperor Jones*, *Sanders of the River*, *Showboat* and *King Solomon's Mines*. In 1943 Robeson starred in the New York stage production of Shakespeare's *Othello*.

Robeson had visited Russia in the 1930s and developed an interest in Marxism and Communism. During the late 1940s he became active in political, civil rights and human rights activities. In the 1950s he was targeted by Senator Joseph McCarthy and the House Un-American Activities Committee. Nevertheless, in 1958, his concert recital sold out Carnegie Hall.

Paul Robeson died on January 23, 1976.

1938: Zydeco musician Rockin' Sidney Simien is born in Louisiana.

In 1985 Simien recorded a song called "My Toot Toot" for a small independent Louisiana label. It was picked up by CBS Records and spurred a renewed interest in zydeco. Soon the whole country was dancing to it.

APRIL 10

1922: Blues guitarist and harmonica player John Brim is born in Hopkinsville, Kentucky.

Brim settled into the Chicago blues scene in 1945. He backed up Muddy Waters, Willie Mabon, Sonny Boy Williamson and others. In 1946 he formed his own band, the Gary Kings, which included Jimmy Reed.

In the late '40s Brim began to record. His best-known piece is "Rattlesnake." Although he never had a hit record, his 1950s recordings are cherished by bluesologists because of the array of talent that accompanies him. The list includes Elmore James, Jimmy Reed, Sunnyland Slim, Little Walter and Roosevelt Sykes.

1928: Singer Roscoe Gordon is born in Memphis.

At the age of 16 Gordon had his own radio show on WDIA, in Memphis. He was a member of the Beale Streeters band, with B. B. King, Johnny Ace and Bobby "Blue" Bland.

Roscoe Gordon hit the R&B charts in 1951, with "I Saddled the Cow (and Milked the Horse)." His other big chart

successes were "Booted" (1952), "No More Doggin'" (1952), "The Chicken" (1956) and "Just a Little Bit" (1960).

APRIL 11

1939: Blues guitarist Luther "Guitar, Jr." Johnson is born in Itta Benna, Mississippi.

Johnson spent 1973 to 1979 as a guitarist and vocalist with the Muddy Waters band. He won a Grammy in 1984 for his rendition of "Walkin' the Dog," which was included in the Atlantic Records anthology *Blues Explosion*. He is currently a popular performer on the national blues club circuit and has made several tours abroad. His best LPs include *I Want to Groove With You* and *Doin' the Sugar Too*. (Note: There are at least two other bluesmen who record under the name Luther Johnson, and popular blues guitarist Lonnie Brooks once recorded under the name of Guitar, Jr.)

APRIL 12

1909: Lionel Hampton is born in Louisville.

Hampton was raised in Birmingham, Alabama. His father was killed in action in World War I. His mother moved the family to Chicago in 1919.

Hampton attended Catholic schools and began playing the drums at age 14. He played drums in the Chicago Defender Newsboys Band and took lessons on the xylophone. He also played in various Chicago bands.

Hampton moved to California in 1927, where he played in the bands of Paul Howard and Les Hite. In the late 1930s he became a member of Benny Goodman's quartet, along with Teddy Wilson and Gene Krupa.

In 1940 Hampton borrowed $10,000 from Louis Armstrong's manager, Joe Glaser, and started his own big band. He also signed with Decca Records. His first big hit came in 1942, with "Flying Home," which featured the tenor sax of Illinois Jacquet. As well as pleasing jazz audiences, Hamp's version of swing also topped the R&B charts and the jukebox playlists. Other big hits of this period were "On the Sunny Side of the Street" (1944), "Salty Papa Blues" (1944), "Evil Gal Blues" (1944), "Hamp's Boogie Woogie" (1944), "Beulah's Boogie" (1945), "Hey: Ba-Ba-Re-Bop" (1946), "Blow Top Blues" (1947), "I Want to be Loved" (1947) and "Rag Mop" (1950).

One of the most interesting aspects of Hampton's band was the roster of young artists it included over the years: Earl Bostic, Dinah Washington, Dexter Gordon, Quincy Jones, Joe Williams, Art Farmer, Clark Terry, Charles Mingus and Arnette Cobb. By the late '40s and early '50s Hampton had trimmed his big band to a small quintet.

More than just a bandleader and musician, Lionel Hampton is an excellent showman. He continues to be among jazz's top attractions.

1917: Bluesman Hound Dog Taylor is born Theodore Roosevelt Taylor in Natchez, Mississippi.

Taylor played on the famed King Biscuit radio show in Helena, Arkansas, before settling in Chicago, in 1942. He became one of the Chicago blues club circuit's most popular performers. He called his band the Houserockers and his music "houserocking music," a mixture of boogie, rock 'n' roll and blues.

In . 1974 Taylor signed with the small, independent, Chicago-based Alligator label. The deal put both Taylor and Alligator on the map. Some of Taylor's best LPs are *Hound Dog Taylor and the Houserockers*, *Natural Boogie*, *Beware of the Dog* and *Genuine Houserocking Music*.

Hound Dog Taylor died of cancer on December 17, 1975, in Chicago.

1940: Herbie Hancock is born in Chicago.

Hancock began studying classical piano at the age of seven. By the time he was 11 he was performing Mozart concertos with the Chicago Symphony.

He first became interested in jazz while in high school. In his early teens he went to New York with trumpeter Donald Byrd, who introduced him to Blue Note Records.

In 1961 Hancock's debut album, *Takin' Off*, was an immediate success and contained Hancock's composition

"Watermelon Man," which became a hit for Mongo Santamaria and has been recorded by over 200 other artists. Two follow-up LPs and lots of session work at Blue Note quickly established Hancock as one of the era's brightest pianists.

Hancock then joined the Miles Davis Quintet, where he remained until 1971, when he formed his own group.

In 1974 Hancock recorded the album *Headhunters*, using an assortment of electronic keyboard instruments and synthesizers. The music on *Headhunters* was a high-energy blend of jazz, pop and funk. The album sold over a million copies, produced the hit single "Chameleon" and introduced Hancock to mainstream pop audiences.

Hancock formed VSOP in 1977, along with Freddie Hubbard, Wayne Shorter, Tony Williams and Ron Carter, playing strictly straight jazz. In 1978 he engaged in a series of duet keyboard concerts with Chick Corea.

In 1983 Hancock recorded the album *Future Shock*, a collection of funk-pop rhythms using hip-hop street techniques. The album produced the hit single and video "Rockit." The video earned Hancock five MTV video awards, and the single gained him a Grammy for best R&B instrumental.

Hancock won an Oscar in 1987 for his soundtrack to the film *Round Midnight*.

HERBIE HANCOCK

He had scored his first film, *Blow Up*, in 1966. Since then he has provided music for such films as *The Spook Who Sat by the Door*, *Death Wish*, *A Soldier's Story*, *JoJo Dancer*, *Your Life Is Calling*, *Action Jackson* and *Colors*.

After almost 30 years as one of the most creative musical forces around, Herbie Hancock shows no signs of slowing down. He is the host of the PBS series "Rock School," which teaches various aspects of the world of modern music.

APRIL 13

1946: Singer Al Green is born in Forest City, Arkansas.

Al Green was one of nine children. At the age of nine he joined his father's gospel group, the Green Brothers. He was tossed out of the devoutly Christian group for listening to Jackie Wilson records. At the age of 16 he formed a pop group, Al Green and the Creations (later the Soul Mates).

Green hit the soul charts in 1967, with "Back Up Train." His career turned to gold when he met producer Willie Mitchel and signed with Memphis-based Hi Records. Mitchel produced all of Green's million-sellers.

Al Green was the top soul heart-throb of the early 1970s. His voice, personality and good looks added up to hits like "Tired of Being Along" (1971), "Still in Love with You" (1972), "You Ought to Be With Me" (1972), "Call Me" (1973), "Here I Am" (1973) and "Sha-La-La" (1974).

In 1974 Green experienced a spiritual awakening. He joined the ministry, purchased a church building in Memphis and was ordained pastor of the Full Gospel Tabernacle.

For several years Green mixed his preaching with his pop-music career, but in 1979 he turned solely to gospel music. Green's first all-gospel LP, *The Lord Will Make a Way*, earned him a Grammy.

In 1982 Al Green appeared with Patti Labelle on Broadway in the gospel musical *Your Arms Too Short to Box with God*. Also in the '80s he released such best-selling gospel LPs such as *He Is the Light* and *Soul Survivor*.

1951: Vocalist and master balladeer Peabo Bryson is born in Greenville, South Carolina.

Bryson cut his soul-music teeth with such club bands as Al Freeman and the Upsetters and Moses Dillard and the Tex-Town Display.

He first hit the charts in 1976, as vocalist for Michael Zager's Moon Band, with "Do It with Feeling." He also provided vocals on the Moon Band's hits "Reaching for the Sky" (1978) and "I'm So Into You" (1978). In 1979 and 1980 he recorded duets with Natalie Cole, "Gimme Some Time" and "What You Won't Do for Love." Bryson's solo hits include "Let the Feeling Flow" and "If Ever You're in My Arms Again."

In the 1980s he recorded a series of duets with Roberta Flack ("Tonight I Celebrate My Love"), Melissa Manchester ("Lovers After All") and Regina Belle ("Without You").

APRIL 14

1925: Tenor saxophonist Gene "Jug" Ammons, son of boogie-woogie piano player Albert Ammons, is born in Chicago.

Ammons played with Billy Eckstine's band from 1944 to 1947 and with Woody Herman's Thundering Herd in 1949. His penchant for R&B produced such hits as "Red Top" (1947), "My Foolish Heart" (1950) and "Jug" (1951). In the '50s he also worked in mainstream jazz with Sonny Stitt's band.

Gene Ammons died on July 23, 1974.

APRIL 15

1895: Bessie Smith is born in Chattanooga, Tennessee. (The date is taken from her tombstone. Most biographies say 1898; her marriage license says 1894.)

Both of Bessie Smith's parents died before she was eight, and she began singing in the streets for pennies. She often performed at storefronts in Chattanooga with her brother.

In the early 1900s she worked with Ma Rainey. She was also a chorus girl in a traveling tent show.

In 1913 she began singing and dancing as part of the vaudeville team of

Smith and Burton at the 81 Theater in Atlanta. She also toured with such outfits as the Pete Worley Florida Cotton Blossoms Minstrel Show and the Silas Green Minstrel Show. By 1918 she had her own show, the Liberty Belles Revue, and was playing club dates.

In 1921 she appeared in the musical comedy *How Come* in Philadelphia.

Bessie Smith was called the empress of the blues. She was essentially black music's first recording superstar. In 1923 she signed an exclusive recording contract with Columbia.

Her first record was "Down-Hearted Blues," which featured only her rough, volcanic voice and the piano accompaniment of Clarence Williams. The record was a smash. It sold 780,000 copies in under six months.

Over the next six years Bessie Smith sold between five and ten million records. She became one of the world's highest-paid entertainers, netting fees of $2,500 a week while touring the United States and Europe. Her biggest hits from this period include "T'aint Nobody's Bizness If I Do," "Bleeding Heart Blues," "Hot Springs Blues," "Backwater Blues," "Empty Bed Blues," "Any Woman Blues" and "Preachin' the Blues."

From 1925 through 1927 she starred in *Harlem Frolics*, and in 1929 she starred in the short film *St. Louis Blues*.

By 1931 her record sales had dropped sharply. Most critics say the decline came because the record-buying public had switched from rough blues to the newer, smoother jazz songs. Throughout the '30s she performed in the Bessie Smith Revue, the Broadway Revue, *Hot Stuff of 1933*, *Blackbird Revue* and *Stars Over Broadway*.

In 1937, while touring the South in a show called *Broadway Rastus*, Bessie Smith was injured in a car accident. She died on September 26 in Clarksdale, Mississippi.

1936: Bluesman Frank Frost is born in Augusta, Arkansas.

Frank Frost plays guitar, harmonica, organ and piano. He has worked in the bands of Sonny Boy Williamson, Albert King, B. B. King, and Little Milton. He

has also worked with such country-music artists as Carl Perkins and Conway Twitty.

As a solo artist, Frank Frost hit the charts in 1966 with "My Back Scratcher."

APRIL 16

1929: Singer Roy Hamilton is born in Leesburg, Georgia.

Hamilton moved to Jersey City, New Jersey, at the age of 14. He studied commercial art and was a heavyweight Golden Gloves boxer. He also had operatic and classical voice training. In 1947 he won first prize in an amateur contest at the Apollo Theater.

In the mid-1950s Hamilton had a run of hits on both the R&B and pop charts. These included "You'll Never Walk Alone" (1954), "If I Loved You" (1954), "Ebb Tide" (1954), "Hurt" (1954), "Unchained Melody" (1955) and "Forgive This Fool" (1955).

In 1956 Hamilton retired from the music business, exhausted. Two years later he returned, hitting the charts with "Don't Let Go" in 1958 and "You Can Have Her" in 1960.

Roy Hamilton died of a stroke on July 20, 1969.

APRIL 17

1961: The Marcels' "Blue Moon" is the number 1 pop single.

The Marcels were made up of lead singer Cornelius Harp, bass Fred Johnson, Ronald Mundy, Gene Bricker and Richard Knauss. The group formed in Pittsburgh and signed with Colpix Records after sending a demo tape to producer Stu Phillips.

"Blue Moon" was a ballad written in 1935 by the classic songwriting team of Rodgers and Hart. The Marcels came up with the rocking version, and Phillips came up with the famed bass intro.

Later in 1961 the Marcels hit the Top 10 again, with their remake of another '30s ballad, "Heartache."

APRIL 18

1924: Vocalist and guitarist Clarence "Gatemouth" Brown is born in Vinton, Louisiana.

He's usually dubbed a bluesman but his music is basically uncategorizable. It contains bits and pieces of blues, jazz, R&B, country, rockabilly, gospel, bluegrass, soul, rock 'n' roll, and so on.

In the 1930s Brown was the drummer for an outfit called William Benbow's Brown Skin Models. In the late '30s and early '40s he played country & western music. During World War II he served in the Engineer Corps of the U.S. Army.

In 1947 Brown recorded for Aladdin Records. In 1949 he became the first artist that Don Robey signed to his Peacock label. That year he had R&B hits with "Mary Is Fine" and "My Time Is Expensive."

Gatemouth Brown sings, and he plays guitar, fiddle, harmonica, bass, drums and mandolin. His ability to blend blues and country makes him a popular performer in both arenas. He has appeared on such TV shows as "Austin City Limits" and "The Texas Connection." He also did a series of TV commercials for Lone Star Beer.

Brown continues to record. His LP *Alright Again* won him a Grammy. Other albums are *Real Life*, *One More Mile*, *Standing My Guard* and *Pressure Cooker*.

APRIL 19

1963: The Chiffons' "He's So Fine" is the number 1 pop hit.

The Chiffons formed in the Bronx in 1960. The group consisted of Judy Craig, Barbara Lee, Patricia Bennett and Sylvia Patterson. They were initially called the Four Pennies and worked as backup singers, recording for Rust Records. In late 1962 they changed their name and signed with Laurie Records.

After the success of "He's So Fine," the Chiffons hit the Top 10 with "One Fine Day" (1963) and "Sweet Talkin' Guy" (1966).

APRIL 20

1923: Tito Puente is born in Harlem to parents of Puerto Rican origin.

As a child, Puente learned to play piano, drums, timbales, vibes and saxophone.

Tito Puente is the king of Latin music. He has recorded more than 100 albums of Latin dance music. His biggest hit was his 1958 recording of "Dance Mania."

Puente fronts a large band with lots of percussion, a well-oiled horn section and backup vocalists. He often records and performs with Latin music's top female performer, Celia Cruz.

1929: West Coast–based bluesman Johnny Fuller is born in Edwards, Mississippi.

Fuller hit the R&B charts in the mid-1950s, with tunes like "Johnny Ace's Last Letter" (1955), "Sister Jenny" (1956), "Don't Slam That Door" (1956) and "Haunted House" (1959).

In the late '50s he toured Europe and Hawaii as part of package shows headlined by Paul Anka and Frankie Avalon. In the late '60s he was one of the West Coast blues circuit's most popular performers.

Johnny Fuller died on May 20, 1985, in Oakland.

1951: Romantic balladeer Luther Vandross is born in New York City.

Vandross began as a session vocalist and commercial jingle singer in the early 1970s. He sang behind the likes of David Bowie, Bette Midler, Carly Simon and Chaka Khan.

In the late '70s he put together his own group, called Luther. The group first hit the charts in 1976, with "It's Good for the Soul" and "Funky Music."

Vandross was the dominant black male vocalist of the 1980s. His best-selling albums include *Never Too Much*, *Forever, For Love, For Always*, *Busy Body*, *The Night I Fell in Love*, *Give Me the Reason* and *Any Love*.

His top single hits include "Never Too Much" (1981), "If This World Were Mine" (with Cheryl Lynn, 1982), "Bad Boy" (1982), "How Many Times Can We Say Goodbye" (with Dionne Warwick, 1983), "Til My Baby Comes Home" (1985), "It's Over Now" (1985), "Give Me the Reason" (1986), "Stop to Love" (1986), "There's Nothing Better Than Love " (with Gregory Hines, 1987) and "Here and Now" (1990).

Vandross is also a top-flight songwriter, producer and arranger. He produced Aretha Franklin's *Jump to It* LP and Dionne Warwick's *How Many Times Can We Say Goodbye* album.

APRIL 21

1924: Gospel singer Clara Ward, the daughter of gospel singer Mother Gertrude Ward, is born in Philadelphia.

Ward made her national debut at the age of 19, singing at the national Baptist convention.

She former her own group, the Clara Ward Singers, in the late '40s. Ward herself had a powerful voice and an exciting stage presence. She was, without a doubt, the most flamboyant and charismatic singer in the history of gospel music and the first black gospel-music star—and the Clara Ward Singers were electrifying. They wore high-fashion wigs and gaudy robes and outfits, and their performances shook the rafters. In 1947 Marion Williams joined, an addition that gave the group two powerful lead singers. The group had million-selling gospel hits with "Surely God Is Able" and "Packin' Up."

Sometimes Ward's flamboyance and business practices alienated her fans and her fellow performers. Although she formed several groups of Clara Ward Singers, most of them performed without her. Promoters had to specifically

THE CHIFFONS

ask for Clara Ward lest they get just a group of Ward Singers. In 1958 the main group of Ward Singers, including Marion Williams, split from Clara Ward and formed the Stars of Faith.

In 1961 Ward shocked gospel-music fans by signing a 40-week contract to perform in Las Vegas nightclubs.

Clara Ward died on January 16, 1973.

1973: Gospel great Inez Andrews hits the soul charts, with "Lord, Don't Move the Mountains," a true rocker and hand-clapper. The record crossed over and achieved a respectable position on the national soul charts.

Inez Andrews hails from Birmingham, Alabama. In the early 1950s she joined Dorothy Love Coates and the Gospel Harmonettes. In the mid-1950s she was with the famous Caravans. In the early '60s she formed her own group, the Andrewettes, and went solo in the late '60s.

APRIL 22

1919: Singer Benjamin "Bull-moose" Jackson is born in Buffalo.

Jackson was raised in Cleveland. He formed his first band, the Harlem Hotshots, in high school. In 1943 he joined Lucky Millinder's band.

Bullmoose first hit the R&B charts in 1946, with "I Know Who Threw the Whiskey in the Well." He followed up with top R&B hits like "I Love You, Yes I Do" (1947), "Sneaky Pete" (1948), "All My Love Belongs to You" (1948), "I Can't Go On Without You" (1948), "Little Girl, Don't Cry" (1949) and "Why Don't You Haul Off and Love Me" (1949).

In 1961 he rerecorded "I Love You, Yes I Do" and the new version hit the R&B Top 100.

Jackson's best songs were romantic ballads, but he is best known for double-entendre, raucous rockers like "I Want a Bowlegged Woman" and "Big Ten Inch Record of the Blues." In his heyday, Bullmoose Jackson was one of R&B's top stars. His backup band was called the Buffalo Bearcats.

1922: Jazz bassist Charles Mingus is born in Nogales, Arizona.

Mingus was raised in Los Angeles. He took up the bass at the of 16. He studied piano and music theory and got his first gig with Buddy Collette's group.

In 1942 Mingus worked with the bands of Barney Bigard and Louis Armstrong. He was with the Lee Young Sextet in 1943. He formed his own strings-and-keys trio in 1944 and began recording in 1945. In 1947 and 1948 he toured with Lionel Hampton.

The 1950s saw Charles Mingus emerge as one of the most powerful forces in modern jazz. Along with being a highly regarded bassist, Mingus was a composer of avant-garde jazz, an arranger and bandleader. Mingus was a great student of jazz, and he used his broad knowledge of jazz to mold and shape his compositions.

From 1950 to 1951 Mingus was a member of the Red Norvo Trio. In 1951 he settled in New York, playing with Miles Davis, Billy Taylor, Charlie Parker, Art Tatum, Stan Getz, Duke Ellington and many others. In 1952 he formed his own record company, Debut Records. In 1953 he cofounded the Jazz Composers Workshop, and in 1955 he formed his famous band, the Charles Mingus Jazz Workshop. In 1956 his LP *Pithecanthropus Erectus* drew serious attention throughout the jazz world. Other well-known LPs are *New York Sketch Book*, *The Black Saint . . . Sinner Lady*, *Mingus Dynasty* and *Mingus Revisited*.

In the 1960s Mingus experimented with large bands, but by 1977 he had been halted by multiple sclerosis. He died on January 5, 1979, in Cuernavaca, Mexico.

APRIL 23

1952: Singer, songwriter, drummer and record producer Narada Michael Walden is born in Kalamazoo, Michigan.

Walden is the man who crafted and produced Whitney Houston's best-selling LPs and singles. He was a member of John McLaughlin's Mahavishnu Orchestra from 1974 to 1976. In the 1970s he also worked with rock guitarist Jeff Beck.

As an artist, Walden placed several singles on the pop charts, including "I Don't Want Nobody Else" (1979) and "I Shoulda Loved Ya" (1980).

APRIL 24

1933: Singer Freddie Scott is born in Providence.

Scott was working as a staff songwriter for Screen Gem/Columbia Music Publishers when he recorded the hit ballad "Hey Girl" in 1963. Between 1963 and 1970 Freddie Scott had pop and soul single hits like "Are You Lonely for Me," "Am I Grooving You" and "You Got What I Need."

1937: Jazz saxophonist Joe Henderson is born in Lima, Ohio.

Henderson first came to notice in the early 1960s, when he co-led a group with trumpeter Kenny Dorham. He had worked in the groups of Horace Silver and Herbie Hancock, and he co-led the Jazz Communicators with Freddie Hubbard. In 1971 Henderson had a short stint with the rock-jazz group Blood, Sweat and Tears.

Joe Henderson's *Lush Life* was voted one of 1992's best jazz LPs and was number 1 in *Down Beat* magazine's readers' poll.

APRIL 25

1913: Earl Bostic, king of the R&B sax honkers in the late 1940s and early 1950s, is born in Tulsa.

Bostic attended Xavier University of New Orleans. In the '30s and '40s he worked in the big bands of Bennie Moten, Don Redman, Edgar Hayes, Lionel Hampton and Hot Lips Page. By the mid-1940s he was a sought-after arranger, doing charts for the bands of Artie Shaw, Paul Whiteman, Louis Prima and others.

Bostic's tunes were jazzy, bluesy and danceable. Among his classic hits are "Temptation" (1948), "845 Stomp" (1948), "Serenade" (1950), "Flamingo" (1951), "Sleep" (1952), "Moonglow" (1952) and "Mambolino" (1954). During Bostic's hit years, many young musicians were members of his band, including John Coltrane, Jaki Byard, Blue Mitchell and Stanley Turrentine.

1918: Ella Fitzgerald, first lady of jazz and the world's best-known jazz

singer, is born in Newport News, Virginia.

Fitzgerald was raised in Yonkers, New York. In 1934 she won an amateur-night contest at the Apollo Theater. In 1935 she began her professional career with Tiny Bradshaw's band. In the same year, she became the vocalist with Chick Webb's orchestra and recorded her first tune, "Love and Kisses." In 1938, so the story goes, Chick Webb was ill. To make him feel better, Ella and the band's arranger wrote him a nonsensical nursery-rhyme piece called "A-Tisket, A-Tasket," which Ella recorded in May of that year. It became a huge hit. In 1939, when Webb died, Ella Fitzgerald took over leadership of the band until it broke up, in 1941.

For a while Fitzgerald worked with a vocal group called the Four Keys, and then she went solo.

In the 1940s Ella Fitzgerald popularized the vocal form called "scattin'," or scat singing. In scat, lyrics are replaced by "shoo-bee-doo-bees" and "doo-bops" and are most effectively performed in rhythmic overdrive. Fitzgerald had big hits with "My Heart and I Decided" (1943), "Cow-Cow Boogie" (1944), "Into Each Life Some Rain Must Fall" (1944), "I'm Making Believe" (with the Ink Spots, 1944), "It's Only a Paper Moon" (1945), "The Frim-Fram Sauce" (1946), "Stone Cold Dead in the Market" (1946), "Petootie Pie" (1946), "That's My Desire" (1947), "My Happiness" (1948), "It's Too Soon to Know" (1949), and "Baby, It's Cold Outside" (1949). Several of her best-known '40s songs were duets with the "daddy of R&B," Louis Jordan.

In the 1950s Ella Fitzgerald began recording her "song book" series of albums, dedicated to the works of such songwriters as George Gershwin, Harold Arlen, Johnny Mercer, Cole Porter, Irving Berlin and Duke Ellington. Among her recorded treasures are the LPs *The Best of Ella Fitzgerald*, *Princess of the Savoy*, *Ella in Berlin*, *The Cole Porter Songbook*, *Porgy and Bess*, and *Ella and (Count) Basie: On the Sunny Side of the Street*.

Ella Fitzgerald has won many Grammy awards and numerous popularity awards from *Down Beat* magazine. She has appeared in such films as *Pete Kelly's Blues*, *Ride 'Em Cowboy* (with Abbott and Costello), and *St. Louis Blues*.

ELLA FITZGERALD

1923: Bluesman Albert King is born Albert Nelson in Indianola, Mississippi.

Albert King grew up on a farm outside Forest City, Arkansas. He learned to play guitar on a homemade instrument and got his first real guitar in 1942. From 1949 to 1951 he played with a gospel group called the Harmony Kings.

In 1952 King formed his own blues combo, called the Groove Boys. Later he moved to Indiana and played drums for Jimmy Reed's band.

In 1953 Albert King cut his first record, "Bad Luck Blues," for the Parrot label. The record had little success, and King did not record again for six years.

In the early 1960s King recorded for the small Bobbin label. In 1961 he had a Top 20 R&B hit with "Don't Throw Your Love on Me So Strong." His other hits of the era include "Travelin' to California" and "I've Made Nights by Myself."

In 1966 King signed with the Memphis-based R&B giant, Stax Records. From 1966 to 1974 King hit the R&B and pop charts with songs like "Laundromat Blues" (1966),

"Crosscut Saw" (1967), "Born Under a Bad Sign" (1967), "Cold Feet" (1968), "Everybody Wants to Go to Heaven" (1971) and "That's What the Blues Is All About" (1974).

In 1976 King signed with Utopia Records and produced hits like "Cadillac Assembly Line." During the latter part of the '70s his LPs suffered from overproduction and tinges of disco.

Albert King's trademark guitar was a Gibson Flying V named Lucy. He died of a heart attack on December 21, 1992, in Memphis.

1940: Country singer O. B. McClinton is born in Senatobia, Mississippi.

One of the few black country singers, McClinton was a frequent guest on the "Nashville Now" TV show. He had a string of country hits from 1972 to 1987, including "Don't Let the Green Grass Fool You" (1972), "My Whole World Is Falling Down" (1973) and "Turn the Music On" (1987).

O. B. McClinton had worked as a deejay at Memphis radio station WDIA and at one time was a staff songwriter for Stax Records. He died of stomach cancer on September 23, 1987.

1950: Jazz flutist Bobbie Humphrey is born in Dallas.

Humphrey had a series of jazz-disco hits in the 1970s, including "Chicago Damn" (1974) and "Homemade Jam" (1978).

APRIL 26

1886: Gertrude "Ma" Rainey, the first commercially successful female black blues singer, is born in Columbus, Georgia.

Around 1900 Rainey was working as a singer, dancer and actress in a traveling show called *A Bunch of Blackberries*. She began singing the blues about 1902.

In 1904 she married dancer William "Pa" Rainey. Throughout the early 1900s she worked theater circuits, minstrel shows and carnivals.

In 1917 she formed her own group, billed as Madam Gertrude Rainey and her Smart Sets, and toured throughout the South. In 1923 Ma Rainey began to record but recorded only until 1928.

Her best-known recordings include "Don't Fish in My Sea," "Stack-Olee Blues" and "Farewell Daddy Blues." The best collection of her recordings is an LP called *Ma Rainey's Black Bottom*.

Throughout the 1930s Ma Rainey performed in music halls, theaters and carnivals. She died of a heart attack on December 22, 1939, in Columbus.

1915: Blues singer and guitarist Johnny Shines is born in Frayser, Tennessee.

Shines was a disciple and protégé of the great Robert Johnson. He spent part of 1934 and 1935 playing with Johnson.

Shines arrived in Chicago in the early 1940s. In the mid-1940s he recorded for Columbia Records, but nothing came of his efforts. For most of the late '40s Johnny Shines worked outside the music world.

In the early '50s he signed with Chess Records. Here, Shines ran into another problem: Chess didn't release most of his records because his style so closely resembled that of the label's top blues star, Muddy Waters. Once again Shines got out of the music business.

During the 1960s Johnny Shines found an audience for his music in Europe. In the mid-1960s he recorded for Vanguard Records, and his career took off. He never became a big blues star, but he played the club and festival circuits and was hailed by critics as a major interpreter of authentic Delta blues.

Some of the finest albums by Johnny Shines are *Johnny Shines and Robert Lockwood: Dust My Broom*, *Johnny Shines with Big Walter Hawkins* and *The Johnny Shines Band*.

Johnny Shines died on April 20, 1992.

1926: Bluesman Joseph Benjamin "J. B." Hutto, one of the most popular and exciting of the modern-day electric slide guitarists, is born in Blackville, South Carolina.

Hutto was raised in Augusta, Georgia, and began his career in his family's gospel group, the Golden Crown Gospel Singers.

He moved to Chicago in the 1940s and played with Johnny Ferguson's band. In 1946 he formed his own group, the Hawks.

For the next 20 years J. B. Hutto and the Hawks were a fixture in Chicago blues clubs. In 1965 some of Hutto's material was included in an anthology LP called *Chicago: The Blues Today*. Hutto was booked around the country at blues festivals, and more recordings followed.

J. B. Hutto's best LPs are *Hawk Squat*, *Slideslinger* and *Slippin' and Slidin'*.

J. B. Hutto died on June 12, 1983.

1938: Singer and songwriter Maurice Williams is born in Lancaster, South Carolina.

Maurice Williams first hit the charts in 1957, as lead singer of the Gladiolas. The other members of the group were Earl Gainey, William Massey, Willie Jones and Norman Wade.

The Gladiolas' big hit was a rocking novelty called "Little Darlin'." Their version hit the Top 10 on the R&B chart; the version by the Diamonds was a big pop hit.

Williams changed the name of the group to the Zodiacs. In 1960 the Zodiacs, now made up of Williams, Wiley Bennett, Henry Gaston, Charles Thomas, Albert Hill and Willie Morrow, hit number 1 on the pop charts with the monster smash "Stay." Thirty years later Maurice Williams and the Zodiacs remain one of the top acts on the Eastern Seaboard beach-music circuit.

APRIL 27

1947: Singer Ann Peebles is born in East St. Louis, Illinois.

Ann Peebles began singing at the age of eight in her family's gospel group. She was the top female vocalist on the roster of Hi Records, whose superstar was Al Green. Between 1969 and 1979 Ann Peebles scored 19 chart singles. Her biggest one was 1973's "I Can't Stand the Rain." Others were "Part Time Love" (1970), "I Pity the Fool" (1971), "Breaking Up Somebody's Home" (1972) and "Hanging On" (1974).

APRIL 28

1934: Bluesman Charley Patton dies of heart disease in Indianola, Mississippi.

Patton was born in Edwards, Mississippi—some sources say in 1881, others say in 1885 and still others say in 1887. One of 12 children, Patton worked on a farm for most of his childhood. He is said to have begun playing and singing the blues at the Saturday night shivarees on Will Dockery's plantation in Ruleville. Around 1916 he could be found on the Webb Jennings plantation. By the early 1920s he was a blues-playing hobo, going from plantation to plantation and juke joint to juke joint. He eventually settled in Holly Ridge, Mississippi.

In the mid-1920s Charley Patton started cutting records. In 1929 he recorded one of his best-known songs, "Pea Vine Blues." Other great Charley Patton songs are "Prayer of Death," "Mean Black Moan," "I'm Goin' Home," "Devil Sent the Rain," "Screamin' and Hollerin' the Blues," "Bo Weevil Blues," "Pony Blues" and "High Water Everywhere."

Patton is considered the founder of the form of acoustic country music that today is commonly known as Delta blues. His rough vocal style and powerful rhythmic guitar riffs have spawned legions of disciples and imitators.

APRIL 29

1899: Edward Kennedy "Duke" Ellington is born in Washington, D.C.

Ellington took his first piano lesson in 1906. While in high school he played at the Washington True Reformer Hall and at the Poodle Dog Cafe and wrote his first composition, "The Soda Fountain Rag."

Duke Ellington studied music theory and harmony and played with the bands of Louis Thomas, Daniel Doyle, Oliver Perry and Elmer Snowden. He was one of five pianists with the 34-piece orchestra of Russell Wooding.

In 1924 Ellington took over Snowden's band and named it Duke Ellington and His Washingtonians. He also wrote a revue called *The Chocolate Kiddies* and toured throughout the Northeast.

On December 4, 1927, Duke Ellington began his four-year run

at Harlem's famous Cotton Club. The late '20s also saw Ellington begin to record a series of classics, including "Mood Indigo," "Hot Feet," "Rockin' in Rhythm," "Echoes of the Jungle," "The Cotton Club Stomp," "Solitude," "Caravan," and "It Don't Mean a Thing If It Ain't Got That Swing."

In 1930 the Duke Ellington Orchestra appeared in the film *Check and Double Check*. In the early '30s the orchestra toured the West Coast and England. In 1937 Ellington returned to the Cotton Club and in 1939 he began his collaboration with writer and arranger Billy Strayhorn.

In 1943 Duke Ellington appeared at Carnegie Hall for the first time and introduced his 50-minute suite, *Black, Brown and Beige*. Ellington's biggest hits of the '40s include "Take the A Train," "I Am in a Sentimental Mood," "Sophisticated Lady," "Don't Get Around Much Anymore," "A Slip of the Lip," "Sentimental Lady," "Do Nothin' Till You Hear from Me," "Main Stem," "My Little Brown Book" and "I'm Beginning to See the Light."

A great part of the Duke Ellington Orchestra's success was due to Ellington's use of only the finest musicians. Over the years his top soloists included Cootie Williams, Harry

DUKE ELLINGTON

Carney, Barney Bigard, Johnny Hodges, Juan Tizol, Ray Nance, Jimmy Blanton, Ben Webster, Clark Terry and Louis Bellson. Vocalists included Ivie Anderson, Herb Jeffries, Al Hibbler and Kay Davis. In the 1950s, when money problems forced most big bands to fold, Ellington used his composing royalties to keep his orchestra afloat and touring the world. In the 1960s and 1970s, he toured Europe, the Far East, the Middle East, Africa, Japan and Russia.

Duke Ellington died on May 24, 1974.

1927: R&B saxophonist Big Jay McNeely is born in Los Angeles.

McNeely is considered the originator of the wild honking style of R&B tenor sax playing that was so popular in the late 1940s and early 1950s. McNeely usually worked with a four- or five-piece combo.

In 1949 Big Jay McNeely had a number 1 R&B hit with "Deacon's Hop." Other hits include "Wild Wig" (1949), "Let's Work" (1959) and "There's Something on Your Mind" (with vocal by Little Sonny Warner, 1959).

1934: Bluesman Otis Rush is born in Philadelphia.

Rush is one of the top box-office draws on the Chicago blues circuit. Critics and students of modern blues credit Rush as the creator of the West Side Chicago blues sound.

Otis Rush moved to Chicago in 1948. In 1956 he had a big R&B hit with "I Can't Quit You, Baby." Follow-ups included "All Your Love," "My Love Will Never Die" and "Groaning the Blues," all on the small Cobra label.

Things weren't always great for Rush. After touring Europe in the mid-1960s he signed with Capitol Records and found himself and his blues strictly out of place. His records were over-arranged and underpromoted. With few record sales, he saw his bookings fall off.

By the mid-1970s Rush was back touring Europe and Japan. Otis Rush can currently be spotted playing Chicago clubs like B.L.U.E.S. and the Wise Fools Pub.

1896: Reverend Gary Davis, one of the most influential of the early 12-string guitar players, is born in Laurens, South Carolina.

Davis suffered ulcerated eyes and was blind by the age of two months. He had taught himself to play harmonica, banjo and guitar by the time he was seven. He attended Cedar Spring School for Blind People.

He worked as a street singer around Asheville, North Carolina, in the late 1920s. In the early '30s he became an ordained minister.

Davis settled around Durham, North Carolina. Even though he was deeply religious, he played at parties and fish fries as well as at churches. He began recording around 1935.

In 1940 Davis moved to New York and worked as a minister in the Missionary Baptist Connection Church. He sang in venues ranging from street corners to radio. In the '50s and '60s he was actively recording and appearing at folk festivals.

Davis, along with Blind Blake and Blind Boy Fuller, is credited with founding an East coast blues form called Peidmont blues. Some of his best LPs are *Reverend Gary Davis*, *When I Die I'll Live Again* and *I Am the True Voice*.

Reverend Gary Davis suffered a heart attack on the way to a concert and died on May 5, 1972.

1910: Chicago-based vocalist, guitarist and harmonica player Homesick James is born John Williamson in Somerville, Tennessee.

James took his nickname from his 1952 hit "Homesick." He was reportedly the cousin of Elmore James and of Sonny Boy Williamson (John Lee Williamson). He moved to Chicago in 1939. His best LPs are *Blues on the South Side*, *Ain't Sick No More* and *Homesick James and Snooky Pryor*.

1915: Singer Mabel Scott is born in Richmond, Virginia.

Scott moved to New York in 1921. She made her professional debut in 1932. Ten years later she moved to Los Angeles, where she married popular blues singer Charles Brown. Her biggest R&B hits are "Elevator Boogie" (1948) and "Boogie-Woogie Santa Claus" (1948).

1923: Jazz bassist Percy Heath, a founding member of the Modern Jazz Quartet, is born in Wilmington, North Carolina.

Heath seriously took up the bass after getting out of the service, in 1946. In 1947 he played with Howard McGhee's band and joined Dizzy Gillespie's group.

In the early 1950s Heath recorded with Milt Jackson, Miles Davis, Charlie Parker, Thelonious Monk and many others.

1930: Singer Bobby Marchan is born in Youngstown, Ohio.

Bobby Marchan was working as a female impersonator when he was hired as lead singer for Huey Smith and the Clowns. Marchan sang lead on "Rocking Pneumonia" and other Clowns hits before going solo. His biggest hit was the 1960 single "There's Something on Your Mind."

MAY 1

1890: Pianist and vocalist Ada Brown, star of the music hall and theater circuits of the 1920s and 1930s, is born in Kansas City, Kansas.

Brown appeared in shows like *Plantation Days, Bandannaland, Tan Town Tamales, Brown Buddies, Jangleland* and *Jungle Drums* with such stars as Miller and Lyles and Bill "Bojangles" Robinson. She also appeared with Fats Waller in the classic film *Stormy Weather*.

Ada Brown died on March 31, 1950.

1924: Singer Big Maybelle, one of the classic female R&B shouters of the early 1950s, is born Mabel Louise Smith in Jackson, Tennessee.

She began her career in the late 1930s with Dave Clark's band. In the 1940s she was part of an all-woman band, the Sweethearts of Rhythm, and she also performed with the Christine Chatman Orchestra. She had such hits as "Gabbin' the Blues" (1953), "Way Back Home" (1953), "My Country Man" (1953) and "Candy" (1956).

Big Maybelle died of diabetes on January 23, 1972.

1930: Marion "Little Walter" Jacobs, king of the modern blues harmonica players, is born in Marshville, Louisiana.

He grew up in rural Louisiana. By the age of 12 he was playing blues harp in local clubs around New Orleans.

Little Walter moved to Chicago in the mid-1940s. He worked basically as a street performer. In 1947 he recorded a couple of sides for a short-lived label called Ora Nelle Records. He met bluesman Big Bill Broonzy, who got him club work backing Memphis Slim, Tampa Red and Broonzy himself. In 1948 he joined Muddy Waters's band, a move that brought him to the forefront of the Chicago blues scene.

In 1952 Little Walter signed with Chess Records and produced a series of top blues and R&B chart hits. His best-known ones are "Juke" (1952), "Sad Hours" (1952), "Mean Old World" (1953), "Tell Me, Mama" (1953), "Blues with a Feeling" (1953), "You're So Fine" (1954), "My Babe" (1955), "Roller Coaster" (1955) and "Key to the Highway" (1958). His LPs include *The Best of Little Walter* (Chess 1428) and *Boss Blues Harmonica*.

Little Walter died in Chicago on February 15, 1968, from injuries suffered in a street fight.

1954: Singer, songwriter and guitarist Ray Parker, Jr., is born in Detroit.

Parker gained a reputation as a top session guitarist working with Stevie Wonder and Barry White. In 1977 he formed the group RAYDIO, which produced pop hits like "Jack and Jill" (1978), "You Can't Change That" (1979) and "A Woman Needs Love" (1981).

In 1982 Parker went solo, and the hits kept coming: "The Other Woman" (1982), "Jamie" (1984) and "Girls Are More Fun" (1985). His biggest hit was the million-selling theme from the 1984 movie *Ghostbusters*.

MAY 2

1969: The Fifth Dimension's "Aquarius" is the number 1 pop single.

The Fifth Dimension, one of the most successful pop 'n' soul groups of the late '60s and early '70s, was formed in Los Angeles in 1966 and was first called the Versatiles. The members were Marilyn McCoo, Florence LaRue, Billy Davis, Jr., Lamonte McLemore and Ron Townson.

The group had a string of single chart hits, including "Up, Up and Away" (1967), "Stoned Soul Picnic" (1968), "Sweet Blindness" (1968), "Wedding Bell Blues" (1969), "One Less Bell to Answer" (1970), "Last Night I Didn't Get to Sleep At All" (1971) and "If I Could Reach You" (1972).

In 1969 Marilyn McCoo and Billy Davis, Jr., were married. In 1976 they left the Fifth Dimension and began recording as a duo. They had a million-selling single, "You Don't Have to Be a Star" (1976), and from 1981 to 1984 Marilyn McCoo hosted the TV show "Solid Gold."

THE FIFTH DIMENSION

MAY 3

1928: James Brown—the godfather of soul, soul brother number one, the hardest-working man in show business, the amazing Mr. Please, Please, Please—is born in Macon, Georgia.

He was raised in an Augusta, Georgia, whorehouse. He grew up a natural-born hustler. He formed his first musical group at the age of 13. In 1949 he went to jail for petty theft.

In 1952 Brown and Bobby Byrd began to collaborate, calling themselves the Gospel Starlighters when they sang gospel and the Avons when they did R&B. By 1955 they were the Famous Flames, the hottest thing in Georgia. In January of 1956 James and the Flames signed with King Records.

In 1963 James Brown released his masterpiece LP *Live at the Apollo*. In 1965 "Papa's Got a Brand New Bag" became James Brown's first pop Top 10 hit. By the mid-1960s many of James Brown's songs were dealing with such social issues as education, drugs and black pride.

By 1970 the Famous Flames were no longer. Brown's backup group and band were called the J.B.s.

James Brown has placed over 100 songs on the R&B and pop singles charts and over 30 albums on the LP charts. Brown wrote, produced and arranged the majority of his hits. His biggest singles include "Please, Please, Please" (1956), "Try Me" (1958), "Think" (1960), "Bewildered" (1961), "I Don't Mind" (1961), "Lost Someone" (1961), "Night Train" (1962), "Prisoner of Love" (1963), "I Got You" (1965), "It's a Man's Man's Man's World" (1966), "Don't Be a Dropout" (1966), "Bring It Up" (1967)," Cold Sweat" (1967), "I Can't Stand Myself" (1967), "There Was a Time" (1968), "I Got the Feelin'" (1968), "Lickin' Stick" (1968), "Say It Loud— I'm Black and I'm Proud" (1968) "Git It Up or Turn It Loose" (1969), "I Don't Want Nobody to Give Me Nothing" (1969), "Mother Popcorn" (1969), "Let a Man Come In and Do the Popcorn" (1969) "It's A New Day" (1970), "Brother Rapp" (1970), "Get Up, I Feel Like Being a Sex Machine" (1970), "Super Bad" (1970), "Hot Pants" (1971), "Talking Loud and Saying Nothing" (1971), "Get on the Good Foot" (1972), "I Got Ants in My Pants" (1973), "The Payback" (1974), "My Thang" (1974), "Papa Don't Take No Mess" (1974), "Get Up Offa That Thing" (1976), "Living in America" (1985) and "I'm Real" (1988). James Brown has amassed almost 50 gold records.

James Brown is also one of the world's greatest showmen. His dance routines are unmatched, and his James Brown Revue is among the best live stage shows ever.

In the early 1970s Brown produced records for Lyn Collins and provided soundtracks for the films *Black Caesar* and *Slaughter's Big Ripoff*.

In 1984 Brown recorded "Unity" with rapper Afrika Bambaataa. In 1985 he appeared in the film *Rocky IV*, performing his hit single "Living in America." In the late '80s Brown was arrested for drug and weapons violations and served time in the South Carolina prison system.

In the early 1990s James Brown returned to his old form with a hit LP, a live pay-per-view concert special and a hit video.

MAY 4

1937: Jazz bassist Ron Carter is born in Ferndale, Michigan.

Carter, who holds a master's degree and is a graduate of the Eastman School of Music, played with the Eastman Philharmonic Orchestra before getting his first jazz gig with Chico Hamilton, in 1959. Early in his career he worked with Cannonball Adderley, Eric Dolphy and Jaki Byard.

In 1963 he joined Miles Davis's group. He remained with Davis until 1968. In the 1970s Carter worked with such varied artists as Lena Horne, Michel Legrand, Stanley Turrentine, Hubert Laws and George Benson.

In 1976 he formed his first quartet. In 1977 he joined Herbie Hancock and Tony Williams in the all-star group VSOP.

Carter has also taught jazz history at City College of New York.

1938: Singer Tyrone Davis is born in Greenville, Mississippi.

Davis's first job in show business was as a valet and chauffeur for blues guitarist Freddie King. He first recorded in 1965, billed as Tyrone the Wonder Boy.

Tyrone Davis had a 20-year string of soul and pop chart hits from 1968 to 1988. His best-known hits are "Can I Change My Mind" (1968), "Is It Something You've Got" (1969), "Turn Back the Hands of Time" (1970) "I Had It All the Time" (1972), "Without You in My Life" (1973), "Turning Point" (1975), "Give It Up" (1976) "This I Swear" (1977), "In the Mood" (1979) and "Are You Serious" (1982). In all, he placed over 40 singles on the charts.

1942: Songwriter Nicholas Ashford is born in Fairfield, South Carolina.

Nicholas Ashford and Valerie Simpson are a famous and successful husband-and-wife songwriting team. Over the past 20 years Ashford and Simpson have collected 22 gold and platinum records and more than 50 ASCAP awards as performers, producers and songwriters.

They met in New York in 1964, when Ashford joined the choir of the White Rock Baptist Church, where Simpson was singing and playing piano for the choir. The two began singing and writing songs together. They were soon signed as staff writers for Scepter Records and wrote Ray Charles's hit "Let's Go Get Stoned."

After meeting the Motown production team of Holland-Dozier-Holland, they joined Motown as staff writers. Their first Motown hit was "Ain't No Mountain High Enough," for Marvin Gaye and Tammi Terrell. They followed up with other Gaye/Terrell hits, such as "Ain't Nothing Like the Real Thing," "You're All I Need to Get By" and "Good Lovin' Ain't Easy to Come By."

In 1973 Ashford and Simpson signed with Warner Brothers as recording artists. They recorded eight LPs for the label, three of which went gold, and numerous singles, including "Send It," "Don't Cost You Nothing" and "Love Don't Make It Right." They also wrote and produced for Ben E. King, Chaka Khan, Gladys Knight and the Pips and Quincy Jones.

In 1982 the couple signed with Capitol Records. Their first LP for the label, *Street Opera*, yielded an instant hit, "Street Corner." Their second LP, *High Rise*, went to number 14 on the *Billboard* charts. In 1984, they released *Solid*, their most stylish work, and the title cut became one of the year's most popular songs.

In addition to their musical duties, Ashford and Simpson own the popular New York City restaurant 20/20, at 20 West 20th Street.

MAY 5

1901: Bluesman Blind Willie McTell is born in Thomson, Georgia.

McTell was almost totally blind at birth. He learned to play the guitar from his mother when he was 13. He attended the Georgia State School for the Blind.

McTell ran away from home and played in carnivals and minstrel shows. He hoboed across the eastern U.S., playing anywhere he could.

McTell began recording about 1927. His best early recordings include "T'aint Long for Day," "Crapshooter's Blues," "Death Cell Blues," "Statesboro Blues," "Rollin' Mama Blues" and "Three Women Blues."

McTell toured, hoboed and recorded until the mid-1950s, performing under more than half a dozen different aliases, including Barrelhouse Sammy, Georgia Bill, Red Hot Willie Glaze, Hot Shot Willie and Pig 'n' Whistle Red.

Blind Willie McTell died of a cerebral hemorrhage on August 19, 1950.

BLIND WILLIE McTELL

1938: Singer Johnnie Taylor is born in Crawfordsville, Arkansas.

Taylor began his career in the early 1950s with a Chicago-based gospel group, the Highway Q.C.s. In the mid-1950s he replaced Sam Cooke as lead singer with the Soul Stirrers.

Taylor first hit the R&B charts in 1963, with "Baby, We Got Love." In the mid-1960s he signed with Stax Records. In 1968 he scored a number 1 soul and Top 10 pop hit with the million-seller "Who's Making Love to Your Old Lady (While You Was Out Making Love)." A

number of Stax hits followed, including "Take Care of Your Homework" (1969), "Testify" (1969), "I Could Never Be President" (1969), "Love Bones" (1969), "Steal Away" (1970), "I Am Somebody" (1970), "Jody's Got Your Girl and Gone" (1971), "Hijackin' Love" (1971), "I Believe in You" (1973), "Cheaper to Keep Her" (1973) and "We're Getting Careless with Our Love" (1974).

When Stax went under, Taylor switched to Columbia Records. In 1976 he had a two-million-selling single with "Disco Lady." His other late-1970s hits include "Somebody's Gettin' It" (1976) and "Love Is Better in the A.M." (1977).

Johnnie Taylor currently records for the Malaco label.

MAY 6

1936: Vocalist and producer Sylvia Vanderpool Robinson is born in New York City.

Robinson first came to notice in 1950, when she was billed as Little Sylvia. She recorded with Hot Lips Page.

In 1956 she teamed up with Mickey "Guitar" Baker to record the classic rock 'n' roll song "Love Is Strange."

In 1973 she had a million-selling single with the very sexy "Pillow Talk."

In the late 1970s Robinson formed Sugar Hill Records, the first commercially successful rap music label, producing such groups as the Sugarhill Gang and Grandmaster Flash and the Furious Five.

1989: Teddy Riley and Guy make their pop chart debut.

By the age of 20, in 1988, Teddy Riley was an important songwriter, producer and composer. He is credited with forming the popular musical style called New Jack swing, which combines rap and hip-hop with pop dance music and funk. (The major purveyor of New Jack swing is Bobby Brown.)

Riley produced such hits as Keith Sweat's "I Want Her," Kool Moe Dee's "How You Like Me Now," Johnny Kemp's "Just Got Paid," "Don't You Know," by Heavy D and the Boyz, as well as album cuts for such artists as Billy Ocean, Bobby Brown and Michael Jackson.

Guy, composed of Riley and brothers Aaron and Damian Hall, had a hit in 1989 with the single "My Fantasy." Other hits are "Groove Me," "I Like" and "I Wanna Get with U."

MAY 7

1939: Singer Jimmy Ruffin, brother of the Temptations' David Ruffin, is born in Collinsville, Mississippi.

His biggest hit was "What Becomes of the Broken Hearted" (1966). Other hits include "I've Passed This Way Before" (1966), "Stand By Me" (with David Ruffin, 1970) and "Turn to Me" (with Maxine Nightingale, 1982).

MAY 8

1910: Pianist, composer and arranger Mary Lou Williams is born in Atlanta, Georgia.

Mary Lou Williams first performed in public at the age of six. By the age of 13 she was working in carnivals and vaudeville shows. At 16 she married carny band member John Williams and settled in Memphis, recording with her husband's group, the Synco Jazzers.

In 1929 she became the pianist and chief arranger for Andy Kirk's orchestra. Throughout the 1930s Mary Lou Williams was a freelance arranger, producing charts for such well-known bandleaders as Benny Goodman, Louis Armstrong, Earl Hines, Tommy Dorsey and Glen Gray.

In the early 1940s Williams became a staff arranger with Duke Ellington's band. By 1944 she was a fixture at New York's Cafe Society and became a prolific composer. In 1946 she premiered her extended work *Zodiac Suite* with the New York Philharmonic Orchestra.

In 1952 Williams moved to Europe for two years. In 1957 she appeared with Dizzy Gillespie at the Newport Jazz Festival.

Mary Lou Williams served as artist-in-residence at Duke University from 1977 until shortly before her death, on May 28, 1981.

1911: Robert Johnson, king of the Delta bluesmen, is born in Hazelhurst, Mississippi.

Johnson was one of at least 10 children. His father was named Charles Dodds, but his mother was living with Noah Johnson. Robert Johnson was raised on the Leatherman plantation near Commerce, Mississippi, and received little schooling.

He took up the guitar in the late 1920s, listening to Leroy Carr records and taking up with bluesmen like Son House and Willie Brown. Johnson worked as a farmer.

He married in February of 1929. In April of 1930 he lost both his wife and his child in childbirth.

In the early '30s he hoboed around, playing juke joints, cafes, house parties and fish fries. He traveled basically throughout the South but ventured as far north as New York and as far west as the Dakotas.

In 1936 Robert Johnson signed with the American Record Company. He possessed an impassioned vocal style that mirrored inner torment. His guitar style was powerful and fervent. Johnson had only two recording sessions: one on November 23, 1936, in San Antonio, Texas, and the other on June 19 and 20, 1937, in Dallas. His songs are unmatched blues classics filled with graphic references to hell and devils and his inability to escape from them: "Hell Hound on My Trail," "Me and the Devil," "Terraplane Blues," "Cross Road Blues," "I'm a Steady Rollin' Man," "Preachin' Blues" and "I Believe I'll Dust My Broom."

Robert Johnson was a consistent womanizer, and it reportedly caught up with him on August 16, 1928, when he was either poisoned or stabbed to death by a woman's jealous husband.

1951: Vocalist Philip Bailey is born in Denver.

Bailey was percussionist and co–lead singer of the popular group Earth, Wind and Fire. He had a million-selling pop-rock single in 1984, "Easy Lover." He also released several gospel LPs.

MAY 9

1937: Dave Prater of the vocal duo Sam and Dave is born in Ocilla, Georgia.

Sam Moore and Dave Prater teamed up in 1961. They had a run of pop and soul chart hits that included "You Don't Know Like I Know" (1966), "Hold On, I'm Coming" (1966), "Said I Wasn't Gonna Tell Nobody" (1966), "You Got Me Hummin'" (1966), "When Something Is Wrong with My Baby" (1967), "Soul Man" (1967) and "I Thank You" (1968).

Dave Prater was killed in an auto accident on April 11, 1988.

MAY 10

1935: Singer Larry Williams, one of the most underrated of the early rock 'n' rollers and a label-mate of the famed Little Richard, is born in New Orleans.

Williams worked with Lloyd Price in the early 1950s. He hit the charts with such tunes as "Short Fat Fannie" (1957), "Bony Moronie" (1957), "You Bug Me, Baby" (1957) and "Dizzy Miss Lizzy" (1958). In 1960 he was convicted of drug dealing and spent time in prison.

In the mid-1960s he returned to the charts, teamed with Johnny "Guitar" Watson on songs like "Mercy, Mercy" (1967) and "Nobody" (1968).

Larry Williams committed suicide in Los Angeles on January 7, 1980.

1951: Dramatics lead singer Ron Banks is born in Detroit.

The Dramatics were formed in 1966 and first hit the soul charts in 1967. The group consisted of Banks, William Howard, Larry Demps, Willie Ford and Elbert Wilkins.

In 1971 they recorded a tune based on Flip Wilson's popular TV character Geraldine's catch phrase "whatcha see is whatcha get." The song went to the Top 10 on both the soul and pop charts.

Their biggest hit came in 1972, with "In the Rain." Other Dramatics hits include "Hey You, Get Off My Mountain" (1973), "Me and Mrs. Jones" (1975), "Be My Girl" (1976), "Shake It Well" (1977) and "Welcome Back Home" (1980).

In 1983 Ron Banks went solo. His biggest solo hit was "Make It Easy on Yourself" that same year.

MAY 11

1885: Cornetist and composer Joe "King" Oliver is born in Louisiana.

From 1908 to 1917 King Oliver played in parades and gigged around New Orleans. He performed in various brass bands, including the Magnolia Brass Band, the Original Superior Brass Band and the Olympia Brass Band. From 1917 to 1919 he played with the legendary Kid Ory, who gave him his nickname.

In 1919 Oliver moved to Chicago and joined Lawrence Duhe's band. He toured the West Coast and then returned to Chicago. In 1922 he formed his Creole Jazz Band, which included a young trumpeter named Louis Armstrong. In 1925 he formed the Dixie Syncopators. He stopped touring in the late '20s and concentrated on recording. He returned to the road in 1930. In 1937 he retired from music.

Oliver's best-known compositions are "Dipper Mouth Blues," "Canal Street Blues," "Riverside Blues" and "Working Man Blues."

King Oliver died on April 10, 1938, in Savannah, Georgia.

1933: Songwriter Titus Turner is born in Atlanta.

Turner wrote many of the early R&B and rock 'n' roll classics, including Buddy Holly's "That'll Be the Day," Lloyd Price's "Stagger Lee," Little Willie John's "All Around the World" and the Clovers' "Hey Baby Doll."

MAY 12

1959: The Swan Silvertones, one of the all-time great gospel groups, record their classic rocker "Mary Don't You Weep."

The Silvertones were formed in 1938 by the Reverend Claude Jeter, his brother and two others who were working in the coal mines in West Virginia. They were originally called the Harmony Kings. When they got their own radio show, over WBIR in Knoxville, their sponsor was the Swan Bakery, and so they became the Swan Silvertones.

The Swan Silvertones first recorded in July of 1946 for King Records. By then the group consisted of Jeter, John Myles, Henry Bossard, John Manson and Solomon Womack. The Silvertones had a stunning, exciting sound, with Jeter's dynamic falsetto on one end and Bossard's bass on the other.

In the early 1950s they recorded for specialty records and featured a third lead, a "screamer" named Paul Owens. The Swan Silvertones had hits with "Jesus Remember," "Savior Pass Me Not," "My Rock" and "How I Got Over."

In the mid-1960s Jeter left the Swan Silvertones to pastor a church in Detroit. Since his departure, they have had a succession of lead singers, including Solomon Womack, Percell Perkins, Robert Crenshaw, Dewey Young and Louis Johnson.

1962: The Temptations make their chart debut with "Dream Come True."

The song made it only to number 22 on the R&B charts, but it was the beginning of a fantastic career for Motown's most exciting group. The Temptations have rung up 43 Top 10 hits over the past 30 years.

Their biggest hits include "The Way You Do the Things You Do" (1964), "My Girl" (1965), "It's Growing" (1965), "Since I Lost My Baby" (1965), "My Baby" (1965), "Get Ready" (1966), "Ain't Too Proud to Beg" (1966), "Beauty Is Only Skin Deep" (1966), "I Know I'm Losing You" (1966), "All I Need" (1967), "You're My Everything" (1967), "It's You That I Need" (1967), "I Wish It Would Rain" (1968), "I Could Never Love Another" (1968), "Cloud Nine" (1968), "Runaway Child, Running Wild" (1969), "I Can't Get Next to You" (1969), "Just My Imagination" (1971), "Papa Was a Rolling Stone" (1972), "Masterpiece" (1973), "Treat Her Like a Lady" (1984) and "Lady Soul" (1986).

The group was formed in Detroit in 1960 and was known as the Primes. The original members were Eddie Kendricks, Paul Williams, Melvin Franklin, Otis Williams and Elbridge Bryant. David Ruffin replaced Bryant in 1964. In 1968 he was replaced in turn by Dennis Edwards. In 1971 Eddie Kendricks and Paul Williams left and were replaced by

Richard Street and Ricky Owens. Later members of the group were Damon Harris, Glenn Leonard, Louis Price, Ollie Woodson and Ron Tyson.

Paul Williams died on August 8, 1973. David Ruffin died on June 1, 1991, and Eddie Kendricks died on October 5, 1992.

MAY 13

1911: Jazz vocalist and trombonist Maxine Sullivan is born in Pittsburgh.

Maxine Sullivan began as a radio singer in the 1930s. In the late '30s she had a hit record, "Loch Lomond." She also sang with the big bands of Benny Carter, Benny Goodman and Glen Gray.

Sullivan retired from music in 1942 but returned in the mid-1940s, playing mostly in clubs around New York. In 1954 she retired again, this time to become a nurse, but in 1958 she was back on the bandstand.

In the late 1960s she worked with the World's Greatest Jazz Band. In 1985 she had a best-selling LP, *Music from the Cotton Club.*

Maxine Sullivan appeared in the films *St. Louis Blues* and *Going Places.*

MAXINE SULLIVAN

1943: Singer Mary Wells is born in Detroit.

At the age of 17 Mary Wells approached Berry Gordy, Jr., with a song

called "Bye, Bye Baby," which she had written for Jackie Wilson. It became her first chart record. Wells was Motown's first female recording star and the first person signed to the Motown label. She was also the first Motown artist to chart in England and the first Motown artist to receive a Grammy award nomination.

Mary Wells had a string of early '60s hits, all written and produced by Smokey Robinson, including "The One Who Really Loves You," "You Beat Me to the Punch," "Two Lovers, "Laughing Boy" and "My Guy."

Wells and Motown parted company in 1964, and over the next several years she recorded for several labels, including Atco and Jubilee, but never achieved the same success she had enjoyed with Motown. Her biggest hit of that era was "Dear Lover," in 1966.

Wells was married for a time to Bobby Womack's brother Cecil. She died of cancer on July 26, 1992.

1950: Stevie Wonder is born Steveland Morris in Saginaw, Michigan.

Stevie Wonder was born blind. At the age of 11 he could play drums, piano and harmonica. He was brought to Motown Records by Ronnie White of the Miracles and given the name Little Stevie Wonder by Berry Gordy, Jr. He began his career as "the 12-year-old genius" and has developed into one of the world's most prolific and eloquent singer-songwriters. His first hit, "Fingertips," was recorded live at Chicago's Regal Theater.

Wonder has won numerous awards, including 17 Grammies, and has been inducted into the Songwriters Hall of Fame. He has charted with more than 60 pop and R&B singles. His best-sellers include "Fingertips Part II" (1963), "Uptight" (1965), "Blowin' in the Wind" (1966), "A Place in the Sun" (1966), "I Was Made to Love Her" (1967), "Shoo-be-doo-be-doo-be-doo-dah-day" (1968), "For Once in My Life" (1968), "Ma Cherie Amour" (1969), "Yester Me, Yester You, Yesterday" (1969), "Signed, Sealed, Delivered, I'm Yours" (1970), "If You Really Love Me" (1971), "Superstition" (1972), "You Are the Sunshine of My Life" (1973), '"Higher Ground" (1973),

"Living for the City" (1973), "You Haven't Done Nothing" (1974), "Boogie On, Reggae Woman" (1974), "I Wish" (1976), "Sir Duke" (1977), "Ebony and Ivory" (with Paul McCartney, 1982), "I Just Called to Say I Love You" (1984), "Part Time Lover" (1985) and "That's What Friends Are For" (with Dionne Warwick and friends, 1985). His best selling LPs include *The Twelve-Year-Old Genius, Innervisions, Fulfillingness' First Finale, Original Musicquarium, In Square Circle* and *Characters*.

Stevie Wonder was married to Motown songwriter Syreeta Wright from 1970 to 1972. In August of 1973 he was injured in a near-fatal auto accident. In the early 1980s Wonder took time out from his commercial music endeavors to help promote and establish Martin Luther King's birthday as a national holiday, which is now celebrated on the third Monday in January.

MAY 14

1897: Sidney Bechet, clarinetist, saxophonist and accomplished jazz soloist, is born in New Orleans.

As a teenager, Bechet played with local bands around New Orleans. In 1914 he took up with a traveling show. In 1919 he toured England and Europe with Will Marion Cook's Southern Syncopated Orchestra.

In the early 1920s Bechet recorded with Louis Armstrong. He returned to Europe in 1925, with Josephine Baker's *Revue Nègre*. He worked in Germany, Russia and France (with Noble Sissle).

Bechet returned to the U.S. in 1931 and worked with Sissle and Duke Ellington. In 1932 he formed the New Orleans Feetwarmers Band. He had a hit in 1939, with "Summertime." In 1940 he issued a series of recordings with Muggsy Spanier. He settled in France in 1951.

Sidney Bechet died on May 14, 1959, in Paris.

1934: R&B saxophonist Grady Gaines is born in Waskom, Texas.

Gaines was the leader of the Upsetters, Little Richard's backup band, and one of the best live R&B bands ever. In the classic 1950s rock 'n' roll film *Don't Knock the Rock*, the man standing on Little Richard's piano and wailing on the sax is Grady Gaines.

When Little Richard became a preacher and gave up rock 'n' roll, the Upsetters worked behind such R&B greats as Dee Clark, Little Willie John, Sam Cooke, Solomon Burke and Jackie Wilson. They also served as the backup band for scores of rock 'n' roll package-show tours in the late '50s and early '60s.

Today they still perform and record, under the name Grady Gaines and the Texas Upsetters.

MAY 15

1938: Vocalist Lenny Welch is born in Asbury Park, New Jersey.

In the 1960s smooth-voiced Lenny Welch was one of the best ballad singers around. His best-known recording was his 1963 hit, "Since I Fell for You." His other hits of the period include "You Don't Know Me" (1960) and "Ebb Tide" (1964).

MAY 16

1930: Jazz singer Betty Carter is born Lillie Mae Jones in Flint, Michigan.

Betty Carter began singing in local clubs around Detroit in 1946. Early in her career she worked with Dizzy Gillespie's big band and Charlie Parker's quintet. Hanging out with such far-out cats gained her the nickname Betty

BETTY CARTER

Bebop. Many of Carter's vocals were so improvised and instrumentally conceived that she was considered to be far outside the mainstream of jazz vocalists.

In 1948 she joined Lionel Hampton's big band. In 1951 she went solo, becoming a fixture at Harlem's Apollo Bar. Carter recorded a series of duets with Ray Charles in 1961. In 1969 she formed her own record label, Bet-Car.

Her best LPs include *The Modern Sound of Betty Carter, Whatever Happened to Love, Ray Charles and Betty Carter* and *Inside Betty Carter*.

1944: Jazz drummer Billy Cobham is born in Panama.

Billy Cobham came to New York at the age of three. He started playing drums and percussion as a toddler and attended the High School of Music and Arts.

In 1968 Cobham joined the Horace Silver Quintet. He also worked with the Brecker Brothers and played on Miles Davis's LPs *Bitches Brew, Live-Evil* and *Jack Johnson*.

In 1971 Billy Cobham was a founding member of John McLaughlin's Mahavishnu Orchestra. In 1973 he began leading his own group and recording under his own name. His first LP, *Spectrum*, is one of the early classics of the jazz-rock genre.

Cobham formed the group Spectrum in 1975. It included George Duke on keyboards. In the early 1980s Billy Cobham moved to Europe and joined the group Consortium.

1966: Janet Jackson is born in Gary, Indiana.

A member of the dynamic Jackson family, Janet Jackson was best known nonmusically for her recurring role in the hit TV series "Diff'rent Strokes," on which she played Todd Bridges's girlfriend. She was also a regular on "Fame" before she turned her efforts to recording.

In 1984 Jackson released the album *Dream Street*, on which she worked with several producers, including Jesse Johnson, Giorgio Moroder and Pete Bellotte, as well as her brother Marlon.

The LP was successful and produced a hit single, "Don't Stand Another Chance," but it didn't satisfy Jackson.

She continued to search for the right recording formula for her music. She found it with the Minnesota-based duo of Terry Lewis and Jimmy Jam.

Control, the album she released with them in 1986, produced pop, black and dance-music chart toppers like the title track, "Nasty," "What Have You Done for Me Lately," "The Pleasure Principle" and "Let's Wait Awhile." Each single from the LP was promoted with a slickly produced video, in which Jackson performed hot dance moves choreographed by Paula Abdul. In Jackson's own words, the LP was "one nasty groove after another."

In 1989 Janet Jackson released her follow-up album, *Janet Jackson Rhythm Nation*. It too was a tremendous success, producing such hit singles as "Miss You Much," "Rhythm Nation," "Escapade," "Alright" and "Come Back at Me."

MAY 17

1942: Bluesman Taj Mahal is born Henry Saint Claire Fredericks in New York City.

Taj Mahal attended the University of Massachusetts and earned a B.A. in animal husbandry. He began playing coffeehouses around 1964 and came to prominence during the blues revival of the 1960s and 1970s. He signed with Columbia Records in 1967.

Taj Mahal's concert appearances have included the Newport Folk Festival and the Fillmores East and West.

In 1990 Taj Mahal composed the music for the blues-based Broadway musical *Mule Bone*. His best LPs include *Natch'l Blues*, *Mo' Roots*, *Taj Mahal*, *Regarding the Blues* and *Ooh, Ooh, Sho Good 'n' Blues*.

MAY 18

1911: Big Joe Turner, Big Daddy of all the blues and R&B shouters and one of the paramount figures bridging R&B with early rock 'n' roll, is born in Kansas City, Missouri. Big Joe Turner's classic recordings of the '50s not only delighted black R&B fans, but their gutsy raucousness captured the fancy of white rockin' 'n' rollin' teenagers.

His father was killed when Turner was 15. To help his family, Turner worked at a series of jobs, from shining shoes to cooking to running liquor and bartending in Prohibition Era bootleg joints.

In 1929 he teamed up with boogie-woogie pianist Pete Johnson and played clubs around the Midwest. Talent scout John Hammond brought the duo to New York in 1938 and put them in his *Spirituals of Swing* at Carnegie Hall on Christmas Eve. The next week they began recording for the Vocalion label.

In 1939 Turner and Johnson were recording under the name of Pete Johnson and His Boogie Boys and had a hit called "Cherry Red." In 1940 Turner began recording as a solo artist, as well as with Johnson. Some of his best-known early '40s hits include "Piney Brown Blues" (1941), "Wee Baby Blues" (1941) and "Corrina, Corrina" (1941).

In 1946 Joe Turner signed with National Records and had a huge R&B hit, "My Girl's a Jockey." In 1951 he signed with Atlantic Records and began his string of unforgettable hits with "Chains of Love," which hit the top of the R&B charts and the pop Top 40. He followed with such hits as "Sweet Sixteen" (1952), "Don't You Cry" (1952), "Honey Hush" (1953), "TV Mama" (1954), "Shake, Rattle and Roll" (1954), "Well, All Right" (1954), "Flip Flop and Fly" (1955), "Hide and Seek" (1955), "Morning, Noon and Night" (1956), "The Chicken and the Hawk" (1956), "Corrina, Corrina" (1956) and "Lipstick, Powder and Paint" (1956).

Big Joe Turner appeared in the rock 'n' roll film, *Shake, Rattle and Rock*. He continued to record into the 1980s and died of kidney failure on November 24, 1985.

MAY 19

1952: Flamboyant singer, actress, model and disco queen Grace Jones, one of the few true stars that the disco era of the 1970s produced, is born in Spanishtown, Jamaica.

Jones was raised in Syracuse, New York. She became a top model in Europe and appeared on the covers of *Vogue*, *Elle* and *Der Stern* before turning to a musical career. She hit the soul, pop and disco dance charts with a series of singles that included "Sorry" (1977), "Pull Up to the Bumper" (1981), "Nipple to the Bottle" (1982), "Slave to the Rhythm" (1985), "I Am Not Perfect" (1986) and "Love Is the Drug" (1986).

Jones's appearance and stage act have often bordered on the bizarre, with hints of unisexuality, leather culture and sado-masochistic fantasy. During the disco era Grace Jones was the darling of the New York jet set's "in" crowd and became the first artist to perform live at the famous Studio 54 nightclub. Jones has also appeared in such films as *Gordon's War*, *Conan the Destroyer*, *A View to a Kill* and *Vamp*.

MAY 20

1940: Singer Shorty Long is born Frederick Earl Long in Birmingham, Alabama.

Shorty Long was Motown's party-record animal. Between 1966 and 1968 he recorded such humor-filled funk sides as "Devil with a Blue Dress," "Function at the Junction" and "Here Comes the Judge."

Shorty Long died in a boating accident while fishing on the Great Lakes on June 29, 1969.

MAY 21

1904: Composer Thomas Wright "Fats" Waller is born in New York City.

Waller's father was a minister, and his mother taught him the piano at age six. He took piano lessons from James P. Johnson. In 1918 he won an amateur contest at the Roosevelt Theater. He began recording in 1922 and became resident organist at New York's Lincoln Theater, providing music for silent films. He also toured with such vaudeville acts as Art Jarrett and Brown and Williams.

In the mid-1920s Waller formed his own trio and began a collaboration with lyricist Andy Razaf.

He worked with James P. Johnson in 1928 in the revue *Keep Shufflin'*. In 1929 he composed songs for the show *Hot Chocolate* and in 1930 had his own radio series.

In 1932 Waller toured Europe. In 1934 he began his famous "Fats Waller and His Rhythm" series of recordings and got his own show on CBS radio. Throughout the '30s he continued to tour Europe and the U.S.

Waller formed his own big band in 1941. It broke up a year later. In 1942 he appeared at Carnegie Hall, and in 1943 his show *Early to Bed* opened.

Fats Waller wrote such well-known songs as "Ain't Misbehavin'," "Black and Blue," "I'm Crazy 'Bout My Baby," "I've Got a Feeling I'm Fallin'" and "Honeysuckle Rose." He also appeared in the films *Hooray for Love, King of Burlesque* and *Stormy Weather.*

On December 15, 1943, while on a train traveling from Los Angeles to New York, Fats Waller died of pneumonia.

1983: Rap group Run-DMC makes its chart debut.

The trio, consisting of Joseph Simmons (aka Run), Darryl McDaniels (DMC) and Jason Mizell (Jam Master Jay), is one of the most commercially successful rap crews and was one of the hottest musical acts of the 1980s.

Run-DMC was the first rap act to earn a gold record (for the album *Run-DMC*, in 1984), the first rap act to earn a platinum record (for the LP *Raising Hell*, in 1986), the first to have a video aired on MTV, the first to appear on "American Bandstand," the first to be on the cover of *Rolling Stone*, the first group of nonathletes ever to receive an endorsement contract from Adidas sportswear and the first black group of any kind to sell four million copies of one album (*Raising Hell*) since Prince's *Purple Rain*, in 1984. *Raising Hell* made the Top 10 lists of both the *New York Times* and the *Los Angeles Times* and climbed to number 3 on *Billboard's* top pop albums chart. The album sold 3.3 million copies in the U.S. and nearly a million more overseas. Run-DMC's best-selling singles include "It's Like That" (1983), "Rock Box" (1984), "King of Rock" (1985), "My Adidas" (1986), "Walk This Way" (1986), "You Be Illin'" (1986), "It's Tricky" (1987) and "Run's House" (1988).

The group has appeared on such TV shows as "Saturday Night Live" and "The Late Show, Starring Joan Rivers," as well as in the films *Krush Groove* and *Tougher Than Leather.*

1988: Rappers D.J. Jazzy Jeff (Jeff Towners) and the Fresh Prince (Will Smith) make their pop chart debut.

The two proved that rappers don't have to be gangsters to be successful. They come across as just a couple of middle-class boy-next-door types.

They first hit in 1988, with a million-selling record and video smash, "Parents Just Don't Understand," and followed up with "Nightmare on My Street" (1988), "Girls Ain't Nothing But Trouble" (1988) and "I Think I Can Beat Mike Tyson" (1989).

In 1990 Will Smith became the star of the hit NBC-TV series "The Fresh Prince of Bel Air."

MAY 22

1914: Jazzman Sun Ra, composer and bandleader, is born Herman "Sonny" Blount in Birmingham, Alabama. According to Sun Ra, however, he wasn't really born; he simply arrived on Earth from another galaxy.

Sun Ra majored in music at Alabama A&M University. He settled in Chicago in the mid-1930s. Early in his career he worked with Fletcher Henderson and Coleman Hawkins. In the early 1950s he took the name Sun Ra and formed his first orchestra.

Over the years, Sun Ra gave his group various names: the Solar Arkestra, the Space Arkestra and the Intergalactic Myth-Science Arkestra, for example. He played conventional instruments such as piano, electric keyboard and synthesizer, as well as his own creations, such as the "rahsi-chord" and the "sun harp." His concerts were multimedia stage fantasies featuring musicians, singers, dancers, circus performers, lots of colorful costumes and theatrics.

Sun Ra recorded 115 albums over 30 years, mostly on his own record label. The best-known of them are *Sun Song, The Nubians of Plutonia, The Heliocentric Worlds of Sun Ra, Vols. I and II, Pictures of Infinity* and *Sunrise in Different Dimensions.*

Sun Ra had to be seen and heard to be believed. He died on May 30, 1993.

1928: Singer Roscoe Robinson is born in Dumont, Arkansas.

Robinson grew up in Gary, Indiana, and sang with such well-known gospel groups as the Highway Q.C.s, the Fairfield Four and the Five Blind Boys. In the mid-1960s he had such soul chart hits as "That's Enough" (1966), "How Much Pressure" (1966) and "Oo Wee Baby, I Love You" (1969).

MAY 23

1943: Singer and songwriter General Norman Johnson is born.

General Johnson first hit the R&B charts in 1961, as lead singer of the New Orleans–based Showmen. The group had hits with "It Will Stand" and "39-21-40 Shape."

In 1969 he formed the Chairmen of the Board and signed with the Holland-Dozier-Holland Invictus label. The Chairmen consisted of Johnson, Danny Woods, Harrison Kennedy and Eddie Curtis. The Chairmen had hits with such singles as "Give Me Just a Little More Time" (1970), "Dangling on a String" (1970), "Pay to the Piper" (1970), "Chairmen of the Board" (1971) and "Finders Keepers" (1973). Johnson also wrote and produced hits for other Invictus artists, such as Freda Payne and Honey Cone, and he wrote Clarence Carter's hit "Patches."

For the last decade General Norman Johnson and the Chairmen of the Board have been the biggest live draw on the South Carolina beach-music circuit.

MAY 24

1937: Jazz saxophonist and composer Archie Shepp, who is associated with the "free music" movement of the 1960s, and is also a poet and playwright, is born in Fort Lauderdale, Florida.

Shepp's major influences were such contemporaries as Cecil Taylor and Ornette Coleman. He first recorded with Taylor in 1960. In 1963 he cofounded the New York Contemporary Five. Like the "free jazz" of Coleman and Taylor, Shepp's recordings met with disapproval from the mainstream jazz community, especially because they were so overtly political. But recognition eventually did come. In 1967 his LP *Mama Too Tight* was critically acclaimed, and in 1969 he toured Europe and North Africa.

In 1965 Shepp's play *The Communist* was produced in New York. In the early 1970s his plays *Lady Day: A Musical Tragedy* and *Junebug Graduates Tonight* were produced, and he taught playwriting at the University of Buffalo.

Among Shepp's best LPs are *Ballads for Trane*, *On Green Dolphin Street*, *There's a Trumpet in My Soul* and *Trouble in Mind*.

1944: Singer Patti Labelle is born Patricia Holt in Philadelphia.

Patti Labelle has one of the most electrifying voices in the world of music. In 1961 she formed a group called Patti Labelle and the Blue Belles, with Cindy Birdsong, Sarah Dash and Nona Hendryx. The group had solid hits with songs such as "I Sold My Heart to the Junkman" (1962), "Down the Aisle" (1963), "You'll Never Walk Alone" (1964), "Danny Boy" (1964) and "Take Me for a Little While" (1967).

In 1967 Cindy Birdsong left to join the Supremes, and in 1971 Labelle, Dash and Hendryx became Labelle. Their sound became more hard rock–based, and they scored a million-seller in 1974 with "Lady Marmalade." Other Labelle hits include "What Can I

PATTI LABELLE

Do for You" (1975) and "Messin' with My Mind" (1975).

In 1977 Labelle disbanded, and Patti Labelle became a solo act. Her biggest hits include "If Only You Knew" (1983), "Love Has Finally Come at Last" (with Bobby Womack, 1984), "Love, Need and Want You" (1984), "New Attitude" (1985), "Stir It Up" (1985), "On My Own" (with Michael McDonald, 1986) and "Oh People" (1986).

Patti Labelle has also appeared in the film *A Soldier's Story* and on the TV shows "A Different World" and "Out All Night," her own sitcom.

MAY 25

1878: Dancer Bill "Bojangles" Robinson is born in Richmond, Virginia.

Bojangles Robinson was one of filmdom's best-known tap dancers, probably best remembered by audiences for his work with Shirley Temple in four films. Among the films in which he appeared are *Dixiana*, *Harlem Is Harlem*, *The Little Colonel*, *In Old Kentucky*, *Hooray for Love*, *The Big Broadcast of 1936*, *The Littlest Rebel*, *Curly Top*, *Dimples*, *Rebecca of Sunnybrook Farm*, *The Cotton Club Revue* and *Stormy Weather*.

Bill Robinson died of heart disease on November 25, 1949.

1926: Jazz legend Miles Davis is born Miles Dewey Davis III in Alton, Illinois.

Davis got his first trumpet on his 13th birthday as a present from his father. While still in high school he worked with a band called Eddie Randall's Blue Devils.

In 1944 Davis had a short stint with Billy Eckstine's band, whose ranks also included Charlie Parker and Dizzy Gillespie. In 1945 he went to New York to study at the Juilliard School of Music but soon found himself playing in small New York clubs with Coleman Hawkins and Parker.

Miles Davis first recorded in November of 1945, with Parker's quintet. These recordings are considered the first recorded elements of bebop and contain the classic "Now's the Time." Davis and

Parker worked together until 1948, when Davis formed his own group.

In 1949 he got his first international exposure, at the Paris Jazz Festival. From 1949 to 1953 he did very little performing. In 1955 he put together the first great Miles Davis Quintet, with John Coltrane, Philly Joe Jones, Red Garland and Paul Chambers. His classic LPs of the '50s include *Birth of the Cool*, *Bag's Groove*, *Miles Ahead*, *Porgy and Bess*, *Coolin'*, *Kind of Blue* and *Sketches of Spain*. In 1957 he did the soundtrack for Louis Malle's film *Lift to the Scaffold*.

In 1963 he formed a new quintet, with Herbie Hancock, Ron Carter, Tony Williams and Wayne Shorter. Davis and crew produced the superb live LP *My Funny Valentine* and the equally superb *Miles in the Sky*. In 1968 Davis became interested in fusion, the mixing of jazz with elements of funk, rock and other rhythms and the marriage of jazz to electronic instruments. Beginning in 1969, he recorded the classic LPs *In a Silent Way*, *Bitches Brew*, *Live-Evil*, *Jack Johnson* and *Filles de Kilimanjaro*.

In 1975, beset by drug and health problems, Davis retired, but he returned to performing in 1980, with the LP *The Man with the Horn*. During the 1980s Davis released a pair of brilliant LPs, *You're Under Arrest* and *Tuto*.

During the late '70s and early '80s Davis spent a lot of time in seclusion, writing music and working on the other love of his life, painting. He was married at one time to actress Cicely Tyson.

Miles Davis died on September 28, 1991.

MAY 26

1883: Mamie Smith, the first black blues singer to record solo, is born in Cincinnati.

Mamie Smith went to New York in 1913 with a white vaudeville group, the Four Mitchells. Hustler and composer Perry Bradford became her manager, and she appeared in such shows as *The Smart Set*.

In 1920 she recorded "Crazy Blues." Within six months of its issue, the record had sold a million copies and set off the "race music" explosion. After this success, Smith toured with her own band, the Jazz Hounds, one of whose members was Coleman Hawkins. She also appeared in *The Syncopated Revue*, *Frolicking Around*, *The Sugarcane Revue* and *A Riot of Fun*.

Smith toured Europe in the 1930s. She also appeared in the films *Jail House Blues*, *Paradise in Harlem*, *Murder on Lenox Avenue* and *Sunday Sinners*.

Mamie Smith is thought to have died on September 16, 1946, in Harlem.

MAY 27

1935: Jazz pianist Ramsey Lewis is born in Chicago.

Lewis began piano lessons at the age of six. He studied at Chicago Music College and at DePaul University.

In 1956 he formed the Ramsey Lewis Trio, with bassist Eldee Young and drummer Red Holt, and signed with the Chess Records subsidiary ARGO.

The Ramsey Lewis Trio began hitting the pop and soul charts in 1964, with a series of hit singles that included "The In Crowd" (1965), "Hang On, Sloopy" (1965), "A Hard Day's Night" (1966), "High Heel Sneakers" (1966), "Wade in the Water" (1966) and "Uptight" (1966). All were jazzy versions of pop tunes.

Young and Holt left to form their own group, Young-Holt Unlimited, and were replaced by Cleveland Eaton and Chess Records house drummer Maurice White.

Ramsey Lewis's later LPs include *Love Notes*, *Les Fleurs* and *Ramsey Lewis and Nancy Wilson*.

MAY 28

1898: Bandleader Andy Kirk is born in Newport, Kentucky.

Saxman Andy Kirk was moonlighting as a mailman when he took over the leadership of the Terrence Holders band, the Dark Clouds of Joy, in 1929. Pianist Mary Lou Williams became the band's chief arranger in 1931. In 1936 Andy Kirk and his Clouds of Joy had a hit record, "Until the Real Thing Comes Along," which featured Pha (pronounced Fay) Terrell on vocals. In 1939 the Clouds of Joy replaced Cab Calloway's orchestra at the Cotton Club.

During the 1940s Kirk's band had a great vocal crew, which included June Richmond and the Jubilaires. With their vocals out front, the band had such R&B chart hits as "Take It and Git" (1942), "Hey Lawdy Mama" (1943), "I Know" (1946), "I Don't Know What I'd Do Without You" (1946) and "47th Street Jive" (1949). When the band broke up, in 1948, Andy Kirk retired from performing.

Andy Kirk died in December 1992.

1910: Guitarist Aaron "T-Bone" Walker is born Aaron Thibeaux Walker in Linden, Texas.

Walker taught himself to sing and to play guitar, fiddle and piano. In the 1920s he played in carnivals and medicine shows. He first recorded in 1929, using an acoustic guitar.

During the 1930s he worked with Ma Rainey, Cab Calloway and Milt Larkin. He moved to Los Angeles in 1934.

By the mid-1940s Walker and his electric guitar were hitting the top of the R&B charts, with such tunes as "Bobby Sox Blues" (1947), "Call It Stormy Monday" (1948), "Long Shirt Baby Blues" (1948), "I'm Just Waiting for Your Call" (1948), "Westside Baby" (1948) and "T-Bone Shuffle" (1949).

Walker was one of the most influential guitarists of the postwar period and is sometimes considered the inventor of electric-guitar blues. Most credit Walker with bringing the electric guitar into vogue. He was a masterful showman, playing his guitar across his shoulders and behind his back. He continued to record and tour into the early 1970s.

T-Bone Walker died of bronchial pneumonia on May 16, 1975.

1944: Gladys Knight is born in Atlanta.

At the age of seven, Gladys Knight was a winner on TV's "Ted Mack's Original Amateur Hour." In 1952 Knight and her brother Merald, her sister Brenda and her cousins Edmund and Eleanor Guest formed a group to sing gospel in local churches. In 1957 they turned professional and called themselves the Pips, after their manager, Pip Woods. They got a recording contract with Brunswick Records but failed to

GLADYS KNIGHT AND THE PIPS

have a hit. Brenda Knight and Eleanor Guest left the group and were replaced by Langston George and Edward Patten.

In 1960 the Pips recorded "Every Beat of My Heart" for a small label, which sold it to Vee Jay Records. It became the Pips' first hit in 1961. In 1962 Langston George left the group.

Gladys Knight and the Pips signed with Motown in 1966. In 1977 the group became embroiled in legal hassles with Motown over unpaid royalties, and its members were unable to record together. It took until the early '80s for the contractual problems to be resolved.

Gladys Knight and the Pips have placed more than 50 singles on the pop and soul charts. Their biggest hits include "Letter Full of Tears" (1961), "I Heard It Through the Grapevine" (1967), "The Nitty Gritty" (1969), "Friendship Train" (1969), "If I Were Your Woman" (1970), "Neither One of Us" (1973), "Midnight Train to Georgia" (1973), "I've Got to Use My Imagination" (1973), "Best Thing That Ever Happened to Me" (1974), "On and On" (1974), " I Feel a Song in My Heart" (1974), "Love Finds Its Own Way" (1975), "Landlord" (1980), "Save the Overtime" (1983), "Love Overboard" (1987) and "Lovin' on Next to Nothin'" (1988).

Gladys Knight and the Pips had their own TV variety show in 1975. Gladys Knight starred in the film *Pipe Dreams* in 1976, and she was a member in 1985 of the cast of the TV show "Charlie and Co."

Gladys Knight and the Pips have won several Grammies, NAACP Image awards, and awards from such music-industry publishers as *Billboard*, *Cashbox* and *Record World*.

MAY 29

1943: The Mills Brothers make their chart debut with "Paper Doll."

The Mills brothers hailed from the small town of Piqua, Ohio, and originally consisted of tenors Herb and Don, baritone Harry and bass John Mills, Jr. Billed at first as Four Boys and a Kazoo, they began playing in small theaters around Ohio. Their act originally consisted of doing imitations of musical instruments.

By the early 1930s the Mills Brothers were a hit on national radio and had their first big record, "Glow Worm." On January 23, 1936, John Mills, Jr., died of tuberculosis. His place in the group was taken by his father.

The Mills Brothers' best-known chart hits include "Till Then" (1944), "You Always Hurt the One You Love" (1944), "Put Another Chair at the Table" (1945), "Across the Alley from the Alamo" (1947) and "Mañana" (1948). The Mills Brothers are also noted for "Opus One," "Daddy's

Little Girl," "Smack Dab in the Middle" and "Cab Driver." They appeared in many films, including *The Big Broadcast* (1932), *Twenty Million Sweethearts* (1934), *Broadway Gondolier* (1935), *Reveille with Beverly* (1943) and *Chatterbox* (1943).

Harry Mills died on June 28, 1982. John Mills, Sr., died on December 8, 1967.

MAY 30

1949: "The Hucklebuck," by saxophonist and bandleader Paul Williams, is the number 1 R&B song. It spawned a dance craze by the same name, and the record remained at the number 1 spot on the R&B charts for 14 weeks.

Williams was one of the top R&B instrumentalists of the late 1940s. He formed his first band, the Paul Williams Orchestra, in 1947, after playing in the orchestras of Clarence Dorsey and King Porter. The group featured vocalists Joan Shaw, Connie Allen, Danny Cobb and Jimmy Brown and trumpeter Phil Gilbeau and saxman Noble "Thin Man" Watts.

Williams had such other R&B chart hits as "35-30" (1948), "Walkin' Around" (1949), "House Rocker" (1949) and "Popcorn" (1949).

In the late '50s and early '60s Paul Williams led the backup bands for such rock 'n' roll package shows as the *Shower of Stars* and the *Show of Stars*.

MAY 31

1966: Percy Sledge's "When a Man Loves a Woman," one of the most soulful records ever made, is the number 1 soul chart hit. It hit number 1 on the pop charts, too. The song was written by Sledge, bassist Cameron Lewis and organist Andrew Wright and grew out of an improvisational piece that Sledge performed during his nightclub act.

Percy Sledge was born in Leighton, Alabama, in 1941. He was a cousin of soul singer Jimmy Hughes and worked with a band called the Esquires Combo. Sledge's other hits include "Warm and Tender Love" (1966), "It Tears Me Up" (1966), "Out of Left Field" (1967) and "Take Time to Know Her" (1968).

JUNE 1

1925: Singer Marie Knight is born in Brooklyn.

In the late 1940s and early 1950s Knight and Sister Rosetta Tharpe formed a popular gospel-music duo. In 1949 they had a Top 10 R&B hit with "Gospel Train."

After her breakup with Tharpe, Knight concentrated solely on pop music. She hit the charts in 1965, with a cover of "Cry Me a River."

JUNE 2

1932: Singer Sammy Turner is born in Paterson, New Jersey.

Sammy Turner had a string of R&B and pop hits in 1959 and 1960, including "Lavender Blue," "Always" and "Paradise."

1937: Singer Jimmy Jones is born in Birmingham, Alabama.

In 1960 Jimmy Jones recorded two classic rock 'n' roll oldies, "Handy Man" and "Good Times." Both went to the pop and R&B Top 10.

1943: Singer and songwriter Jimmy Castor is born in New York City.

Before he became a recording star, Jimmy Castor was a music-business jack-of-all-trades. He sang with a doo-wop group called the Juniors, replaced Frankie Lymon in the Teenagers and played sax on Dave "Baby" Cortez's hit instrumental "Rinky Dink."

In 1966 Castor had a Top 40 R&B and pop hit with the Latin-flavored "Hey, Leroy, Your Mama's Callin' You."

In 1972 he formed the Jimmy Castor Bunch. They scored a million-seller in the same year, with the novelty tune "Troglodyte (Cave Man)."

JUNE 3

1897: Memphis Minnie, the most famous female country blues singer ever, is born Lizzie Douglas in Algiers, Louisiana.

Memphis Minnie learned to play the guitar at age 11. She was raised in Mississippi but ran away to become a street performer in Memphis. Throughout the late 1910s and early 1920s she worked bars and joints along Beale Street, along with Kansas Joe McCoy, whom she married.

She began recording in the late 1920s. The roughness of her vocals and her down-home guitar playing set her apart from the other female blues singers of the era. Her first hit was "Bumblebee," in 1930. Her other early hits included "In My Girlish Days," "Black Rat Swing," "Nothing in Rambling" and "I'm So Glad."

In the early 1930s she moved to Chicago and began working local clubs, playing with bluesmen like Big Bill Broonzy and Bumble Bee Slim. Her later hits include "Me and My Chauffeur" (1941) and "Why Did I Make You Cry" (1950).

Memphis Minnie suffered a stroke and died on August 6, 1973.

1906: Josephine Baker is born in St. Louis, Missouri.

To help support her family, Josephine Baker had to go to work at the age of eight. While still in high school, she worked as a dancer in a chorus line.

In 1923, at the age of 17, Baker was a dancer in Noble Sissle's hit show, *Shuffle Along*. In 1925, as a dancer in *La Revue Nègre*, she visited Paris. The French audiences reacted to her so positively that she was signed to star in Paris's famed Folies Bergère. On June 19, 1925, Baker made her debut as the "dark star" of the Folies Bergère at the Casino de Paris.

Josephine Baker became a major star in France. Aside from her nightclub appearances, she starred in such French films as *Zou Zou* (1934), *Princess Tam Tam* (1935), *The French Way* (1940) and *Moulin Rouge* (1944).

Josephine Baker's personal life was marked by two things: her love affairs, and her humanitarian efforts. She was married several times; her husbands included painter Count Heno Abatino and orchestra leader Jo Boullon. She adopted and raised children of all races and was inducted into the French Legion of Honor for her work with the French underground resistance during World War II.

Josephine Baker died of a cerebral hemorrhage on April 12, 1975, in Paris.

JOSEPHINE BAKER

1942: Singer and songwriter Curtis Mayfield is born in Chicago.

In 1957 Mayfield, along with Jerry Butler, Sam Gooden, Arthur Brooks and Richard Brooks, formed a group called the Roosters. In 1958 the Roosters, now called Jerry Butler and the Impressions, had a top R&B hit with the ballad "For Your Precious Love." The success of the record led Butler to go solo. Mayfield wrote such songs as "He Will Break Your Heart" for Butler and worked as his guitarist and backup singer.

In 1961 Mayfield reorganized the Impressions, with Sam Gooden and

Fred Cash, and signed with ABC-Paramount Records. Over the next nine years the Impressions placed more than two dozen singles on the pop and soul charts, almost all written by Curtis Mayfield: "Gypsy Woman" (1961), "It's All Right" (1963), "Talking About My Baby" (1964), "I'm So Proud" (1964), "Keep on Pushing" (1964), "Amen" (1965), "People Get Ready" (1965), "Woman's Got Soul" (1965), "We're a Winner" (1968), "This Is My Country" (1968) and "Choice of Colors" (1969).

In 1970 Mayfield went solo. His hits included "If There's a Hell Below, We're All Going to Go" (1970), "Freddie's Dead" (1972), "Superfly" (1972), "Kung Fu" (1974), "So in Love" (1975) and "Only You, Babe" (1976). Mayfield also continued to write hit songs for other artists: "Find Yourself Another Girl" and "I'm Telling You," for Jerry Butler; "The Monkey Time, "Um, Um, Um, Um, Um, Um" and "Rhythm" for Major Lance; and "It's All Over" for Walter Jackson. He also scored such films as *Superfly*, *Claudine*, *A Piece of the Action* and *Short Eyes*.

On August 14, 1990, while appearing at an outdoor concert in Brooklyn, Curtis Mayfield was paralyzed from the neck down when a lighting scaffold fell on him.

1946: Singer Eddie Holman is born in Norfolk, Virginia.

Eddie Holman first hit the soul charts in 1965, with "This Can't Be True." In 1969 he had a million-seller with the ballad "Hey There, Lonely Girl."

1951: Singer Deneice Williams is born in Gary, Indiana.

Williams began singing as a child in her local church choir. From 1972 to 1975 she was a member of Stevie Wonder's backup vocal group, Wonderlove, and she had a solo on Wonder's "Ordinary Fool," from his *Songs in the Key of Life* LP.

In 1975 Williams signed with CBS Records. Her first hit came in 1976, with the single "Free." In the late 1970s she teamed up with Johnny Mathis and scored a number 1 pop hit with "Too Much, Too Little, Too Late," which sold a million copies. They also had a hit with

"You're All I Need to Get By" and provided the theme for the hit TV series "Family Ties."

In 1982 Williams had a number 1 black chart single with "It's Gonna Take a Miracle." In 1984 she had a number 1 pop single, "Let's Hear It for the Boy," from the soundtrack of the film *Footloose*. Her other hits include "Silly" (1981), "Do What You Feel" (1983), "I'm So Proud" (1983) and "Never Say Never" (1987). Deneice Williams also recorded the popular gospel LP *So Glad I Know*, in 1986.

JUNE 4

1945: Jazz saxophonist Anthony Braxton is born in Chicago.

Braxton studied harmony and composition at the Chicago School of Music and philosophy at Roosevelt University. He is fluent on alto and soprano saxes, clarinet, flute, accordion, percussion and harmonica. He also composes, arranges and sings.

In 1968 Braxton recorded the LP *For Alto*, a double record of solo alto-sax pieces. The set was not released until 1971.

In 1969 he went to Paris and played with the Creative Construction Company. In 1970 he joined Chick Corea's band, Circle.

Anthony Braxton's most acclaimed LPs include *The Complete Braxton*, *New York Fall 1974*, *Five Pieces* and *Alto Sax Improvisations*.

1961: DeBarge lead singer Eldra "El" DeBarge is born in Grand Rapids, Michigan.

With his good looks and unusual voice, El DeBarge quickly sprang to the forefront of the group. In 1985 he embarked on a solo career. He scored in 1986 with the theme from the film *Short Circuit*, "Who's Johnny." He later became embroiled in controversy when a woman in Michigan filed charges of sexual assault against him.

Besides El DeBarge, the group DeBarge was made up of brothers James, Mark and Randy and their sister Bunny. The group leapt onto the black and pop music charts in the early 1980s with a series of love ballads. DeBarge, discov-

ered and brought to Motown Records by Jermaine Jackson, was reminiscent of such earlier mellow Motown groups as the Miracles, the Originals and Bobby Taylor and the Vancouvers. DeBarge topped the charts with "All This Love," "Time Will Reveal," "Rhythm of the Night" and "Who's Holding Donna Now."

In 1984 James DeBarge eloped with and married Janet Jackson, but the marriage was quickly annulled. Later in the '80s another member of the family, Chico DeBarge, made his recording debut. Minus El and Bunny, DeBarge regrouped with the help of brother Bobby, who in the '70s had recorded with the soul group Switch.

JUNE 5

1950: Singer Ronnie Dyson is born in Washington, D.C.

Dyson was raised in Brooklyn and appeared in the Broadway musical *Hair*. He also appeared in the film *Putney Swope*. His best-remembered pop hit was 1970's "(If You Let Me Make Love to You Then) Why Can't I Touch You?"

Ronnie Dyson died of heart failure on November 10, 1990.

JUNE 6

1902: Bandleader Jimmie Lunceford is born in Fulton, Missouri.

Lunceford attended Fiske University and City College of New York. He formed his first band in 1927, the Chickasaw Syncopaters. In 1934 his band signed with Decca Records and took up residence in the famed Cotton Club.

Lunceford played sax, guitar and trombone but usually stuck to conducting. At the height of its popularity, from 1935 to 1943, the band featured such musicians as Sy Oliver, Paul Webster, Eddie Durham, Joe Thomas, Moses Allen and Gerald Wilson. The band had hit records with "Uptown Blues," "Swingin' on C," "Blues in the Night (My Mama Done Tol' Me)," "It Had to Be You," "Easy Street" and "I'm Gonna Move to the Outskirts of Town." Vocalists included Joe Thomas, Trummy Young, Willie Smith and Dan Grissom.

The Jimmie Lunceford Orchestra was the daddy of all the black swing bands of the '30s and '40s. During the war years, however, Lunceford's popularity fell. He lost most of his best players to the service and had trouble replacing them. In 1945 Lunceford and his orchestra came back with an R&B hit, "The Honeydripper," featuring the Delta Rhythm Boys on vocals.

While touring the Pacific Northwest, Jimmie Lunceford suffered a heart attack. He died on July 12, 1947, in Astoria, Oregon.

1939: Gary "U.S." Bonds is born Gary Anderson in Jacksonville, Florida.

Bonds was among the best of the 1960s black rock 'n' rollers. His hits include "New Orleans" (1960), "Quarter to Three" (1961), "School Is Out" (1961), "Dear Lady Twist" (1961) and "Twist, Twist Señora" (1962). His records were produced in Norfolk, Virginia, by Frank Guida and featured wild sax breaks by Gene "Daddy G" Barge.

In the 1970s Bonds wrote the country-and-western hit "Friend, Don't Take Her" for Johnny Paycheck. In the '80s he recorded and performed with Bruce Springsteen.

JUNE 7

1945: Singer Billy Butler, younger brother of the "Iceman," Jerry Butler, is born in Chicago.

Butler formed a group called the Enchanters at Wells High School. In 1963 they were signed by Okeh Records, and their name was changed to Billy Butler and the Chanters. The other members were Errol Batts and Jesse Tillman. Their soul chart hits included "I Can't Work No Longer," "Nevertheless" and "Right Track." The group broke up in 1966.

In 1969 Butler formed Infinity, with Errol Batts, Phyllis Knox and Larry Wade. Infinity hit the charts with such songs as "Get On the Case" (1969), "I Don't Want to Lose You" (1971) and "Hung Up on You" (1973).

1958: Prince is born Rogers Nelson in Minneapolis.

Prince first made the recording scene in April 1978, with an LP titled *For You* on Warner Brothers Records. The music

was nothing more than standard black Top 40 fare, but the unique thing was that Prince had written, arranged and produced the LP himself, playing all 27 instruments on it.

His second effort appeared in October of the following year and was simply titled *Prince*. Critics' and censors' eyes opened when they saw the LP cover photo of a partially nude Prince and heard the album's most risqué track, "Sexy Dancer."

His next work, *Dirty Mind*, came in 1980. Its themes were heavily sexual, and so were its lyrics. It was followed in 1981 by the aptly titled *Controversy*.

Prince's career hit the mainstream in late 1982 and early 1983. The title cut from his LP *1999* landed at number 12 on the singles chart, and its follow-up, "Little Red Corvette," though filled with graphic sexual innuendoes, got lots of radio play and made it to number 6.

During this period Prince was becoming noted for his high-energy live concerts, which contained street language, sexually oriented dance routines, scantily clad women and an even more scantily clad Prince. Also in this period, Prince developed his best-known back-up band, the Revolution, featuring Wendy and Lisa, and began producing albums for such protégés as Morris Day and the Time and Vanity Six. Former Prince sidemen Andre Cymone and Jesse Johnson also began releasing their own versions of Prince-style rock/funk 'n' roll on their solo projects.

Prince's next project was the multimedia *Purple Rain* film and soundtrack. The film was very successful, and the soundtrack was a multiplatinum effort. It also gave Prince two number 1 hits, "When Doves Cry" and "Let's Go Crazy." The title track went to number 2.

Prince then released the LPs *Around the World in a Day* (1985) and *Parade* (1986), which gave him Top 10 singles in "Raspberry Beret" and "Kiss," but they never attained the success of "Purple Rain." During this period Prince disbanded the Revolution.

He went on to star in two more films. The self-directed *Under the Cherry Moon* was a dreadful bomb. *Sign o' the*

Times is one of the best and tightest concert films ever produced. Through 13 songs, with accompanying dramatics and choreography. Prince and his backup band, led by drummer Sheila E., maintain a faster-than-life pace. The film and its soundtrack gave Prince such Top 10 hits as "You Got the Look" and "I Could Never Take the Place of your Man."

Controversial in his look, his dress, his relationships, his music, his lyrics, his films, his concerts, his women friends and the cast of characters with whom he surrounds himself, Prince is also noted for his mentorship. Former associates like Jesse Johnson, Andre Cymone, Vanity, Morris Day, Sheila E. and Wendy and Lisa have gone on to successful solo careers. Former Time members Jimmy Jam and Terry Lewis became the mid-1980s' hottest record producers, working with Janet Jackson. Prince has also written hit songs for other artists, such as "Sugar Walls" for Sheena Easton and "Manic Monday" for the Bangles.

PRINCE

JUNE 8

1923: Vocalist and impressionist George Kirby is born in Chicago.

In the 1960s Kirby delighted nightclub and TV audiences with his impersonations of Nat "King" Cole, Count Basie, Sammy Davis, Jr., and Billy Eckstine. His masterpiece was his takeoff on Pearl Bailey. He performed on all the top TV variety shows of the era. He also recorded an LP, *The Real George Kirby*, on which he sings in his own voice.

JUNE 9

1929: Johnny Ace is born John Marshall Alexander, Jr., in Memphis.

Johnny Ace's father was a minister. He had eight brothers and sisters. He learned to play the piano as a child. By his teens he was proficient on both piano and organ.

After attending Booker T. Washington High School, in Memphis, Ace enlisted in the U.S. Navy. He returned to Memphis after his tour of duty and was hired as the keyboard player for a band called the Beale Street Blues Boys. The group was led by sax player Adolph Duncan and included such soon-to-be notables as lead singer Robert Calvin, Bobby "Blue" Bland, lead guitarist Riley B. "B. B." King and drummer Earl Forest. At the time, Ace was only the piano player, but things changed. In 1951 Bland was drafted. The following year saw King, who had been recording on his own while with the Beale Streeters, leave to pursue a solo career. The band had its own radio show on Memphis's WDIA. That's where Johnny Ace moved from being the piano player to becoming lead vocalist. He began recording for Duke, a small local label owned by one of the deejays at WDIA. When the label was bought by a Texan, Don Robey, and given national distribution, Johnny Ace became its hottest property.

Ace hit number 1 on the R&B charts in 1952, with "My Song." He followed up in 1953 with another number 1, "The Clock." He also had hits with "Cross My Heart," "Saving My Love for You," "Please Forgive Me" and "Never Let Me Go."

Johnny Ace was at his peak on December 24, 1954, when he was to headline an R&B show at the City Auditorium in Houston. According to reports, he began playing a backstage game of Russian roulette. A .22-caliber bullet to the right temple ended his life.

Ace's untimely death led to a plethora of Johnny Ace memorial records, some by such notable R&B artists as Varetta Dillard, Johnny Moore's Three Blazers,

Johnny Fuller and Johnny Otis. Almost a month to the day after his death, Johnny Ace's biggest hit and best-known recording, "Pledging My Love," hit the charts. It went to number 1 on the R&B charts and to the Top 20 on the national pop charts.

1934: Jackie Wilson is born in Detroit.

At the age of 16 Wilson was a Golden Gloves boxing champion. He also sang with local gospel groups and was a solo performer in local clubs.

His break came in 1953, when he joined the group Billy Ward and the Dominoes, whose lead singer, Clyde McPhatter, had left to form his own group, the Drifters. Jackie Wilson sang lead on such Dominoes hits as "You Can't Keep a Good Man Down."

In 1957 Wilson went solo and signed with Brunswick Records. His first chart single, "Reet Petite," written by Berry Gordy, Jr., only reached number 62 on the pop charts, but it was the beginning of a phenomenal string of chart hits for Jackie Wilson.

In all, Wilson placed over 50 singles on the pop and R&B charts, including a half-dozen number 1 R&B hits. His biggest hits include "To Be Loved" (1958), "Lonely Teardrops" (1958), "That's Why (I Love You So)" (1959), "I'll Be Satisfied" (1959), "You Better Know It" (1959), "Talk That Talk" (1959), "Doggin' Around" (1960), "The Tear of the Year" (1961), "Baby Workout" (1963), "Danny Boy" (1965), "Whispers (Gettin' Louder)" (1966), "Higher and Higher" (1967) and "This Love Is Real" (1970).

Wilson was an outstanding performer. His concerts drew women fans by the thousands. It was common to see a cadre of huge bodyguards attempting to protect Jackie from onrushing throngs of adoring women who tried to pull him from the stage. Despite such precautions, however, Wilson was shot and seriously wounded in 1961 by a woman fan in New York.

On September 25, 1975, Wilson suffered a stroke while performing in Camden, New Jersey. He spent the rest of his life in a coma and died on January 21, 1984.

1951: The Clovers, one of the all-time great R&B doo-wop and rock 'n' roll vocal groups, make their chart debut.

The Clovers were formed in 1946. They signed with Atlantic Records in 1951. Between 1951 and 1959 the Clovers placed over 20 singles at the top of the R&B charts. Their greatest hits included "Don't You Know I love You" (1951), "Fool, Fool, Fool" (1951), "One Mint Julep" (1952), "Middle of the Night" (1952), "Ting-a-Ling" (1952), "Hey Miss Fannie" (1952), "Good Lovin'" (1953), "Lovey Dovey" (1954), "Your Cash Ain't Nothin' But Trash" (1954), "Nip Sip" (1955), "Devil or Angel" (1956) and "Love Potion Number Nine" (1959).

The original Clovers were made up of lead singer John "Buddy" Bailey, Matthew McQuater, Harold Lucas, Harold Winley and guitarist Bill Harris. Later members include Charlie White and Billy Mitchell. A unit of the Clovers still appears on the beach-music and oldies circuits.

JUNE 10

1895: Actress and singer Hattie McDaniel, the first African-American to receive an Academy Award, in 1939, is born in Wichita, Kansas.

McDaniel began her career in vaudeville. In the 1920s, under the name Hi Hat Hattie, she was a singer and drummer. She recorded for Okeh Records and performed on radio. She worked the theater and vaudeville circuits and appeared in the road-company production of the hit show *Showboat*.

Hattie McDaniel made more than 50 motion pictures, including *Gone With the Wind*, for which she won her Oscar as best supporting actress. Her other films include *Blonde Venus, I'm No Angel, Imitation of Life, The Little Colonel, Showboat, They Died with Their Boots On, The Male Animal* and *Song of the South*. She also starred in both the radio and TV versions of the series "Beulah."

Hattie McDaniel died on October 26, 1952.

1910: Blues singer Howlin' Wolf is born Chester Arthur Burnett in West Point, Mississippi.

Howlin' Wolf worked as a farmer and played juke joints and fish fries as a young man in Mississippi. In the 1930s he worked with such bluesmen as Sonny Boy Williamson, Robert Johnson and Robert J. Lockwood. He served in the U.S. Army. When he got out he went back to work as a farmer. In 1948 he moved to West Memphis, Arkansas, and formed his own group.

He got this own radio show on KWEM and cut some sides for Sam Phillips's Sun label. In 1951 he began recording for Chess. Howlin' Wolf's first big record was "Moanin' at Midnight," in the winter of 1951. He also had a hit with "How Many More Years" at about the same time.

In 1952 Howlin' Wolf moved to Chicago and began to record a string of classic blues tunes, including "No Place to Go" (1954), "Evil" (1954), "Who Will Be Next" (1955), "Smokestack Lightnin'" (1957), "Sitting on Top of the World" (1957), "Spoonful" (1960), "Back Door Man" (1960) and "The Red Rooster" (1961).

Howlin' Wolf was the blues' most explosive singer. He stood six feet, three inches and weighed over 275 pounds. His personality was enigmatic and often explosive. His vocal style is best described as rough and primitive.

In the early 1960s Howlin' Wolf was credited as an inspiration to many of the "British invasion" rock bands, especially the Rolling Stones. As a result, his music found a new audience. He appeared on TV shows like "Shindig," toured Europe, played such pop-culture palaces as the Electric Circus and the Café à Go-Go and made the rounds on the folk and blues festival circuits. His best LPs include *The Real Folk Blues*, *Moanin' in the Moonlight*, *His Greatest Sides* and *Back Door Wolf*.

Howlin' Wolf died of cancer on January 10, 1976.

1944: Shirelles lead singer Shirley Owens Alston is born in Passaic, New Jersey.

The Shirelles were one of the most famous girl groups of the 1960s. Their biggest hits include "I Met Him on a Sunday" (1958), "Tonight's the Night" (1960), "Will You Still Love Me Tomorrow" (1960), "Dedicated to the One I Love" (1961), "Mama Said" (1961), "Baby, It's You" (1961), "Soldier Boy" (1962) and "Foolish Little Girl" (1963).

Besides Alston, the group consisted of Beverly Lee, Doris Jackson and Micki Harris. They formed the group while they were in junior high school and first called themselves the Poquellos. In 1958 they signed with the small Tiara label. Their first hit, "I Met Him on a Sunday," was originally released on Tiara and picked up by Decca Records. In 1959 the Shirelles signed with Scepter Records.

Micki Harris died on June 6, 1982.

1970: Organist, pianist and vocalist Earl Grant dies in an auto accident.

Grant was one of the most popular nightclub and variety-show performers of the 1960s. He was born in Oklahoma City in 1931. He began recording for Decca in 1957 and had chart hits with "The End" (1958), "Evening Rain" (1959), "Swingin' Gently" (1962) and "Sweet Sixteen Bars" (1962). Grant also appeared in the films *Tender Is the Night*, *Imitation of Life* and *Tokyo Night*.

JUNE 11

1934: Spaniels' lead singer James "Pookie" Hudson is born in Gary, Indiana.

When the Spaniels were formed, at Roosevelt High School in 1952, they wanted to be different. Most of the current crop of R&B groups were named after either birds or cars, so they named themselves after a dog. Along with Pookie Hudson, the original lineup consisted of Ernest Warren, Opal Courtney, Willie Jackson and Gerald Gregory. Just before graduation, deejay Vivian Carter heard the Spaniels singing at a high school dance. She quickly made them the first artists to be signed to her newly formed Vee Jay record label. Their first hit came in the fall of 1953, with "Baby, It's You." Their biggest hit was the classic ballad "Goodnight, Sweetheart, Goodnight," in 1955.

JUNE 12

1941: Armando "Chick" Corea, one of the jazz world's most prolific

keyboardists and composers, is born in Chelsea, Massachusetts.

Corea started playing piano at the age of four. By his early teens he was playing in his father's band at local clubs. His musical training included short stays at both Columbia University and the Juilliard School of Music. He opted to forgo additional formal training and became a professional musician.

His first important jobs were in the Latin bands of Willie Bobo and Mongo Santamaria. In 1967 he recorded with Stan Getz and started leading his own group. From 1968 to 1970 he worked with Miles Davis. In 1970 Corea and bassist Anthony Holland formed the group Circle. In 1972 Corea formed the band Return to Forever, which included Airto Moreira and Flora Purim. Return to Forever was a jazz-pop group with a Latin flavor.

Return to Forever went through many personnel changes before breaking up, in 1980. Throughout his career, Corea has balanced his recording output between acoustic and electric piano. Among Chick Corea's most critically acclaimed LPs and CDs are *Chick Corea and the Electric Band*, *Chick Corea and the Akoustic Band*, *My Spanish Heart*, *Inner Space*, *ECM Works*, *Early Days* and *Piano Improvisation, Volume 2*.

1948: Singer Lyn Collins is born in Lexington, Texas.

Collins joined the James Brown Revue in 1969 and remained until the mid-1970s. She hit the soul and pop charts in 1972, with "Think (About It)," which was produced by James Brown. In the same year she had a successful duet with Brown, "What My Baby Needs Now Is a Little More Lovin'." Her other well-known singles include "Mama Feel Good" (1973), "Take Me As I Am" (1973) and "Rock Me Again and Again and Again" (1974).

1982: Rapper Afrika Bambaataa's "Planet Rock" makes its chart debut.

Afrika Bambaataa is a pioneer of rap and hip-hop music. He called his group the Soulsonic Force, and his followers were called the Zulu Nation.

"Planet Rock" was one of the first successful hip-hop records to be released and one of the best jam-box records ever. Released as a 12-inch single, it sold over a million copies.

Followups to "Planet Rock" include "Looking for the Perfect Beat" (1983) and "Renegades of Funk" (1984).

In 1984 Afrika Bambaataa recorded the single "Unity" with his funk mentor, James Brown. Afrika Bambaataa has also appeared in the film *Beat Street*.

JUNE 13

1940: Singer Bobby Freeman is born in San Francisco.

Freeman formed his first vocal group at the age of 14. In 1958 he had a Top 10 rock 'n' roll hit, "Do You Want to Dance?" In 1964 he hit the Top 10 again, with "C'mon and Swim." His other hits include "Betty Lou Got a New Pair of Shoes" (1958), "Shimmy, Shimmy" (1960) and "The Mess Around" (1961).

1942: Singer James Carr, one of the true treasures of soul music, is born in Memphis.

Carr's records of "You've Got My Mind Messed Up" (1966), "Pouring Water on a Drowning Man" (1966) and "The Dark End of the Street" (1967) are classics. Thoroughly underpromoted, Carr's best records did well enough on the soul charts but languished near the bottom of the pop charts. He got out of the music business in the 1970s but has returned to performing in the 1990s.

JUNE 14

1964: The Dixie Cups' "Chapel of Love" is the number 1 soul chart hit.

The Dixie Cups hailed from New Orleans. The members were Joan Marie Johnson, Barbara Ann Hawkins and Rosa Lee Hawkins. The group was originally called Little Miss and the Muffets and was discovered and managed by singer Joe ("You Talk Too Much") Jones.

The Dixie Cups were signed by the legendary rock 'n' roll songwriter-producer team of Jerry Leiber and Mike Stoller for their Red Bird label. The group followed up the success of "Chapel of Love" with "People Say" (1964) and "Iko Iko" (1965).

JUNE 15

1921: Pianist Erroll Garner, best known as the composer of the jazz standard "Misty," is born in Pittsburgh.

Garner was recognized as a gifted musician in early childhood. At the age of 10 he was performing on the radio. In 1944 he moved to New York and found immediate success on the nightclub circuit.

Garner spent most of his career playing clubs, hotels and concerts around the world. Early in his career he played with the well-known jazz drummer Art Blakey, also from Pittsburgh.

Garner recorded many LPs. His best include *The Complete Savoy Sessions*; *Play It Again, Erroll*; *Concert by the Sea*; and *Contrasts*, which contains his recording of "Misty."

Erroll Garner died on January 2, 1977.

1922: Jazzman Jaki Byard, equally at home on the piano or the saxophone, is born in Worcester, Massachusetts.

Byard's professional career began when he was 15. After serving in the U.S. Army, during World War II, Byard played with Earl Bostic's band and Hugh Pomeroy's band. In 1959 he replaced Joe Zawinul in Maynard Ferguson's orchestra. He also had two stints with Charles Mingus, 1962 to 1965 and 1970.

Jaki Byard's best LPs include *Blues for Smoke*, *Family Man*, *Live*, *Giant Steps* and *The Jaki Byard Experience*.

THE DIXIE CUPS

JUNE 16

1941: Singer, songwriter and producer Lamont Dozier is born in Detroit.

Lamont Dozier was a member of the highly respected Motown producer-writer team of Holland-Dozier-Holland, with Eddie and Brian Holland. The three of them wrote all of the initial, best-known hits by Diana Ross and the Supremes, including "Where Did Our Love Go," "Baby Love," "Come See About Me," "Stop! In the Name of Love," "Back in My Arms Again," "I Hear a Symphony," "My World Is Empty Without You," "You Keep Me Hangin' On," "You Can't Hurry Love," "Love Is Here and Now You're Gone," "The Happening" and "Reflections." They also wrote and produced hits for other Motown artists: "Come and Get These Memories" and "Heatwave," for Martha and the Vandellas; "I Can't Help Myself" and "It's the Same Old Song," for the Four Tops; and "I'm a Roadrunner," for Junior Walker.

Holland-Dozier-Holland left Motown in 1968 and founded their own Invictus and Hot Wax labels, which featured such artists as Freda Payne, the Honeycones and the Chairmen of the Board.

Lamont Dozier also found a measure of success as a solo recording artist. His chart hits include "Why Can't We Be Lovers" (1972), "Trying to Hold On to My Woman" (1973), "Fish Ain't Bitin'" (1974) and "Let Me Start Tonight" (1974).

1942: O'Jays lead singer Eddie LeVert is born in Canton, Ohio.

The O'Jays were formed in 1958 at McKinley High School, in Canton. Besides LeVert, the original group consisted of Walter Williams, William Powell, Bobby Massey and Bill Isles. They were originally called the Triumphs. When they got their first record contract, in 1961, they changed their name to the Mascots. They changed their name again, to the O'Jays, in honor of the famous Cleveland disc jockey Eddie O. Jay.

The O'Jays had their first chart hit in 1963, with "Lonely Drifter." Throughout the '60s and early '70s they recorded for such labels as Imperial, Bell and

Neptune. Their hits of the period included "Lipstick Traces" (1965), "Stand in for Love" (1966) and "I'll Be Sweeter Tomorrow" (1967). They also found work as backup singers for recording sessions. Bobby Massey left the group in 1971.

In 1972 the O'Jays signed with Gamble and Huff's Philadelphia International Records and began a tremendous run of top chart hits, starting with the million-selling "Back Stabbers." Follow-ups included "Love Train" (1973), "Time to Get Down" (1973), "Put Your Hands Together" (1973), "For the Love of Money" (1974), "Give the People What They Want" (1975), "I Love Music" (1975), "Livin' for the Weekend" (1976), "Message in Our Music" (1976), "Darlin' Darlin' Baby" (1976), "Work on Me" (1977), "Used to Be My Girl" (1978), "Sing a Happy Song" (1979), "Forever Mine" (1979), "Girl Don't Let It Get You Down" (1980), "Lovin' You" (1987) and "Let Me Touch You" (1987).

In 1975 William Powell retired from the group because of illness, and he died on May 26, 1987. Powell was replaced by Sammy Strain.

In the late 1980s Eddie LeVert's sons Gerald and Sean formed the successful group LeVert.

JUNE 17

1977: K. C. and the Sunshine Band's "I'm Your Boogie Man" is the number 1 pop chart hit.

K. C. and the Sunshine Band were one of the top-selling groups of the disco era. They were unique in being a black band with a white lead singer, Harry Wayne "K. C." Casey, who formed the group in Florida in 1973. At times, the group carried as many as 11 pieces.

Casey, along with bass player Richard Finch, wrote, produced and arranged all of the Sunshine Band's biggest hits, including five number 1 pop singles: "Get Down Tonight" (1975), "That's the Way I Like It" (1975), "Shake Your Booty" (1976), "I'm Your Boogie Man" (1977) and "Please Don't Go" (1979).

JUNE 18

1884: Blues singer Sara Martin is born in Louisville.

In the 1920s Sara Martin was billed as the blues sensation from the West. She toured with Fats Waller, working the theater and vaudeville circuits and appearing in such shows as *Up and Down* and *Jump Steady*. In 1931 she turned her attention to gospel music, working with the Reverend Thomas Dorsey. She retired from the music business in 1932.

Sara Martin died on May 24, 1955.

1938: Singer and guitarist Don "Sugarcane" Harris is born in Pasadena, California.

Sugarcane Harris and pianist Dewey Terry teamed up as Don and Dewey and had a string of 1950s R&B hits, including "Jungle Hop" (1957), "Leavin' It All Up to You" (1957), "Justine" (1958), "Big Boy Pete" (1958) and "Farmer John" (1959).

JUNE 19

1936: Singer Shirley Goodman is born in New Orleans.

In the 1950s Shirley Goodman and Leonard Lee teamed up to record as Shirley & Lee. Billed as the sweethearts of the blues, they had such top R&B hits as "I'm Gone" (1952), "Feel So Good" (1955), "Let the Good Times Roll" (1956), "I Feel Good" (1956) and "When I Saw You" (1957). Shirley & Lee broke up in 1963. Leonard Lee died of a heart attack on October 23, 1976.

After her separation from Lee, Shirley Goodman moved to the West Coast. Her voice was unusual, high-pitched and almost childlike, and she found work as a backup vocalist.

In 1975 Shirley Goodman returned to recording and scored a top soul, pop and disco hit with "Shame, Shame, Shame" on the Shirley and Company label.

1939: Singer Al Wilson is born in Meridian, Mississippi.

Wilson moved to California in the late 1950s and performed with such groups as the Rollers and Johnny Harris and the Statesmen. He first hit the R&B and pop charts in 1968. In 1973 he had a million-selling single, "Show and Tell." His other hits include "The Snake," (1968), "Touch and Go" (1974) and "I've Got a Feeling" (1976).

1962: Singer, dancer and choreographer Paula Abdul is born in Van Nuys, California.

Abdul began taking dance classes at the age of eight. By her teens, she was proficient in ballet, jazz, modern dance and tap.

Paula Abdul began her career as an L.A. Lakers cheerleader, while still a student at Cal State Northridge. Before embarking on her recording career, Abdul was one of the most sought-after film and video choreographers in Hollywood. She won an American Video Award for her work on the ZZ Top video "Velcro Fly," and she staged and choreographed Janet Jackson's exciting *Control* video sequences. She also worked with such artists as Michael Jackson, Duran Duran, Kool and the Gang, the Pointer Sisters and Dolly Parton. Abdul also staged numbers for motion pictures like Arnold Schwarzenegger's *The Running Man* and Eddie Murphy's *Coming to America*, television's "The Tracy Ullman Show" and the Jackson Brothers' 1984 tour.

Paula Abdul's debut LP, *Forever Your Girl*, released in mid-1988, was the third best-selling album of 1989. It produced a pair of that year's ten best-selling singles, "Straight Up" and "Cold Hearted." The album also included the hits "Knocked Out," "Opposites Attract" and the title cut.

JUNE 20

1928: Jazzman Eric Allan Dolphy is born in Los Angeles.

Dolphy played sax, flute and clarinet in various West Coast groups after high school. He also played in a U.S. Army band. After he got out of the service he worked with the bands of Gerald Wilson and Buddy Collette.

In 1958 he joined the Chico Hamilton Quintet. In 1959 he worked with Charles Mingus, both in small-group and big-band settings. He also recorded with Max Roach and did a solo tour of Europe.

In 1961 Dolphy played on Oliver Nelson's LP *The Blues and the Abstract Truth* and became a member of John Coltrane's group. He then worked with John Lewis's orchestra. In 1964 he returned to the Mingus group.

Dolphy's best LP is *Out to Lunch*. His others include *At the Five Spot, Vols. 1 and 2* and *Music Matador*.

Eric Dolphy died in Berlin on June 29, 1964, most likely of undiagnosed diabetes.

ERIC DOLPHY

1933: Blues harp player Lazy Lester is born Leslie Johnson in Torras, Louisiana.

Lazy Lester, who is mostly just laid back, first came to notice in the 1950s, on the "Swamp Blue" Excello Records label. He has also recorded on his own and played with the likes of Lightnin' Slim, Slim Harpo and Silas Hogan. His biggest hits were "They Call Me Lazy" and "I'm a Lover, Not a Fighter."

Lazy Lester is the most underrated of the modern blues harp players, maybe because he has been based in Louisiana instead of Chicago. He retired from music in 1966 but returned in 1988. His best LPs include *Lazy Lester, True Blues, Lazy Lester Rides Again* and *Harp and Soul*.

1946: Concert pianist Andre Watts is born in Nuremburg, Germany.

Andre Watts made his first public appearance at the age of nine, with the New York Philharmonic Orchestra, under Leonard Bernstein. He attended Albright College and the Peabody Conservatory of Music.

In 1963 Watts made his European debut, with the London Philharmonic Orchestra. In the mid-1960s he toured Asia and Europe for the U.S. State Department. In the early 1970s he toured the Soviet Union with the San Francisco Symphony Orchestra.

1949: Lionel Richie is born is Tuskegee, Alabama.

At Tuskegee, Richie was an economics major who had considered becoming an Episcopal minister. He spent a dozen years as the lead singer, songwriter and saxman for the award-winning R&B group the Commodores, which he cofounded in the late 1960s. In the early 1970s the Commodores were hired by a Motown vice president, basically as a backup group and opening act for the Jackson Five. They were eventually given a Motown recording contract. Their first single, "Machine Gun," landed at number 22 on the pop charts in 1974.

Over the next few years the group charted with hits like "Slippery When Wet" (1975), "Sweet Love" (1976), "Easy" (1977) and "Brick House" (1977). The Commodores were also becoming a top black-music concert attraction. In 1978 the band hit number 1 with "Three Times a Lady," a beautiful ballad that Richie had written for his parents' wedding anniversary. They also appeared in the disco film *Thank God It's Friday* with Donna Summer. During this period Richie began drifting in a different direction. He wrote and produced "Lady" for country-pop king Kenny Rogers, a record that eventually sold 15 million copies worldwide.

In 1981 he wrote and recorded, with Diana Ross, "Endless Love," the theme song from the Franco Zeffirelli film of the same name. By this time Richie had made a clean break with the Commodores and released his first LP as a solo artist, simply titled *Lionel Richie*. The album went platinum and produced such hit singles as "Truly," "You Are" and "My Love." In 1982

Richie won a Grammy for best pop male vocal and an NAACP Image award for best male artist.

In 1983 Richie's album *Can't Slow Down* racked up 14 million copies in sales, becoming Motown's all-time bestseller and providing the hit singles "All Night Long" and "Running with the Night." It also won a Grammy for album of the year in 1984. In 1985 Richie contributed a great love ballad "Say You, Say Me," to the film *White Knights*.

JUNE 21

1936: Vocalist O. C. Smith is born in Mansfield, Louisiana.

Smith worked with Count Basie's band in the early 1960s. In 1968 he had a million-seller with "Little Green Apples." Other hits include "The Son of Hickory Holler's Tramp" (1968), "Honey" (1969), "Daddy's Little Man" (1969) and "Brenda" (1984).

1941: Gospel singer Mitty Collier is born in Birmingham, Alabama.

Collier won a talent contest at Chicago's Regal Theater and signed a contract with Chess Records in 1961. She had several R&B hits in the 1960s: the soulful ballad "I'm Your Part-Time Love" (1963), "I Had a Talk with My Man" (1964), "No Faith, No Love" (1965) and "Sharing You" (1966). She then returned to gospel singing.

1946: Singer Brenda Holloway is born in Atascadero, California.

Holloway had a string of hits for Motown in the mid-1960s: "Every Little Bit Hurts" (1964), "When I'm Gone" (1965), "Operator" (1965), "Just Look What You've Done" (1967) and "You've Made Me So Very Happy" (1967).

JUNE 22

1923: Singer Ella Johnson is born in Darlington, South Carolina.

Johnson was the chief vocalist for her brother Buddy Johnson's big band in the 1940s and 1950s. Her hits include "Please, Mr. Johnson" (1941), "When My Man Comes Home" (1944), "That's the Stuff You Gotta Watch" (1945) "Hittin' on One" (1953), "I'm Just Your Fool" (1954), "Gotta Go Upside Your Head" (1955) and "Alright, Okay, You

Win" (1955). Johnson also toured with the orchestra in many of the R&B and rock 'n' roll package shows and appeared in several of Alan Freed's rock 'n' roll shows. Ella Johnson retired from music in the early 1960s.

JUNE 23

1910: Milt Hinton, "the bassist of the stars," is born in Vicksburg, Mississippi.

In the early 1930s Hinton played in the bands of Eddie South, Tiny Parham and Jabbo Smith. In 1936 he joined Cab Calloway's orchestra and remained until 1951. He then worked with Dizzy Gillespie, Count Basie and Louis Armstrong.

In 1954 he took a job as staff musician at CBS and often recorded with Billie Holiday. He also provided the bass licks for Bobby Darin's classic "Mack the Knife."

Milt Hinton worked with Sam Jones, Ron Carter and Richard Davies in the New York Bass Violin Choir and toured with such greats as Pearl Bailey and Bing Crosby.

1913: Jazz and blues singer Helen Humes is born in Louisville.

Humes cut her first record at the age of 14 for the famous Okeh label. In the 1930s she worked with the bands of Stuff Smith, Jonah Jones and Big Al Sears.

In 1938 she was hired by Count Basie to replace Billie Holiday. She stayed with the Basie band until 1941, providing vocals on such tunes as "Don't Worry About Me" (1939).

Humes later sang with the bands of Teddy Wilson, Art Tatum and Pete Brown. She had such R&B chart hits as "Unlucky Woman" (1942), "He May Be Your Man" (1945), "Be-Baba-Leba" (1945), "Today I Sing the Blues" (1948), "Million Dollar Secret" (1950) and "I Ain't in the Mood" (1952).

In the '50s and '60s Humes toured with the R&B package shows. She appeared with the Red Norvo group in Australia, where she moved in 1964. She returned to the U.S. in 1967. In 1973 she played the Newport Jazz Festival.

Helen Humes died on September 9, 1981.

1962: The Orlons make their chart debut with "The Watusi."

The song hit number 2 on the pop charts and was followed by such hits as "Don't Hang Up" (1962), "South Street" (1963), "Not Me" (1963), "Crossfire" (1963) and "Shimmy, Shimmy" (1964).

The Orlons were labelmates of Chubby Checker, Bobby Rydell and Dee Dee Sharp at Philadelphia's Cameo/Parkway Records. The members of the group were lead singer Rosetta Hightower, Marlena Davis, Steve Caldwell and Shirley Brickley. The Orlons disbanded in 1968.

JUNE 24

1942: Singer Garland Green is born in Leland, Mississippi.

Green attended the Chicago Conservatory of Music. He had a big pop and soul hit single in 1969, "Jealous Kind of Fella." He continued to chart in the 1970s with such tunes as "Plain and Simple Girl" (1971), "Let the Good Times Roll" (1974) and "Bumpin' and Stompin'" (1975).

JUNE 25

1925: Zydeco king Clifton Chenier is born in Opelousa, Louisiana.

The late Clifton Chenier and his Red Hot Louisiana Band were the undoubted kings of zydeco. Until his death, on December 12, 1977, in Lafayette, Louisiana, Chenier, through his records and especially his personal appearances, did more to foster the worldwide growth and acceptance of zydeco than did any other artist.

In his early 20s Chenier began playing the accordion and performed as a duo with his brother Cleveland. In the early 1950s he moved to Houston, where he played blues and R&B. Unsatisfied, he returned to his home state and to the Cajun bayou music he loved. In 1954 he scored his first success, with a record called "The Clifton Blues." A decade later he scored again, with "Louisiana Blues."

By the 1970s Chenier had taken zydeco worldwide and was regarded as the musical "foreign ambassador" of the culture. In 1984 he was awarded a Grammy for his LP *I'm Here* and a National Heritage Fellowship from the National Endowment for the Arts.

In the early 1980s Chenier's constant touring with his Red Hot Louisiana Band had begun to take a physical toll on him. He developed diabetes and eventually lost one of his feet to the disease. He also developed kidney disease. Through it all he continued to play his music. In fact, he was scheduled to play a club date on the day he died, December 12, 1987. A selected Clifton Chenier discography includes *Classic Clifton*, *Sixty Minutes with the King of Zydeco*: *Live at the Montreux Jazz Festival*, *I'm Here*, *Black Snake Blues*, *Bon Ton Roulet*, *King of the Bayou* and *Out West*.

CLIFTON CHENIER

1935: Singer and songwriter Eddie Floyd is born in Montgomery, Alabama.

Floyd was raised in Detroit. In 1955 he cofounded a group called the Falcons, who had a number 2 R&B and Top 20 pop hit, "You're So Fine," in 1959, with Floyd on lead vocals. Follow-up singles included "Just for Your Love" (1959) and "The Teacher" (1960). In 1960 the Falcons were joined by Wilson Pickett, who sang lead on their 1962 hit "I Found a Love."

When the Falcons broke up, in 1963, Floyd turned his attention to songwriting. He joined Stax Records as a staff writer and cowrote Wilson Pickett's hit "634-5789" and "99½ Won't Do." He also signed with Stax as a recording artist.

Floyd hit the charts with "Knock on Wood" in the fall of 1966. Later hits were "Raise Your Hand" (1967), "I've Never Found a Girl" (1968), "Bring It On Home to Me" (1968), "California Girl" (1970) and "Blood Is Thicker Than Water" (1971).

1988: Rapper Ice T makes his chart debut with the theme from the film *Colors*.

Ice T was born Tracy Morrow. He grew up on the streets of South Central Los Angeles. According to various reports, he was a car thief and gang leader before turning to music. He took his name and inspiration from the writings of pimp and author Iceberg Slim. Ice T released his first LP, *Rhyme Pays*, in 1987. His other LP releases include *Power* (1988), *Freedom of Speech* (1989) and *Original Gangsta* (1991).

Ice T is one of the most controversial figures in pop music. He is the foremost "gangsta" rapper, and many of his songs deal with street life and death, usually dealt from the barrel of a pistol or an Uzi. In 1992 his song "Cop Killer" caused a furor in the media and brought such pressure from the police that his record company pulled it from the shelves.

Ice T, one of the few rappers to appear with a live band (a heavy-metal outfit called Body Count), has also acted in the films *Breakin'*, *New Jack City* and *Trespass*.

JUNE 26

1893: Bluesman William Lee Conley "Big Bill" Broonzy is born in Scott, Mississippi.

One of 17 children, Broonzy moved to Chicago in 1920 and was instrumental in developing the famous Chicago blues scene. He worked as a guitar player, accompanying many musicians on recordings, and began himself to record in 1927, for Paramount Records. His first song was "The House Rent Stomp," and in 1928 he had a hit with "Big Bill's Blues."

Broonzy is reputed to have recorded over 300 sides during his career, some with Lil Green, Washboard Sam and Sonny Boy Williamson. He recorded for the Paramount, Okeh, Bluebird, Columbia and Chess labels.

After World War II Broonzy's rough style of blues fell into disfavor with the blues-buying public, which now preferred the smoother R&B-flavored styles. In 1949 Broonzy was working as a janitor.

In the early 1950s he made a comeback, singing his old Southern gruff blues and billing himself as the last blues singer. He also toured Europe, Africa and Australia.

Big Bill Broonzy died of cancer on August 15, 1958, in Chicago.

1943: Singer Jean Knight is born in New Orleans.

In 1971 Knight scored a Top 10 soul and pop hit with "Mr. Big Stuff." In 1985 she scored again, with a version of Rockin' Sidney's zydeco tune "My Toot Toot." Her other chart hits include "You Think You're Hot Stuff" (1971) and "You Got the Papers (but I Got the Man)" (1981).

JUNE 27

1977: The Emotions' "Best of My Love" is the number 1 soul chart hit.

The song was one of two million-selling singles that Chicago-born sisters Wanda, Sheila and Jeanette Hutchinson scored. The other was a 1979 collaboration with Earth, Wind and Fire called "Boogie Wonderland."

The Hutchinson sisters began their musical career as children, singing gospel music under the name the Heavenly Sunbeams. In 1968 they switched to pop music and became the Emotions. In 1969 they signed with Volt Records and hit the charts with the soulful ballad "So I Can Love You."

Other top Emotions hits include "Show Me How" (1971), "Don't Ask My Neighbor" (1977) and "You're the One" (1984).

At times the group also included another sister, Pamela Hutchinson, and a cousin, Theresa Davis.

JUNE 28

1915: Bluesman David "Honey Boy" Edwards is born in Shaw, Mississippi.

Edwards learned from the best. In the '30s and '40s he worked with Charley Patton, Robert Johnson, Big Walter Horton and Little Walter. In the early '50s he recorded for Chess, with very little commercial success. Most noted for his club performances across America and Europe for the past 40 years, Edwards is based in Chicago.

JUNE 29

1945: Singer Little Eva is born Eva Narcissus Boyd in Bellhaven, North Carolina.

Little Eva was discovered while working as a babysitter for the 1960s songwriting duo of Carole King and Gerry Goffin. In 1962 she had a number 1 hit with "The Locomotion." Her chart run lasted only a couple of years and included "Keep Your Hands Off My Baby" (1962) and "Let's Turkey Trot" (1963).

1960: Vocalist Evelyn "Champagne" King is born in the Bronx.

Rumor has it that King was discovered while singing to herself as she helped her mother clean up a Philadelphia recording studio. In 1978 she scored a million-selling pop Top 10 hit with her debut single, a disco-flavored dance tune called "Shame." Her other chart hits include "I Don't Know if It's Right" (1978), "I'm in Love" (1981), "Love Come Down" (1982), "Betcha She Don't Love You" (1982), "Your Personal Touch" (1985) and "Flirt" (1988).

JUNE 30

1917: Singer and actress Lena Horne is born in Brooklyn.

Horne began her career as a dancer, at Harlem's famous Cotton Club, in 1934. Her big break came in 1935, when she was hired as chief vocalist for Noble Sissle's orchestra.

In 1941 she joined Charlie Barnet's band and made some of her best recordings with Barnet's crew. Her early '40s hits include "You're My Thrill," "Good for Nothin' Joe," "Love Me a Little," "Don't Take Your Love from Me," "Haunted Town" and "Stormy Weather." She also sang with Artie Shaw's big band before becoming a solo artist, appearing in only the best cafes. Horne was also a

LENA HORNE

star of Armed Forces radio broadcasts during World War II.

Lena Horne appeared in the films *Panama Hattie* (1942), *Cabin in the Sky* (1943), *Stormy Weather* (1943), *Ziegfeld Follies* (1946), and *Till the Clouds Roll By* (1946). In the early '50s her association with Paul Robeson got her blacklisted by the film world, but she did appear later in *Death of a Gunfighter* (1969) and *The Wiz* (1978).

In the early 1980s Lena Horne's one-woman Broadway show brought her renewed popularity. In 1989 she was awarded a lifetime-achievement Grammy award.

1951: Jazz bassist Stanley Clarke is born in Philadelphia.

Clarke studied violin and cello as a child and took up the bass in his teens, playing in local rock and R&B bands. In 1970 he joined Horace Silver's band and then worked with Joe Henderson, Pharaoh Sanders, Stan Getz, Art Blakey and Dexter Gordon. Clarke was first noticed in 1972, when he joined Chick Corea's band, Return to Forever.

In 1976 he began his solo career, playing jazz rock and commercial pop. His albums include *Stanley Clarke, Journey to Love, School Days* and *I Wanna Play for You*. He also teamed up with George Duke to form the Clarke-Duke Project.

Stanley Clarke has also had such pop and black-music chart singles as "Silly Putty" (1976), "Sweet Baby" (1981) and "Heroes" (1983).

JULY 1

1899: The Reverend Thomas Andrew Dorsey, father of black gospel music and the genre's greatest songwriter, is born in Villa Rica, Georgia.

Dorsey grew up under the influence of two types of music: the blues, and the music of the Baptist Church. He became interested in playing the piano while working as a soft-drink vendor at Atlanta's 81 Theater. The theater's barrelhouse piano players taught him to read music and play. He briefly attended Morehouse College. By the time he was 17 he had developed a reputation as a blues pianist.

In 1916 he headed for Chicago, where he formed his own band and worked local nightclubs. He attended the College of Composition and Arranging, worked for a music publisher and toured with such acts as Will Walker's Whispering Syncopaters and Ma Rainey's show.

At the age of 22 he joined the Pilgrim Baptist Church and began writing gospel songs. In 1928 he began recording blues under the name of Georgia Tom. That year he also teamed up with guitarist Tampa Red and recorded the smash hit "It's Tight Like That." Thomas Dorsey continued to write gospel songs all the while he was a top blues singer. In 1929 he abandoned the blues for full-time gospel work.

In 1930 he formed the Thomas A. Dorsey Gospel Songs Music Publishing Company. In fact, it was Dorsey, along with Sallie Martin, who developed the gospel-music publishing industry, created the gospel-music concert circuit and gave many gospel-music greats their start, including Professor Alex Bradford and Roberta Martin.

In 1932 Dorsey wrote his masterpiece, "Precious Lord, Take My Hand," which has been translated into over 30 languages and recorded by countless gospel singers. In 1932 he also formed his first choir and toured with his gospel-music show, *An Evening with Dorsey*.

Dorsey's best-known songs include "A Little Talk with Jesus," "If You See My Savior," "Peace in the Valley," "Search Me, Lord" and "Tell Jesus Everything." His books include *Inspirational Thoughts*, *My Ups and Downs* and *Dorsey's Book of Poems*.

Thomas Dorsey died of Alzheimer's disease on January 23, 1993, in Chicago.

1915: Singer, songwriter, producer and bassist Willie Dixon is born in Vicksburg, Mississippi.

Dixon got his start in the early 1930s, writing songs and selling them to local country bands. He also sang with the Jubilee Gospel Singers. In 1936 he moved to Chicago and took up boxing. He won the Illinois state Golden Gloves heavyweight championship in 1937.

In 1940 he made his first record, as a member of the Five Breezes. In 1941 he refused induction into the Army and spent time in jail. Afterward he formed a group called the Four Jumps of Jive.

In 1945 Dixon, along with Leonard Caston and Bernardo Dennis, formed the Big Three Trio, which scored with R&B chart hits like "The Signifying Monkey" (1947), "You Sure Look Good to Me" (1948) and "Ebony Rhapsody" (1948).

Willie Dixon was much in demand as a session bassist. He played on such classic R&B records as Chuck Berry's "Maybelline," BoDiddley's "Hey Bo-Diddley," Jimmy Reed's "Big Boss Man," Little Walter's "My Babe" and Muddy Water's "I'm Your Hoochie Coochie Man" (both of which Dixon also wrote), and Howlin' Wolf's "Spoonful." When the Big Three broke up, Dixon signed with Chess Records as artist, songwriter, arranger and session man.

Dixon has been called the poet laureate of the blues. He wrote hundreds of blues songs, including such classics as "Back Door Man," "Wang Dang Doodle," "Spoonful," "Little Red Rooster," "You Can't Judge a Book" and "Evil." His songs have been recorded by Howlin' Wolf, BoDiddley, Chuck Berry, Koko Taylor, Led Zeppelin, Hank Williams, Jr., the Allman Brothers, Etta James, the Rolling Stones and countless others.

It was Willie Dixon who founded the Blues Heaven Foundation to help older blues performers and promote scholarships for young blues players. Dixon's best LP is *I Am The Blues*, which is also the title of his autobiography.

Willie Dixon died of heart failure on January 29, 1992.

1935: Blues harmonica player James Cotton is born in Tunica, Mississippi.

Cotton learned his trade from Sonny Boy Williamson, with whom he played in the late 1940s. In the early 1950s Cotton moved to Memphis, where he worked on local radio shows and as a session player for Sun Records. Cotton also had a couple of regional blues hits, "Cotton Crop Blues" and "Hold Me in Your Arms." In 1954 he replaced Little Walter in Muddy Waters's band. This gave him his greatest exposure to audiences and to the top blues musicians of the era.

Over the years James Cotton has recorded some excellent LPs. They include *From Cotton with Love*, *High Compression*, *Mighty Long Time* and *Live From Chicago*.

In 1988 James Cotton was nominated for a Grammy for his album *James Cotton Live*.

1939: Singer Syl Johnson is born Syl Thompson in Holly Springs, Mississippi.

Syl Johnson worked with such blues greats as Magic Sam, Junior Wells and Jimmy Reed in the 1950s. In 1959 he formed his own group, the Deacons, and signed with Federal Records.

In the mid-1960s Johnson began hitting the R&B charts. His best-known songs are "Come On, Sock It to Me" (1967), "Different Strokes" (1967), "Is It Because I'm Black" (1969), "Back for a Taste of Your Love" (1973) and "Take Me to the River" (1975).

1942: Gospel singer Andre Crouch is born in Los Angeles.

Andre Crouch bridged the gap between white and black gospel music. He infused rhythm and blues, soul, funk, rock and Latin music into his gospel music.

Crouch began playing and singing gospel music at the age of nine. He formed the group Andre Crouch and the Disciples and had his first hit LP, *Take the Message Everywhere*, in 1969, appearing on TV's "The Tonight Show."

Andre Crouch scored huge hits with "Everything Changed," "Satisfied" and "I'll Be Thinking of You." His recording trademark was a slick pop-music sound, using the latest recording techniques.

In 1981 Crouch disbanded the Disciples after top vocalist Danniebelle Hall left.

Andre Crouch received Grammy awards in 1976, 1978 and 1979. His recording of "Jesus Is the Answer" sold a million copies. He also composed the theme for the 1980s TV show "Amen."

In 1982 Crouch was arrested for drug possession, but the charges were later dropped. His twin sister, Sandra Crouch, is also a top gospel performer.

JULY 2

1927: R&B sax player Lee Allen is born in Pittsburgh.

Allen was one of the top New Orleans session players in the heyday of that city's R&B explosion, during the 1950s. His work can be heard on records by such artists as Fats Domino and Little Richard.

In 1958 Lee Allen hit the charts with one of the best rock 'n' roll instrumentals ever, "Walkin' with Mr. Lee."

1930: Jazz pianist Ahmad Jamal is born Fritz Jones in Pittsburgh.

Since forming his first group, in 1949, Jamal has been a consistent jazz club performer. He first recorded in

1951 and has had several hit singles, including "Secret Love" (1958) and "Don't Ask My Neighbor" (1980).

His most acclaimed albums include *The Awakening*, *At the Pershing*, *Live at the Alhambra*, *Portfolio* and *Live at the Montreal Jazz Festival*.

JULY 3

1893: Legendary bluesman and influential blues guitarist Mississippi John Hurt is born in Teoc, Mississippi.

Hurt moved to Avalon, Mississippi, when he was two. He taught himself a three-finger style of guitar playing at the age of nine. While working at odd jobs and farming, he played local dances.

In 1928 he recorded a few songs for Vocalion Records, getting about $20 a song. Meanwhile, he farmed and raised 14 children.

In 1963 a record collector and promoter, Tom Hoskins, heard Hurt's recordings and traveled to Avalon to persuade Hurt to resume recording. Hurt did, and he played folk and blues festivals, but his career lasted only three years.

There are several collections of Hurt's works. The best are *1928 Sessions*, *Avalon Blues* and *The Best of Mississippi John Hurt*.

Mississippi John Hurt died on November 2, 1966.

1940: Singer Fontella Bass is born in St. Louis, Missouri.

Bass began by singing in church choirs. Her mother was a member of the Clara Ward Singers. Bass worked with Oliver Sain's band and was working with Little Milton's Blues Revue in 1964 when she signed a contract with Chess Records.

Her first chart hits were two duets with Bobby McClure, "Don't Mess Up a Good Thing" and "You'll Miss Me," in 1965. In the same year Fontella Bass also hit the soul and pop Top 10 with the classic "Rescue Me," whose thumping bass signature was provided by Chess session player Louis Satterfield.

1954: The Chords make their R&B chart debut with "Sh-Boom." The record peaked at number 2 on the R&B charts and number 5 on the pop charts. The Chords consisted of lead singer Carl

Feaster, Jimmy Keys, Floyd McRae, Claude Feaster, William Edwards and Rupert Branker. "Sh-Boom" was their only hit.

"Sh-Boom" started the "cover records" craze, in which record companies took R&B hits by black artists, cut out the funk and released milquetoast versions of the songs by white artists for white rock 'n' roll audiences. "Sh-Boom" was covered by the Crewcuts. A cover of Fats Domino's "Ain't That a Shame" became Pat Boone's first number 1 hit, and there was a watered-down version of Big Joe Turner's "Shake, Rattle and Roll" that Bill Haley and the Comets took to number 1.

JULY 4

1900: Traditional birthdate of jazz trumpeter Louis Daniel "Satchmo" Armstrong. (He was actually born August 4, 1901, in New Orleans.)

Armstrong formed his first vocal quintet in his early teens. In January of 1913 he was sent to the Colored Waifs' Home after being arrested for firing a pistol in the street. He played trumpet in the Waifs' Home band. After being released, he worked several jobs before forming a band to play local honky tonks.

In 1919 he replaced King Oliver in Kid Ory's band. In mid-1919 he joined Fate Marable's band and played riverboats until 1921. In 1922 he joined King Oliver's band in Chicago. With Oliver's band, Louis Armstrong cut his first record, on March 23, 1923. In February of 1924 he married Lil Hardin. In the same year he also played with Fletcher Henderson's orchestra but soon left to front Lil Armstrong's Dreamland Syncopators. In 1925 he began recording as a group leader and issued his series of *Hot Five* and *Hot Seven* recordings. In 1927 he formed his own group, Louis Armstrong and His Stompers. In 1929 he played such New York clubs as Connie's Inn and appeared in the show *Hot Chocolate*.

In 1931 Armstrong played California. The following year he made his first European tour. In 1935 he formed the Louis Armstrong Big Band. In the late 1930s he appeared in the films *Pennies from Heaven* and *Artists and Models*.

Later film appearances included roles in *Cabin in the Sky, Atlantic City, New Orleans, The Glenn Miller Story, High Society* and *Paris Blues*.

The Big Band broke up in 1947, and Armstrong formed a smaller group, the All Stars. He recorded some of his best-known LPs with the All Stars, including *Louis Armstrong Plays W. C. Handy, Louis Armstrong Plays Fats (Waller)* and *At the Crescendo*. Armstrong and his All Stars toured the world until he suffered a heart attack, in 1959. In 1964 Armstrong scored a number 1 pop hit with "Hello, Dolly."

There are many collections of Armstrong's material. Some of the best are *Great Original Performances, The Silver Collection, Ella and Louis* and *Singing 'n' Playing*.

Louis Armstrong died on July 6, 1971.

LOUIS ARMSTRONG

1910: Blues singer and pianist William Thomas "Champion Jack" Dupree is born in New Orleans.

Dupree's parents were killed in a fire, and he was raised in the same Waifs' Home where Louis Armstrong was. He moved to Chicago in 1930, where he got his nickname because of his pugilistic exploits. Dupree served in the Navy as a cook and began recording in 1940.

In 1944 Dupree settled in New York. In 1953 he signed with King Records. In 1960 he moved to Europe, where he continued to record and perform. His R&B chart hits include "Chain Gang Blues" (1940), "The Dupree Shake Dance" (1941), "Shake Baby Shake" (1953), "Shim Sham Shimmy" (1954) and "Walking the Blues" (1955).

Champion Jack Dupree died on January 21, 1992.

1938: Singer and songwriter Bill Withers is born in Slab Fork, West Virginia.

Withers composed and recorded a trio of million-sellers in the early 1970s: "Ain't No Sunshine," "Lean on Me" and "Use Me." In 1981 he had a Top 10 hit, "Just the Two of Us," with saxophonist Grover Washington, Jr.

1987: Gospel singers Benjamin (Bebe) and Priscilla (Cece) Winans make their chart debut with "I.O.U Me."

The Detroit-based brother-and-sister duo exploded onto the national scene in 1987, with a self-titled LP that won a Grammy. That year Cece also won a Grammy for best female gospel performance. The LP remained on the charts for 63 weeks and reached as high as number 49 on *Billboard*'s black LP chart.

Their 1988 LP, *Heaven*, became the first gospel album to reach the Top 10 on *Billboard*'s urban-music chart. It sold over a million copies. In 1989 Bebe and Cece won the Gospel Music Association's award for group of the year; *Heaven* won an award for contemporary album of the year.

In 1991 they released the controversial LP *Different Lifestyles*, which mixed elements of rap and hip-hop with traditional gospel music.

JULY 5

1913: Blues singer Smiley Lewis is born in Union, Louisiana.

In the late 1940s and early 1950s Lewis worked in the New Orleans area's top R&B and blues nightclubs, places like the Dew Drop Inn and El Morocco. He began recording in 1947, under the name Smiling Lewis. His biggest hits were "Bells Are Ringing"

(1952), "I Hear You Knocking" (1955), "One Night" (1956) and "Please Listen to Me" (1956). His version of the song "Shame, Shame, Shame" was featured on the soundtrack of the 1956 film *Baby Doll*.

Smiley Lewis died of cancer on October 7, 1966.

JULY 6

1931: Singer and actress Della Reese is born Delloreese Patricia Early in Detroit.

From 1945 to 1949 Reese worked in gospel music with the troupe of Mahalia Jackson. In the early 1950s she got a job as vocalist with Erskine Hawkins's orchestra.

In 1957 she went solo and scored her first hit record, a Top 20 pop tune called "And That Reminds Me." In 1959 her recording of "Don't You Know" landed at number 2 on the pop charts. Other single hits include "Sermonette" (1959), "Not One Minute More" (1959), "And Now" (1960) and "Bill Bailey" (1961).

Reese has also been a popular TV performer. In 1970 she had her own series, "Della," and was in the cast of the popular sitcom "Chico and the Man" from 1976 to 1978. She appeared in the films *Let's Rock* and *Harlem Nights*.

1937: Singer Gene Chandler is born Eugene Dixon in Chicago.

Chandler is called the Duke of Earl, after his number 1 R&B and pop smash hit of the same name, in 1962. In 1957 Dixon had joined a group called the Dukays as lead singer. Then he went into the service. In 1960 he rejoined the group. The Dukays recorded a pair of tunes, "Night Owl" and "The Duke of Earl." Their label, Nat Records, decided to release only "Night Owl." The producer then took "The Duke of Earl" to Vee Jay Records, which bought the song. He offered Dixon the choice of remaining with the Dukays or going solo with "The Duke of Earl," under the name Gene Chandler.

Chandler went on to place over 30 singles on the charts. His biggest hits include "You Threw a Lucky Punch" (1962), "Rainbow" (1963), "Man's Temptation"

(1963), "Just Be True" (1964), "Bless Our Love" (1964), "Nothing Can Stop Me" (1965), "Rainbow '65" (1965), "I Fooled You This Time" (1966), "To Be a Lover" (1967), "Groovy Situation" (1970) and "Get Down" (1978).

JULY 7

1913: Blues pianist Joe Willie "Pinetop" Perkins is born in Belzoni, Mississippi.

The talents of Pinetop Perkins came to light for national blues audiences in 1970, when he replaced Otis Spann in Muddy Waters's band. He remained with the band until Waters's death. Before his stint with Waters, Perkins had spent most of his time playing in the South, especially in Mississippi and Arkansas. From 1943 to 1948 he was the regular piano player on the famed King Biscuit show from Helena, Arkansas. In the early 1950s Perkins was a session player around Memphis, working with Ike Turner and others. Some of his best LPs are *After Hours* and *Pinetop Is Just Top*.

1937: Count Basie records "One O'Clock Jump."

There are a couple of things that were unique about Count Basie's orchestra. One is that Basie took the rhythm section from the back of the band and put it in the forefront. The other is that most of the Basie band's arrangements were designed to show off the talents of the individual members. When Basie recorded "One O'Clock Jump" his band consisted of Buck Clayton, Ed Lewis and Bobby Moore on trumpets; Dan Minor and George Hunt on trombones; Earl Warren and Jack Washington on alto sax; Herschel Evans and Lester Young on tenor sax; Count Basie on piano; Freddie Green on guitar; Walter Page on bass; and Joe Jones on drums. Count Basie also recorded another version of "One O'Clock Jump," in 1941.

JULY 8

1908: Singer and saxophonist Louis Jordan, the father of rhythm and blues and the father of rock 'n' roll, is born in Brinkley, Arkansas.

Louis Jordan's father taught him music as a child. Jordan ran errands to pay for his first saxophone and played his first gig as a teenager, in Hot Springs, Arkansas. He attended Arkansas Baptist College, where he majored in music. His first full-time job as a musician came with the Rabbit Foot Minstrels and with the bands of pianist Jimmy Pryor and singer Ruby Williams.

In 1932 Jordan headed north to Philadelphia, where he joined Charlie Gaines's band. He recorded with the Gaines band in 1934. In 1936 he joined the Chick Webb Orchestra as soprano and alto saxophonist, vocalist and announcer. (The orchestra featured Ella Fitzgerald at the time.) With Webb, Jordan's forte was novelty songs.

In 1938 Jordan formed his own group, a nine-piece band called the Tympany Five. The band played at Harlem's Elks' Rendezvous and in Chicago, where it was the opening act for the Mills Brothers. In December 1938 Jordan signed with Decca and cut his first solo records.

Jordan's success as a recording artist was phenomenal. Between 1940 and 1954 he placed over 80 singles on the R&B charts, including 18 number 1 records. His biggest seller was 1946's "Choo Choo Cha Boogie," which reportedly sold over two million copies. He also recorded a series of popular duets with Ella Fitzgerald.

Louis Jordan's songs were almost always humorous. He appeared in the films *Meet Miss Bobby Sox* and *Swing Parade of 1946*. He also starred in the black musical films *Beware*, *Reet Petite* and *Gone*.

Jordan was as popular with white audiences as he was with black ones. A decade before Alan Freed popularized the term "rock 'n' roll," Jordan's jazz-flavored jump blues and boogie fit the beat and structure of the music that came to have that name.

Jordan cut back on his extensive touring during the late '50s and early '60s. In October 1974 he suffered a heart attack while performing in Sparks, Nevada. After another heart attack, Jordan died in Los Angeles, on February 4, 1975. In 1991–92 the Broadway musical *Five Guys Named Moe* was based on the music of Louis Jordan.

1914: William Clarence "Billy" Eckstine, "Mr. B.," is born in Pittsburgh.

Mr. B. defined the word "suave." From 1939 to 1943 he sang, mostly ballads, with the orchestra of Earl "Fatha" Hines. He had a hit with the bluesy "Jelly Jelly."

In 1944 he formed his own big band. Several legendary jazz performers got their start in Eckstine's band, including Dizzy Gillespie, Charlie Parker, Gene Ammons, Miles Davis and Sarah Vaughan. Eckstine broke the band up in 1947.

Throughout the '40s and early '50s Eckstine had R&B and pop hits like "I Stay in the Mood for You" (1944), "Last Night and Now Tonight Again" (1945), "Lonesome Lover Blues" (1945), "A Cottage for Sale" (1945), "Prisoner of Love" (1946), "You Call It Madness" (1946), "Fools Rush In" (1949), "Bewildered" (1949), "Temptation" (1949), "Sitting by the Window" (1950), "I Apologize" (1951) and "Kiss of Fire" (1952).

Billy Eckstine died on March 8, 1993.

JULY 9

1966: The Intruders, one of the best and most successful of the "Philadelphia Sound" groups of the 1960s and 1970s, make their chart debut with "United."

The group was made up of Sam "Little Sonny" Brown, Eugene Daughtry, Phil Terry and Robert "Big Sonny" Edwards. Their biggest and best-known hits were written and produced by Kenny Gamble and Leon Huff. These included "Together" (1967), "Cowboys to Girls" (1968), "Love Is Like a Baseball Game" (1968), "When We Get Married" (1970), "I'll Always Love My Mama" (1973) and "I Wanna Know Your Name" (1973).

JULY 10

1899: Bandleader and composer Noble Sissle is born.

Sissle formed his first band in 1914, in Indianapolis. In 1915 he moved to Baltimore and worked in Bob Young's band with Eubie Blake. In 1916 he joined the U.S. Army and served as an officer with the 369th Division Band. After World War I Sissle formed a partnership with Blake, in 1919. Sissle and Blake spent the next several years writing and producing such hit shows as *Shuffle Along* and *Chocolate Dandies*.

In 1926, they played London. Two years later Sissle returned to England as a solo act. He spent most of the late '20s and early '30s touring Europe. In 1938 he became bandleader at New York's Diamond Horseshoe Club. During World War II he formed his own USO group and entertained U.S. Troops.

Noble Sissle died on December 17, 1975.

1905: Ivie Anderson, main vocalist with Duke Ellington's band, is born in Los Angeles.

Anderson joined Ellington in 1931 and sang on his 1932 hit "It Don't Mean a Thing." One of the centerpieces of the Ellington show was the jive dialogue between Anderson and drummer Sonny Greer. Anderson's biggest hits included "I've Got It Bad and That Ain't Good" (1941), "Hayfoot-Strawfoot" (1942), "I Don't Mind" (1944) and "Mexico Joe" (1944). Later in the 1940s

IVIE ANDERSON

Anderson left Ellington to go into the restaurant business.

Ivie Anderson died on December 28, 1949.

1938: Jazz trumpeter Lee Morgan is born in Philadelphia.

At the age of 18 Morgan joined Dizzy Gillespie's big band and stayed for two years. From 1958 to 1961 he was with Art Blakey's Jazz Messengers. In 1964 he had a big hit with a self-composed piece, "Sidewinder." Morgan's best LPs were *Sidewinder*, *Rumproller* and *At the Lighthouse*.

On February 19, 1972, Lee Morgan was shot and killed during an argument with a woman in a New York nightclub where he was performing.

JULY 11

1897: Bluesman Blind Lemon Jefferson, said to have founded the Texas blues and coined the phrase "rock 'n' roll," is born in Couchman, Texas.

Jefferson was born blind on a farm in Freestone County, Texas. Around 1912 he was playing on the streets and at parties around Wortham, Texas. By 1917 he was working the barrelhouses in Dallas and hoboing across the South.

Jefferson possessed a clear blues voice and well-defined guitar stylings highly influenced by the flamenco guitar he had heard in Texas. In the early 1920s he arrived in Chicago, where he first recorded. His first recordings were in the gospel vein.

He began recording blues for the Paramount and Okeh labels around 1926. His best-known records include "Jack of Diamonds," "Matchbox Blues," "Broke and Hungry" and "See That My Grave Is Kept Clean."

In 1927 he returned to Texas and worked in Dallas, Waco and Fort Worth. In December 1929 he went back to Chicago, intending to record again. According to some sources, he attended a party and then tried to find his way home in a heavy snowstorm. He got lost and died, either of exposure or of a heart attack.

1951: Singer Bonnie Pointer is born in East Oakland, California.

Bonnie Pointer left the famous sister act in 1978 to go it alone. She signed with Motown Records and charted with singles like "Free Me from My Freedom" (1978), "Heaven Must Have Sent You" (1979) and "I Can't Help Myself" (1979).

JULY 12

1938: Comedian and actor Bill Cosby is born in Philadelphia.

Best known as Heathcliffe Huxtable on the award-winning TV series "The Cosby Show" and for his many best-selling comedy LPs, "the Cos" has occasionally dabbled in pop music and jazz. In 1967 he hit the pop Top 10 with a take-off on Stevie Wonder's "Uptight," called "Little Ole Man." Cosby has also hit the singles charts with tunes like "Hooray for the Salvation Army Band" (1967), "Funky North Philly" (1968), "Grover Henson Feels Forgotten" (1970) and "Yes, Yes, Yes" (1976).

Bill Cosby's jazz LPs include *My Appreciation* and *Where You Lay Your Head*.

JULY 13

1936: Jazz saxophonist Albert Ayler is born in Cleveland.

Ayler began playing the saxophone at the age of seven. The U.S. audience for his unconventional music was small, and so he moved to Sweden in 1962.

Ayler was proficient on alto, tenor and soprano sax. Charlie Parker was such a strong influence on him that he had been dubbed "Little Bird" around his native Cleveland. In 1963 he released the LP *My Name is Albert Ayler*, which critics hailed as an immediate classic.

He returned to the U.S., played with Cecil Taylor, became a member of the Jazz Composers Guild and formed his own group. In the mid 1960s Ayler recorded his best and most influential LP, *Bells*, at New York's Town Hall. Ayler was still controversial, however, and many jazz critics and fans didn't know how to take his ultraimprovisational music.

In 1968 he released the LP *New Grass*, which featured heavy gospel overtones. The LP was a commercial success, and many of his "free jazz" colleagues accused him of selling out. Other Ayler LPs are *Vibrations, Witches and Devils* and *Spiritual Unity*.

On November 25, 1970, Albert Ayler drowned in New York's East River.

JULY 14

1919: The Trenier Twins, one of the most underrated of the pre–rock 'n' roll R&B acts, are born in Mobile, Alabama.

Claude and Clifford Trenier began their career in 1944, with Jimmie Lunceford's band. In the late '40s they recorded for the Mercury label; in the '50s they recorded for Okeh. Their R&B chart hits include "Go! Go! Go!" (1951), "Old Woman Blues" (1951), "Hadacal, That's All" (1952), "Rockin' on Saturday Night" (1952), "Rockin' in Our Burners" (1953), "Rock-a Beatin' Boogie" (1953) and "Get Out of the Car" (1955).

After their "hit record" days, the Treniers settled in as one of the top nightclub acts in Las Vegas.

JULY 15

1910: Bluesman Washboard Sam is born Robert Brown in Walnut Ridge, Arkansas.

Instead of the guitar or the harp, Brown's instrument was a washboard. He moved to Chicago in 1932 and worked with Sleepy John Estes, Hammie Nixon and Big Bill Broonzy. In the early 1940s he had R&B hits with "Diggin' My Potatoes" and "Gonna Hit the Highway."

Washboard Sam died of heart disease on November 13, 1966, in Chicago.

1923: Jazz drummer Philly Joe Jones is born in Philadelphia.

Jones worked with Joe Morris, Zoot Simms, Lee Konitz and Tadd Dameron before joining Miles Davis's group, in 1952. He remained with Davis until 1962. He was also a member of the Bill Evans Trio in the '60s and '70s. Jones is credited with having developed the unique rhythm patterns of Davis's classic early quintet.

Philly Joe Jones died on August 30, 1985.

1940: Bluesman Willie Cobbs is born in Monroe, Arkansas.

In the early 1950s Cobbs played with Little Walter and Muddy Waters. After a hitch in the U.S. Marines he recorded such songs as "While in Korea." He also became a club owner in Chicago and Arkansas.

1944: Singer Millie Jackson is born in Thompson, Georgia.

Jackson moved to Newark, New Jersey, in 1958 and began her professional singing career in 1964. She scored her first big hit in 1972, with "Ask Me What You Want." Jackson has placed over three dozen singles on the charts, including "My Man, A Sweet Man" (1972), "Hurts So Good" (1973), "The Rap" (1975), "Leftovers" (1975), "If You're Not Back in Love by Monday" (1977), "Hot! Wild! Unrestricted! Crazy Love" (1986) and "Love Is a Dangerous Game" (1987).

Millie Jackson's specialty is live performance, which features her X-rated raps. Her best LPs include *Feelin' Bitchy, Live and Uncensored* and *Back to the Shit*.

JULY 16

1939: Singer William Bell is born in Memphis.

Bell recorded one of the best R&B singles ever, the soulful ballad "You Don't Miss Your Water Till the Well Runs Dry" (1962). His career was interrupted by a hitch in the U.S. Army. When he got out, in 1966, he resumed his recording career and charted with such singles as "Share What You Got" (1966), "Everybody Loves a Winner" (1967), "A Tribute to a King" (1968) and "Trying to Love Two" (1976). In 1968 he had a pair of successful duets with Judy Clay, "Private Number" and "I Forgot to Be Your Lover."

1939: Singer Denise LaSalle is born in LeFlore County, Mississippi.

LaSalle moved to Chicago in the early 1950s and began recording in 1967. Her first chart hit was a million-seller, in 1971: "Trapped by a Thing Called Love." Her follow-up hits include "Now Run and Tell That" (1972), "Man-Sized Job" (1972), "What It Takes to Get

a Good Woman" (1973) and "Love Me Right" (1977).

Today Denise LaSalle works as a record producer and records for the Malaco label.

JULY 17

1925: Blues singer and guitarist Peppermint Harris is born Harrison D. Nelson in Texarkana, Texas.

Harris was discovered by Texas blues legend Lightnin' Hopkins in 1948. He hit the R&B charts with "Raining in My Heart" (1950), "I Got Loaded" (1951) and "Have Another Drink and Talk to Me" (1952).

1935: Singer and actress Diahann Carroll is born in the Bronx.

Carroll attended New York University. In 1962 she won a Tony for her performance in the Broadway show *No Strings*. From 1968 to 1971 she starred in the hit TV show "Julia." She was also in the cast of the prime-time soap opera "Dynasty."

Carroll's film credits include *Carmen Jones*, (1954), *Porgy and Bess* (1959), *Goodbye Again* (1960), *Paris Blues* (1961), *Hurry Sundown* (1967), *The Split* (1968) and *Claudine* (1974). She also portrayed Whitley Gilbert's snooty mama in the TV series "A Different World."

1959: Billie Holiday dies in New York City.

Holiday made her final public appearance at the Phoenix Theater in New York on May 25, 1959. She entered Metropolitan Hospital and, on what was to be her death bed, was placed under arrest for possession of narcotics.

JULY 18

1929: Singer Screamin' Jay Hawkins is born in Cleveland.

Hawkins only had one big hit, a 1956 rock 'n' roll classic called "I Put a Spell on You." As part of his stage act, Hawkins was rolled onstage in a coffin. He would leap out of the coffin wearing a Dracula-like cape and carrying a skull. His antics drove white audiences wild, but black folks didn't care a whole lot for the coffin bit.

1941: Singer Martha Reeves is born in Detroit.

MARTHA AND THE VANDELLAS

Reeves had been in a group called the Del-Phis when she got a job as a secretary at Motown Records. Part of her job was singing on demo records. When one backup singer couldn't make a recording session, Martha Reeves took her place. As more studio work developed, she brought in members of her old group. In 1962 they sang backup on Marvin Gaye's hit "Stubborn Kind of Fellow."

Along with Annette Beard and Rosilyn Ashford, Reeves formed Martha and the Vandellas. Between 1963 and 1972 they placed two dozen singles on the R&B and pop music charts. Their first hit was "Come and Get These Memories" (1963). Others include "Heatwave" (1963), "Quicksand" (1963), "Dancing in the Street" (1964), "Nowhere to Run" (1965), "My Baby Loves Me" (1966), "I'm Ready for Love (1966), "Jimmy Mack" (1967) and "Honey Chile" (1967).

In 1964 Annette Beard left the group and was replaced by Betty Kelly. In 1969 the group broke up but formed again in 1971, with Martha Reeves, Lois Reeves and Sandra Tilley.

Martha Reeves went solo in 1972. Her biggest hit was "Power of Love," in 1974.

JULY 19

1895: Vaudevillian Butter Beans is born Jody Edwards in Pensacola, Florida.

The duo of Butter Beans and Susie, one of the first male-female teams, was a top draw on the vaudeville and Theater Owners' Booking Association circuits. Susie was Susie Edwards, the wife of Butter Beans. She was born in Florida in 1896. The pair first teamed up in 1915 as Edwards and Edwards, doing comedy, singing and dancing.

In 1921 they worked with Ethel Waters. Throughout the '20s they toured with the Rabbit Foot Minstrels and recorded for the Okeh label. They appeared with the Black and White Revue, the Okeh Revue and their own Butter Beans and Susie Revue. In the '30s they worked again with Waters and with Bessie Smith. They also appeared at the Cotton Club and starred in such shows as *Harlem Bound*, *Ease on Down* and *Hot Stuff of 1933*. In the '40s and '50s they often appeared at Harlem's Apollo Theater.

Butter Beans died on October 27, 1967. Susie Edwards died on December 5, 1963.

JULY 20

1963: "Easier Said Than Done," by the Essex, hits number 1 on the R&B charts. The song also eventually hit number 1 on the pop charts.

The members of the Essex were lead singer Anita Humes, Walter Vickers, Rodney Taylor, Billie Hill and Rudolph Johnson. All were U.S. Marines stationed at Camp Lejeune, North Carolina. Vickers and Taylor had started the group while stationed on Okinawa, in Japan.

This was one group that needed special permission from the U.S. Marine Corps to go on tour. The Essex performed "Easier Said Than Done" on "American Bandstand," wearing their Marine dress blues. They went on to have another pop hit, "A Walkin' Miracle," later in 1963.

JULY 21

1921: Jazz pianist Billy Taylor is born in Greensboro, North Carolina.

Taylor moved to New York in the early 1940s. He worked with such jazz artists as Ben Webster, Dizzy Gillespie and Stuff Smith. He was the bandleader at Birdland and founded his own trio in the early 1950s. Later in his career he worked as a writer, radio disc jockey, TV musical director and educator.

Billy Taylor also wrote the 1982 book *Jazz Piano*.

JULY 22

1937: Singer Chuck Jackson is born in Winston-Salem, North Carolina.

Jackson began his career in a gospel group called the Raspberry Singers. He then joined the Dell Vikings. When the group split up, in 1959, Jackson began his solo career.

He began hitting the national R&B charts in 1961. His biggest records include "I Don't Want to Cry" (1961), "I Wake Up Crying" (1961), "Any Day Now" (1962), "Tell Him I'm Not Home" (1963), "Beg Me" (1964) and "Something You Got" (1965).

In the 1960s Chuck Johnson was a top concert draw, and his performances featured one of the best show bands of the day.

1940: Funkmaster George Clinton is born in Plainfield, Ohio.

Clinton grew up in Detroit, where in the early 1960s he formed the original Parliaments, who hit the soul charts with "I Just Wanna Testify" in the mid-1960s.

With the assistance of such musicians as William "Bootsy" Collins, Bernie Worrell, Eddie Hazel, Fred Wesley and many others, Clinton conceived and recorded such groups as Funkadelic, the Parliaments, the P-Funk All Stars and the Brides of Dr. Funkenstein. He threw them all together for worldwide tours that were theatrically staged, four-hour funk extravaganzas complete with explosions, light shows and huge spaceships landing on stage. He also produced albums with such titles as *The Clones of Dr. Funkenstein*, *The Mothership Connection*, *Funkentelechy Versus the Placebo Syndrome* and *Maggot Brain*. The latter two featured top soul hits: "Tear the

Roof Off the Sucker," "Free Your Mind and Your Ass Will Follow" and "One Nation Under a Groove."

Clinton's two main groups, the Parliaments and Funkadelic, were basically the same personnel under two different names and under contract to two different record companies—the Parliaments to Casablanca, and Funkadelic to Warner Brothers. This practice finally caught up with Clinton. By 1981 he found himself up to his funky ears in lawsuits. He worsened his problems by seeking solace in drugs. Within a couple of years, however, Clinton had cleared up both his legal and drug problems and was back recording. He stepped back into his former groove and issued a series of LPs: *You Shouldn't Nuf Bit Fish*, *Some of My Best Jokes Are Friends* and *R&B Skeletons in My Closet*. His biggest single hit of the eighties was "Atomic Dog," in 1983.

JULY 23

1935: Penguins lead singer Cleve Duncan is born in Los Angeles.

In 1954, while they were students at Fremont High School in Los Angeles, Duncan, Dexter Tisby, Curtis Williams and Bruce Tate named their singing group after Willie the Penguin on the Kool cigarette pack.

The Penguins signed a contract with Dootone Records and in December 1954 hit the charts with "Earth Angel." The record, considered one of the all-time great R&B classics and one of the most-played rock 'n' roll songs, soared to the Top 10 on both the R&B and pop charts.

JULY 24

1910: Jazz trumpeter Charles Melvin "Cootie" Williams is born in Mobile, Alabama.

Williams joined Duke Ellington's orchestra in 1929 and remained until 1940. Early in his career he had played with various other bands, including those of Fletcher Henderson and Chick Webb.

With Ellington, Williams displayed a variety of talents. He soloed on such early Ellington pieces as "Rockin' in

Rhythm," did scat vocals on "Hot Feet" and composed "Echoes of the Jungle."

After leaving Duke Ellington, Cootie Williams joined Benny Goodman's orchestra. He then formed his own big band, which became a staple at the Savoy Ballroom throughout the 1940s. The band featured pianist Bud Powell and tenor saxmen Eddie "Lockjaw" Davis and Cleanhead Vinson. Williams had R&B hits with "Cherry Red Blues" (1944), "Is You Is or Is You Ain't " (1944) and "Somebody's Got to Go" (1945). In 1948 Williams cut down to a small band. He worked solo and with a quintet after the Savoy closed.

In the late '50s he toured Europe. He played with Benny Goodman in the early '60s. In 1962 he returned to Duke Ellington.

Cootie Williams died on September 15, 1985.

JULY 25

1907: Jazz saxophonist Johnny Hodges is born in Cambridge, Massachusetts.

Hodges joined Duke Ellington's band in May 1928 and remained until 1951. His solos can be heard on such Ellington classics as "Echoes of the Jungle," "Double Check Stomp" and "Time's a Wastin'." While still a member of the Ellington band, Johnny Hodges also recorded on his own. His best-known solo pieces include "Hodge Podge," "Empty Ballroom Blues," "Jeep's Blues" and his 1944 R&B chart hit "Going Out the Back Way." Hodges earned the nickname Rabbit because of his affinity for lettuce-and-tomato sandwiches. He was a master of both alto and soprano sax. Some critics have called him the first soul sax player because of the feeling and energy that radiated from his horn.

In 1951 Hodges formed his own band and had a successful four-year run. He returned to the Ellington outfit in 1955.

His health began to deteriorate in the mid-1960s. He was advised to slow down but didn't.

Johnny Hodges died while visiting his dentist on May 11, 1970, in New York City.

JULY 26

1914: Trumpeter and composer Erskine Hawkins is born in Birmingham, Alabama.

Hawkins began playing drums at the age of seven and trumpet at the age of 13. He attended State Teachers College in Montgomery, Alabama, and was appointed band leader of the State Collegians Band. In 1934 the band went to New York and became known as the Erskine Hawkins Orchestra.

Hawkins and the band had a big following throughout the '30s and '40s. They also had a string of R&B and pop hits, including "Tuxedo Junction" (1939), "Bicycle Bounce" (1942), "Don't Cry, Baby" (1943), "Cherry" (1944), "Tippin' In" (1945), "Caledonia" (1945), "Fifteen Years and I'm Still Servin' Time" (1945), "Sneakin' Out" (1946), "I've Got a Right to Cry" (1946), "After Hours," (1946), "Hawk's Boogie" (1947), "Cornbread" (1949) and "Tennessee Waltz" (1950). Their main stomping grounds were the Harlem Opera House and the Savoy Ballroom. In later years Hawkins cut the band down to a quartet, which he led until the 1970s.

1941: Singer and songwriter Bobby Hebb is born in Nashville.

At the age of 12 Hebb played and sang at the Grand Ole Opry. In 1966 he had a million-selling Top 10 pop hit, "Sunny."

1942: Singer and songwriter Dobie Gray is born in Brookshire, Texas.

Gray moved to Los Angeles in 1960. In 1965 he had a pop and soul hit with the single "The In Crowd." In 1973 he sold a million copies of his Top 10 hit "Drift Away."

Gray appeared in the L.A. production of the musical *Hair*. In the mid-1980s he hit the country charts with songs like "That's One to Grow On" and "The Dark Side of Town." He currently works in Nashville as a country songwriter.

JULY 27

1927: Harvey Fuqua, best known as lead singer of the Moonglows, is born in Louisville.

The Moonglows were one of the best and most successful of the R&B and rock 'n' roll doo-wop groups. The members, besides Fuqua, were co–lead singer Bobby Lester, Alexander Graves, Prentiss Barnes and guitarist Billy Johnson. They were originally called the Crazy Sounds but were renamed by famed disc jockey Alan Freed. Their biggest hits were "Sincerely" (1954), "Most of All" (1955), "We Go Together" (1956), "See Saw" (1956), "Please Send Me Someone to Love" (1957) and "The Ten Commandments of Love" (1958).

In 1958 Fuqua left the original group and formed Harvey and the Moonglows, which included Marvin Gaye. Fuqua went on to establish his own record label. In 1961 he helped create and produce the Spinners. In the '60s Harvey Fuqua also worked as a writer and producer for Motown Records. He produced such hits as "How Sweet It Is," by Junior Walker and the All Stars, and "Ain't No Mountain High Enough," by Marvin Gaye and Tammi Terrell.

JULY 28

1981: Frankie Smith's "Double Dutch Bus" is the number 1 black chart single.

Philadelphia-born Frankie Smith's only hit record was a two-million-selling ode to the art of rhythmically jumping a pair of twirling ropes. The record sold a million copies as both a regular 7-inch single and as one of the newly popularized 12-inch singles.

JULY 29

1916: Jazz guitarist Charlie Christian is born in Dallas.

Christian's professional career began in Oklahoma in 1934, with the Anna Mae Winburn band. By 1937 he was specializing in the electric guitar with Lesley Sheffield's band. He was introduced to the king of swing, Benny Goodman, by talent scout John Hammond and was hired as the star of Goodman's sextet. Goodman took him to New York.

Christian was a consummate musician. His career lasted less than a decade, but he is regarded as jazz's most influential guitarist. When he wasn't playing with Goodman's group, he was

playing solo in a club somewhere, and after that he was jamming all night long in somebody's basement. He played as hard as he worked.

In late October of 1940 Christian was diagnosed as having tuberculosis. He was admitted to New York's Bellevue Hospital and, later, to the SeaVue Sanitarium. Some of his buddies sneaked him out one night and took him to a party. Charlie Christian contracted pneumonia and died on March 2, 1942.

JULY 30

1936: Blues guitarist George "Buddy" Guy is born in Lettsworth, Louisiana.

At the age of 13 Buddy Guy made his own guitar and taught himself to play it. In the early 1950s he played with Big Poppa John Tilly's band and sat in with Slim Harpo and Lightnin' Slim. In 1957 Guy moved to Chicago. He won the Battle of the Blues at Chicago's Blue Flame Club, defeating Junior Wells, Otis Rush and Magic Sam. That year he also recorded with Magic Sam and, for the first time, as a solo artist. He released the singles "Sit and Cry the Blues" and "This Is the End." In 1960 he signed with Chess Records, and in 1962 he had his first R&B chart hit, "Stone Crazy."

BUDDY GUY

Guy's main influences were T-Bone Walker, Lightnin' Hopkins, Lightnin' Slim and Guitar Slim. He eventually teamed up with harmonica player Junior Wells and toured England. He also bought a club in Chicago, and for a dozen years he did not record, but in 1992 he released a highly successful LP, *Damn Right I Got the Blues*. Other albums are *I Was Walkin' Through the Woods*; *Buddy Guy on Chess, Volume 1*; *This Is Buddy Guy*; and *Buddy Guy and Junior Wells: Drinkin' TNT 'n' Smoking Dynamite*. He can often be found playing at his successful Chicago night spot, Buddy Guy's Legend, one of the Windy City's best blues clubs.

JULY 31

1907: Singer Roy Milton is born in Tulsa.

In the late 1940s and early 1950s Roy Milton and His Solid Senders were one of the most popular and successful R&B acts around. Milton was often called the West Coast Louis Jordan. Popular vocalist and pianist Camille Howard belonged to his group.

Milton formed his first band in 1930s and first recorded in 1945. Between 1946 and 1953 he had 19 Top 10 R&B singles, including "R. M. Blues" (1946), "Milton's Boogie" (1946), "True Blues" (1947), "Thrill Me" (1947), "Everything I Do Is Wrong" (1948), "Hop, Skip and Jump" (1948), "Information Blues" (1950), "Oh Babe" (1950), "Best Wishes" (1951) and "Night and Day" (1952). "R. M. Blues" was reportedly the first R&B record to sell a million copies, and Milton claimed that he was the inventor of the rock 'n' roll beat.

Roy Milton died of a stroke in September 1983.

1959: Jazz guitarist Stanley Jordan is born in Palo Alto, California.

Jordan began piano training at the age of six and took up the guitar when he was 11. He studied music at Princeton University and graduated in 1981.

He recorded his own album, *Touch Sensitive*, and sold it at his club gigs. In 1984 he played the Kool Jazz Festival and the Montreux Jazz Festival. In 1985 he released his first major-label album, *Magic Touch*. Jordan's other LPs include *Standards, Volume 1*; *Cornucopia*; *Stanley Jordan Live*; and *Flying Home*.

Critics seem to have a love-hate relationship with Stanley Jordan. A point of controversy surrounding Jordan is his revolutionary guitar technique. He plays the strings much the way one would finger a keyboard.

AUGUST 1

1953: Blues singer and guitarist Robert Cray is born in Columbus, Georgia.

In 1974 Cray formed a band to back up blues guitarist Albert Collins. By 1980 the group was on its own and called the Robert Cray Band. The band released its first LP, *Who's Been Talking*, in the same year.

The blues world took note of Cray in 1983, when his LP *Bad Influence* won four W. C. Handy Blues Awards—for best contemporary album and single of the year, song of the year (both for "Phone Booth") and best contemporary male blues artist. The LP also made the "best" lists in England and Japan. In 1985 Cray's LP *False Accusations* made *Newsweek* magazine's best-of-the-year list. On the strength of these albums, both released on small independent labels, Cray signed with Mercury Records.

Cray's first Mercury LP, *Strong Persuader*, was released in 1986. Some sources list it as the biggest-selling blues LP of all time. Cray's other best-selling

ROBERT CRAY

LPs include *Don't Be Afraid of the Dark*, *Midnight Stroll* and *Who's Been Talking*.

Cray's music is a pleasing blend of blues, R&B and pop. It has managed to capture the fancy of hard-core blues fans and rock-music listeners alike. It is closer to the Memphis R&B of Stax than to the hardcore Delta gutbucket fare. Robert Cray, along with Stevie Ray Vaughan, is largely responsible for the renewed popularity of the blues during the 1980s.

1981: MTV (Music Television) debuts, offering 24 hours a day of music videos.

Early on there was little if any black music played, which drew the ire of the black-music community. In response, MTV began playing videos by black crossover artists, such as Michael Jackson, Prince, Lionel Richie and the Pointer Sisters. Jackson and Prince were among the first MTV superstars.

By the late 1980s MTV was showing more and more black artists, concentrating on dance music and rap, genres in which the majority of music is made by black artists. MTV has also had its share of black veejays, including J. J. Jackson, Downtown Julie Brown, Dr. Dre and Ed Lover and Fab Five Freddy.

AUGUST 2

1941: Stax songwriter Homer Banks is born in Memphis.

Memphis-based R&B giant Stax Records had several top songwriting teams in its heyday. From 1968 until its demise, one of Stax's most prolific teams was Homer Banks, Betty Crutcher and Raymond Jackson, collectively known as "we three." Their biggest hit was "Who's Making Love to Your Old Lady." They also wrote for the Staple Singers, and Banks also wrote Luther Ingram's "If Loving You Is Wrong."

1980: Singer, songwriter and producer Leon Huff makes his

chart debut with the single "Tight Money."

Huff, with his partner, Kenny Gamble, was largely responsible for creating and honing what was called the Philly sound during the 1960s and 1970s. Gamble and Huff wrote, produced and arranged a string of hits for such artists as the Intruders, the O'Jays, Harold Melvin and the Blue Notes, the Three Degrees, Archie Bell and the Drells, Billy Paul, Jerry Butler, Wilson Pickett, Teddy Pendergrass and MFSB (Mother Father Sister Brother). Most of their best work was done at Sigma Sound Studio in Philadelphia.

Gamble had sung with a group called the Romeos, and Huff had been a staff writer at Cameo Parkway Records. They first teamed up in 1965. Their first big hit was "Expressway to Your Heart," by the Soul Survivors.

Some of the best tunes Gamble and Huff wrote and produced were "Cowboys to Girls" (the Intruders), "Me and Mrs. Jones" (Billy Paul), "The Love I Lost" (Harold Melvin and the Bluenotes), "Used to Be My Girl" (the O'Jays), "Love Train" (the O'Jays), "United" (the Intruders) and "Hey Western Union Man" (Jerry Butler).

Leon Huff's foray into singing was short-lived. "Tight Money" peaked at number 68 on the soul charts.

AUGUST 3

1915: Vocalist and pianist Mercy Dee Walton is born in Waco, Texas.

Walton moved to Oakland, California, in the late 1930s and worked with Big Jay McNeely's band. He recorded under the name Mercy Dee. His style is best described as sweet blues. Walton's biggest R&B hits were "Lonesome Cabin (Log Cabin Blues)" (1949), "One-Room Country Shack" (1953), "Rent Man Blues" (1953) and "Dark Muddy Bottom" (1954).

Mercy Dee Walton died on December 2, 1962.

1917: Charlie Shavers, one of the best-known trumpeters of the big-band era, is born in New York City.

Shavers began his career as a teenager, playing piano and dancing in a Harlem rib joint called Tilly's Chicken Shack. At 18 he joined Tiny Bradshaw's band.

He joined John Kirby's band in 1937. Shaver became the band's chief composer and arranger and wrote the hit tunes "Pastel Blue" and "Undecided." He stayed with Kirby until 1944.

In 1945 he joined Tommy Dorsey's band. Over the next 11 years he left and rejoined several times, and he also played in the bands of Lucky Millinder, Van Alexander, Sonny Burke and Red Norvo. In the early 1950s he worked with Benny Goodman. In the 1960s he worked with Frank Sinatra, Jr., touring Vietnam, Japan and Hong Kong.

Charlie Shavers died of throat cancer on July 8, 1971.

1937: The Golden Gate Quartet records "Golden Gate Gospel Train."

The Golden Gate Quartet of Norfolk, Virginia, is generally credited with inventing and popularizing the rhythmic spiritual style of quartet gospel singing called "jubilee." The group was composed of Willie Johnson, Henry Owens, William Langford and Orlandus Wilson and began recording for the Bluebird label in 1936.

1951: The Swallows make their chart debut.

The Swallows were formed in 1946 as the Oakaleers and consisted of Norris "Bunky" Mack, Eddie Rich, Irving Turner, Earl Hurley, Junior Denby and Frederick Johnson. Later members were Dee Bailey, Buddy Bailey and Cai Kollette.

The Swallows had Top 10 R&B chart hits with "Will You Be Mine" (1951) and "Beside You" (1952), but they are best remembered for a 1951 double-entendre ditty called "It Ain't the Meat, It's the Motion."

AUGUST 4

1961: Bobby Lewis's "Tossin' and Turnin' " is the number 1 pop single and became the best-selling single of 1961. Bobby Lewis had only one other Top 10 hit, "One Track Mind."

AUGUST 5

1957: Lee Andrews and the Hearts make their chart debut with "Long, Lonely Nights."

Lee Andrews and the Hearts, formed in Philadelphia in 1953, were among the mellowest of the doo-wop groups. Their best-known other hits were "Teardrops" (1958), "Try the Impossible" (1958) and "Why Do I" (1958). Apart from Andrews, the group included Roy Calhoun, Wendell Calhoun, Ted Weems and Butch Curry.

AUGUST 6

1963: Little Stevie Wonder's "Fingertips, Part 2" is the number 1 soul chart hit.

"Fingertips" was the record that introduced the "12-year-old genius" to the world. It was written by Motown session players Clarence Paul and Henry Cosby and recorded live in late 1962 at Chicago's Regal Theater, where Stevie Wonder was on tour with the Motortown Revue.

The most intriguing aspect of the record is its "false ending," followed by the famous question "Hey, Stevie, what key?" Here's what happened: After Stevie Wonder finished playing the "Mary Had a Little Lamb" riff, the number was supposed to have ended. In fact, the emcee

STEVIE WONDER

can be heard calling out, "Take a bow, Stevie." But instead of leaving, Stevie Wonder cranked up "Fingertips" again. Meanwhile, the rhythm section for the next act, Mary Wells, was setting up. It was Wells's bassist, Joe Swift, who hollered, "What key?" (For trivia buffs, the key was C minor.)

AUGUST 7

1936: Rahsaan Roland Kirk, master of the tenor sax, flute, clarinet, manzello, stritch and assorted other whistles and horns, is born in Columbus, Ohio.

Kirk was blinded soon after birth. he was educated at the Ohio State School for the Blind and played sax and clarinet in the school band. At age 15 he had his own R&B band, playing dances around Ohio. At 16 he discovered two obscure woodwind instruments, the manzello and the stritch. He took the name Rahsaan after being instructed to do so in a dream.

Kirk recorded his first LP in 1956. In 1960, with the help of Ramsey Lewis, he signed with Chess Records. In 1961 he recorded and toured with Charles Mingus. He formed his own band, the Vibration Society, in 1963. His best LPs include *We Free Kings*, *Domino*, *Roland Kirk in Copenhagen* and *The Inflated Tear*.

In 1975 Rahsaan Roland Kirk suffered a stroke, which paralyzed one side of his body. On December 5, 1977, he suffered a second stroke and died.

1937: Bluesman Magic Slim is born Morris Holt in Grenada, Mississippi.

He attended school with fellow blues player Magic Sam, who gave him his "Magic" nickname. He played in Sam's Chicago-based group in the mid-1950s and 1960s. In 1967 he formed his own group, the Teardrops, and he released his first LP, *Born on a Bad Sign*, in 1975. Other LPs include *Raw Magic* and *The Highway Is My Home*.

Magic Slim has been called the best Chicago blues discovery of the 1970s. He is currently one of the best draws and most exciting performers on the Chicago blues circuit.

1970: "Soul Train" makes its TV debut.

The hippest trip in America, and the world's longest-running TV dance party, began as a local show on WCIU-TV in Chicago. The program was the brain-child of its host and producer, Don Cornelius, who at the time was a local radio deejay. "Soul Train" has been the major television venue for black music acts for the past 20 years.

It features the latest dances, the hottest live acts and such special features as the famous "Soul Train" line.

AUGUST 8

1908: Bandleader Lucius "Lucky" Millinder is born in Anniston, Alabama.

Millinder grew up in Chicago and worked as an emcee at various ballrooms during the 1920s. In 1931 he fronted a band for a tour on the R.K.O. theater circuit. In 1933 he took over and led Doc Crawford's band at the Harlem Opera House and toured Europe. Later in 1933 he took over the Mills Blue Rhythm Band and renamed it the Lucky Millinder Band. In 1937 he began fronting the band of pianist Bill Doggett, eventually taking it over, too. In 1939 the band went bankrupt.

Millinder formed his most successful orchestra in 1940. This outfit lasted until 1952. Over the years, it included such musicians as Bill Doggett (who did most of the arranging), Dizzy Gillespie, Charlie Shavers and Tab Smith. Featured vocalists included Sister Rosetta Tharpe, Wynonie Harris, Bullmoose Jackson, John Greer and Annisteen Allen.

Millinder and his band racked up four number 1 R&B hits in the '40s: "When the Lights Go On Again" (featuring Gillespie, 1942), "Apollo Jump" (1943), "Sweet Slumber" (1943) and "Who Threw the Whiskey in the Well" (1945). Other Millinder hits included "Shorty's Got to Go" (1946), "D'Natural Blues" (1949), I'll Never Be Free" (1951) and "I'm Waiting Just for You" (1951).

Millinder was not really a musician, but he was a great showman. After retiring from the band business, Millinder worked in radio, as a disc jockey, and in public relations.

Lucky Millinder died on September 28, 1966, in New York City.

1907: Jazz saxophonist Benny Carter, well known both as arranger and a musician, is born in New York City.

During the '20s and early '30s Carter had stints with the big bands of Earl "Fatha" Hines, Duke Ellington, Billy Fowler, Horace Henderson, Fletcher Henderson, Chick Webb and Don Redman. He was also musical director for McKinney's Cotton Pickers band. Carter also began arranging in the early '30s. he did scores for the bands of Duke Ellington, Teddy Hill and Fletcher Henderson and for the Mills Blue Rhythm Band. In 1934 he began arranging for Benny Goodman. In 1936 he became staff arranger for the London-based Henry Hull Orchestra.

He formed his own big band in 1940 and played New York's Savoy Ballroom. During the early '40s Carter's band was a fixture at the Apollo Theater. The band featured trombonist J. J. Johnson and singer Savannah Churchill and had hit records with "Hurry, Hurry" (1944), "Poinciana" (1944) and "I'm Lost" (1944). In the late '40s Carter began working as a composer and arranger in the film industry. His music can be heard on the soundtracks of *The Snows of Kilimanjaro*, *As Thousands Cheer* and *Clash by Night* and on such old TV shows as "M Squad" and "Alfred Hitchcock Presents." Carter is fluent on alto and tenor sax, trumpet, clarinet, piano and trombone.

1933: Singer Joe Tex is born Joseph Arrington, Jr., in Rogers, Texas.

Joe Tex won a recording contract in an Apollo Theater contest in 1954. His earliest hit was "Davy, You Upset My Home" (1955). In 1964 Joe Tex signed with Dial Records. With "Hold On to What You've Got" (1965), he began a string of over two dozen R&B and pop chart hits. His biggest include "You Got What It Takes" (1965), "I Want To (Do Everything for You)" (1965), "A Sweet Woman Like You" (1965), "The Love You Save" (1966), "S.Y.S.L.J.F.M."

(1965), "I Believe I'm Gonna Make It" (1966), "Skinny Legs and All" (1967), "Men Are Gettin' Scarce" (1968), "I Gotcha" (1972) and "Ain't Gonna Bump No More (with No Big Fat Woman)" (1977).

Joe Tex was a master showman and always injected a sense of humor into his hit records. He was one of the first soul "rappers"; that is, many of his songs included spoken verse. Joe Tex was exciting to watch onstage. One of his best stage gimmicks was falling to his knees and catching a teetering microphone before it hit the floor. His shows were backed by a great R&B band, Clyde Williams and the Hornets.

In 1972 Joe Tex converted to the Muslim faith and changed his name to Joseph Hazzifz. He gave up recording for five years and spent that time preaching. He returned to the record charts in 1977.

Joe Tex died of a heart attack on August 13, 1982.

AUGUST 9

1942: Jazz drummer Jack DeJohnette is born in Chicago.

DeJohnette studied classical piano for ten years and graduated from the American Conservatory of Music. In the mid-1960s he played behind singers Betty Carter and Abbey Lincoln. From 1966 to 1969 he was with Charles Lloyd's group. He also joined Miles Davis's group and played on such Davis LPS as *Bitches Brew*, *Live-Evil* and *Live at the Fillmore*.

DeJohnette first led his own group in 1968. In the 1970s he became house drummer for EMC Records. Jack DeJohnette's most acclaimed albums are *Special Edition*, *New Directions in Europe* and *Earth Walk*.

1947: Singer Barbara Mason is born in Philadelphia.

Mason first charted in 1965. Her biggest hit was "I'm Ready," that same year. Her other hits include "Give Me Your Love" (1972), "From His Woman to You" (1974) and "Shakin' Up" (1975).

1959: Rapper Kurtis Blow is born Kurt Walker in New York City.

Kurtis Blow was one of the first rappers to take his show on the road. Before rap became mainstream, he played 2,500-seat arenas with 60 people in them and took abuse because he didn't have a live band.

Nevertheless, he was one of rap music's first successful recording artists. In 1980 he had a million-selling 12-inch single, "The Breaks." His other rap hits include "Basketball" (1985), "America" (1985) and "If I Ruled the World" (1985).

1963: Singer Whitney Houston is born in Newark, New Jersey.

Houston began her singing career at the age of 11 in the choir of the church where her mother, legendary gospel singer Cissy Houston, was minister of music. By the time she was 15 she was part of her mother's act and was also doing backup vocals on records for artists like Lou Rawls and Chaka Khan. By the time she was 18 Houston had developed into a top model, appearing on the covers of *Glamour* and *Seventeen*.

She reached superstardom after releasing her very first album, *Whitney Houston*, in 1985. The LP sold over eight million copies in the U.S. and more than 14 million copies worldwide. It brought Houston four number 1 singles, a Grammy and seven American Music Awards. It also made her one of the most publicized and photographed personalities in show business.

In 1987 Houston released her second LP, *Whitney*. With this LP she became the first female artist to have an album debut at the number 1 spot on the charts. Houston is also the only artist to have seven consecutive number 1 pop singles: "Saving All My Love for You" (1985), "How Well I Know" (1985), "Greatest Love of All" (1986), "I Wanna Dance with Somebody" (1987), "Didn't We Almost Have It All" (1987), "So Emotional" (1987) and "Where Do Broken Hearts Go" (1988). Other number 1 hits by Houston are "I'm Your Baby Tonight" (1990), "All the Man I Need" (1991) and "I Will Always Love You" (1992).

In 1992 Whitney Houston starred in her first film, *The Bodyguard*, with Kevin Costner. Throughout her career she has benefited from the tutelage and guidance of her famous cousin, vocalist Dionne Warwick. Houston is married to hip-hop idol Bobby Brown.

AUGUST 10

1918: Saxophonist Arnette Cobb is born in Houston.

Cobb and Illinois Jacquet are the daddies of a sax style commonly called Texas tenor. Cobb played with the Texas-based groups of Chester Boone and Milt Larkin before succeeding Jacquet with Lionel Hampton's band, in 1942. He stayed with Hampton until 1947 and then formed his own seven-piece group. In 1951 he had a hit with "Smooth Sailin'."

In 1956 Arnette Cobb was severely injured in a car crash. In the late '50s and early '60s he led a Texas-based big band.

1948: Jazz, jingle and pop singer Patti Austin is born in New York City.

Austin made her debut at age five on the stage of Harlem's Apollo Theater. During the 1970s she recorded a series of jazz LPs for the legendary CTI label, and she has cut commercial jingles for clients like Coca-Cola, McDonald's, Burger King, TWA, 7-Up, Budweiser, Avon and a host of others.

Austin's biggest hits of the '80s came in a series of duets with James Ingram. Their 1983 hit "Baby, Come to Me" went to number 1 on the pop charts and was one of the year's best-sellers.

Patti Austin's best LPs are *End of the Rainbow*, *Live at the Bottom Line*, *The Real Me* and *Carry On*.

1945: Ronettes lead singer Veronica "Ronnie" Bennett-Spector is born in New York City.

The Ronettes were the centerpiece of producer Phil Spector's "wall of sound" recordings: "Be My Baby" (1963), "Baby, I Love You" (1963), "Do I Love You" (1964), "Walking in the Rain" (1964), "I Can Hear Music" (1966) and others. The members besides Ronnie Bennett-Spector were her sister Estelle Bennett and their cousin Nedra Talley-Ross.

The Ronettes were formed in 1958, when they were in junior high school. They danced at Murray the K's rock 'n' roll shows at the Brooklyn Fox Theater and at the Peppermint Lounge. In 1961, under the name Ronnie and the

Relatives, they recorded for Colpix Records. They began their association with Phil Spector in 1962, doing background vocals. At one point they were an opening act for the Beatles in the U.S.

The Ronettes disbanded in 1966. From 1968 to 1974 Ronnie Bennett-Spector and Phil Spector had a stormy marriage. Today she still plays clubs and rock 'n' roll revivals around New York.

THE RONETTES

AUGUST 11

1977: "Strawberry Letter #23," by the Brothers Johnson, is the number 1 black chart single.

George and Louis Johnson began playing music in childhood. In the mid-1970s they were fronting their own band when they were discovered by Quincy Jones. They provided the vocal tracks for Jones's 1975 hit "Is It Love That We're Missing."

They began hitting the charts, with "I'll Be Good To You" (1976), "Get the Funk Out Ma Face" (1976), "Ain't We Funkin' Now" (1978), "Stomp" (1980), "The Real Thing" (1981) and "You Keep Me Coming Back" (1984).

AUGUST 12

1920: Singer and songwriter Percy Mayfield, known as the poet of the blues, is born in Minden, Louisiana.

Mayfield moved to Los Angeles in 1942. He had such self-penned R&B hits as "Please Send Me Someone to Love" (1950), "Strange Things Happening" (1951), "Lost Love" (1951), "What a Fool

I Was" (1951), "Praying for Your Return" (1951), "Cry Baby" (1952) and "Big Question" (1952). He also wrote tunes for Jimmy Witherspoon and Lowell Fulson.

Mayfield was one of the best R&B songwriters of the 1950s. His best-known and biggest-selling composition was "Hit the Road, Jack," for Ray Charles. He became a staff writer for Charles after a 1952 auto accident that altered his voice. Mayfield returned to recording in the 1960s, however.

Two Mayfield collections, *The Best of Percy Mayfield* and *Percy Mayfield, Poet of the Blues*, are essential for any connoisseur of rhythm and blues.

Percy Mayfield died of a heart attack on August 11, 1984.

1926: Singer Joe Jones is born in New Orleans.

Jones worked as B. B. King's valet during the 1950s. In 1960 he had a Top 10 R&B and pop hit, "You Talk Too Much." He is not to be confused with jazz drummer Jo Jones or Philly Joe Jones.

1989: Singer, songwriter and producer Baby Face debuts on the pop chart with "It's No Crime."

Baby Face (Kenneth Edmonds) and Antonia "L.A." Reid are one of the hottest current writer-producer duos. Megahits that the pair have turned out include "Girlfriend" (for Pebbles), "Rock Steady" (for the Whispers), "The Lover in Me" (for Sheena Easton), "Every Little Step" (for Bobby Brown), "All the Man That I Need" (for Whitney Houston) and "Secret Rendezvous," "The Way You Love Me" and "Superwoman" (for Karyn White). They also produced several hits for Baby Face as a recording artist, including "Tender Lover" (1989) and "Whip Appeal" (1990).

Edmonds and Reid began writing and producing together in the 1980s, when they were members of the Deele. That band recorded for the Solar label and had such black chart hits as "Body Talk" (1983), "Two Occasions" (1987) and "Shoot-'Em-Up Movies" (1988).

AUGUST 13

1921: Jimmy McCracklin, one of the best-known West Coast blues singers, is born in St. Louis.

After settling in Los Angeles, in the 1940s, Jimmy McCracklin was a professional boxer for a time.

In 1958 McCracklin had a Top 10 pop and R&B hit, "The Walk." His other hits include "Just Got to Know" (1961), "Shame, Shame, Shame" (1962) and "Think" (1965). His best LPs are *Rockin' Man*, *I'm Gonna Have My Fun* and *You Deceived Me*.

1938: Rock 'n' roll organist Dave "Baby" Cortez is born in Detroit.

Cortez's 1959 hit, "The Happy Organ," was one of the few rock 'n' roll instrumentals to hit number 1 on the pop charts. Cortez had been a member of the 1950s doo-wop groups the Pearls and the Valentines. In 1962 he scored another Top 10 pop hit, "Rinky Dink."

1942: Chicago blues guitarist and singer Frank "Son" Seals is born in Osceola, Arkansas.

His father, Jim Seals, was a member of the famed Rabbit Foot Minstrels. At the age of 13 Son Seals was playing drums for bluesman Robert Nighthawk. At 18 he had his own band, playing in Memphis and around Arkansas. Later in the 1960s he backed up Earl Hooker and Albert King.

Son Seals recorded his first LP, *The Son Seals Blues Band*, in 1973. His second, *Midnight Son*, was released in 1977 and is considered a classic. Other great Seals LPs are *Live and Burning*, *Chicago Fire*, *Bad Axe* and 1991's *Living in the Danger Zone*.

Son Seals can be found playing the blues in Chicago clubs like the Wise Fools Pub, B.L.U.E.S. and Rosa's, and he often tours Europe.

AUGUST 14

1946: Vocalist and bassist Larry Graham is born in Beaumont, Texas.

From 1966 to 1972 Graham was bassist for the hit-making funk-rock group Sly and the Family Stone. In 1973 he formed Graham Central Station and had solid disco, soul and pop hits with "Can You Handle It" (1974), "Your Love" (1975), "Now Do U Wanta Dance" (1977) and "My Radio Sure Sounds Good to Me" (1978).

He went solo in 1980 and scored a million-seller with "One-in-a-Million You."

Other hits are "When We Get Married" (1980) and "Just Be My Lady" (1981).

AUGUST 15

1911: Blues singer and harmonica player Buster Brown is born in Cordele, Georgia.

In 1959 he had a number 1 R&B hit, "Fannie Mae." Buster Brown died on January 31, 1976.

1925: Oscar Peterson, master of the traditionally developed jazz piano since the 1950s, is born in Montreal.

As a child, Peterson was taught by his sister, a classical pianist. At the age of 14 he won $250 in a talent contest and bought his own piano. His chief influences were Art Tatum and Nat "King" Cole.

Peterson was introduced to U.S. audiences in 1949 and began recording in 1950. He formed his first Oscar Peterson Trio with Ray Brown on bass and Irving Ashley on guitar. In 1952 Barney Kessell replaced Ashley. Herb Ellis later replaced Kessell, and when Ellis left, in 1959, drummer Ed Thigpen was added. Since the 1970s Peterson has not maintained a regular trio but appears often in trio format and often performs solo.

Oscar Peterson's best LPs are *A Jazz Portrait of Frank Sinatra*, *Very Tall*, *We Get Requests*, *The Trio*, *In Concert* and *Exclusively for My Friends*.

1930: Singer Jackie Brenston is born in Clarksdale, Mississippi.

Brenston was a vocalist and saxophonist with Ike Turner's Kings of Rhythm. In 1951 he recorded what many pop students consider the first rock 'n' roll hit record, "Rocket 88." It was a number 1 R&B single.

The record was cut at the Sun Records studio, along with three others on the same day. Two of the four had Brenston doing vocals, and the other two featured Ike Turner singing. Sam Phillips of Sun labeled two as Ike Turner and His Kings of Rhythm and two as Jackie Brenston and His Delta Cats, and he sold them all to Chess Records. When "Rocker 88" hit number 1, Ike Turner was less than happy, and he and Brenston parted company. Brenston never had another hit.

Jackie Brenston died on December 15, 1979.

1934: Singer Bobby Byrd, James Brown's right-hand man, is born in Toccoa, Georgia.

Byrd and Brown formed the Famous Flames. When Brown became a star, the Flames were his backup vocal group.

Byrd himself had several R&B chart records, most produced by James Brown. His biggest hits were "I Found Out" (1963), "Baby Baby Baby" (with Anna King, 1964), "We Are in Love" (1965), "I Need Help" (1970) and "I Know You Got Soul" (1970).

1964: The Four Tops make their chart debut with "Baby, I Need Your Loving," which began a monumental run of super-smash pop and R&B hits for the group. In all, they have placed over 50 titles on the national singles charts. Their biggest and most unforgettable hits include "Ask the Lonely" (1965), "I Can't Help Myself" (1965), "It's the Same Old Song" (1965), "Something About You" (1965), "Shake Me, Wake Me" (1966), "Reach Out, I'll Be There" (1966), "Standing in the Shadows of Love" (1966), "Bernadette" (1967), "Seven Rooms of Gloom" (1967), "Still Water (Love)" (1970), "Just Seven Numbers" (1971), "Keeper of the Castle" (1972), "Ain't No Woman" (1973), "Are You Man Enough" (1973), "One Chain Don't Make No Prison" (1974), "Catfish" (1976) and "When She Was My Girl" (1981). The Four Tops consist of lead singer Levi Stubbs,

THE FOUR TOPS

Renaldo Benson, Lawrence Payton and Duke Fakir. They were formed in 1954 in Detroit, as the Four Arms. The Four Tops have had no personnel changes in their forty-year history.

The Four Tops first recorded in 1956 for Chess Records. They signed with Motown in 1963. They left in 1972 but returned in the early 1980s.

Levi Stubbs provided the voice for the man-eating plant Audrey II in the 1986 film *Little Shop of Horrors*.

1981: Morris Day and the Time make their chart debut.

Day's association with superstar Prince dates back to when they were teenagers and Day played drums in Prince's band, Grand Central. In 1981, after his solo success, Prince decided to create and produce a group. The basis of the group would be an already existing Minneapolis band called Flyte Time, which included guitarist Jesse Johnson, bassist Terry Lewis, keyboardist Jimmy Jam Harris and comically cool Jerome Benton. Prince put in his old buddy Day as front man and dubbed the troup the Time.

The Time hit it big with the release of their second LP, *What Time Is It*, in August 1982. The album gave the band such top soul chart hits as "The Walk" and "777-9311."

Radio play and TV appearances brought notice to Day as the group's leader. Day was also picked to play Prince's rival in the film *Purple Rain*. In conjunction with the film, in 1984, the Time released its third LP, *Ice Cream Castles*. A clip of the group performing "Jungle Love" constitutes one of the better musical sequences in the film. Acclaimed for his performance in *Purple Rain*, Day left the Time and Prince's fold and embarked on a solo career.

Day's initial LP, *The Color of Success*, went Top 10 and gave him single hits with the title track and "The Oak Tree." In 1988 Day's *Daydreaming* album yielded him top pop and video success with the song "Fishnet." He also appeared in the Richard Pryor film *Movin'*.

Guitarist Jesse Johnson made his mark on the black-music charts of the 1980s as a performer and producer. He

formed the Jess Johnson Revue after the breakup of the Time and signed with A&M Records. Johnson then released a pair of successful LPs, *Jesse Johnson Revue* and *Schockadelica*. His music tends toward heavy funk, without the pop overtones so evident in Prince's music. Johnson also found success as a producer with the Minneapolis-based band Tamara and the Seen.

In 1987 Jimmy Jam and Terry Lewis picked up a Grammy for their production efforts on Janet Jackson's monster hit LP *Control*, which established Jam, Lewis and their Flyte Time Productions as the hottest production outfit around. Other artists they have produced include Alexander O'Neal, Cherelle, Gladys Knight and the Pips, the S.O.S. Band, Cheryl Lynn, Klymaxx and Herb Alpert. The duo began writing and producing in 1983, when it was obvious that the Time was on its way out.

AUGUST 16

1915: Singer Al Hibbler is born in Little Rock, Arkansas.

Hibbler was blind at birth. He studied voice at the Little Rock Conservatory for the Blind and worked with Jay McShann's band in the early 1940s. He did the vocals on McShann's hit "Get Me On Your Mind."

In 1942 Hibbler joined Duke Ellington's orchestra and sang on such Ellington chart hits as "I Ain't Got Nothin' but the Blues" (1945) and "Don't Be So Mean to Baby" (1948). He remained with Ellington until 1951. While with Ellington, Hibbler also recorded solo. His biggest hits of the era were "Trees" (1948), "Lover Come Back to Me" (1949), "Danny Boy" (1950) and "What Will I Tell My Heart" (1951). In 1955 Al Hibbler had his biggest hit, "Unchained Melody," which went to number 1 on the R&B and pop Top 10.

1922: Pianist and arranger Ernie Freeman is born in Cleveland.

In the 1950s Freeman had such R&B instrumental hits as "Jivin' Around" (1956), "Lost Dreams" (1956) and "Raunchy" (1957). He also recorded under the pseudonym B. Bumble and the Stingers and had the hit instrumental "Bumble Boogie" in 1961.

Freeman is best known as a top session musician and arranger. He has worked with Frank Sinatra, Dean Martin, Sammy Davis, Jr., and Connie Francis. Before retiring in the late 1970s he was musical director for Reprise Records.

Ernie Freeman died of a heart attack on May 16, 1981.

1928: Blues singer and guitarist Eddie Kirkland is born in Jamaica.

Eddie Kirkland was raised in Dothan, Alabama. He learned the harmonica and played on the streets for tips as a child.

As a guitarist, he worked in the backup bands of John Lee Hooker, King Curtis and Otis Redding. His best LPs include *It's The Blues Man* and *Have Mercy*.

1934: Singer Ketty Lester is born Reyvolda Frierson in Hope, Arkansas. In 1962 Ketty Lester had a most soulful one-shot; a Top 10 pop and R&B ballad called "Love Letters."

1942: Singer Barbara George is born in New Orleans. Her one big hit was "I Know," in 1961. The horn played on the record is a cornet, and the player is Melvin Lastie.

AUGUST 17

1939: Blues vocalist and guitarist Luther Allison is born in Mayflower, Arkansas.

Allison began his career playing with his family's gospel group. He moved to Chicago in the early 1950s and played in the bands of such noted bluesmen as Jimmy Dawkins, Freddie King, Magic Sam and Sunnyland Slim.

Allison is one of the most rock-oriented of the modern blues guitarists. He enjoys greater popularity in Europe than he does in the U.S. His talent came to notice in the late 1960s, on the strength of his performances on a 1967 blues anthology recording called *Sweet Home Chicago* and at the 1968 Ann Arbor Blues Festival.

Allison cut his first solo LP, *Love Me, Mama*, in 1968. He was also one of the few blues artists to sign with Motown Records.

His best LPs are *Life Is a Bitch*; *Love Me, Papa*; and *Live in Paris*. Today he

continues to record prolifically, mostly in France and England.

AUGUST 18

1923: Singer Jimmy Witherspoon is born in Gurdon, Arkansas.

Witherspoon sang in his church choir as a child. He first sang the blues while in the U.S. Navy. Upon his release, he settled on the West Coast and toured and recorded with Jay McShann's band.

In 1948 Witherspoon formed his own band. In the late '40s and early '50s he had several R&B hits. On many of his recordings he was backed by Roy Milton and His Solid Senders. The biggest hits of Witherspoon's career were "Ain't Nobody's Business" (1945), "In the Evening When the Sun Goes Down" (1949), "No Rollin' Blues" (1949), "Big Fine Girl" (1949) and "Wind Is Blowing" (1952).

For most of the middle and late '50s Witherspoon was hardly heard from. In 1959 he played the Monterey Jazz Festival, and in 1961 he toured Europe with Buck Clayton's band.

1951: The Five Keys make their chart debut with "The Glory of Love."

The Five Keys were formed in Newport News, Virginia, as the Sentimental Four. In 1949 they changed their name to the Five Keys. The group consisted of Maryland Pierce, Dickie Smith, Rudy West, Bernie West and Ripley Ingram. "The Glory of Love" hit number 1 on the R&B charts in the fall of 1951. In 1953 Rudy West and Dickie Smith went into the Army and were replaced by Ramon Loper and Ulysses K. Hicks.

In 1954 the group signed with Capitol Records and had hits like "Ling, Ting, Tong" (1955), "Close Your Eyes" (1955), "The Verdict" (1955), " 'Cause You're My Lover" (1955), "Out of Sight, Out of Mind" (1956), "Wisdom of a Fool" (1956) and "Let There Be You" (1957).

1945: Singer Nona Hendryx is born in Trenton, New Jersey.

From 1961 to 1977 Hendryx was a member of Patti Labelle and the Blue Belles and Labelle. Since going solo, she has had such single hits as "Keep It Confidential" (1983), "Transformation"

(1983), "I Sweat" (1984) and "Why Should I Cry" (1987). Nona Hendryx's music is best described as high-energy metal soul. She is noted for her unusually daring stage costumes.

AUGUST 19

1940: Singer Johnny Nash is born in Houston.

Johnny Nash got his start on local TV at the age of 13. From 1956 to 1963 he sang on Arthur Godfrey's radio and TV shows. During this period he had Top 40 pop hits with "A Very Special Love" (1957) and "The Teen Commandments" (1958). In 1959 he appeared in the film *Take a Giant Step*.

In the late 1960s he began recording in Jamaica and produced a series of reggae-flavored pop hits, including "Hold Me Tight" (1968), the million-seller "I Can See Clearly Now" (1972) and "Stir It Up" (written by Bob Marley, 1973).

AUGUST 20

1942: Singer, songwriter, keyboardist and producer Isaac Hayes is born in Covington, Tennessee.

Hayes went to Stax Records as a session musician and teamed up with David Porter to write many of that label's biggest hits over the next few years. Hayes-Porter compositions included "B-A-B-Y," for Carla Thomas, and "Hold On, I'm Coming," "I Thank You," "Soul Man" and "When Something Is Wrong with My Baby," for Sam and Dave.

In 1969 Hayes released the LP *Hot Buttered Soul*, which contained extended versions of pop songs complemented by "raps." He continued in this style on his 1970 album *The Isaac Hayes Movement*, which produced such single hits as "Walk On By," "By the Time I Get to Phoenix," "I Stand Accused" and "Never Can Say Goodbye." (Hayes has been called "the black Moses," perhaps because he led black recording artists out of the confinement of the two-minute, 30-second single record.) His concerts featured his Isaac Hayes Movement Band, augmented by strings from local symphonies, and were sold out coast to coast.

In 1970 Hayes hit his peak, with the release of the soundtrack LP from the "blaxploitation" film thriller *Shaft*. The theme from that film became the nation's number 1 pop single.

In August of 1972 Hayes headlined the annual Watts Festival in Los Angeles. The concert was filmed and released under the title *Wattstax*, and the soundtrack for the film sold over a million copies.

Hayes left Stax Records in 1975 over a disagreement about royalties. He then formed his own Hot Buttered Soul label and continued to record into the late 1980s. His post-*Shaft* hits include "Do Your Thing" (1972), "Joy" (1973), "Don't Let Go" (1979) and "Ike's Rap" (1986). He also recorded duets with Dionne Warwick and Millie Jackson and composed the scores for the films *Tough Guys* and *Truck Turner*.

AUGUST 21

1904: William "Count" Basie, the man who put the "swing" in the Swing era, is born in Red Bank, New Jersey.

Basie began his career playing piano behind touring vaudeville acts. Throughout the 1920s he worked with such acts as Kate Crippen and Her Kids, *The Hippity Hop Show*, Sonny Thompson, Ganzelle White and the Whitman Sisters. In the late '20s he worked in bands like Walter Page's Blue Devils and Elmer Payne and His Ten Royal Americans. The Payne band included vocalist Jimmy Rushing and trumpeter Hot Lips Page.

In 1929 Basie joined Bennie Moten's orchestra and remained until 1934, when he formed his first band with Moten's help. When Moten died, in 1935, Basie took the nucleus of the Moten orchestra, including Jimmy Rushing, Buster Smith and Lester Young, and added such talents as Buck Clayton and Jo Jones to form the first famous Count Basie Orchestra. The Basie group took up residence in Kansas City's Reno Club and broadcast over radio station WXBY.

The Count Basie Orchestra was discovered by John Hammond, who arranged a national tour. In December 1936 the group debuted in New York

City, at Roseland, and in 1938 debuted at the Savoy Ballroom. By now the band included guitarist Freddie Green and saxophonist Earl Warren.

The Count Basie Orchestra cut its first sides for Decca Records in January 1937. Later that year Count Basie had his first hit, "One O'Clock Jump." Other classics followed: "Pennies from Heaven" (1937), "Honeysuckle Rose" (1937), "Sent for You Yesterday" (1938) and "Jive at Five" (1939).

The Basie group hit the R&B charts with "I Want a Little Girl" (1940), "Goin' to Chicago Blues" (1941), "Rusty Dusty Blues" (1943), "Jimmy's Blues" (1945), "Red Bank Boogie" (1945), "The Mad Boogie" (1946), "Open the Door, Richard" (1947) and "I Ain't Mad at You" (1947). Other vocalists who appeared with Count Basie included Joe Williams, Billie Holiday and Helen Humes. Musicians on the band's roster included Sweets Edison, Buck Clayton, Don Byas, Illinois Jacquet, J. J. Johnson, Clark Terry, Thad Jones and Frank Foster.

Count Basie maintained his big band throughout the 1940s. In January 1950 he broke it up and began performing with a smaller group. He reorganized the big band in 1952.

The Basie outfit performed with superstars like Frank Sinatra, Ella Fitzgerald, Jackie Wilson, the Mills Brothers and Sammy Davis, Jr., recording scores of albums. The best include *Basie in Europe*, *Count Basie and the Kansas City Seven*, *The Atomic Mr. Basie*, *The Best of Basie*, *88 Basie Street*, *The Kansas City Seven*, *Basie Big Band*, *Basie Boogie*, *Sixteen Swinging Men* and *Basie at Birdland*. Basie and the band also appeared in such films as *State Door Canteen*, *Made in Paris*, *Cinderfella* and *Sex and the Single Girl*. The Count Basie band still swings today, under the direction of Frank Foster.

Count Basie died on April 26, 1984.

1920: Singer Savannah Churchill is born in Colfax, Louisiana.

Churchill moved to Brooklyn in 1926. After her husband was killed in an auto accident, in 1941, she took up a singing career to support her two children. She sang with Benny Carter's band and

toured with Nat "King" Cole. In 1956 her career was halted when she was injured in a freak nightclub accident: a drunk fell out of the balcony and landed on top of her, breaking her pelvis.

Churchill's biggest hits include "Daddy Daddy" (1945), "I Want to Be Loved" (1947), "Time Out for Tears" (1948) and "I Want to Cry" (1948).

Savannah Churchill died of pneumonia on April 20, 1974.

1928: Jazz trumpeter Art Farmer is born in Council Bluffs, Iowa.

Farmer was brought up in Phoenix, Arizona, and moved to Los Angeles in 1945. In the late '40s he played in the R&B bands of Johnny Otis and Jay McShann and the jazz bands of Benny Carter and Gerald Wilson.

In the early '50s he was with Wardell Gray and Lionel Hampton. Farmer began recording in 1953 with Clifford Brown and members of Lionel Hampton's band. He is a master of both trumpet and flugelhorn. He spent 1954 to 1956 with Gigi Gryce, 1956 to 1958 with Horace Silver and 1958 to 1959 with Gerry Mulligan. In 1959 he formed a jazztet with Benny Golson.

In 1965 he formed a quintet with Jim Hall. In the late 1960s Farmer moved to Europe but returned to the U.S. in 1975. Some of Art Farmer's best LPs are *Mirage*, *Maiden Voyage*, *Ambrosia*, *Sing Me Softly of the Blues* and *Moose the Mooche*.

AUGUST 22

1920: Bluesman John Lee Hooker is born in Clarksdale, Mississippi. (Some sources list the date as 1917.)

At the age of 14 Hooker ran away from home to Memphis and soon was playing juke joints with such bluesmen as Robert Nighthawk. From the mid-1930s into the early 1940s Hooker worked with gospel groups: the Big Six, the Delta Big Four and the Fairfield Four. In 1943 he moved to Detroit and began playing clubs. He signed with Modern Records in 1948 and began hitting the R&B charts with tunes like "Boogie Chillun" (1949), "Hobo Blues" (1949), "Hoogie Boogie" (1949), "Crawling King Snake Blues" (1949), "I'm in the Mood" (1951),

JOHN LEE HOOKER

"Union Stadium Blues" (1952), "It's My Own Fault" (1954), "I Love You, Honey" (1958), "No Shoes" (1960) and "Boom Boom" (1962).

Hooker's "boogie blues" sound is one of a kind, and his guitar style is one of the most copied. In the 1960s, when the British bands invaded America, the Animals and the Rolling Stones listed John Lee Hooker as one of their major influences. In the 1970s American blues-rock groups like ZZ Top and the J. Geils Band did likewise.

John Lee Hooker has recorded numerous albums for many different record labels. Some of the best are *The Anniversary Album*, *Boogie Chillun*, *House Rent Boogie*, *Mad Man Blues*, *Never Get Out of These Blues Alive* and the current LPs *The Healer* and *Mr. Lucky*. *The Healer* went gold in six countries, including England and Canada. Hooker won the W. C. Handy Award for best traditional blues artist six years in a row, and in 1990 he was named by *Down Beat* magazine as number 1 blues artist. In October 1990, in Madison Square Garden, scores of blues and rock performers, including Bonnie Raitt, BoDiddley and Johnny Winter, gathered to pay tribute to John Lee Hooker with a massive concert featuring his music.

AUGUST 23

1964: "Where Did Our Love Go," by the Supremes, is the number 1 pop chart single.

The Supremes were the top female group of the rock era. They scored 10 number 1 pop singles between 1964 and 1969; "Where Did Our Love Go" was the first. The Supremes also became the first act to score five consecutive number 1 pop hits since Elvis Presley accomplished that feat in the mid-1950s.

The Supremes were the first Motown act to grace the cover of *Ebony* magazine. At the height of their career, a bakery in Michigan produced Supreme Bread, which featured the group's photo on the wrapper.

AUGUST 24

1905: Bluesman Arthur "Big Boy" Crudup is born in Forrest, Mississippi.

In the early 1940s Crudup sang with a gospel group, the Harmony Four. He also worked with bluesmen like Elmore James and Sonny Boy Williamson. He signed with Blue Bird Records and had R&B hits with "Rock Me, Mama" (1945), "Who's Been Foolin' You" (1945), "Keep Your Arms Around Me" (1945), "So Glad You're Mine" (1946), "Ethel Mae" (1946) and "I'm Gonna Dig Myself a Hole" (1951). In 1953 Crudup quit the music business.

Elvis Presley listed Big Boy Crudup as one of his major influences. In fact, Presley seems to have been the only one to give Crudup the credit he is due as one of the early formulators of the music that was to become rock 'n' roll. Crudup returned to music in 1959, when Presley arranged a recording session for him.

Big Boy Crudup died of a stroke on Mary 28, 1974.

1915: Singer Wynonie Harris is born in Omaha.

Harris worked as a drummer, dancer and comic before being hired by the Lucky Millinder band as a vocalist, in 1944. He performed the vocals in Millinder's hits "Who Threw the Whiskey in the Well" (1945) and "Shorty's Got to Go" (1946).

In 1946 he began his solo career and had an incredible run of R&B chart hits that included "Wynonie's Blues" (1946), "Playful Baby" (1946), "Good Rockin' Tonight" (1948), "Lollypop Mama"

(1948), "Grandma Plays the Numbers" (1949), "I Feel That Old Age Coming On" (1949), "Drinking Wine, Spo-Dee-O-Dee, Drinking Wine" (1949), "All She Wants to Do Is Rock" (1949), "I Want My Fanny Brown" (1949), "Sittin' On It All the Time" (1950), "I Like My Baby's Pudding" (1950), "Good Morning, Judge" (1950), "Oh Babe" (1950), "Bloodshot Eyes" (1951) and "Lovin' Machine" (1952). Suddenly his string of hits stopped, and Harris was out of the music business by 1953. According to some critics, "Good Rockin' Tonight" was the first rock 'n' roll record.

Harris had been a flamboyant performer. In fact, someone once wrote that Elvis Presley at his wildest was a watered-down version of Wynonie Harris. He attracted women like a magnet, and he played to them. There are tales that after club and concert performances Harris would have several limos parked at the stage door and let the collected throng of female fans decide which one he should ride in. Harris attempted a couple of comebacks, but they came to nothing.

Wynonie Harris died of cancer on June 14, 1969.

1929: Harptones lead singer Willie Winfield is born in New York City.

The other group members were William James, William Galloway, Bill Brown, Nicky Clark and vocal arranger Raoul Cita. In 1953 the Harptones assured themselves of a place in the doo-wop hall of fame with a beautiful ballad called "I Want a Sunday Kind of Love." Their other charted records include "My Memories of You" (1954), "Life is But a Dream" (1955) and "On Sunday Afternoon" (1956).

AUGUST 25

1933: Wayne Shorter, currently the jazz world's number 1 soprano saxophonist, is born in Newark, New Jersey.

Shorter studied music at New York University. He served in the U.S. Army from 1956 to 1958.

From 1959 to 1963 he was a member of Art Blakey's Jazz Messengers. In 1964 he joined Miles Davis's group and stayed until 1970. Shorter's compositions became part of the group's repertoire.

In 1970 Wayne Shorter and pianist Joe Zawinul formed the group Weather Report, which became one of the most important and influential fusion bands of the 1970s. They had such critically acclaimed LPs as *Mysterious Traveler*, *Sporting Life* and *Night Passage*. Wayne Shorter's best LPs and CDs include *Introducing Wayne Shorter*, *Joy Rider*, *Night Dreamer*, *Speak No Evil* and *Native Dancer*.

AUGUST 26

1902: Singer Jimmy Rushing, known as "Mr. Five-by-Five" because of his height and girth, is born in Oklahoma City.

Rushing began singing in clubs in the Midwest. From 1923 to 1924 he worked with Jelly Roll Morton in California. In 1927 he worked with Walter Page's band, and in 1929 he joined Bennie Moten's orchestra. He and Count Basie worked in the Moten organization until Moten's death. When Basie formed his own band, Rushing became its chief vocalist. Rushing provided the vocals on such Basie hits as "Sent for You Yesterday" (1938), "Boogie Woogie" (1937), "Pennies From Heaven" (1937), "I Want a Little Girl" (1940), "Goin' to Chicago Blues" (1941), "Rusty Dusty Blues" (1943) and "Jimmy's Blues" (1945).

Rushing left Basie in 1948. He returned in 1949 but in 1950 formed his own band. In 1952 he became a solo performer, touring the U.S. and Europe. In 1958 he worked the Brussels World's Fair with Benny Goodman. In the mid-1960s he toured Europe with Count Basie. In 1969 he appeared in the film *The Learning Tree*. There are several first-rate CD collections of Rushing's recorded material, including *Jimmy Rushing*, *The Bluesway Sessions* and *Good Morning Blues*.

Jimmy Rushing died on June 8, 1972.

1960: Jazz saxophonist Branford Marsalis is born in New Orleans.

Marsalis is the eldest of six sons born to pianist Ellis Marsalis and his wife, Delores. He grew up in the shadow of his brother Wynton, who was an honor student and an acclaimed musical genius and who by the age of 14 was a trumpet soloist with the New Orleans Philharmonic Orchestra. Branford Marsalis began taking piano lessons at the age of four. By age six he was playing clarinet. At 15 he turned his attention to the alto sax. He was an all-state saxophonist in high school and began playing in local pop-funk bands. He soon turned his attention to jazz. He studied at Southern University and at Boston's Berklee School of Music.

In 1980 and 1981 he played with such outstanding jazz greats as Art Blakey, Lionel Hampton and Clark Terry. Later in 1981 he joined his brother Wynton's group and played on Wynton's first album. He also made the tenor sax his primary instrument.

In 1984 Marsalis recorded his first solo project, *Scenes in the City*, but it drew little reaction from disc jockeys, critics or record buyers. Marsalis then left his brother's group to play with rock star Sting's band. He spent nearly two years on the road with Sting's worldwide *Dream of the Blue Turtles* tour. That period in his life did two things for Marsalis: it game him a much-needed break from jazz, and it gave fans and critics the world over a chance to notice his musical ability.

When he recorded his second solo LP, *Royal Garden Blues*, in 1986, he found a ready audience. That year he also released the album *Romances for Saxophone*, with the English Chamber Orchestra, conducted by Andrew Litton. The following year came his highly acclaimed *Renaissance* LP.

On his later recordings, produced by his brother Delfeayo, Branford is accompanied by first-rate sidemen like pianist Kenny Kirkland, bassists Ron Carter and Bob Hurst and drummer Tony Williams. His 1990s recordings include *The Beautiful Ones Are Not Yet Born* and *I Heard You Twice the First Time*.

In 1992, when the Johnny Carson "Tonight Show" era ended and Jay Leno took over, Branford Marsalis became the leader of the "Tonight Show" band.

AUGUST 27

1909: Jazz saxophonist Lester Young, often credited with being the first to make the saxophone a true reed instrument and an important element in jazz, is born in Woodville, Mississippi.

Young's father taught him to play trumpet, alto sax, drums and violin. In 1920 the family moved to Minneapolis.

After touring with his family band, Young met bandleader Art Bronson, who introduced him to the tenor sax.

In 1928 and 1929 Young played with Bronson's Bronsoneans. In 1933 he joined Bennie Moten's group and became a member of Count Basie's first band. He worked for a short time with the bands of Fletcher Henderson and Andy Kirk before rejoining Basie, in 1936. He stayed with Basie until 1940.

In 1941 Lester Young formed his own orchestra, which he disbanded in 1943. In 1944 Young had a string of R&B chart hits, including "Sometimes I'm Happy," "Just You, Just Me" and "Lester Leaps Again." In the same year, Young was drafted, and the Army turned out to be a bad experience. Young was court martialed for marijuana use. Then he became ill and was discharged, in 1945.

In 1946 Young began a long association with Norman Granz's *Jazz at the Philharmonic* shows and formed his own small combo. In 1951 he played Carnegie Hall. Young's best LPs include *The Savoy Recordings* and *The Jazz Giants*. He was also featured in the 1944 film *Jamming the Blues*.

By the late 1950s his health was a major problem. Lester Young died on March 15, 1959, in New York City.

AUGUST 28

1976: LTD makes its chart debut.
LTD (Love, Togetherness and Devotion) was formed in North Carolina as a backup band for Sam and Dave. In 1971 LTD moved to California to back Merry Clayton.

With Jeffrey Osborne singing lead, LTD had such black and pop hits as "Love Ballad" (1976), "Back in Love Again" (1977), "Never Get Enough of Your Love" (1978), "Holding On" (1978) and "Where Did We Go Wrong" (1980).

When Osborne went solo, in 1980, Leslie Wilson became LTD's lead vocalist. The group's biggest post-Osborne hit was "Kickin' Back," in 1981.

AUGUST 29

1920: Saxophonist Charlie "Bird" Parker, arguably the greatest instrumental soloist in the history of jazz, is born in Kansas City, Kansas.

Parker was raised in Kansas City and got his first sax at the age of 11. As a teenager he saw Count Basie's band and was blown away by the sax work of Lester Young. Parker quit school in order to concentrate all his efforts on mastering the saxophone.

In 1936 he joined Tommy Douglas's band. In 1937 he joined Buster Smith's band and was hired in 1938 by Jay McShann.

In 1939 Parker met Dizzy Gillespie, who was touring with Cab Calloway's orchestra.

Parker went to New York City and began jamming with local jazz musicians. He rejoined McShann's band from 1940 to 1942, making his first appearance on records. In 1942 he joined Gillespie in Earl "Fatha" Hines's band. He also worked briefly in the bands of Andy Kirk and Noble Sissle before joining Gillespie in the band of Billy Eckstine.

In 1944 and 1945 Parker and Gillespie were instrumental in establishing the jazz genre of bebop in small-group settings with other musicians, like Kenny Clarke and Milt Jackson. Parker's first recording session as a leader came in December 1945, for Savoy Records.

Gillespie and Parker took bebop to the West Coast, where they recorded and were featured in the *Jazz at the Philharmonic* shows in 1946. Gillespie returned to New York, and Parker stayed in California.

In 1946 Parker recorded the bebop classics "Ornithology," "Yardbird Suite" and "Night in Tunisia." He also spent six months in Camarillo State Hospital, trying to kick a drug habit.

In early 1947 he returned to New York and formed a quintet that included Miles Davis, Duke Jordan, Tommy Potter and Max Roach. In 1948 he signed a long-term contract with *Jazz at the Philharmonic* mogul Norman Granz.

In 1949 he played the Paris Jazz Festival. In 1950 he recorded with strings.

Parker also toured and guested with the bands of Woody Herman and Stan Kenton in the early 1950s. Parker recorded prolifically, and there are many LPs, tapes and CDs of his work. Some of the best are *Bird/The Savoy Recordings*; *Bird and Diz*; *Now's the Time*; *Charlie Parker on Dial, Vol. 1*; *One Night in Birdland*; *Summit Meeting in Birdland*; *Bird on Verve*; *The Essential Charlie Parker*; and *Bird—The Complete Charlie Parker*.

At the age of 34, also suffering from cirrhosis of the liver, Charlie Parker died of heart failure on March 12, 1955, in New York City.

CHARLIE PARKER

1924: Dinah Washington, one of the most uncategorizable vocalists ever, is born Ruth Jones in Tuscaloosa, Alabama.

Washington moved to Chicago in 1927. At the age of 15 she won an amateur contest at Chicago's Regal Theater.

In 1940 and 1941 she sang with Sallie Martin's gospel singers. From 1941 to 1943 she sang in local nightclubs like the Garrick Bar and the Flame Show Bar.

In 1943 she was hired by Lionel Hampton. That year she also cut her first records, using musicians from Hampton's band. Washington performed the vocals on such Hampton hits as "Salty Papa

Blues" (1944), "Evil Gal Blues" (1944) and "Blowtop Blues" (1947).

Dinah Washington went solo in 1946. In 1948 she began a run of R&B chart hits with "Ain't Misbehavin'." Late in 1948 she hit number 1 on the R&B charts with "Am I Asking Too Much."

Over the next 13 years Washington compiled a long list of top R&B and pop singles. Her best-sellers include "It's Too Soon to Know" (1948), "Baby, Get Lost" (1949), "Long John Blues" (1949), "I Only Know" (1950), "I'll Never Be Free" (1950), "I Won't Cry Anymore" (1951), "Cold, Cold Heart" (1951), "Wheel of Fortune" (1952), "TV Is the Thing" (1953), "I Don't Hurt Anymore" (1954), "Teach Me Tonight" (1954), "What a Difference a Day Makes" (1959), "This Bitter Earth" (1960) and "September in the Rain" (1961). In 1960 she and Brook Benton hit number 1 on the R&B charts twice, with the duets "Baby (You Got What It Takes)" and "Rockin' Good Way."

There are also several great collections of Washington's recordings, including *The Essential Dinah Washington*, *What a Difference a Day Makes*, *The Bessie Smith Songbook*, *Dinah Jams*, *If You Don't Believe I'm Leaving* and *A Slick Chick on the Mellow Side*.

On December 14, 1963, Dinah Washington died from an overdose of alcohol and diet pills.

1958: Michael Jackson is born in Gary, Indiana.

Jackson became a superstar at the age of 11, as lead singer for the Jackson Five. Michael and his brothers were discovered by Diana Ross and became the 1970s darlings of the Motown stable. They ran up a string of number 1 hits in 1970 and 1971.

While still a part of the family group, Michael Jackson had solo hits with "Got to Be There" and "Rockin' Robin." In 1972, he became the youngest performer ever to hit number 1, when "Ben" reached the top of the charts.

In 1976 Jackson costarred with Ross in the Motown-produced musical *The Wiz*. He left the Jacksons and Motown in 1979 to record solo for the Epic label. His first LP, *Off the Wall*, was a harbinger of things to come—namely, the 1983 *Thriller* album.

Thriller, produced by Jackson and Quincy Jones, totally dominated the 1983 Grammy awards and netted Jackson awards in several categories. It also produced a string of monster single releases—the title cut and "Billie Jean," "Beat It," "P.Y.T. (Pretty Young Thing)" and "The Girl Is Mine." He had able assistance on the project from the likes of guest stars Paul McCartney, Eddie Van Halen and Vincent Price.

The series of videos that accompanied the project made Jackson the first music-video superstar. The dynamically choreographed "Beat It" and the 15-minute mini–monster movie "Thriller," directed by John Landis, stand out.

After the release of *Thriller* Jackson took part in the much-ballyhooed Jacksons' *Victory* tour. The tour was conceived by Jackson's father and then-manager, Joe Jackson, and it was preceded by a seemingly endless stream of press reports detailing problem after problem. Tickets were sold by lottery. Before it was over, it involved promoters ranging from boxing mogul Don King to the owner of the New England Patriots football team. Once on the road, it was apparent that it was Michael Jackson's show.

In 1987 Jackson released his *Bad* LP, spawning yet more Michaelmania. "Bad," "The Way You Make Me Feel" and "The Man in the Mirror" all hit number 1. Michael's video magic was also apparent once again in the title video (directed by Martin Scorsese) and the hauntingly reflective "The Man in the Mirror," which featured a video collage of children from around the world. In late 1987 Jackson embarked on his *Bad* tour, his first solo excursion ever, accompanied by a 15-piece backup group, 700 tons of equipment and an entourage of 120. He landed first in Japan and Australia, to rave reviews and near riots, before hitting the United States in March 1988 to much the same reaction.

Critics say that Michael Jackson's greatest magic, or "badness," is in his live performances. His unbridled energy manifests itself in stage productions that rival Broadway shows. Jackson has unmatched vocal stylings and is a master dancer as well. His appreciation and admiration for such screen dance sensations as Fred Astaire and Gene Kelly, along with his natural talent, make Jackson's choreography one of a kind. He also claims the dancing of James Brown as a strong influence.

Jackson is often in the news because of relationships with friends like Elizabeth Taylor and child actor Emmanuel Lewis, his private zoo, his oxygen chamber and his much-talked-about cosmetic surgery. He is also known for his charitable and humanitarian efforts. He was one of the creators of the *We Are the World* LP, recorded to benefit starving people in Africa. He donated a burn unit to a California hospital. Through benefit concerts and direct donations, Michael Jackson is also one of the all-time top contributors to the United Negro College Fund.

AUGUST 30

1982: Zapp's "Dance Floor" is the number 1 black chart single.

Zapp was one of the premier funk bands of the early 1980s. The nucleus of the group was made up of brothers Roger, Lester, Tony and Larry Troutman. Zapp had such other hits as "More Bounce to the Ounce" (1980), "I Can Make You Dance" (1983) and "Computer Love, Part 1" (1986). Roger Troutman has also recorded as a solo artist. He hit the number 1 spot on the black charts with "I Heard It Through the Grapevine" (1981) and "I Want to Be Your Man" (1987).

AUGUST 31

1900: Pianist, arranger and bandleader Todd Rhodes is born in Hopkinsville, Kentucky.

Rhodes had one of the best R&B bands in the late 1940s. Among his band's vocalists was LaVern Baker.

Rhodes played with McKinney's Cotton Pickers from 1921 until 1934. He organized his own band in 1946 and had such R&B hits as "Blues for the Red Boy" (1948) and "Pot Likker" (1949). His group also backed Wynonie Harris on several of his late hits.

Todd Rhodes died in 1975.

1940: Bassist and saxophonist Wilton Felder is born in Houston.

Felder is a founder of the Crusaders. He also enjoys a successful solo recording career. His biggest hit single came in 1985, with "I'll Still Be Looking Up to You." His LPs include *We All Have a Star*, *Gentle Fire* and *Secrets*.

SEPTEMBER 1

1944: Singer Archie Bell is born in Henderson, Texas.

In 1968 Archie Bell and the Drells burst on the scene with a million-selling number 1 soul and pop hit called "The Tighten Up." When the song first hit, Bell was in the U.S. Army, stationed in Germany. The Drells on "The Tighten Up" were Huey Butler, Joe Cross and James Wise. For most of their chart hits, the Drells were James Wise, Lee Bell and Willie Parnell.

Archie Bell and the Drells placed records on the charts until the late 1970s. Their biggest hits include "I Can't Stop Dancing" (1968), "There's Gonna Be a Showdown" (1968), "Girl, You're Too Young" (1969), "Dancing to Your Music" (1973) and "Let's Groove" (1976).

1956: The Five Satins make their chart debut with "In the Still of the Night," one of the songs that defined the doo-wop era. It sold over a million copies and today is one of radio's most requested oldies.

The Five Satins were lead singer Fred Parris, Al Denby, Jim Freeman, Eddie Martin and Jessie Murphy. Parris was in the Army in Japan when the song became a hit. The group's follow-up, "To the Aisle" (1957), featured the lead vocal of Bill Baker. Parris returned to the group in 1958. Later Five Satins hits were "Shadows" (1959) and "I'll Be Seeing You" (1960).

SEPTEMBER 2

1928: Jazz pianist and composer Horace Silver is born in Norwalk, Connecticut.

Silver came to notice in 1950 with Stan Getz's group. In 1952 and 1953 he was in Lester Young's band. In 1954 he recorded with Miles Davis, and in 1955 he co-led a group with drummer Art Blakey. The group was the nucleus of what was to become Blakey's famed Jazz Messengers.

That group recorded one of Silver's best-known pieces, "The Preacher."

Silver left the band and formed his own quintet. Over the years, the Horace Silver Quintet has featured such musicians as Art Farmer, Blue Mitchell, Randy and Michael Brecker and Joe Henderson.

Horace Silver's best LPs include *A Song for My Father, Blowin' the Blues Away* and *Horace Silver Live.*

HORACE SILVER

1943: Singer Joe Simon is born in Simmesport, Louisiana.

Simon began his career as a gospel singer. In 1962 he had a moderate hit with "My Adorable One," for Vee Jay Records. In the mid-1960s he met famed WLAC disc jockey John "R" Richburg and signed with his Sound Stage 7 label.

Simon, with his super voice and soulful material, is nevertheless one of the most underrated male soul singers of the '60s and '70s. Between 1965 and 1981 he placed about 50 singles on the soul and pop charts, including a trio of million-sellers: "The Chockin' Kind" (1969), "Drowning in a Sea of Love"

(1971) and "Power of Love" (1972). Other hits include "Teenager's Prayer" (1966), "Nine-Pound Steel" (1967), "Hangin' On" (1968), "Farther On Down the Road" (1970), "Your Love" (1970), "Your Time to Cry" (1970), "Trouble in My Home" (1972), "Step by Step" (1973), "Theme from *Cleopatra Jones*" (1973), "River" (1973), "Get Down, Get Down" (1975), "Music in My Bones" (1975) and "I Need You, You Need Me" (1976).

1957: The Bobbettes make their chart debut with "Mr. Lee."

The Bobbettes were one of the earliest successful female R&B and rock 'n' roll groups. They hailed from New York City and were originally called the Harlem Queens. The group consisted of sisters Emma and Jannie Pought and Laura Webb, Helen Gathers and Heather Dixon. All were between the ages of 11 and 15. The girls wrote "Mr. Lee" about their school principal. It went Top 10 on both the R&B and pop charts. The Bobbettes also had a few other chart records, including "I Shot Mr. Lee" (1960) and "Dance with Me, Georgie" (1960).

SEPTEMBER 3

1915: Vocalist and pianist Memphis Slim is born Peter Chatmon in Memphis.

Memphis Slim taught himself to play piano at the age of seven and was working cafes and juke joints around Memphis by the age of 16.

He moved to Chicago around 1937 and worked with Big Bill Broonzy and Washboard Sam. He cut his first sides in 1940, for Okeh Records. Some of his earliest records were "Beer-Drinking Woman" and "Grinder Man Blues."

Throughout the early 1940s Memphis Slim played clubs and theaters. By the mid-1940s he had his own band, the Houserockers.

In 1948 Memphis Slim began hitting the R&B charts regularly. Some of his best-known hits were "Messin' Around" (1948), "Blue and Lonesome" (1949), "Help Me Some" (1949), "Angel Child" (1949), "Mother Earth" (1951) and "The Comeback" (1953). Among his best albums are *Memphis Slim USA*, *Rockin' the Blues*, *Memphis Slim* and *Southside Reunion*.

In the late 1950s Memphis Slim recorded and toured with Willie Dixon. He also played Carnegie Hall and the Newport Folk Festival.

Memphis Slim also acquired quite a following abroad. In 1961 he moved to Paris. He recorded, made TV appearances and toured throughout England and the rest of Europe. He was especially popular in France and Germany, and he established the United Black Artists Booking Agency to bring other artists to Europe.

Memphis Slim died of kidney failure on February 24, 1988, in Paris.

1934: Blues guitarist Freddie King is born in Gilmer, Texas.

King settled in Chicago in 1950 and worked clubs with the bands of Little Sonny Cooper and Hound Dog Taylor. He formed his own group, the Every Hour Blues Boys, and began recording about 1956.

In 1960 he signed with Federal Records and became one of the few hard-core bluesmen to hit the pop charts. He did it with a series of instrumentals: "Hide Away" (1961), "Lonesome Whistle Blues" (1961), "San Hozay" (1961) and "I'm Tore Down" (1961). Some of his best LPs are *Hideaway*, *Freddie King Sings* and *Just Pickin'*.

Freddie King died on December 28, 1976.

SEPTEMBER 4

1905: Meade "Lux" Lewis, the most famous of all the boogie-woogie piano players, is born in Chicago.

As a child Lewis was dubbed the Duke of Luxembourg, hence the nickname Lux. He studied violin and then took up piano, playing in clubs and bars in Chicago.

In 1928 he recorded a song called "Honky Tonk Train Blues," but the record had little success. Lewis quit playing and went to work for the federal Works Progress Administration. He was also a taxi driver.

In 1935 a talent scout, John Hammond, discovered the record and traced Lewis, and Lewis began performing again in 1938. Hammond took him to New York to play with two other top boogie-woogie pianists, Albert Ammons and Pete Johnson. In 1941 Lewis made California his base of operations when he was not touring.

Meade "Lux" Lewis died in an auto crash on June 7, 1964, in Minneapolis.

1961: Solomon Burke, gospel-inspired soul singer, makes his chart debut with "Just Out of Reach."

Burke came from a deeply religious family and received his early vocal training in church. He became a soloist at the age of nine. By the time he was 12 he was known as the "wonder-boy preacher." He had his own church, Solomon's Temple, and his own radio show.

Burke was signed by Apollo Records in the early 1950s. He had a spiritual hit with the song "Christmas Present from Heaven," which he wrote for his grandmother.

Burke quit preaching and recording to study to become a mortician, but he returned in 1960 and signed with Atlantic Records. Beginning in 1961 and continuing into the late 1970s, Burke had a run of over 30 pop and R&B hits. His best-sellers include "Cry to Me" (1962), "If You Need Me" (1963), "You're Good for Me" (1963), "Goodbye, Baby" (1964), "Got to Get You Off My Mind" (1965), "Tonight's the Night" (1965), "Keep a Light in the Window Until I Come Home" (1967), "Take Me" (1967) and "Midnight and You" (1974).

In the mid-1970s he experimented with a sound best described as country soul. In 1981 Burke recorded the LP *Soul Alive*. He has also recorded such gospel LPs as *Lord, I Need a Miracle Right Now* and *This Is His Song*.

SEPTEMBER 5

1907: Blues pianist Sunnyland Slim is born Albert Luandrew in Vance, Mississippi.

In the 1920s and 1930s he played with Ma Rainey and Sonny Boy Williamson; in the late 1940s, with Little Walter and Muddy Waters, when he began his recording career. His best LPs are *Sunnyland Slim*, *The Devil Is a Busy Man*, *Sad and Lonesome* and *Slim's Got a Thing Goin' On*. While he has toured the world, his main stomping ground is the Chicago club circuit, where he has been playing for nearly 50 years.

1946: Rock drummer Buddy Miles is born in Omaha.

In the late '60s and early '70s he was one of the hottest rock drummers around. With his band, the Buddy Miles Express, he had such hits as "Memphis Train" (1969), "Them Changes" (1970) and "Wholesale Love" (1971). Miles was also one of the busiest and most sought-after session musicians of the era. In 1963 he worked as a drummer for the *Dick Clark Caravan of Stars*, and from 1965 to 1966 he was with Wilson Pickett's band.

Miles got into the hard-rock scene in 1967, when he joined Michael Bloomfield's Electric Flag. In 1969 and 1970 he was a member of the Jimi Hendrix–led supergroup Band of Gypsies.

BUDDY MILES

1964: Singer and songwriter Don Covay makes his chart debut with "Mercy, Mercy."

Covay was born in Orangeburg, South Carolina, in 1938 and was raised in Washington, D.C. In 1958 he joined a group called the Rainbows, which included Marvin Gaye and Billy Stewart.

He became a staff writer for Roosevelt Music and had songs recorded by Jerry Butler and Gladys Knight. Covay also composed such chart smashes as "Pony Time," for Chubby Checker; "Sookie Sookie," for Roy Thompson; and "Chain of Fools," for Aretha Franklin.

In 1960 he formed the band the Goodtimers and signed with Atlantic Records. As a recording artist, Don Covay has had hits with "See Saw" (1965), "I Was Checkin' Out and She Was Checkin' In" (1973) and "It's Better to Have" (1974).

SEPTEMBER 6

1877: Cornet player Buddy Bolden, said to be the first jazz musician, is born in New Orleans.

It is believed that Bolden was raised on First Street in New Orleans and learned the cornet from a friend of his mother. He started playing in Charlie Galloway's dance band around 1897.

Bolden was a charismatic performer and a unique improvisationalist. By 1900 he was playing clubs and dance halls all over New Orleans. By 1904 he was called King Bolden.

In 1906, according to reports, during his performance in the Labor Day parade, Bolden underwent a complete nervous breakdown. He never played again, and in May 1907 he was committed to the Jackson Mental Institute, where he remained until his death, on November 4, 1931. Buddy Bolden never recorded.

1925: Blues singer, songwriter, guitarist and harmonica player Jimmy Reed is born Mathis James Reed in Dunleith, Mississippi.

Reed began singing in church choirs around the age of seven. He was taught guitar by a boyhood friend and future blues singer named Eddie Taylor.

He moved to Chicago in 1943. He served in the U.S. Navy in 1944 and 1945 and returned to Mississippi after his discharge. In the late 1940s he moved to Gary, Indiana, and began playing in clubs with John Brim's band.

During the late '40s and early '50s he had a band made up basically of himself; his wife, Mary Lee "Mama" Reed; Eddie Taylor; and Albert King, who was then a drummer.

Jimmy Reed began recording in 1953. He signed with Vee Jay Records and began hitting the R&B and pop charts, becoming the most successful of the era's hard-core bluesmen. He scored more chart hits than either Muddy Waters or Howlin' Wolf. His biggest hits included "You Don't Have to Go" (1955), "Ain't That Lovin' You, Baby" (1956), "You've Got Me Dizzy" (1956), "Little Rain" (1957), "Honest I Do" (1957), "Baby, What Do You Want Me To Do" (1960), "Big Boss Man" (1961) and "Bright Lights, Big City" (1961). His best LPs are *Big Boss Blues*, *The Best of Jimmy Reed*, *High and Lonesome* and *Upside Your Head*.

Because he eschewed the formula 12-bar blues, Reed is ranked among the most influential of blues artists, although insiders and bluesologists claim that much of the credit for Jimmy Reed's songs and style must go to his wife.

Jimmy Reed constantly toured the U.S. and Europe. He played venues that ranged from the Playboy Club to the Apollo Theater, from the Ann Arbor Blues Festival to the British pop TV show "Ready, Steady, Go."

He began suffering from epilepsy in 1957. On August 29, 1976, he had an epileptic seizure and died.

SEPTEMBER 7

1929: Jazz saxophonist Theodore Walter "Sonny" Rollins is born in New York City.

Rollins had set out to be a painter, but he took up the tenor sax in high school. By 1947 he was working recording sessions with singers Babs Gonzalez, J. J. Johnson and Bud Powell.

In the late '40s and early '50s Rollins recorded and played live with Thelonious Monk, Art Blakey, Miles Davis and Tadd Dameron.

He began recording as a solo artist and group leader in 1951. In 1954 Rollins left the New York music scene and moved to Chicago to try to kick his

drug habit. In 1955, he joined the Max Roach–Clifford Brown quintet.

In 1956 Rollins issued his critically acclaimed LP *Saxophone Colossus*. In the late '50s he took two years off from performing to study.

In 1961 he formed the quartet Sonny Rollins and Company and signed with RCA Records. Over the decades, Rollins has turned out such classic jazz LPs as *Sonny Rollins Plus Four*, *Way Out West*, *The Bridge* and *Sunny Days, Starry Nights*. With the coming of CDs, Sonny Rollins currently has over four dozen works in print, including his early work with Monk, Davis and John Coltrane.

1934: Blues singer Little Milton is born Milton Campbell, Jr., in Inverness, Mississippi.

He formed his first band in Memphis, in 1951, and recorded for the Sun label in the early 1950s. He has also recorded for such top labels as Checker, Stax, Glades, MCA and Malaco.

His biggest sellers include "We're Gonna Make It" (1965), "Who's Cheating Who" (1965), "Feel So Bad" (1967), "Grits Ain't Groceries" (1969), "If Walls Could Talk" (1969), "Baby, I Love You" (1970), "That's What Love Will Do" (1972), "A Friend of Mine" (1976) and "Age Ain't Nothing But a Number" (1983).

Little Milton's blues style is closely akin to that of Bobby "Blue" Bland, which is one reason for his commercial R&B and pop success. Over the years, Little Milton has placed nearly 30 hits on the singles charts.

1939: Singer Latimore is born Benjamin Latimore in Charleston, Tennessee.

Latimore was one of the top artists on the hot Florida-based Glades label of the 1970s. His biggest hits were "Let's Straighten It Out" (1974), "Keep the Home Fires Burning" (1975) and "Something About Cha" (1976).

Latimore has a knack for choosing songs with unique lyrics. He is a truly underrated and underpromoted talent. He currently records for Malaco.

1949: Singer Gloria Gaynor, one of the most popular and successful

performers of the disco era, is born in Newark, New Jersey.

Her biggest hits include "Never Can Say Goodbye" (1974), "Do It Yourself" (1975) and "I Will Survive" (1979).

SEPTEMBER 8

1927: Harmonica Fats, billed as "320 pounds of the blues," is born Harvey Blackson in McDade, Louisiana.

He taught himself to play the harp as a youngster working on his grandfather's farm. He began playing clubs around Los Angeles in the mid-1940s. In 1961 he hit the R&B charts with a song called "Tore Up."

Harmonica Fats is still performing. He had a small part in the Oliver Stone film *The Doors*, and his current LP is called *I Had to Get Nasty*.

SEPTEMBER 9

1937: Jazz drummer Elvin Jones, brother of jazzmen Hank and Thad Jones, is born in Pontiac, Michigan.

After getting out of the service, in 1949, Jones played with the Detroit-based group of Billy Mitchell. In 1955 he moved to New York, where he recorded with Miles Davis, Charles Mingus and Sonny Rollins. In 1956 he joined J. J. Johnson's quintet.

Jones also became part of John Coltrane's famed quartet, remaining with Coltrane until 1966. Later that year he formed his own group.

Elvin Jones is one of jazz's most dynamic drummers, equally at home in mainstream jazz, free jazz and fusion.

1941: Otis Redding is born in Macon, Georgia.

It is sad to note that Otis Redding, one of the world's truly legendary R&B singers, was discovered by most of Top 40 Middle America only on the occasion of his death. Redding became national news when he and several members of the vocal-instrumental group the Barkays perished in the crash of a chartered plane on December 10, 1967, in Lake Momona, near Madison, Wisconsin.

With his memory fresh in the nation's mind, Volt released what was to be Otis Redding's biggest record, in mid-

January 1968. The record was "(Sitting on the) Dock of the Bay," a wistful, almost folksy upbeat ballad, which Redding had written with Booker T. and the MGs guitarist Steve Cropper and recorded only three days before his death. "Dock of the Bay" went to number 1 on the pop charts, sold over a million copies, stayed on the charts for more than four months and today is considered a pop classic. During his lifetime, the best any of Redding's records had ever done on the national Top 40 music charts was number 21—"(I've Been) Loving You Too Long (to Stop Now)," in the summer of 1965. His best-known black-music chart toppers, songs such as "These Arms of Mine," "Mr. Pitiful," "Respect," "Satisfaction" and "Fa-Fa-Fa-Fa-Fa (Sad Song)," had made only brief appearances on the *Billboard* and *Cashbox* Hot 100 charts or had languished near the middle or bottom. Also ironic is the fact that, with Redding's posthumous popularity, "Dock of the Bay" debuted on the pop charts two weeks before it hit the black charts, on which he had been a constant presence for the previous five years.

Otis Redding was a large, muscular man who stood over six feet tall and weighed in at around 210 pounds. He was ruggedly handsome and flashed a broad grin. The blues were deeply ingrained in his vocals and songwriting, but he did not exhibit the traditional sulky brooding of a bluesman.

Redding was a consummate entertainer. His voice was made for the plaintive wailing, pleading style of pop blues that became his trademark. Onstage he moved, danced, glided, dropped to his knees or ran in place to the drummer's beat, especially during the upbeat vamp near the closing of "Loving You Too Long."

Redding first became interested in music by singing in church choirs. Later he sang at local clubs and dances. A childhood friend, Phil Walden (later to become head of Capricorn Records and manager of the Allman Brothers), got Redding a gig as a combination vocalist and roadie with a recording group known as Johnny Jenkins and the Pinetoppers,

in 1959. Redding first recorded with the Pinetoppers in 1960, for a small independent label called Confederate Records. In 1962 the Pinetoppers had booked recording time in the Stax Records studios. When they finished recording their material, there was still some studio time left, so Redding cut two of his own songs. One of them was the ballad "These Arms of Mine."

The soulful sound caught the ear of Stax president Jim Stewart, who signed Redding to the Stax subsidiary label Volt Records. "These Arms of Mine" entered the R&B charts in March 1963 and reached number 20, making Redding an instant success. Over the next two years he released other R&B hits: "Pain in My Heart" (1963), "Security" (1964), "Chained and Bound" (1964) and "Mr. Pitiful" (1965). In mid-1965 he recorded and released the aforementioned "Loving You Too Long," reportedly written by Redding and Jerry Butler backstage between shows at the Apollo Theater. The ballad sailed into the R&B Top 5 and into the Top 20 on some pop charts around the country.

Redding followed "Loving You Too Long" with "Respect," the torrid rocker that later would become an anthem for the queen of soul, Aretha Franklin, and with a soul-stirring remake of the Rolling Stones' hit "Satisfaction."

By this time Redding had become a black-music superstar on records and in person. He headlined the Stax/Volt Revue in England in 1965, and he sold out clubs and concerts in the U.S. In 1966 Redding had such hits as "My Lover's Prayer," "Sad Song" and "Try a Little Tenderness."

In 1967 Redding began to expand his horizons and move into other musical avenues. He recorded an album of duets with Stax Records top vocalist Carla Thomas. The album contained a funkily refreshing, tongue-in-cheek version of bluesman Lowell Fulson's "Tramp" and a rendition of Eddie Floyd's "Knock on Wood." That year Redding also made an appearance at the Monterey Pop Festival, a signal event in the newborn hippie counterculture and the newly emerging underground and psychedelic music trends. Redding performed along with such new acts as Jimi Hendrix and Janis Joplin. Audience members who had previously dismissed contemporary black music were taken with the charisma and high energy of Redding's performance at Monterey, which was captured on film in *Monterey Pop*, currently available on videocassette.

Otis Redding had a unique sound. His music was deeply rooted in gospel and country blues, but he was also influenced by the mellow pop sound of Sam Cooke. Redding was able to combine all of this into his vocals, which were ably backed up by the Memphis Horns and the laid-back funk of the Booker T. and the MGs rhythm section, which served as the standard Stax/Volt recording combo of the 1960s. Redding also wrote most of his material.

Otis Redding recorded in an era when the emphasis was on singles, but several of his LPs are classics: *Pain in My Heart*, *Otis Redding's Dictionary of Soul*, *Otis Redding Live in Europe* and his best hit compilation, *The History of Otis Redding*, released in 1967, before his death.

OTIS REDDING

1942: Singer Inez Foxx is born in Greensboro, North Carolina.

Foxx hit the pop and R&B charts in the summer of 1962, with the single "Mockingbird," which featured her brother Charlie on backup vocals. She continued to record into the 1970s, but "Mockingbird" was her only hit.

1945: Singer Dee Dee Sharp is born Dione La Roux in Philadelphia.

Sharp was working as a backup vocalist at Cameo Parkway Records when she gained national attention for her work on Chubby Checker's hit "Slow Twistin'" in 1962. She was immediately signed to a recording contract and began hitting the pop Top 10 with hits like "Mashed Potato Time" (1962), "Gravy" (1962), "Ride" (1962) and "Do the Bird" (1963). She appeared in the film *Don't Knock the Twist* and toured with the *Dick Clark Caravan of Stars*. She continued to hit the charts, with such tunes as "Wild" (1963), "Where Did I Go Wrong" (1964), "Willyam Willyam" (1964) and "I Really Love You" (1966).

In 1967 Dee Dee Sharp married record producer Kenny Gamble. She recorded several LPs in the 1970s for her husband's labels, TSOP and Philadelphia International.

1946: Vocalist and keyboardist Billy Preston is born in Houston.

Preston was considered a keyboard wizard by the age of 10. He worked with Mahalia Jackson in 1956 and appeared in the 1958 film *St. Louis Blues*. He was also a member of the band in the 1960s TV music show "Shindig." He caught the ear of the Beatles and can be heard on "Get Back" and "Let It Be." Preston has been a sought-after session player as well.

As a recording artist, Preston scored three million-selling singles: "Outa Space" (1972), "Will It Go Round in Circles" (1973) and "Nothing from Nothing" (1974). In the early 1980s Billy Preston turned to gospel music. In 1982 he had a best-selling gospel LP, *Behold*.

1989: Rap group 2 Live Crew makes its chart debut.

2 Live Crew is the brainchild of rapper, writer, producer and record-label owner Luther Campbell, whose rap name was Luke Skywalker (film director George Lucas sued Campbell and he had to stop using the name of the hero of *Star Wars*). Campbell started 2 Live Crew in the early 1980s with David "Mr. Mix" Hobbs, Chris "Fresh Kid Ice" Won Wong and Marquis Ross. In 1986 they recorded the LP *2 Live Crew Is What We Are*. In 1988 they released *Move Something*.

Between the lyrics on the 1990 LP *Nasty As They Wanna Be* and their concert performances, they sparked a national furor and a debate over censorship. A judge in Florida deemed the LP obscene, and it was pulled from record-store shelves. Several store owners who continued to sell it were arrested, and 2 Live Crew were arrested during a nightclub performance. The album sold a million copies, as did a single called "Me So Horny." 2 Live Crew also recorded a response to the controversy, "Banned in the USA," which likewise became a million-seller.

SEPTEMBER 10

1925: Singer and pianist Roy Brown, considered one of the originators of the New Orleans R&B sound, is born in New Orleans.

As a youth, Brown picked cotton, chopped sugarcane and harvested rice. At the age of 13 he organized a gospel quartet. He attended high school in Houston and at the age of 17 went to Los Angeles to become a boxer. He won first prize at amateur night at Los Angeles's Million Dollar Theater.

Brown's first professional job was at the Palace Park Club in Shreveport, Louisiana, where he sang mostly ballads like "Stardust." During this period he began writing and singing the blues.

In 1948 Brown returned to New Orleans and wrote "Good Rockin' Tonight." He approached Wynonie Harris (who later had the biggest hit with the song) about recording it but was turned down. Brown recorded "Good Rockin' Tonight," and it hit the R&B Top 20. Some say "Good Rockin' Tonight" was the first rock 'n' roll record.

Brown's next song, "Long About Midnight," hit number 1 on the R&B charts in the fall of 1948. He followed up with a string of more hits: "Fore Day in the Morning" (1949), "Rainy Weather Blues" (1949), "Rockin' at Midnight" (1949), "Miss Fanny Brown" (1949), "Please Don't Go" (1949), "Boogie at Midnight" (1949), "Hard Luck Blues" (1950), "Love Don't Love Nobody" (1950), "Long About Sundown" (1950),

"Cadillac Baby" (1950), "Big Town" (1951) and "Barroom Blues" (1951).

Roy Brown died on May 25, 1981.

1940: Jazz vibraphonist Roy Ayers is born in Los Angeles.

In the 1960s Ayers played with Herbie Mann's group. In 1970 he formed his own group, Ubiquity.

Ayers managed to capture the attention of rock and disco fans alike and had a run of soul chart singles that included "Running Away" (1977), "Freaky Deaky" (1978), "Don't Stop the Feeling" (1979) and "Hot" (1986).

1949: Brother Joe May records "Search Me, Lord."

In the late 1940s and early 1950s vibrant gospel singer Brother Joe May was called the Thunderbolt of the Midwest. May received his gospel-music training from the famed Willie Mae Ford Smith and sang with the electrifying power of a holiness preacher. He signed with Specialty Records in the late '40s. "Search Me, Lord" was his biggest hit. Others were "Old Ship of Zion" and "He'll Understand."

Throughout he '50s Brother Joe May was one of the most commercially successful gospel acts. In the late '50s he recorded for Nashboro Records. In the 1960s he toured Europe in *Black Nativity*.

SEPTEMBER 11

1902: Bluesman Barbeque Bob is born Robert Hicks in Walnut Grove, Georgia.

Barbeque Bob's recording career only lasted three years, from 1927 to 1930. He was one of the most popular of that era's bluesmen and took his name from the fact that he had a day job as a cook at Tidwell's Barbeque. He had a unique "hammering" bottleneck guitar style. His best collections of songs are on the LPs *Chocolate to the Bone* and *Barbeque Bob.*

Barbeque Bob died of pneumonia on October 21, 1931.

1961: The Marvelettes make their chart debut with "Please, Mr. Postman."

The Marvelettes were Motown's first hit "girl group." They were also the first Motown artists to hit number 1 on the pop charts.

The group was made up of co–lead singers Gladys Horton and Wanda Young, Katherine Anderson, Juanita Cowart and Georgeanna Tillman. The Marvelettes were formed in 1960 at Inkston High School in Inkston, Michigan, and got an audition with Motown after appearing in a school talent show.

"Please, Mr. Postman" hit number 1 on both the pop and R&B charts. Other best-selling Marvelettes singles are "Playboy" (1962), "Beachwood 4-5789" (1962), "Some Day, Some Way" (1962), "Strange, I Know" (1962), "Too Many Fish in the Sea" (1964), "Don't Mess with Bill" (1966), "The Hunter Gets Captured by the Game" (1967), "When You're Young and in Love" (1967) and "My Baby Must Be a Magician" (1967).

Early on Juanita Cowart left the group because she didn't like life on the road. In 1967 Gladys Horton left, and the group disbanded in 1969. Georgeanna Tillman died of sickle cell anemia in January 1980.

SEPTEMBER 12

1900: Bluesman Alger "Texas" Alexander is born in Jewett, Texas.

Not a lot is known about Texas Alexander. For most of his life he was an itinerant musician in Texas and Oklahoma. He spent 1940 to 1945 in prison for killing his wife.

Some have called Alexander the voice of Texas blues because it is said that his rough blues shouts, field hollers and chain-gang moans captured more of the feel and intensity of Texas sharecroppers and prisoners than did the work of any other artist.

Alexander was strictly a singer. He did not play guitar, but he worked with some of the best players of the era, including Blind Lemon Jefferson, Lonnie Johnson and Lightnin' Hopkins.

Alexander began recording in 1927. One of his earliest hits was "Penitentiary Moan Blues." His best material can be found on a series of LPs released by Matchbox Records and titled *Texas Alexander, Vols. 1, 2 and 3.*

Texas Alexander died of syphilis on April 16, 1964.

1944: Singer, songwriter, producer and arranger Barry White is born in Galveston, Texas.

White grew up in Los Angeles. As a child he taught himself to play several instruments. At the age of 11 he played piano on Jesse Belvin's hit "Goodnight, My Love."

In 1960 he joined a vocal group called the Upfronts. White also began doing session work for small labels around Los Angeles. In the 1960s he arranged such R&B hits as "Harlem Shuffle," by Bob and Earl, and "The Duck," by Jackie Lee. In the mid-1960s he became head of the Artist and Repertoire Division for Mustang Records.

In 1972 White discovered the group Love Unlimited, which consisted of sisters Glodean and Linda James and Diane Taylor. He became their manager and wrote and produced their million-selling hit "Walkin' in the Rain with the One I Love." On July 4, 1974, White married Glodean James.

White secured a recording contract for the group and himself from Twentieth Century Records. His first hit came in early 1973, with the million-selling single "I'm Gonna Love You Just a Little More, Baby." He followed with a succession of hits written and produced by himself and arranged with Gene Page.

Throughout the 1970s White was the undeniable king of bedroom soul. His hits were all lavishly produced and lushly arranged, and they all dealt with his favorite subjects, love and romance. His best-sellers include "I've Got So Much to Give" (1973), "Never Never Gonna Give Ya Up" (1973), "Can't Get Enough of Your Love, Babe" (1974), "You're the First, the Last, My Everything" (1974), "What Am I Gonna Do with You" (1975), "I'll Do for You Anything You Want Me To" (1975), "Let the Music Play" (1975), "It's Ecstasy When You Lay Down Next to Me" (1977) and "Your Sweetness Is My Weakness" (1978).

White also conducted, arranged and produced the 40-piece Love Unlimited Orchestra, which had a million-selling single in 1973 called "Love's Theme." White also wrote the theme for the 1977 film remake of *King Kong.*

Barry White's hits declined in the early 1980s. He had a moderate hit with "Sho You Right," in 1987, and was heard on the Quincy Jones single "The Secret Garden" in 1990.

SEPTEMBER 13

1910: Jazz saxophonist Leon "Chu" Berry is born in Wheeling, West Virginia.

Chu Berry was one of the most popular tenor sax players of the big-band era. He played in the bands of Fletcher Henderson, Benny Carter and Cab Calloway. He got his nickname from a musician named Billy Stewart, who said Berry looked like a "Chu-chin Chow."

Chu Berry died on October 30, 1941, of injuries suffered in a car wreck.

1922: Singer and pianist Charles Brown is born in Texas City, Texas.

Brown studied classical piano in high school and earned his B.S. degree from Prairie View Agricultural and Mechanical College. In 1942 he taught at George Washington Carver High School, in Baytown, Texas. He moved to Los Angeles the following year. In 1943 he won an amateur contest at the Lincoln Theater, and later he worked in the theater's house band.

In 1944 he joined Johnny Moore's Three Blazers. Brown sang lead on the Blazers' biggest records, including "Drifting Blues," "Sunny Road," "New Orleans Blues" and "Merry Christmas, Baby."

In 1948 he formed his own band and began recording as a solo performer. Brown is the most important and most influential of the West Coast blues singers. His style is suave and sophisticated when compared to the styles of the Delta and Chicago blues shouters. His early hits include "Get Yourself Another Fool" (1949), "Long Time" (1949), "Trouble Blues" (1949), "In the Evening When the Sun Goes Down" (1949), "Homesick Blues" (1949) and "My Baby's Gone" (1950).

Brown recorded and toured throughout the 1950s. In 1951 he recorded his R&B classic "Black Night." He continued to chart with such hits as "I'll Always Be in Love with You" (1951), "Seven Long Days" (1951) and "Hard Times" (1952). In 1960 he released the classic "Please Come Home for Christmas."

Brown also has a roster of excellent LPs. His best include *Driftin' Blues*, *Sunny Road*, *Racetrack Blues*, *Legend*, *All My Life*, *One More for the Road*, *Sail On* and *Hard Times and Cool Blues*.

Charles Brown is still recording and performing today.

CHARLES BROWN

SEPTEMBER 14

1955: Chuck Berry's "Maybelline" is the number 1 R&B single and Berry's first hit record.

Such other Berry classics as "School Days" and "Sweet Little Sixteen" also hit the top of the R&B charts, but none made it to the number 1 spot on the pop charts. "Sweet Little Sixteen" (1958) landed at number 2, and "Maybelline" made it to number 5.

SEPTEMBER 15

1911: Bluesman Silas Hogan is born in Westover, Louisiana.

Hogan spent most of his life just playing music on the side. He signed with Excello in the late 1950s and was 51 years old when he recorded his first hit. His best-known hits are "Lowdown Blues," for the "Swamp Blues" Excello label in the 1960s, and "Trouble at Home Blues," "I'm Gonna Quit You Baby" and "Everybody Needs Somebody."

1921: Blues singer and harmonica player James Edward "Snooky" Pryor is born in Lambert, Mississippi.

Pryor has been a constant player on the Chicago blues scene for nearly 50 years. He first arrived in Chicago in 1940. After serving in the U.S. Army, he returned and played with Sonny Boy Williamson and Homesick James.

In 1946 he began recording. He recorded for nearly 20 years, without much commercial success. Disgusted, he quit the business. In 1971 he came back, recording and touring with Homesick James.

Snooky Pryor's best LPs are *Real Fine Boogie* and *Homesick James and Snooky Pryor*.

1924: Pianist and vocalist Bobby Short is born in Danville, Illinois.

Short is one of the world's top cabaret performers. He has been performing for nearly 50 years. For the past 25 years he has performed at New York's Cafe Carlyle.

Bobby Short has recorded many great LPs. Among them are *Bobby Short at Town Hall*, *Fifty From Bobby Short* (a CD collection), *Live at the Cafe Carlyle*, *Bobby Short Loves Cole Porter* and *Krazy for Gershwin*.

1928: Jazz saxophonist Julian Edwin "Cannonball" Adderley is born in Tampa, Florida.

Adderley taught music in the Fort Lauderdale school system and played jazz on the side. In 1955 he moved to New York and gained a reputation as a progressive player. He first recorded that year as well, with a group led by drummer Kenny Clarke.

Adderley joined Miles Davis in 1957 and played on such classic Davis recordings as "Milestones" and "Kind of Blue."

In 1959 Adderley left Davis and formed his own group with his brother Nat, a top-flight cornetist. In the early 1960s Adderley flirted with the pop charts when two of his songs, "African Waltz" and "The Jive Samba," did well on the black music charts and cracked *Billboard* magazine's Hot 100.

In January 1967 Adderley landed in the Top 20 with an instrumental piece, "Mercy, Mercy, Mercy." The tune, a gritty fusion of jazz, pop, soul and funk, spent 11 weeks on the charts. There was also a vocal version by the Chicago-based pop group the Buckinghams.

It was most unusual to see a mainstream jazz artist on the national pop charts in the 1960s. Adderley was a proponent of what was then called "soul jazz." Performed almost exclusively by black artists, soul jazz was a genre that combined straight jazz with overtones of funk, gospel and other forms of black popular music. Many claim that from the purveyors of soul jazz came the popular term "soul brother." Milt Jackson and Jimmy Smith were two other musicians identified with soul jazz.

Among Cannonball Adderley's best-known and critically acclaimed albums are *The Cannonball Adderley Quintet in San Francisco* (1959), *Know What I Mean* (1961), *Cannonball Adderley and Nancy Wilson* (1961) and *Spontaneous Combustion* (1955, with Kenny Clarke).

Cannonball Adderley suffered a stroke and died on August 8, 1975.

1945: Soprano Jessye Norman, one of the world's top opera stars, is born in Augusta, Georgia.

Norman studied at Howard University, the University of Michigan and the Peabody Conservatory of Music. She made her opera debut at La Scala, in Milan, in 1972.

Norman has performed in *Die Walküre*, *L'Africaine*, *The Marriage of Figaro*, *Aida*, *Don Giovanni*, *Götter-dammerung* and *Oedipus Rex*. As a recitalist, she has appeared with the Los Angeles Philharmonic, the New York Philharmonic, the London Philharmonic and the Vienna Philharmonic.

SEPTEMBER 16

1921: Jazz vocalist Jon Hendricks, the best vocal arranger in jazz, is born in Newark, Ohio.

Hendricks was brought up in Toledo and began singing on the radio as a child. He performed throughout his high school years and served in the U.S. Army from 1942 to 1946. Hendricks was attending law school and singing on the side when Charlie Parker convinced him to sing full-time.

In the early 1950s Hendricks formed his own band and worked part-time as a songwriter. One of his songs, "I Want You to Be My Baby," was recorded by

Louis Jordan. In 1957 Hendricks recorded lyricized versions of the instrumentals "Four Brothers" and "Cloudburst."

He teamed up with Dave Lambert and Annie Ross in 1958, and they began recording as Lambert, Hendricks and Ross. The trio's style anticipated what Bobby McFerrin does today. (Hendricks only popularized the "vocalese" style, however. Credit for inventing it goes to a 1940s singer, Eddie Jefferson. It was also used by King Pleasure, who had the 1952 R&B hit "Moody's Mood for Love." The story goes that Jefferson originally created the style when the bandleader for whom he was working wouldn't let him scat.) Lambert, Hendricks and Ross had hits with such songs as Horace Silver's "Doodlin'," Neal Hefti's "Li'l Darlin' " and tunes by Miles Davis and Count Basie. The three were a hit in person as well as on record. In 1962 Yolande Bavan replaced Annie Ross, and in 1964 the trio disbanded.

In the late 1960s Hendricks moved to Europe and worked with Annie Ross and pop singer Georgie Fame. Jon Hendricks returned to the U.S. in the late 1970s and has worked with Bobby McFerrin and especially with Manhattan Transfer. He did much of the vocal arrangements for the Manhattan Transfer hit LP *Vocalese*.

1925: Riley "B. B." (for Blues Boy) King is born in Itta Bena, Mississippi.

King was born on a plantation outside Itta Bena. His grandfather was a bottleneck-guitar player. His parents were both singers. King began singing in church at the age of four. He taught himself to play guitar and formed a gospel quintet. He served briefly in the U.S. Army and then performed on the radio with a gospel group in Greenwood, Mississippi.

When King was working as a farmhand, so the story goes, he borrowed $30 from his boss to buy his first electric guitar, from Sears and Roebuck. In 1946 King hitchhiked to Memphis. He played in local amateur shows and, in 1947, joined a band called the Beale Streeters, which included Bobby "Blue" Bland and

B. B. KING

Johnny Ace. In 1948 King appeared on KMEW radio in West Memphis, Arkansas. In 1949 he got his own radio show on WDIA in Memphis, where he was dubbed the Beale Street Blues Boy.

King cut his first record in 1949, "Miss Martha King," for an outfit named Bullet Records. His career took off in 1951, when he hit number 1 on the R&B charts with "Three O'Clock Blues." Over the next decade or so King had such hits as "You Know I Love You" (1952), "Please Love Me" (1953), "Please Hurry Home" (1953), "You Upset Me Baby" (1954), "Every Day I Have the Blues" (1955), "Ten Long Years" (1955), "Bad Luck" (1956), "Sweet Little Angel" (1956), "Please Accept My Love" (1958), "Sweet Sixteen" (1960), "Peace of Mind" (1961), "Don't Answer the Door" (1966) and "Paying the Cost to Be the Boss" (1968). In 1970 the pop and rock-music worlds discovered B. B. King, and his single "The Thrill Is Gone" hit the Top 20.

King, with his famous guitar, Lucille, has recorded 55 albums, placed more than 70 singles on the R&B charts, won five Grammy awards and performed in 57 countries since his career began. He has appeared on every major TV show.

The best of his LPs are *The Best of B. B. King, Volumes 1* and *2*; *Live at the Regal*; *Live at Cook County Jail*; *Now Appearing at Ole Miss*; *Indianola*; *Mississippi Seeds*; and *Live at San*

Quentin. In 1992 MCA released a boxed set of King's recordings, which covers his career from 1949 to the late 1980s.

King was given the Grammy lifetime-achievement award in 1987. In 1990 he was given the Presidential Medal of Freedom. In the same year, he was given a star on Hollywood's Walk of Fame. Today King continues to work about 200 concerts a year.

1931: Bluesman Little Willie Littlefield is born in El Campo, Texas.

Littlefield began recording in 1946. In 1949 he settled in Los Angeles and signed with Modem Records. He had R&B charts hits with "It's Midnight" (1949), "Farewell" (1949) and "I've Been Lost " (1951). In 1952 Little Willie Littlefield recorded "K. C. Lovin'," which became a huge rock 'n' roll hit for Wilbert Harrison under the title "Kansas City."

1953: Jazz guitarist Earl Klugh is born in Detroit.

Klugh taught himself to play. By the age of 16 he was giving lessons at a local music store. At 17 he was hired by flutist Yusef Lateef. He then played with George Benson's group and with Chick Corea's Return to Forever. In 1974 he toured with George Shearing, and in 1975 he went solo.

In this age of domination by the electric guitar, Earl Klugh prefers the acoustic approach to jazz. Among his best LPs are *Living Inside Your Love*, *Late Night Guitar*, *Earl Klugh and Bob James: One on One* and *Earl Klugh and Bob James: Two of a Kind*.

SEPTEMBER 17

1926: Jazz organist Brother Jack McDuff is born in Champaign, Illinois.

McDuff worked in the 1950s with the band of R&B saxophonist Willis "Gator Tail" Jackson and formed his own trio in 1961. He has been recording and touring ever since. His best LPs include *The Honey Dripper*, *Screamin'*, *Greatest Hits*, *At the Jazz Workshop* and *Tuff Duff*.

1983: Vanessa Williams becomes the first black Miss America.

Williams was forced to resign in July 1984 when *Penthouse* magazine pub-lished nude photos of her. This was a crushing blow, but Williams went on to appear on such television shows as "The Love Boat" and "T. J. Hooker" and in the films *The Pickup Artist* and *The Sex Tapes*.

In 1988 she released her first album, *The Right Stuff*. It yielded a pair of Top 20 black chart singles, the title cut and its follow-up, "He's Got the Look." In 1992 her LP *The Comfort Zone* hit number 1 on the pop charts.

SEPTEMBER 18

1970: Rock guitar legend Jimi Hendrix dies in London.

The cause of death was a combination of drug overdose and suffocation. Jimi Hendrix was 27 years old.

1992: Earl Van Dyke dies of prostate cancer.

Van Dyke was born in 1928. His nickname was Chunk of Funk. For over 30 years he was one of Motown Records' chief staff musicians. As a keyboardist, he performed on hits by Stevie Wonder, the Supremes, the Four Tops and the Temptations.

When the touring Motown Revue changed its backup band from the 18-piece Choker Campbell Orchestra to a sextet, Earl Van Dyke became its musical conductor. When Motown shifted its base of operations to the West Coast, Van Dyke retired and remained in Detroit.

Van Dyke also recorded several instrumental LPs, including *That Motown Sound* and *The Earl of Funk*.

SEPTEMBER 19

1887: Pianist and arranger Cora Calhoun "Lovie" Austin is born in Chattanooga, Tennessee.

Austin studied music at Roger Williams College and Knoxville College. She began working in vaudeville, as a pianist for her husband's act. She toured with such shows as Irving Miller's *Blue Babies* and *Sunflower Girls*.

A pioneering woman in jazz, Austin formed her own band, the Blues Serenaders, and directed her own show, *Lovie Austin's Revue*.

She settled in Chicago, where she became musical director at the Monogram Theater and worked as house pianist for Paramount Records. There she recorded with such blueswomen as Ma Rainey, Ida Cox and Ethel Waters. She also wrote Bessie Smith's hit "Graveyard Blues."

During World War II she gave up music and went to work in a munitions factory. After the war she returned to recording and performing. Her music is captured on a collection called *Lovie Austin's Blues Serenades (1924–1926)*.

Lovie Austin died on July 10, 1972.

1921: Dominoes leader Billy Ward is born in New York City.

Billy Ward and the Dominoes were one of the earliest, best and most successful doo-wop groups. The group was formed in 1950 by Ward and talent agent Rose Marks. The other original members were lead singer Clyde McPhatter, tenor Charlie White, baritone Joe Lamont and bass Bill Brown. They won a talent contest at the Apollo Theater and appeared on Arthur Godfrey's TV show.

The group was signed to Federal Records in late 1950 and first charted in 1951, with "Do Something for Me." In mid-1951 the Dominoes scored with a million-selling R&B classic, "Sixty-Minute Man." They had a string of hits, including "I Am with You" (1951), "That's What You're Doing to Me" (1952), "Have Mercy, Baby" (1952), "I'd Be Satisfied" (1952), "The Bells" (1953), "Pedal Pushin' Papa" (1953) and "These Foolish Things Remind Me of You" (1953).

In 1953 Clyde McPhatter left to form his own group, the Drifters, and Bill Brown left to form the Checkers. McPhatter's lead vocals were assumed by a young Detroiter named Jackie Wilson, who remained with the group until 1957. After Wilson left, Eugene Mumford became the Dominoes' lead singer.

Later Dominoes hits include "You Can't Keep a Good Man Down" (1953), "Rags to Riches" (1953) and "Star Dust" (1957). The Dominoes disbanded in the early 1960s.

1931: Singer and songwriter Brook Benton is born Benjamin Franklin Peay in Camden, South Carolina.

In the early 1950s Benton was singing with gospel quartets. In 1953 he signed with Okeh Records. When nothing came of his recordings, he quit singing and started driving a truck.

Benton then met songwriter Clyde Otis, and the two formed a songwriting partnership. In 1958 they had two big hits: "Looking Back," by Nat "King" Cole, and "A Lover's Question," by Clyde McPhatter.

Benton signed with Mercury Records and hit the Top 10 on both the R&B and pop charts with "It's Just a Matter of Time" in 1959. He quickly followed up with "Endlessly," "So Close," "Thank You, Pretty Baby" and "So Many Ways," all in the same year.

In 1960 Benton had a pair of hit duet singles with Dinah Washington, "Baby, You've Got What It Takes" and "A Rockin' Good Way." That year he also had solo hits with "Kiddo" and "Fools Rush In." Throughout the early 1960s Benton consistently topped the charts with such tunes as "For My Baby" (1961), "Think Twice" (1961), "The Boll Weevil Song" (1961), "Lie to Me" (1962), "Hotel Happiness" (1962), "I've Got What I Wanted" (1963) and "My True Confession" (1963). In early 1970 Benton released his only million-seller, "Rainy Night in Georgia."

Brook Benton died on April 9, 1988, from complications of spinal meningitis.

1939: The Dixie Hummingbirds, one of black gospel music's greatest and most successful quartets, record for the first time.

They were organized in South Carolina in the mid-1930s by James B. Davis. In 1939 they signed with Decca Records and were taken to New York to record. Of the 16 sides that came out of that session, the Dixie Hummingbirds got one hit, "Joshua Journeyed to Jericho." Also in 1939 the Dixie Hummingbirds acquired Ira Tucker as their lead singer. Tucker was a dynamic performer who shouted and leapt from the stage into the audience.

The Dixie Hummingbirds moved to Philadelphia in 1942. They performed not only in churches but also in such secular venues as New York's Cafe Society.

By 1944 the group consisted of Tucker, James Davis, William Bobo, Beachey Thompson and guitarist Howard Carroll, whom some call gospel's answer to B. B. King. They had hits with "I'm Still Living on Mother's Prayer," "Let's Go Out to the Programs" and "Christian's Automobile."

In 1966 the Dixie Hummingbirds appeared at the Newport Folk Festival. In 1973 they sang backup on Paul Simon's "Loves Me Like a Rock," and they hit the soul music charts with their own version of the song.

1945: Singer Freda Payne is born in Detroit.

In the early 1960s Payne worked with Duke Ellington, Pearl Bailey and Quincy Jones. In 1969 she signed with Holland-Dozier-Holland's newly created Invictus label. She scored with a pair of million-selling singles, "Band of Gold" (1970) and "Bring the Boys Home" (1971). Freda Payne also hosted the syndicated TV show "For You, Black Woman," in the early 1980s.

Her sister Scherrie Payne sang with the Supremes after Diana Ross's day.

1952: Record producer Nile Rodgers is born in New York City.

Rodgers and Bernard Edwards were one of the most successful record-producing teams of the 1970s and 1980s. They burst on the scene in 1977 as members of the group Chic, which scored a pair of million-selling singles: "Dance, Dance, Dance" (1977) and "Good Times" (1979), as well as a platinum single, "Le Freak," in 1978.

Rodgers and Edwards produced seven Chic LPs between 1978 and 1983. Their success with Chic made them much sought after as producers. They produced the hit LPs *Koo Doo* (for Debbie Harry), *Diana* (for Diana Ross) and *We Are Family* (for Sister Sledge).

As a solo producer, Nile Rodgers crafted David Bowie's *Let's Dance* LP, as well as projects for such artists as INXS and Southside Johnny.

SEPTEMBER 20

1960: "The Twist," by Chubby Checker, is the number 1 pop single.

"The Twist" hit number 1 on September 19, 1960, and remained

there for a week. On January 13, 1962, "The Twist" was back as the number 1 song in the nation. This time it hung on to the spot for two weeks, until it was booted out by another twist record, "The Peppermint Twist," by Joey Dee and the Starliters.

Except for Bing Crosby's "White Christmas," Chubby Checker's ode to this sacroiliac-wrenching dance craze is the only single ever to have hit number 1, left the charts and then reentered and landed at number 1 again after an absence of a year of more.

SEPTEMBER 21

1914: Jazz bassist Leroy "Slam" Stewart is born in Englewood, New Jersey.

Stewart studied at the Boston Conservatory of Music and played with Peanuts Holland's band before teaming up with Slim Gaillard. They had the jivey 1937 hit song "Flat Foot Floogie." They also had their own radio show over WNEW and played together off and on until Gaillard was drafted, in 1942.

Stewart then worked with the bands of Van Alexander, Art Tatum and Tiny Grimes. He appeared in the 1943 film *Stormy Weather*. In 1945 he joined Benny Goodman's band. In the 1950s he led his own trio and toured Europe several times. In the 1970s he taught at Yale University and made several appearances on the "Today Show."

1921: Jazz drummer Chico Hamilton is born in Los Angeles.

Hamilton first came to prominence as a member of the original Gerry Mulligan Quartet in 1952. Hamilton had spent the early 1940s playing in the bands of Floyd Ray, Lionel Hampton and Slim Gaillard. He served in the U.S. Army from 1942 to 1946. When he got out he played in the bands of Jimmy Mundy, Count Basie and Lester Young. In 1948 he became Lena Horne's regular tour drummer. In 1955 Hamilton formed his own quintet. In the 1970s he branched out into writing commercials and jingles.

Chico Hamilton is considered one of jazz's most creative drummers and a master of the brushes. His best LPs are *The Dealer* and *Chic, Chic Chico*.

1959: The Isley Brothers make their pop chart debut with "Shout," for RCA Records.

Rudolph, Ronald and O'Kelly Isley hailed from Cincinnati. In the early 1950s they formed a gospel group with another brother, Vernon, who later was killed in an auto wreck. After his death, the Isley Brothers stopped performing but regrouped a year later.

In 1957 they moved to New York and, after recording for several small labels, signed with RCA.

Not until 1962 did they muster a successful follow-up to "Shout"—with 1962's Top 20 hit "Twist and Shout." They switched labels again, this time signing with Motown subsidiary Tamla Records. The Isley Brothers' association with Tamla was largely unsuccessful. It produced only one hit single, "This Old Heart of Mine," in 1966.

In 1969 the Isley Brothers formed their own label, T-Neck. Their first T-Neck single was a monster million-seller, "It's Your Thing." That began a string of hits, which included "Love the One You're With" (1971), "Lay Away" (1972), "Pop That Thing" (1972), "That Lady" (1973), "Fight the Power" (1975), "The Pride" (1977), "Take Me to the Next Phase" (1978), "I Wanna Be with You" (1979), "Inside You" (1981), "Between the Sheets" (1983) and "Smooth Sailing Tonight" (1987).

In the mid-1970s the Isley Brothers added their younger brothers Ernie and Marvin and their cousin Chris Jasper to

THE ISLEY BROTHER

the group. Ernie Isley was an outstanding rock guitarist. He, Marvin Isley and Chris Jasper recorded as Isley, Jasper and Isley in the mid-1980s. O'Kelly Isley died of a heart attack on March 31, 1986.

In 1990 Ronald Isley rerecorded "This Old Heart of Mine" with Rod Stewart, and the record hit the Top 10.

SEPTEMBER 22

1953: Faye Adams's "Shake a Hand" is the number 1 R&B single.

Faye Adams was born Faye Tuell in Newark, New Jersey. At the age of five she and her two older sisters formed a gospel music trio.

In 1952 she joined the Joe Morris Blues Cavalcade, and in the early 1950s she had number 1 R&B singles with "I'll Be True" (1953) and "Hurts Me to My Heart" (1954).

At one time Faye Adams also recorded under the name Faye Scruggs.

SEPTEMBER 23

1907: Pianist Albert Ammons, a founding father of the "beat me, Daddy, eight to the bar" boogie-woogie piano style, is born in Chicago.

Ammons often performed with boogie-woogie masters "Lux" Lewis and Pete Johnson. He started playing the piano at the age of 10 and worked in clubs around Chicago as a soloist. In the 1930s he played with William Barbee and Louis Banks. In 1934 he formed his own combo. He moved to New York in 1938, to play places like Cafe Society with Johnson and Lewis.

In 1941 Ammons cut off the tip of one of his fingers and did not play for a while. In the mid-1940s he suffered paralysis in both hands. In the last few years of his life, however, Albert Ammons was a mainstay at such Chicago clubs as the Beehive and Mama Yancey's. His son, Gene "Jug" Ammons, was a noted sax player.

Albert Ammons died on December 2, 1949.

1926: Jazz saxophonist John William Coltrane is born in Hamlet, North Carolina.

Coltrane moved to Philadelphia after graduating from high school. He studied saxophone and mastered alto, tenor and

soprano sax. He began playing local gigs, mostly on alto sax. He spent 1945 and 1946 in the U.S. Navy band. Then he toured with the R&B band of King Kolax and Eddie "Cleanhead" Vinson. He joined Dizzy Gillespie's big band in 1949. When Gillespie reduced the outfit to a sextet, Coltrane remained with him and stayed until 1951. Around this time he also switched to tenor sax.

Between 1952 and 1955 he played in the bands of Gay Crosse, Earl Bostic and Johnny Hodges. In 1955 he joined the Miles Davis Quintet.

Coltrane underwent a spiritual awakening in 1957. He kicked his drug and alcohol habits. In the same year, he played with Thelonious Monk. In 1958 he rejoined Miles Davis.

After switching to soprano sax he left Davis, in early 1960, to form his classic John Coltrane Quartet, with drummer Elvin Jones, pianist McCoy Tyner and bassist Steve Davis. In the mid-1960s he radically changed the personnel. He added Pharoah Sanders on tenor, Rashied Ali on drums and his wife, Alice, on piano.

"Trane" was a jazz explorer, one of the great innovators of modern music. He was constantly searching for unexplored territory. He was interested in free jazz and Indian scales. He also tried new and different approaches to playing. At one stage he took the concept of chord changes to its logical conclusion, playing every possible combination of notes against each chord before progressing to the next. Among Coltrane's best LPs are *Love Supreme, My Favorite Things, Lush Life, Africa, John Coltrane and the Giants of Jazz, Soultrane, Countdown, Live in Stockholm, Giant Steps* and *Ascension.* There are also several Coltrane CD collections, including *The Prestige Recordings* and *Retrospective: The Impulse Years.*

1930: Ray Charles is born Ray Charles Robinson in Albany, Georgia.

They call "it" the genius of Ray Charles. "It" is a universally known musical styling that encompasses elements of jazz, blues, gospel, pop and even country music to form an unmistakably unique and successful sound.

Since debuting on records in the late 1940s, Ray Charles has placed over 80 singles on the national black music charts, more than 70 on the national pop Top 100 charts and at least a dozen on the country charts. Over the past five decades, Ray Charles has become one of the world's best-known performers.

Charles was raised in the town of Greenville, Florida. He contracted glaucoma and was partially blind by the age of five. Two years later his sight was completely gone. He had shown some musical talent, and so his mother sent him to the Florida State School for Deaf and Blind Children, in St. Augustine. He remained there until 1945, studying classical piano, clarinet, saxophone and arranging.

His mother's death forced Charles to leave school and seek a living as a musician with a series of Florida bands. As a road musician Charles traveled throughout the Southeast, playing every type of music there was: pop, jazz, bebop, blues and even country. At one point he was the featured player in Lowell Fulson's band.

By the time he was 17 Charles had formed his own trio. He left the South and headed for Seattle, where he landed a spot on local television in 1948, the same year he cut his first records. His major influence at that time was Nat "King" Cole, whose soft, jazzy ballads had made him the most successful black recording artist of the era. Charles's first recorded efforts were also in this vein.

Ray Charles and his trio first hit the R&B charts in early 1949, with a tune called "Confession Blues" on Downbeat Records. The song was a major jukebox hit and climbed to number 2 on the *Billboard* juke chart. Though he recorded for several small West Coast labels, Charles's major output between 1949 and 1952 was on Swingtime, a Los Angeles–based label owned by Jack Lauderdale. Charles hit the *Billboard* R&B polls with such Swingtime releases as "Baby, Let Me Hold Your Hand," in 1951, and "Kiss Me, Baby," in 1952. It was his success on the small Swingtime label that gained Charles the notice and interest of one of the country's most progressive black labels—Atlantic Records.

In 1952 Atlantic purchased Ray Charles's contract from Jack Lauderdale for a reported $2,000, but success on Atlantic was not immediate or automatic for Ray Charles. Atlantic released several records by Charles in 1953, and none sold. In 1954 things began to change. In the spring of that year Charles hit with "It Should've Been Me," and he followed up with a summertime hit, "Don't You Know." During this period Charles's musical direction also changed: he left his "King Cole" phase behind and replaced his small combo with a big band. It had a full horn section, and its roots were closer to blues and gospel than to the big-band jazz of the 1940s.

Charles displayed his new band and new sound on his classic "I've Got a Woman," released in January 1955. It became his first number 1 R&B hit. Critics and record buyers hailed the sound of the throaty vocals, set against the jump-rhythm backgrounds and accentuated by big-band horn riffs. This was something new and exciting in the R&B world.

Ray Charles had a banner year in 1955. He followed up "I've Got a Woman" with a year-long string of Top 10 hits: "Come Back," "This Little Girl of Mine," "Blackjack" and "Greenbacks." Later that year he added another important ingredient to what we know as the Ray Charles sound: sassy, husky-voiced female backup singers who didn't just hum in the background but took turns accentuating, urging, cajoling, or even reprimanding Charles in his vocalizations. Charles initially used the Atlantic recording trio the Cookies, composed of Margie Hendricks, Dolly McCrea and Doretta Jones. The initial result of this collaboration was "Drown in My Own Tears," released in February 1956, which quickly soared to number 1 and remained at the top of the R&B charts for 12 weeks. The same recording session produced the church music–like classic hit "Hallelujah, I Love Her So." Charles rounded out 1956 with another Cookies collaboration, "Lonely Avenue."

Although he had run up a string of black chart hits, Charles had yet to hit the

RAY CHARLES

mainstream pop charts. He finally accomplished that feat in October 1957, with "Swanee River Rock," which peaked at number 34 on the *Billboard* pop chart. Charles finally had his foot in the door, in time for the rock 'n' roll craze.

By now Charles was constantly on the road, touring and playing across the United States. He was different from most other black artists in the way he took his music live to his fans. Instead of joining the 1957 *Shower of Stars* tour, with Chuck Berry and 15 other top recording stars, Charles had his own self-contained show, which featured the 15-piece Ray Charles Orchestra. Instead of the Cookies, Ray brought along his own Raelettes. Instead of the 20-minute set the package show would have afforded him, he gave his audiences what they craved: over two solid hours of Ray Charles.

He scored his first pop Top 10 hit in midsummer of 1959, with the rocking classic "What'd I Say." In 1960 Charles left Atlantic for ABC-Paramount, which reportedly offered him complete creative control of his recording sessions and allowed him to keep 75 cents on every dollar his recordings earned. This was an arrangement quite unheard-of in the recording business, and an offer that Atlantic could in no way match.

It was during his tenure with ABC-Paramount that Charles established himself as an American musical treasure. In September 1980 Charles hit number 1 nationwide, with "Georgia on My Mind," a remake of a 1930s Hoagy Carmichael ballad. "Georgia" also hit the top of the European charts and established Charles internationally. He hit number 1 again the next year, with a song that has now become a pop standard—"Hit the Road, Jack." He also scored Top 10 hits with "Unchain My Heart" and the pop-jazz instrumental "One Mint Julep."

In 1962 Charles rattled a few cages throughout the music world by recording an album of country-and-western tunes. *Modern Sounds in Country and Western* contained Charles's renditions of such country classics as "'Your Cheating Heart." The album took the nation by storm. It produced the number 1 single "I Can't Stop Loving You" and such Top 10 hits as "You Don't Know Me" and "You Are My Sunshine." "I Can't Stop Loving You" became Ray Charles's first million-seller. On the basis of the album and its singles, Charles sold an estimated $8 million worth of records in 1962.

Throughout the remainder of the sixties Charles turned out a roster of Top 10 hits that included such unforgettables as "Take These Chains from My Heart" (1963), "Busted" (1963), "Crying Time" (1965), "Together Again" (1965), "Let's Go Get Stoned" (1966), "Here We Go Again" (1967) and a remake of the Beatles' "Yesterday" (1967). Charles became a regular performed on TV, guesting on many variety shows and hosting his own specials. He also turned his attention to motion pictures, providing theme music for such feature films as the Sidney Poitier thriller *In the Heat of the Night* and Clint Eastwood's *Any Which Way You Can*.

In 1984 Charles hit the number 1 spot on the *Billboard* country charts, with "Seven Spanish Angels," a duet with country superstar Willie Nelson. In 1986 the world of pop music gave Ray Charles its supreme accolade, inducting him into the Rock 'n' Roll Hall of Fame.

1935: Blues guitarist and vocalist Fenton Robinson is born in Greenwood, Mississippi.

Robinson moved to Memphis in 1953 and played guitar behind Bobby "Blue" Bland and Roscoe Gordon. In the late '50s he recorded for Duke Records.

In the early '60s he moved to Chicago and played with Junior Wells, Otis Rush and Sonny Boy Williamson. In 1964 he formed his own band.

Robinson is one of the most creative of the modern bluesmen, but he has never been able to land a recording contract with a major label. He records sporadically and has released two of the best modern blues LPs ever: *Somebody Loan Me a Dime* and *I Hear Some Blues Downstairs*. His other albums include *Night Flyte* and *The Mellow Blues Genius*.

Fenton Robinson divides his time between Chicago and the Deep South.

1938: Singer Ben E. King is born Benjamin Earl Nelson in Henderson, North Carolina.

King moved to New York in 1947. He worked for a short time with the Moonglows while still in high school and joined a group called the Five Crowns in 1957. In 1959 that group became the Drifters. He co-wrote and sang lead on their hit "There Goes My Baby" and sang lead on such Drifters hits as "Save the Last Dance for Me," "I Count the Tears," "Dance with Me" and "This Magic Moment."

In 1960 Ben E. King went solo and recorded several classic soul hits, beginning with "Spanish Harlem" in early 1961. His biggest hits were "Stand By Me" (1961), "Amor" (1961), "Don't Play That Song" (1962), "How Can I Forget" (1963), "I Who Have Nothing" (1963), "Seven Letters" (1965), "Supernatural Thing" (1975) and "Do It in the Name of Love" (1975).

In 1986 Ben E. King's recording was used as the theme song for the film *Stand By Me*. The record was rereleased and landed in the Top 10 once again.

SEPTEMBER 24

1916: Singer and actor Herb Jeffries, best known for his film work as a singing cowboy in the late 1930s, is born.

Jeffries was singing with Earl "Fatha" Hines's band when he got the call from Hollywood. He starred in such films as *The Bronze Buckaroo* and *Harlem Rides the Range*. In the 1940s Jeffries sang with Duke Ellington's orchestra. He did the vocals on such Ellington hits as "Flamingo" (1941) and "My Little Brown Book" (1944). In 1945 he had a solo hit with "I Left a Good Deal in Mobile."

1935: Blues singer Z. Z. Hill is born Arzell Hill in Naples, Texas.

Hill began his singing career with a gospel group called the Spiritual Five. He first hit the R&B charts in 1964, with a song called "You Were Wrong." In the early 1970s he began hitting the charts with songs like "Don't Make Me Pay for His Mistakes" (1971), "Love Is So Good When You're Stealing It" (1977), "Down Home Blues" (1980) and "Cheating in the Next Room" (1982).

For some reason, Hill got lost in the shuffle, despite the fact that he was an excellent singer and performer and hit the R&B charts consistently for almost a decade and a half. Some of his best music can be found on the LP *Z. Z. Hill: In Memoriam*.

Z. Z. Hill died of a heart attack on April 27, 1984.

SEPTEMBER 25

1975: "It Only Takes a Minute," by Tavares, is the number 1 black chart single.

The group was made up of Ralph, Cubby, Butch, Pooch and Tiny Tavares and hailed from New Bedford, Massachusetts. The brothers Tavares had a string of pop and black chart hits from the early '70s to the early '80s. They had a million-seller with "Heaven Must Be Missing an Angel" in 1976. Their other top hits include "Check It Out" (1973), "She's Gone" (1974), "Remember What I Told You to Forget" (1975), "Whodunit" (1977), "I Never Had a Love Like This Before" (1978) and "Deeper in Love" (1983).

SEPTEMBER 26

1937: Bessie Smith dies in Clarksdale, Mississippi.

The death of Bessie Smith is one of the incidents most talked and written about in the history of American music. According to the most common story, Smith was taken to a white hospital after being severely injured in an auto accident; she was refused treatment because she was black, and she bled to death.

The facts are somewhat different. On September 25, 1937, while touring with a show called *Broadway Rastus*, Smith was severely injured in an auto crash near Coahoma, Mississippi, about 10 miles north of Clarksdale. There was a white hospital nearby, but Smith was taken to the colored hospital in Clarksdale, where she received treatment that included amputation of her right arm. Her injuries were so massive that she died the next day.

There were 7,000 people at her funeral, but she went without a headstone until one was purchased by singer Janis Joplin. Bessie Smith is buried in Mount Lawn Cemetery, Sharon Hill, Pennsylvania.

SEPTEMBER 27

1969: The Originals' classic ballad "Baby, I'm for Real" is released, perhaps the greatest piece of pure soul ever to come from Motown Records. The song was written and produced by Marvin Gaye and made it to number 1 on the soul charts.

The Originals were formed in Detroit in 1966 by Freddie Gorman, Crathman Spencer, Henry Dixon and Walter Gaines. Gorman was a successful songwriter, having penned such hits as "Please, Mr. Postman" for the Marvelettes and "Just Like Romeo and Juliet" for the Reflections.

Other hits by the Originals included "The Bells" (1970), "We Can Make It, Baby" (1970) and "God Bless Whoever Sent You" (1971).

SEPTEMBER 28

1910: Bluesman Houston Stackhouse is born in Wesson, Mississippi.

Houston Stackhouse was a postwar Mississippi bluesman. In his early days he worked with Robert "Junior"

Lockwood, Robert Nighthawk and Sonny Boy Williamson and was a regular on such Deep South radio blues shows as those sponsored by Mother's Best Flour and King Biscuit. In the 1960s and 1970s he toured the U.S. and Europe, playing folk and blues festivals. One reason for his relative anonymity is that he never had what was considered to be a hit record.

Houston Stackhouse is believed to have died in 1981 in Crystal Springs, Mississippi.

1935: Chicago-based blues singer Koko Taylor is born Cora Walton in Memphis.

Taylor was raised in Memphis and began singing in her church choir at the age of 15. At 19 she and her husband moved to Chicago, where she began singing in a nightspot called the Beale Street Club. In the 1950s she worked with bluesmen Buddy Guy, Junior Wells and J. B. Lenore.

In 1965 she signed with Checker Records and was taken under the wing of blues singer, songwriter and producer Willie Dixon. "Wang Dang Doodle" (1966) was one result of the collaboration between Taylor and Dixon. The record gave Taylor worldwide attention and, in essence, got her out of South Side Chicago clubs and onto TV and the international blues festival circuit. She is an electrifying performer who constantly tours the world, has recorded more than a dozen blues LPs and picked up a Grammy in 1984.

In 1974 Taylor signed with Alligator Records and began to issued a series of critically acclaimed LPs, including *Queen of the Blues*, *From the Heart of a Woman*, *The Earthshakers* and *Jump for Joy*. In 1991 she released a performance video entitled "Koko Taylor, Queen of the Blues."

1957: Jazz pianist Kenny Kirkland, best known for his work with jazz trumpeter Wynton Marsalis and rock star Sting, is born in Brooklyn.

Kirkland attended the Manhattan School of Music. He got his start in jazz touring Europe with Michal Urbaniak. He joined the Marsalis group in 1982.

1991: Miles Davis dies in Santa Monica, California, where he had been hospitalized for several weeks after a stroke.

For many fans and musicians, Davis was as much a spiritual leader as a musical leader. He spent much of his nonperforming time in seclusion—meditating, painting and writing music.

On October 5, 1991, a memorial service was held for Miles Davis. Speakers at the service included the Reverend Jesse Jackson, Bill Cosby, Quincy Jones and Herbie Hancock.

MILES DAVIS

SEPTEMBER 29

1970: Diana Ross's "Ain't No Mountain High Enough" is the number 1 pop single and Ross's first number 1 hit as a solo artist. It was written by Nick Ashford and Valerie Simpson and was originally recorded by Marvin Gaye and Tammi Terrell, in 1967.

SEPTEMBER 30

1922: Jazz bassist Oscar Pettiford is born in Okmulgee, Oklahoma.

In the 1940s Pettiford worked with the live and recording bands of Charlie Shavers, Roy Eldridge, Coleman Hawkins, Earl "Fatha" Hines and Ben Webster. In 1944 he co-led a quintet with Dizzy Gillespie. In 1945 he joined Duke Ellington's orchestra and remained until 1948.

In the late 1940s and early 1950s, when not leading his own group, he played with Woody Herman, Louis

Bellson and again with Charlie Shavers. The 1950s also saw Pettiford with Art Blakey and Thelonious Monk, and he led his own big band for a while.

In 1958 he toured Europe with a package show called *Jazz from Carnegie Hall*. During the early '50s Pettiford had begun using the cello in his jazz performances, plucking its strings as if it were a standup bass.

Some of his best LPs are *Bohemia After Dark*, *Blue Brothers* and *The Oscar Pettiford Orchestra in HiFi*.

Oscar Pettiford died on September 8, 1960, in Copenhagen.

1935: Johnny Mathis is born in San Francisco.

Mathis began studying opera at the age of 13. He attended San Francisco State College on a track scholarship. He went to New York in 1956 and was signed by Columbia Records. Mathis initially recorded as a jazz singer but was persuaded by Columbia A&R chief Mitch Miller to concentrate on romantic ballads.

Since the late 1950s Mathis has been one of the world's most popular and successful male vocalists. Mathis has placed over 60 LPs on the *Billboard* album charts. His million-selling albums include *Warm*, *Johnny's Greatest Hits*, *Swing Softly*, *Heavenly* and *Feelings*. His best-selling singles include "Wonderful, Wonderful" (1957), "It's Not for Me to Say" (1957), "Chances Are" (1957), "The Twelfth of Never" (1957), "A Certain Smile" (1958), "Gena" (1962) and "What Will My Mary Say" (1963). In 1978 Johnny Mathis teamed up with Deneice Williams for the million-selling single "Too Much, Too Little, Too Late" and the theme song for the hit TV show "Family Ties."

1942: Singer Frankie Lymon is born in New York City.

In 1955, when Lymon was 12, he joined a singing group called the Teenagers. The other members were Joe Negroni, Herman Santiago, Jimmy Merchant and Sherman Garnes. They caught the attention of record producer Richard Barrett, who decided to have the group record a song the members had written, "Why Do Fools Fall in Love." Santiago was supposed to do the lead vocal, but on the day of the recording session he was sick. Lymon sang lead instead.

The record was an instant hit. Early in 1956 it made the Top 10, and the group became Frankie Lymon and the Teenagers. Other chart hits followed: "I Want You to Be My Girl," "I Promise to Remember," "Who Can Explain" and "The ABC's of Love," all in 1956.

In 1957 Lymon went solo. He was a dynamite performer. He caused some controversy when he danced with a white girl on Dick Clark's "American Bandstand." He had a hit single, "Goody, Goody," in the summer of 1957.

Lymon's record label went bankrupt, and he didn't hit the charts again until 1960, with a version of "Little Bitty Pretty One," which was moderately successful. Throughout the 1960s Lymon battled heroin addiction. He tried rehabilitation several times, without success.

Frankie Lymon died of a heroin overdose on February 28, 1968.

1954: Vocalist and keyboardist Patrice Rushen is born in Los Angeles.

While still in her teens, Rushen was a sought-after session musician, working with such artists as Melba Liston and the Sylvers. She attended the University of Southern California and began playing with jazz artists like Jean-Luc Ponty, Lee Ritenour, Stanley Turrentine and Donald Byrd.

In the late 1970s Patrice Rushen began hitting the black singles charts with songs like "Hurry It Up" (1978), "Haven't You Heard" (1979), "Forget-Me-Nots" (1982), "Feels So Real" (1984) and "Watch Out" (1987).

OCTOBER 1

1936: Bluesman Georgie "Wild Child" Butler is born in Autaugaville, Alabama.

Butler got his nickname from his mother. He picked up his first harmonica at the age of six.

In the 1950s he played with Sonny Boy Williamson and worked the club circuit in Chicago, Detroit and Houston. In the mid-1960s he was with Junior Wells's band. He recorded for Jewel Records in the late '60s. His best LPs include *Open Up Baby, Lickin' Gravy* and *These Mean Old Blues*. Wild Child Butler currently works the blues festival and club circuit.

1945: Singer and songwriter Donny Hathaway, one of the brightest talents of the 1970s and an accomplished arranger, keyboardist and record producer, is born in Chicago.

Hathaway began singing gospel music at the age of three. He attended Howard University in Washington, D.C., on a fine-arts scholarship, where one of his classmates was Roberta Flack. He majored in music theory and, upon graduation, got a staff production job with Curtis Mayfield's Custom Records, producing and writing for such artists as Jerry Butler, Carla Thomas and the Staple Singers. Later, in the mid-1970s, he also produced several songs for Aretha Franklin.

With the help of soul saxophonist King Curtis, Hathaway signed with Atlantic Records in 1970. He released his first LP, *Everything Is Everything*, in early 1971. It yielded the hit single "The Ghetto."

In the same year, he began collaborating with Roberta Flack. Their partnership produced a pair of million-selling singles, "Where Is the Love" (1972) and "The Closer I Get to You" (1978), as well as such other hits as "You've Got a Friend" (1971), "You Are

My Heaven" (1980) and "Back Together Again" (1980).

On January 13, 1979, Donny Hathaway committed suicide in New York City.

OCTOBER 2

1948: "Cornbread," by Hal Singer, is the number 1 R&B single.

Tenor saxophonist Hal Singer was one of the originators of the honkin' R&B and rock 'n' roll styles of sax playing. Before forming his own band, Singer spent time in the orchestras of such notables as Ernie Fields, Jay McShann, Roy Eldridge, Earl Bostic, Lucky Millinder and Duke Ellington.

Uniquely, on this date in 1948 "Cornbread" was tied for the top spot on the R&B charts with another instrumental, "Late Freight," by pianist and bandleader Sonny Thompson. Alfonso "Sonny" Thompson was born in Chicago on August 22, 1923. He had a list of R&B hits that included "Long Gone" (1948), "Blue Dreams" (1949), "Mellow Blues" (1952), "I'll Drown in My Own Tears" (1952) and "Let's Call It a Day" (1952).

OCTOBER 3

1932: Blues singer and guitarist Albert Collins, known as the master of the Telecaster and the Houston Twister, is born in Leona, Texas.

Collins grew up in Houston's Third Ward, with future blues guitarist Johnny Copeland and Johnny "Guitar" Watson. He started playing guitar at 18. The first tune that he learned was John Lee Hooker's "Boogie Chillun."

In the mid-1950s he worked the Houston club circuit with a 10-piece band called the Rhythm Rockers.

He cut his first single in 1958 and in 1961 had a million-selling single, "Frosty." In 1968, with the help of the blues-rock group Canned Heat, Collins

signed with Imperial Records and began opening for such rock acts as the Allman Brothers and Frank Zappa. In 1971 he signed with Alligator Records.

Collins is one of the most visible blues performers today. He has been seen on "Austin City Limits" and the PBS special "American Guitar Heroes." He also did the "Nobody Gets Outa Here Without Singing the Blues" sequence in the 1987 film *Adventures in Babysitting*. In 1985 he played the Live Aid Concert in Philadelphia.

Collins has recorded more than a dozen LPs. The best include *Cold Snap, Ice Pickin', Don't Lose Your Cool, Frozen Alive, Live in Japan* and *Albert Collins*. In 1978 *Ice Pickin'* was named best blues album of the year at the Montreux Jazz Festival and was nominated for a Grammy. *Don't Lose Your Cool* won the W. C. Handy Award for best contemporary blues LP of 1983. Albert Collins was named contemporary male blues artist of the year in 1980 and 1981 by the Memphis Blues Foundation.

ALBERT COLLINS

1941: Chubby Checker, who almost singlehandedly sparked the 1960s Twist craze, is born Ernest Evans in Philadelphia.

Chubby Checker (his stage name was a takeoff on Fats Domino) grew up in Philadelphia and once worked as a chicken plucker. He signed with Cameo/Parkway Records in 1959 and released a single called "The Class," in which he did impersonations of such rock performers as Domino and Elvis Presley.

"The Twist," written and first recorded by Hank Ballard, hit number 1 in the late summer of 1960 after Checker recorded it. The song remained on the charts for 18 weeks. In the fall of 1961 the record reappeared on the charts and returned to number one, the only record besides Bing Crosby's "White Christmas" ever to do so after an absence of a year or more.

There were several factors involved in the immense popularity of the Twist. It was easy to do, it (and Checker) got a lot of exposure on TV's "American Bandstand" and Checker himself had great charisma.

Over the next few years Chubby Checker introduced such other dance crazes as the Pony, the Hucklebuck, the Popeye, the Limbo and the Fly. The records named for these dances were best-selling singles. Others include "Let's Twist Again" (1961), "Slow Twistin'" (1962), "Limbo Rock (1962), "Twenty Miles" (1963), "Birdland" (1963), "Loddy Lo" (1963) and "Hey Bobba Needle" (1964). Checker also starred in the film *Don't Knock the Twist.*

Chubby Checker is still performing today.

1950: Vocalist and saxophonist Ronnie Laws is born in Houston.

Laws comes from a musical family. His brother Hubert and his sisters Eloise and Debra all hit the black and jazz charts in the '70s and '80s.

Laws spent the early '70s as a member of Earth, Wind and Fire. In 1975 he formed his own jazz-rock group, Pressure. His best-known singles include "Always There" (1975), "Every Generation" (1980) and "Stay Awake" (1981). In 1981

he and his sister Debra had a best-selling black chart hit, "Very Special."

1951: Blues harmonica player Billy Branch is born in Great Lakes, Illinois.

Branch grew up in Los Angeles but returned to Chicago. He played in the bands of Paul Butterfield and Willie Dixon before forming his current band, the Sons of the Blues. Billy Branch is currently the hottest harp player on the Chicago blues circuit.

OCTOBER 4

1945: Actor, singer and songwriter Clifton Davis, best known as the Reverend Rubin Gregory on the TV series "Amen," is born in Chicago.

Davis has appeared in such Broadway shows as *Two Gentlemen of Verona* (for which he received a Tony nomination) and *Do It Again.* He acted in the films *Together Forever* and *Lost in the Stars* and in the TV series "Love American Style" and "That's My Mama." Clifton Davis also wrote the Jackson Five's big hit "Never Can Say Goodbye."

OCTOBER 5

1941: Chantels lead singer Arlene Smith is born in the Bronx.

The Chantels recorded the classic R&B ballad "Maybe" in 1957. It went to number 2 on the R&B charts and to the Top 20 on the pop charts. The Chantels had several follow-ups, including "Every Night" (1958), "I Love You So" (1958) and "Look in My Eyes" (1961).

Besides Smith, the group was made up of Sonia Goring, Lois Harris, Jackie Landry and Renee Minus. They were all students at St. Anthony's High School and took their group name from a rival high school's basketball team. They auditioned for Richard Barrett, the same man who discovered Frankie Lymon, and were signed to End Records.

1974: The Mighty Clouds of Joy, one of gospel music's most rocking groups, hit the soul singles chart, with "Time."

They have continued to hit the charts over the years, with such singles as

"Mighty Cloud of Joy" (1975), "Mighty High" (1976), "There's Love in the World" (1977) and "Glow Love" (1982).

The Mighty Clouds of Joy were formed in Los Angeles in 1959 by Ermant Franklin, Jr. The original group consisted of Franklin, Elmer Franklin (no relation), Richard Wallace, Willie Joe Ligon, Leon Polk and Johnny Martin.

In the '60s they recorded for Peacock Records. In the '70s they signed with ABC/Dunhill Records and began hitting the pop charts. The lead vocals on their most popular tunes are handled by Johnny Martin and Willie Joe Ligon.

The Mighty Clouds of Joy have recorded numerous albums. Among their best are *The Mighty Clouds Live at the Music Hall, The Best of, Truth Is the Power, The Mighty Clouds Alive* and *Catching On.*

OCTOBER 6

1951: The Cardinals make their R&B chart debut with "Shouldn't I Know."

The Cardinals were formed in Baltimore in 1946 and were first called the Mellotones. The members were Ernie Warren, Prince Brothers, Leon Hardy and Donald Johnson. Their other hits were "The Wheel of Fortune" (1952) and "The Door Is Still Open" (1955).

OCTOBER 7

1957: "American Bandstand" makes its network TV debut.

"American Bandstand" began in Philadelphia in 1955 as a local "dance party" show hosted by Dick Clark. It was a showcase for talent, dances, fads and fashion in the rock 'n' roll culture. It was equally important for black music. The show helped bring scores of black recording artists into the mainstream. In many cases it was the only show on TV where black entertainers of the day could be seen.

"American Bandstand" was also important for the variety of music it featured. Mixed in with Elvis Presley, Chubby Checker and Paul Anka were records by such blues artists as B. B.

King and Slim Harpo and even country artists like Patsy Cline.

"American Bandstand" lasted until the late 1980s and spawned many imitators.

OCTOBER 8

1950: Kool and the Gang leader Robert "Kool" Bell is born in Jersey City, New Jersey.

In the early 1970s there was always the question, in pop circles, of which combo had the hottest horn section: Chicago or Blood, Sweat and Tears? The latter used jazzy horn interjections; Chicago's hornmen had proved beyond a doubt that they could really rear back and blow. But the best answer to that question was squarely at the top of the so-called soul charts, a straight-ahead little funk band called Kool and the Gang.

The band, first formed as the Jazzaics in 1964 by brothers Ronald and Robert "Kool" Bell, had put together a string of popular hits that were composed mostly of hard-funk riffs and vocal chants. Songs like "Jungle Boogie," "Hollywood Swinging," "Funky Stuff" and "I Want to Take You Higher" had made Kool and the Gang a major force in black music and had given them "crossover" berths in the pop Top 40.

First hitting the charts in 1969, by the late 1970s Kool and the Gang were becoming a mainstream pop act. One of their Top 10 black chart singles, "Open Sesame," was included on the monstrously successful *Saturday Night Fever* soundtrack album.

During this period the band members made three major changes. First, having previously produced most of their own records, they opted to bring in an outside producer for future projects. Second, they toned down their usual rough-edged funk sound in favor of a more mellow pop sound. Third, they recruited smooth-voiced James "J. T." Taylor as lead singer.

These new pieces fit together nicely for the 1979 LP *Ladies' Night*. The title track hit number 8 on the pop charts, and the album produced two hot singles, "Too Hot" and "Hangin' Out."

In 1981 the song "Celebration," from the *Celebrate* LP, was the number 7 best-selling single of the year and spent more than seven months on the national Hot 100.

Something Special, in 1981, became the group's third consecutive platinum-selling album and produced three hit singles: "Steppin' Out," "Get Down On It" and "Take My Heart." Their *As One* album featured another pair of high-charting singles, "Let's Go Dancin'" and "Big Fun."

In 1984 and 1985 Kool and the Gang soared to an all-time high in record sales and popularity. Their smash hit "Joanna" was one of the songs most played in 1984, and in 1985 they placed three songs on the list of the year's best-sellers: "Cherish," "Misled" and "Fresh." In 1989 Taylor left the group and went solo.

At the height of their popularity, Kool and the Gang had Robert "Kool" Bell on bass, Taylor on lead vocals, Robert Mickens and Michael Ray on trumpet, Dennis Thomas on alto sax, Ronald Bell on tenor sax, Clifford Adams on trombone, Amir Bayyan on keyboards, Charles Smith on guitar and George Brown on drums.

OCTOBER 9

1934: Jazz pianist and saxophonist Abdullah Ibrahim is born in Cape Town, South Africa. For much of his career Abdullah Ibrahim performed under the name Dollar Brand. Ibrahim is a vocalist and composer, as well as a top-flight performer on piano, soprano saxophone, cello and the Indian-African flute.

He began taking piano lessons at the age of seven and was influenced by American gospel music, Louis Jordan and Duke Ellington. His first professional job in music was with a singing group called the Streamline Brothers. In 1960 he formed his own group, the Jazz Epistles, which included Hugh Masakela and was the first black group in South Africa to record an album.

Ibrahim moved to Europe in 1962 and settled in Zurich. He attracted the attention of Duke Ellington, who arranged for him to record. With Ellington's help, he toured Europe and came to the U.S. in 1965. He worked in the mid-1960s "free jazz" movement with Don Cherry, Ornette Coleman and John Coltrane. In 1966 he was with the group of drummer Elvin Jones. In 1968 Ibrahim returned to Africa.

He spent most of the 1970s shuttling among Africa, the U.S. and Europe. In 1977 he moved to the U.S. He often worked solo during this period but also used a trio or a quintet and performed with his wife, jazz vocalist Sathima Bea Benjamin.

In 1980 he composed *Kalahari Liberation Opera*, a collage of music, dance and drama. In the mid-1980s he formed the seven-piece band Ekaya.

Abdullah Ibrahim's best LPs include *African Sketchbook*, *Good News from Africa*, *Africa Tears and Laughter*, *At Montreux*, *Zimbabwe* and *Ekaya*.

1939: Soul singer Overton Vertis "O. V." Wright is born in Leno, Tennessee.

Before concentrating on pop music, Wright sang with such gospel groups as the Highway Q.C.s, the Sunset Travelers and the Spirits of Memphis. Wright recorded for Backbeat and Hi Records in the 1960s and 1970s. His biggest hits included "You're Gonna Make Me Cry" (1965), "Eight Men, Four Women" (1967), "Heartaches, Heartaches" (1967), "Ace of Spade" (1970), "A Nickel and a Nail" (1971) and "I'd Rather Be Blind, Crippled and Crazy" (1973).

O. V. Wright died on November 16, 1980.

1954: Shirley Gunter and the Queens make their R&B chart debut, the first black all-female R&B group to do so.

The group was formed in Los Angeles and included Zola Taylor, who became a member of the Platters. Their big hit was called "Oop Shoop."

1976: Rose Royce makes its chart debut with the theme song from the movie *Carwash*, hitting number 1 on both the soul and pop charts. The single sold over two million copies.

The group was formed in Los Angeles, under the name Total Concepts

Unlimited, and backed Edwin Starr, Yvonne Fair, the Temptations and Undisputed Truth. The members were Kenji Brown (guitar) Victor Nix (keyboards), Kenny Copeland and Freddie Dunn (trumpets), Michael Moore (sax), Duke Jobe (bass), Henry Garner and Terral Santiel (drums) and Gwen Dickey (vocals).

Most of Rose Royce's early hits were written and produced by Norman Whitfield. The group had a string of best-selling singles: "I Wanna Get Next to You" (1977), "I'm Going Down" (1977), "Do Your Dance" (1977), "Ooh Boy" (1977), "I'm in Love" (1978) and "Love Don't Live Here Anymore" (1979).

In 1980 Dickey and Brown left the group.

OCTOBER 10

1914: Singer and songwriter Ivory Joe Hunter is born in Kirbyville, Texas.

During the 1930s Hunter sang gospel music, recorded for the Library of Congress and had his own radio show in Beaumont, Texas. He moved to the West Coast in 1942 and recorded for his own labels before signing with King Records, in 1947.

Between 1945 and 1958 Hunter placed over 20 singles on the national R&B charts. His biggest hits were "Blues at Sunrise" (1945), "Pretty Mama Blues" (1948), "Waiting in Vain" (1949), "Guess Who" (1949), "Jealous Heart" (1949), "I Almost Lost My Mind" (1950), "I Need You So" (1950), "Since I Lost My Baby" (1956) and "Empty Arms" (1957). Hunter was fond of country music, and "Jealous Heart," although it hit number 2 on the R&B chart, was essentially a country song. Toward the end of his career, Hunter became a country-music performer.

Ivory Joe Hunter died of lung cancer on November 8, 1974.

1915: Jazz trumpeter Harry "Sweets" Edison is born in Columbus, Ohio.

From 1938 to 1950 Edison was one of the main players in the fantastic Count Basie Orchestra. His solos can be heard on such top Basie recordings as "Shorty George," "Jive at Five" and "Sent for You Yesterday."

Before joining Basie, Edison had played with Earl Hood and Lucky Millinder. In 1950, when Count Basie cut his big band down to a smaller combo, Sweets Edison worked as musical director for Josephine Baker and with Frank Sinatra. He also became a cherished session musician, as well as a fixture in the "Jazz at the Philharmonic" programs. In the mid-1950s he began recording on his own.

In the 1970s, when not recording or touring, Sweets Edison taught at Yale University.

1968: Singer, songwriter and producer Michael Bivins is born in Boston.

Bivins was a member of the hit group New Edition and its spinoff, the equally popular Bell-Biv-Devoe. Michael Bivins was also responsible for discovering and producing the top 1990s group Boyz II Men.

OCTOBER 11

1917: Pianist Thelonious "Sphere" Monk, one of the godfathers of modern jazz, is born in Rocky Mount, North Carolina. He was known for his creativity, his technique and the mysterious aura that surrounded him.

Monk moved to New York at the age of five. He took piano lessons at the age of 11 and by the age of 14 was playing at Harlem rent parties and for his mother's church choir. He formed his own trio and then spent two years touring with an evangelist.

In 1939 Monk joined the Keg Purnell Quartet. From 1940 to 1942 he was with Kenny Clarke at the famed "cradle of modern jazz," Minton's Playhouse. In 1942 he played in Lucky Millinder's band. In 1943 he joined the Coleman Hawkins Sextet.

Monk had his first real recording session with the Hawkins band, in 1944. In 1945 he was in the Skippy Williams band, and in 1946 he was with Dizzy Gillespie's big band.

Monk began recording on his own in 1947 and playing at Minton's and the Village Vanguard in New York. His early

sidemen included Milt Jackson, Art Blakey and Sonny Rollins. In the late 1940s Monk recorded some of his signature tunes—"Round Midnight, "Ruby My Dear" and "Straight, No Chaser"—for the Blue Note label.

In 1951 Monk was arrested for drug possession. He was found innocent but still lost his cabaret card, which meant that he couldn't play New York clubs. For the next few years Monk continued to record but rarely played live gigs. During this time he recorded for the Prestige and Riverside Jazz labels.

In 1956 he released an album of his own tunes, *Brilliant Corners*. He regained his cabaret card in 1957 and formed a quartet with John Coltrane, Philly Joe Jones and Wilbur Ware. In 1959 he played Town Hall with a big band.

In 1961 Monk toured Europe. He performed at Lincoln Center in 1963. He played Japan and the Monterey Jazz Festival in 1964. He toured Europe again in 1967 with a band that included Thelonious Monk, Jr., on drums.

By the late 1960s and early 1970s Monk was accepting fewer and fewer engagements. One of his last appearances was at the 1970 Newport Jazz Festival. In 1970 and 1971 he toured with the Giants of Jazz. In the last six years of his life he did not perform in public.

Monk's most highly recommended albums include *The Genius of Modern*

THELONIOUS MONK

Music, Pure Monk, The Man I Love, The Unique Thelonious Monk, Brilliant Corners, Monk's Music (this LP cover is a classic), *Thelonious Monk with John Coltrane, Alone in San Francisco* and *Thelonious Monk and Max Roach: European Tour.*

Thelonious Monk died of a stroke on February 17, 1982, in Englewood, New Jersey.

1919: Jazz drummer Art Blakey is born in Pittsburgh.

Blakey began as a self-taught pianist. By the age of 15 he was leading his own club group. When a pianist named Erroll Garner joined the band, Blakey switched to drums.

During the early and mid-1940s he played in the bands of Mary Lou Williams and Fletcher Henderson and spent three years with Billy Eckstine. In 1947 Blakey formed his own big band, the Seventeen Messengers, and recorded for the Blue Note label. After the band folded, he freelanced into the early 1950s, working with Thelonious Monk, Charlie Parker, Miles Davis, Horace Silver, Lucky Millinder and Buddy DeFranco.

Blakey founded the Jazz Messengers in 1954, with Silver, Kenny Dorham, Hank Mobley and Davey Watkins. The group had first assembled as sidemen for Silver's recording of "The Preacher." Over the next 30 years the Jazz Messengers included such noted players as Wayne Shorter, Bobby Watson, Freddie Hubbard, Lee Morgan, Cedar Walton, Keith Jarrett, Chick Corea and Wynton Marsalis.

There are many, many superb albums by Art Blakey and the Jazz Messengers. Among the most highly recommended are *For Minors Only, Night in Tunisia, Live at Ronnie Scott's, Album of the Year, Art Blakey and Max Roach: Percussion Discussion, Art Blakey and the All-Star Jazz Messengers, At Cafe Bohemia, With Thelonious Monk* and *A Night at Birdland, Volumes 1* and 2.

Although Blakey played most of his live gigs with the Jazz Messengers, he frequently recorded with such other artists as Sonny Rollins, Milt Jackson

and Cannonball Adderley. In 1971 and 1972 he toured with the Giants of Jazz.

Art Blakey died on October 16, 1990.

1941: Trumpeter, vocalist, composer and percussionist Lester Bowie, best known as a founder of the jazz theatrical group Art Ensemble of Chicago, is born in Frederick, Maryland.

Bowie was raised in Little Rock, Arkansas, and St. Louis, Missouri. He began playing music at the age of five.

In the mid-1960s he was a session man at Chess Records. He played in Roscoe Mitchell's band, and later he and Mitchell formed the Art Ensemble of Chicago. In the late '60s and early '70s he composed for and conducted the 50-piece Baden-Baden Free Jazz Orchestra, in Germany. In 1979 he played New York with a 50-plus-piece band called the Sho Nuff Orchestra.

Lester Bowie is one of jazz's most flamboyant performers. He is also married to vocalist Fontella ("Rescue Me") Bass.

OCTOBER 12

1929: Blues shouter Nappy Brown is born Napoleon Culp Brown in Charlotte, North Carolina.

Brown got his start in gospel music. He sang with such groups as the Golden Bell Quartet, the Selah Singers and the Heavenly Lights.

In the 1950s Brown was one of the hardest R&B rockers and shouters around. He had best-selling hits such as "Don't Be Angry" (1955), "Pitter Patter" (1955), "It Don't Hurt No More" (1958) and "I Cried Like a Baby" (1959).

In the 1960s he returned to gospel music, but in the 1980s he came back to his rocking R&B style. Nappy Brown's best current LP is *Something Gonna Jump Out the Bushes.*

1935: Sam Moore, of Sam and Dave, is born in Miami.

Sam Moore and Dave Prater teamed up in Miami in 1961. Moore had been in a gospel group, and Prater had been a solo club act. Early in their careers they recorded for such labels as Roulette and Alston but had little luck.

In 1965 they signed with Stax Records and scored a long list of chart hits, including "You Don't Know Like I Know," "Hold On, I'm Coming," "Said I Wasn't Gonna Tell Nobody," "You Got Me Humming," "Soul Man" and "I Thank You."

In 1970 the duo broke up to pursue solo careers. In April 1988 Dave Prater was killed in an auto accident. Sam Moore had been working with other partners and as a solo performer. He is a frequent guest on the TNN cable show "Nashville Now."

OCTOBER 13

1910: Jazz pianist Art Tatum is born in Toledo, Ohio.

Tatum suffered from cataracts, which left him with only partial vision in one eye. He attended the Cousino School for the Blind in Columbus, Ohio, and studied piano and violin. He also attended the Toledo School of Music.

In 1926 he formed a small band and began playing clubs around Toledo. In the late 1920s he was in Speed Webb's band, and in 1929 he began broadcasting over radio station WSPD in Toledo. In 1932 he became the accompanist for singer Adelaide Hall, playing clubs around New York. Also in 1932 he recorded "Tiger Rag." The following year he began recording for the Decca

ART TATUM

label. In the late 1930s Tatum worked as a soloist in New York, Hollywood, Chicago and England.

Tatum formed a trio with bassist Slam Stewart and guitarist Tiny Grimes in 1943. In 1945 he began his annual concert tours, which lasted until 1954.

During the last few years of his life Tatum recorded over a dozen LPs of solo pieces. His most recommended LPs and CD collections are *Solo Masterpieces*; *Pure Genius*; *Group Masterpieces, Volume 1*; and *Groovy Masterpieces, Volume 6*.

Art Tatum's last big appearance came at the Hollywood Bowl, on August 15, 1956. He died on November 3, 1956.

1938: Evangelist Shirley Caesar, today's top female gospel singer, is born in Durham, North Carolina.

Caesar was one of 12 children. She began her gospel-music career at the age of 10, performing in the Carolinas and Virginia as Baby Shirley. At the age of 12 she recorded for the Federal label.

In 1958 Caesar auditioned for Albertina Walker and became a member of Walker's superstar gospel group, the Caravans. She remained with the Caravans for eight years and then left to become an evangelist.

Her first LP, *I'll Go*, was released on Hob Records. Her first big hit was "The Stranger on the Road." From Hob, she went to the Roadshow label, where she became known as the first lady of gospel music. Her best-selling LPs include *Live in Chicago*, *Celebration*, *Love Parade*, *Sailin'*, *Rejoice*, *I Love Calling Your Name*, *Go*, *The Best of Shirley Caesar* and *Greatest Hits, Volumes 1* and *2*.

In 1971 Caesar won her first Grammy, for "Put Your Hand in the Hand of the Man from Galilee." She has won four other Grammy awards and five Dove awards (gospel music's Grammy) and has at least three million-selling LPs.

Since the mid-1970s Caesar has hosted her own radio series. In 1984 she graduated from Shaw University with a bachelor's degree in business administration. She operates the Shirley Caesar Outreach Ministries, which administers a food program for the needy. She also donates a portion of the receipts from her sold-out concerts to buy food, clothing, toys and shelter for the needy.

1940: Jazz saxophonist Pharaoh Sanders is born in Little Rock, Arkansas.

Sanders began playing flute and sax at the age of 16. He played in R&B bands and, later, in the jazz groups of Vi Redd and Philly Joe Jones.

In 1962 he moved to New York and worked with Sun Ra, Don Cherry and several other avant-garde jazz performers. In the late '60s he worked with John Coltrane. After Coltrane's death he worked with Alice Coltrane until 1969, before forming his own group.

The best Pharaoh Sanders LPs include *Thembi*, *The Heart Is a Melody*, *Shukura* and *Live*.

1926: Jazz bassist Ray Brown is born in Pittsburgh.

Brown was just 19 when he joined Dizzy Gillespie's band, but he has been one of the jazz world's most prominent bassists ever since. In 1947 he formed his own trio, to back singer Ella Fitzgerald, whom he married in 1949. The marriage ended in 1952. From 1951 to 1966 Ray Brown belonged to the Oscar Peterson Trio.

1979: The song "Rapper's Delight" makes its chart debut.

"Rapper's Delight" was the song that brought rap music, break dancing and hip-hop culture out of the streets and clubs of the Bronx and Harlem and into the mainstream of American pop culture. It was performed by the Sugarhill Gang, whose members were Michael "Wonder Mike" Wright, Guy "Master Gee" O'Brien and Henry "Big Bank Hank" Jackson. They were given their names by their record label, Sugar Hill Records. The Sugarhill Gang's follow-up raps included "Eighth Wonder" (1980) and "Apache" (1981).

OCTOBER 14

1924: Vocalist and guitarist Jimmy Liggins is born in Newby, Oklahoma.

Liggins had such R&B chart hits as "Tear Drop Blues" (1948), "Careful Love" (1949), "Don't Put Me Down" (1949) and "Drunk" (1953). He was a professional boxer who trained with Archie Moore and got into show business while driving the bus for his older brother's band, Joe Liggins and the Honeydrippers.

Joe Liggins and the Honeydrippers were one of the major R&B acts of the late 1940s. Joe Liggins was a pianist and vocalist. In 1945 he reportedly had a million-selling single, "The Honeydripper." He also had top R&B hits with "Left a Good Deal in Mobile" (1945), "Got a Right to Cry" (1946), "Tanya" (1946), "Blow, Mr. Jackson" (1947), "Sweet Georgia Brown" (1948), "Pink Champagne" (1950) and "Little Joe's Boogie" (1951). He was born in 1915 and died on August 1, 1987.

1924: Blues guitarist James "Son" Thomas is born in Eden, Mississippi.

Thomas is one of the Deep South's best-known bluesmen. His stomping ground is the Mississippi Delta blues club circuit, where he carries on the tradition of hardline Delta blues. He was the subject of the 1969 film documentary *Delta Blues Singer: James "Sonny Ford" Thomas* and appeared on the PBS program "Mississippi Folk Roots: Delta Blues." Son Thomas's best LP is *Highway 61 Blues*.

OCTOBER 15

1906: Blues singer and pianist Victoria Spivey, one of the best of the 1920s blues queens, is born in Houston.

In her teens she worked as a pianist at the Lincoln Theater in Dallas, and later she worked with Blind Lemon Jefferson and L. C. Tolen's band. In the '20s she signed with Okeh Records. Her first hit was "Black Snake Blues," in 1926. She also recorded "Dope Head Blues," "Murder in the First Degree" and "T.B. Blues."

Throughout the '30s and '40s Spivey stared in such theatrical shows as *Dallas Tan Town Revue* and *Hellzapoppin'*. She also appeared in the all-black musical film *Hallelujah*.

In the late '40s and early '50s Spivey did radio, clubs and theaters. In the '60s she formed her own company, to record and promote young blues talent. In the '70s she played rock clubs like Max's Kansas City, in New York.

Victoria Spivey continued to perform right up until her death, on October 3, 1976.

1915: Vocalist and pianist Nellie Lutcher is born in Lake Charles, Louisiana.

In the late 1940s Lutcher had a string of jazz-flavored R&B chart hits, including "Hurry On Down" (1947), "He's a Real Gone Guy" (1947), "The Song Is Ended (But the Melody Lingers On)" (1948), "Fine Brown Frame" (1948), "Come and Get It, Honey" (1948), "Cool Water" (1948) and "For You, My Love" (1950).

Nellie Lutcher recorded into the 1960s and was once featured on the TV show "This Is Your Life."

1925: Vocalist and guitarist Mickey Baker is born in Louisville.

Baker was one of the most prolific session guitarists of R&B and early rock 'n' roll. His work can be heard on such labels as King, Savoy and Atlantic.

In 1956 he teamed up with singer Sylvia Vanderpool (Robinson) to record a rock 'n' roll classic, "Love Is Strange." The song hit the Top 10 on both the pop and the soul charts. The duo had one more hit, "There Oughta Be a Law," the following year.

1938: Singer Marv Johnson is born in Detroit.

Several of Johnson's early hits were produced by Berry Gordy, Jr. His biggest were "Come to Me" (1959), "You Got What It Takes" (1959), "I Love the Way You Love" (1960), "Move Two Mountains" (1960), "Happy Days" (1960) and "Merry Go Round" (1961). Johnson also worked in record promotion for Motown.

Marv Johnson died on May 16, 1993, after a stroke suffered backstage at a performance in South Carolina.

OCTOBER 16

1935: Sugar Pie DeSanto, one of the hardest-wailing female soul singers of the 1960s, is born Umpeylia Marsema Balinton in Brooklyn.

DeSanto worked with the Johnny Otis Rhythm and Blues Caravan Show in the 1950s and with James Brown's show in 1959 and 1960. Her biggest hits in the 1960s included "I Want to Know" (1960), "Slip in Mules" (1964), "I Don't Want to Fight" (1965) and "In the Basement" (with Etta James, 1966).

OCTOBER 17

1909: Jazz drummer William Randolph "Cozy" Cole, best known to pop fans for his Top 10 1958 instrumental hit "Topsy, Part 2," is born in East Orange, New Jersey.

Cole had a long and varied career. In the 1930s he played in the bands of Benny Carter, Stuff Smith and Jonah Jones. He spent 1938 to 1942 with Cab Calloway and then joined Raymond Scott's CBS radio network orchestra. In the mid-1940s he was the house drummer at Billy Rose's Ziegfield Theater. He also worked with Benny Goodman. In 1949 he joined Louis Armstrong's band.

Cozy Cole died on January 29, 1981.

OCTOBER 18

Chuck Berry is born Charles Edward Anderson Berry in San Jose, California.

Berry grew up in St. Louis. He worked as a house painter and hairdresser. With pianist Johnnie Johnson and drummer Ebby Harding, he formed a trio to play clubs in St. Louis and, eventually, Chicago, where he met Muddy Waters, who took him to Chess Records.

On May 21, 1955, Chuck Berry recorded a song he had written, originally called "Ida May." Record producer Leonard Chess suggested another title. "Maybelline" was an instant hit, landing at number 1 on the R&B charts and number 5 on the pop charts.

As Berry toured, audiences soon discovered that he was an exciting performer. He wielded his guitar like a machine gun, moving around the stage and doing splits and duckwalks.

Berry ran up a string of rock 'n' roll hits, classics like "Wee Wee Hours" (1955), "Thirty Days" (1955), "Roll Over Beethoven" (1956), "Too Much Monkey Business" (1956), "Brown-Eyed Handsome Man" (1956), "School Days" (1957), "Rock 'n' Roll Music" (1957), "Sweet Little Sixteen" (1958), "Johnny B. Goode" (1958), "Carol" (1958), "Almost Grown" (1959), "Little Queenie" (1959) and "Back in the USA" (1959).

In 1959 Berry was arrested for a violation of the Mann act, in an incident involving a 14-year-old girl. In 1962 he was convicted, and he served two years in prison. Upon his release he rocked right back onto the charts, with "Nadine" (1964), "No Particular Place to Go" (1964), "You Never Can Tell" (1964) and "Promised Land" (1964). Berry scored his only number 1 pop single and only million-selling single in 1972, with the novelty tune "My Ding-a-Ling."

There is a boxed set of Chuck Berry's music available, but for a few dollars less *The Great 28* is an excellent buy.

Berry has appeared in several films, including *Rock, Rock, Rock* (1956), *Go Johnny, Go* (1958) and the documentary *Hail, Hail Rock 'n' Roll* (1987). In 1984 Chuck Berry was awarded a lifetime-achievement Grammy, and in 1986 he was inducted into the Rock 'n' Roll Hall of Fame.

CHUCK BERRY

1961: Wynton Marsalis is born in New Orleans.

Marsalis was given his first trumpet at age six by Al Hirt, but he didn't take the instrument seriously until he began studying classical music, at age 12. He played first trumpet in the New Orleans Civic Orchestra throughout high school and was admitted into the Berkshire Music Center at Tanglewood at age 17. At 18 he entered Juilliard. He performed as a pit musician in the Broadway production of *Sweeney Todd* and played with the Brooklyn Philharmonic. During the same period, he joined Art Blakey and the Jazz Messengers and was soon signed to Columbia Records.

In the summer of 1981 he took a leave of absence from Blakey to go on the road with the Herbie Hancock Quartet, playing on the West Coast, in Japan and at the Newport Jazz Festival.

In January of 1982 his self-titled debut album was issued. The album was voted best jazz LP of the year in magazines like *Down Beat* and *Stereo Review* and earned Marsalis a Grammy nomination. His second LP, *Fathers and Sons*, was released the same year. *I Think of One* was released in June 1983.

At the 1984 Grammy award ceremonies Marsalis became the first instrumentalist to win back-to-back awards in the categories of jazz and classical music. He also won the coveted Edison award in Holland and France's Grand Prix du Disque. In 1984 Marsalis also began his first full-scale classical music tour, performing 24 concerts with orchestras across the U.S. and Canada and in Hawaii and London, and his *Hot House Flowers* album was released.

In 1985 he again won back-to-back Grammy awards in jazz and classical music. In 1986 his *Black Codes* won Grammy awards for best jazz instrumental in both the soloist and group categories. In 1987 he collected his seventh Grammy, for the LP *J. Mood*.

Marsalis is undoubtedly the most acclaimed jazz artist of the 1980s. He set an all-time record in *Down Beat* magazine's readers' poll when he was voted jazz musician of the year seven years in a row, 1982 to 1988. Wynton Marsalis's father, Ellis, is a widely respected musician, composer and educator. His brother Branford is a top-notch jazz saxophonist and leader of the "Tonight Show" band. Another brother, Delfeayo, is a respected jazz record producer.

OCTOBER 19

1944: Singer George McCrae is born in West Palm Beach, Florida.

Some critics see McCrae's 1974 release "Rock Your Baby" as the first disco record. McCrae had several hits, all written and produced by Harry Wayne Casey of K. C. and the Sunshine Band. They include "I Can't Leave You Alone" (1974) and "I Get Lifted" (1974). He also recorded a pair of duets with his wife, Gwen McCrae, "Honey I" (1975) and "Winners Together or Losers Apart" (1976).

George McCrae died of cancer on January 24, 1986.

1944: Reggae singer and songwriter Peter Tosh is born Winston Hubert McIntosh in Kingston, Jamaica.

By the time he was a teenager, Tosh was already adept at playing guitar, steel guitar and keyboards. Tosh, Bob Marley and Bunny Livingstone formed reggae's most influential group, the Wailers. The trio split up in 1974, and Marley went on to become the guru of reggae music.

As a songwriter Tosh's favorite subjects were politics, religion and civil rights. Two of his earliest solo hits, "March of the Beast" and "Legalize It," were banned in his homeland, and his 1977 LP *Equal Rights* was considered a radical work.

In 1978 Tosh signed with Rolling Stones Records. Tosh, reggae bassist Sly Dunbar and drummer Robbie Shakespeare were guests on the Rolling Stones' American tour of that year. Also in 1978 his album *Bush Doctor* produced a hit single, "Don't Look Back." In 1981 he had a successful duet single with Gwen Guthrie, "Nothing But Love."

On September 11, 1987, Peter Tosh was fatally shot during a robbery at his home in Kingston.

1960: Singer Jennifer Holliday is born in Riverside, Texas.

Holliday sang in the church choir and on local radio and TV shows. She made her Broadway debut at the age of 17.

She won a Tony award and two Grammies for her show-stopping performance in the Broadway musical *Dream Girls*, and she has also performed in the Broadway musicals *Your Arms Too Short to Box With God* and *Sing, Mahalia, Sing*. She has placed several singles on the pop charts, including "And I Am Telling You I'm Not Going" (from *Dream Girls*, 1982) and "I Am Love" (1983). In 1992 she sang at the Democratic National Convention.

OCTOBER 20

1885: Pianist Jelly Roll Morton is born Ferdinand Joseph Lementhe in New Orleans. (Some sources give the year of his birth as 1890.)

Morton (that was his stepfather's name) learned to play piano, trombone and guitar as a child. In the early 1900s he angered his respectable family by playing piano in the whorehouses of the Storyville district in New Orleans.

In 1906 Morton left New Orleans and traveled around playing piano throughout Mississippi and Louisiana. In 1909 he joined a minstrel show. He worked in St. Louis and Kansas City. In Chicago he led his own club band. In 1915 he played San Francisco's Panama-Pacific Exposition. In 1917 he settled in the Los Angeles area, where he ran his own club and formed another band. He also played briefly in Tijuana, Mexico.

Morton moved to Chicago in 1923 and recorded with a band called the New Orleans Rhythm Kings, in July of that year. Over the next couple of years he recorded his famous "King Porter Stomp," a string of piano solos. He also played with a trio that included clarinetist Johnny Dodds and drummer Baby Dodds. In 1926 Morton recorded the first of his "Red Hot Peppers" sessions. He also worked as staff arranger for Melrose Publishers.

In 1928 he moved to New York City and formed his own big band, called the Red Hot Peppers or, at the time, the Chicago Syncopators.

Hard times befell Morton in the 1930s. His popularity waned, and he lost most of his money in an ill-fated business venture. In 1936 he settled in Washington, D.C., and was out of the music field until 1938, when he recorded for the Library of Congress. He then returned to New York and formed a publishing company.

The best CD collection of Morton's music is called *Great Original Performances, 1926–1934*. His music is currently being celebrated in the Broadway musical *Jelly's Last Jam*. He was also one of the first jazz recording artists to use written musical arrangements.

In 1940 Morton moved back to California. His health began to fail, and he entered a private sanitarium in June 1941. Jelly Roll Morton died of a heart condition on July 10, 1941, in Los Angeles.

1936: Jazzman Eddie Harris, master of tenor sax, piano, organ and trumpet, is born in Chicago.

Harris began his career as keyboardist for Gene Ammons's band. Harris came to notice in 1961, when he hit the Top 40 with his version of the theme from the movie *Exodus*. His other single chart hits include "Listen Here" (1968), "Cold Duck" (1970), and "Is It In" (1974).

Over most of his career Harris's music has been considered too jazzy for rock, and too rock-oriented for jazz. His best LPs include *The Best of Eddie Harris*, *The Electrifying Eddie Harris*, *Live at Newport* and *E.H. in the U.K.*

1962: The Tams make their chart debut with "Untie Me."

The Tams hailed from Atlanta. The members were lead singer Joseph Pope, Charles Pope, Robert Smith, Floyd Ashton and Horace Key. Their biggest hits were "What Kind of Fool" (1963), "You Lied to Your Daddy" (1964), "Hey Girl, Don't Bother Me" (1964), "Silly Little Girl" (1964) and "Be Young, Be Foolish, Be Happy" (1968).

The Tams were extremely popular in the Southeast. A unit of the group still performs today.

OCTOBER 21

1912: Jazz saxophonist Don Byas is born in Muskogee, Oklahoma.

In the early 1930s Byas played in the bands of Bennie Moten and Walter Page. In the mid-1930s he was with Lionel Hampton and Buck Clayton on the West Coast.

In 1937 he moved to New York and played in the big bands of Don Redman, Lucky Millinder, Andy Kirk and Benny Carter. In 1941 he replaced Lester Young in Count Basie's orchestra. He played in Dizzy Gillespie's first small group, in 1944, and later in Charlie Parker's band. In the mid-1940s he visited Europe and gained a following there. He settled in France and played the 1949 Paris Jazz Fair. He returned to the U.S. only once, in 1970. His best LPs include *Midnight at Minton's* and *Savoy Jam Party*.

Don Byas died of lung cancer in Copenhagen on August 24, 1972.

1917: John Birks "Dizzy" Gillespie is born in Cheraw, South Carolina.

Gillespie took up the trumpet as a child. By the age of 14 he was leading his own band. He gained a music scholarship to Laurinburg Institute but left before his senior year. He moved to Philadelphia in 1935.

He began his professional career in the band of Bill Doggett, but it was a short gig: Doggett fired him for not being able to read chart arrangements. His next job was with Frank Fairfax's orchestra. In 1937 Teddy Hill hired Gillespie to replace Roy Eldridge. Gillespie joined Cab Calloway's band in 1935.

He began formulating what was to become bebop around 1940, while touring with the Calloway band. In 1941 Gillespie and some other young musicians, including Charlie Parker, Thelonious Monk and Kenny Clarke, began jamming together at a Harlem club called Minton's Uptown Playhouse. Out of these rhythmically improvisa-

tional jam sessions was born the jazz genre of bebop. Gillespie's tenure with Calloway ended in September 1941, when the two men got into a knife fight onstage during a gig at the State Theater, in Hartford.

After splitting with Calloway, Gillespie spent the next few years with Coleman Hawkins, Benny Carter, Les Hite, Lucky Millinder, Ella Fitzgerald, Earl "Fatha" Hines and Duke Ellington.

In 1944 he joined the newly formed Billy Eckstine band, and in 1945 he cut his first records as a group leader. These included "Night in Tunisia" and "Groovin' High" (with Charlie Parker), as well as "I Can't Get Started," "Good Bait," "Salt Peanuts," "Bebop," "Dizzy Atmosphere" and "All the Things You Are."

In 1946 Gillespie organized a big band that included Sonny Stitt, Ray Brown, Milt Jackson and Kenny Clarke. By 1947 Gillespie was intermingling Afro-Cuban rhythms, with the help of conga player Chano Pozo.

Gillespie broke up the big band in 1956 and began recording with small groups on his own Dee Gee Record label. When the label folded, Gillespie and Parker recorded for the Verve label.

In 1952 Gillespie, Parker and Monk performed at Manhattan's Birdland. Gillespie then toured Europe and, in 1953, joined Parker, Bud Powell, Max Roach and Charles Mingus for the famed concert at Massey Hall, in Toronto. It was also in 1953 that someone fell on Gillespie's trumpet, bending it skyward. He thought it sounded better that way and left it as it was.

In the 1950s Gillespie recorded with Sonny Rollins, Sonny Stitt and Stan Getz. In 1956 he formed another big band and toured South America and Asia for the U.S. State Department. In 1974 Gillespie signed with Pablo Records and began recording prolifically again. He won Grammy awards in 1974 and 1980. Among the best Gillespie LPs and CDs are *Dee Gee Days (the Savoy Sessions)*, *Dizzy in Paris*, *A Portrait of Duke Ellington*, *The Giant*, *New Faces*, *Body and Soul* and *Dizzy Gillespie, Volumes 1 and 2*,

1946–1949. His autobiography, *Dizzy: to Be or Not to Bop*, was published in 1979.

Dizzy Gillespie died on January 6, 1993, in Englewood, New Jersey.

DIZZY GILLESPIE

OCTOBER 22

1986: "Word Up," by Cameo, is the number 1 black chart single.

Cameo was formed in 1974, as the New York Players. The group's leader was vocalist and drummer Larry "Mr. B" Blackmon. Over the years the act has included such members as Gregory Johnson, Wayne Cooper, Tomi Jenkins, Gary Dow and Arnett Leftenant. By 1985 Cameo was a trio, composed of Blackmon, Jenkins and Nathan Leftenant.

Cameo had a string of funk 'n' soul hits that included "I Just Want to Be" (1979), "Sparkle" (1979), "Shake Your Pants" (1980), "Keep It Hot" (1980), "Freaky Dancin'" (1981), "Flirt" (1982), "Alligator Woman" (1982), "She's Strange" (1984), "Attack Me with Your Love" (1985), "Single Life" (1985), "Candy" (1986) and "Back and Forth" (1987).

OCTOBER 23

1892: Blues pianist Rufus "Speckled Red" Perryman is born in Monroe, Louisiana.

Speckled Red's piano playing was closer to boogie-woogie than it was to blues. His best-known piece was a naughty thing called "The Dirty Dozens." He also performed as Detroit Red.

Speckled Red's brother, William Perryman, is known to rock 'n' roll music fans as Doctor Feelgood. With his group, the Interns, he had the 1982 pop hits "Doctor Feelgood" and "Right String but the Wrong Yo-Yo."

Speckled Red died on January 2, 1973. William Perryman died on July 25, 1985.

1930: Wilson "Boozoo" Chavis, a pioneer in zydeco, is born in Louisiana.

Chavis's music is less pop-oriented than that of the current zydeco bands. His best LPs include *Paper in My Shoe* and *Zydeco Homebrew*.

OCTOBER 24

1911: Blues singer and harmonica player Sonny Terry is born in Greensboro, Georgia.

Terry taught himself the harmonica at the age of eight. He was accidentally blinded in both eyes, one in 1922 and the other in 1927.

In the late 1920s and early 1930s he hoboed through North Carolina, playing streets, medicine shows and tobacco warehouses. In 1934 he teamed up with Blind Boy Fuller and recorded for Vocalion Records.

Terry is best known for his partnership with Brownie McGhee. He met McGhee in 1939 in Burlington, North Carolina. They started by playing on the streets in Durham. By 1940 they were recording for the Okeh label.

During the 1940s, along with McGhee, Terry worked and recorded with such artists as Leadbelly, Woody Guthrie and Champion Jack Dupree. Terry and McGhee appeared in *Finian's Rainbow* and *Cat on a Hot Tin Roof*, on radio WNYC's jazz festival and in the films *Whooping*, *The Blues* and *Blues Under the Skin*. They also did soundtracks for the films *Cisco, Pike*, *Buck and the Preacher* and *Book of Numbers*. The duo worked together right up until Sonny Terry's death, on March 11, 1986.

1925: Blues singer Willie Mabon is born in Hollywood, Tennessee.

Mabon went to Chicago in 1942 and first recorded in 1949, under the name Big Willie. For Chess Records, in the 1950s, he had R&B chart hits with "I Don't Know" (1953), "I Don't Care" (1953) and "Poison Ivy" (1954).

Willie Mabon died on April 19, 1985, in Paris.

1936: Blues guitarist Jimmy "Fast Fingers" Dawkins is born in Chychula, Mississippi.

Dawkins, one of the best and most popular acts on the current Chicago blues scene, first attracted attention in 1968, for his guitar work on the LP *Chicago Blues*, by Johnny Young and Big Walter Hawkins. In 1970 he recorded his first LP, *Fast Fingers*, and played the Ann Arbor Blues Festival. His other LPs include *Hot Wire*, *Blistering* and *All for Business*.

1942: *Billboard* magazine begins its Harlem Hit Parade chart.

Records made for and marketed to black audiences have been a viable and profitable product since the 1920s, but no sales or popularity polls were kept on this market until *Billboard*, the bible of the recording industry, began its Harlem Hit Parade. The system for charting single records included sales and jukebox play. In 1949 the chart was renamed Rhythm and Blues. In 1968 it became Soul Music, and in 1982 it became Black Music.

1942: The Ink Spots make their R&B chart debut.

The group was formed in Indianapolis in 1931. It was originally called King Jack and Jesters, but the name was changed to the Ink Spots the following year. The original members were Deek Watson, Charlie Fuqua, Orville "Happy" Jones and Jerry Daniels. In 1936 Jerry Daniels left the group and was replaced by Bill Kenny. They first recorded for the Victor label in 1935.

At first the Ink Spots favored jazz-flavored "jive" tunes but didn't have much success. In 1939 they signed with Decca Records and began concentrating on ballads. The combination of a single guitar background, Jones's deep bass and Kenny's lead vocals spelled success. Their first records for Decca were "Stompin' at the Savoy," "Keep Away from My Doorstep," "Sing High, Sing Low" and "Let's Call the Whole Thing Off."

In 1940 they had a string of hits: "Memories of You," "When the Swallows Come Home to Capistrano," "Stop Pretending," "I'll Never Smile Again" and "My Echo, My Shadow and Me." In 1941 they scored with "Java Jive," "Until the Real Thing Comes Along," "I Don't Want to Set the World on Fire" and "Don't Tell a Lie About Me and I Won't Tell a Lie About You."

In 1942, when *Billboard* magazine instituted its Harlem Hit Parade chart, the Ink Spots leapt onto it with three hits: "Don't Get Around Much Anymore," "Every Night About This Time" and "Just as Though You Were Here."

Over the next few years the Ink Spots had chart hits with "If I Cared a Little Bit Less" (1943), "I Can't Stand Losing You" (1943), "Cow Cow Boogie" (with Ella Fitzgerald, 1944), "I Can Get By" (1944), "Into Each Life Some Rain Must Fall" (1944), "I'm Making Believe" (with Ella Fitzgerald, 1944), "The Gypsy" (1946), "To Each His Own" (1946), "Prisoner of Love" (1946), and "The Best Things in Life Are Free" (1948).

Orville Jones died in 1944. Deek Watson left in 1945 to form his own group. Jones's place was taken by Herb Kenny, and Watson's was filled by Billy Bowen. Bill Kenny went solo in 1952. He died in 1978.

1944: Singer Bettye Swann is born in Shreveport, Louisiana.

Swann's biggest hits were "Don't Wait Too Long" (1965), "Make Me Yours" (1967), "Don't Touch Me" (1969) and "Victim of a Foolish Heart" (1972).

1962: James Brown records *Live at the Apollo*, on a Wednesday, midway through his weekly run at the theater.

Brown's recording company did not like the LP and shelved it for nearly a year before releasing it. *Live at the Apollo* quickly shot to number 2 on the LP charts.

James Brown's stage show was spectacular. Aside from Brown himself, the show's centerpiece was the James Brown Orchestra, which over the years featured such musicians as Maceo Parker, Fred Wesley, Nat Kendrick, Bernard Odum, Clyde Stubblefield and St. Clair Pinckney. Backup vocals were provided by the Famous Flames. The most noted Flames lineup was the mid-1960s crew of Bobby Byrd, Bobby Bennett and "Baby Lloyd" Stallworth. The show also featured the singers Anna King, Yvonne Fair, Tammy Montgomery (Tammi Terrell), Sugar Pie DeSanto, Lyn Collins, Vickie Anderson and the Jewels. Other members of Brown's troupe included singer James Crawford, comic Clay Tyson, female dancers called the Brownies and emcees Fats Gonder, Al Clark and Danny Ray, the guy with whom James Brown did his famous "cape" bit.

OCTOBER 25

1934: R&B saxophonist Sam "The Man" Taylor is born.

Taylor is best remembered as half of the sax duo that fronted the orchestra at Alan Freed's live rock 'n' roll shows in the 1950s. The other half of the honkin' duo was Big Al Sears.

Taylor had a series of instrumental R&B hits, including "Harlem Nocturne" (1955), "Hit the Road" (1956), "Look Out" (1956) and "Big Question" (1958).

OCTOBER 26

1911: Mahalia Jackson is born in New Orleans.

Jackson's mother died when Mahalia was five. She was raised by her aunt. She began singing in church as a child. She had to quit school in the eighth grade.

Jackson was surrounded from infancy by two very different styles of music: gospel and blues. Her father was a preacher, and she had two cousins who toured in the "black bottom" troupe of Ma Rainey. Jackson's own heroine was the great Bessie Smith.

Jackson moved to Chicago in 1927. She soon became a lead singer in the choir of the Greater Salem Baptist Church. She got her first professional

singing experience when her pastor's son, Robert Johnson, formed a group called the Johnson Gospel Singers and asked her to join.

By the mid-1930s Jackson was working as a solo artist under the name Halie Jackson and was winning an audience throughout the Midwest. On May 21, 1937, Jackson cut her first record for the Decca label. Her first songs were "Oh My Lord," "Keep Me Every Day" and "God Shall Wipe All Tears Away." The recordings gained Mahalia Jackson a huge following, especially in the South.

In the early 1940s Jackson worked with the Reverend Thomas A. Dorsey. She became the top gospel attraction on the circuit. Instead of the usual five or six songs that most gospel artists performed, Jackson did 15 or 20.

In 1946 Jackson signed with Apollo Records, where she began her long association with her famous accompanist, pianist Mildred Falls. In 1947 Jackson recorded "Move On Up a Little Higher," which reportedly sold over a million copies.

On October 4, 1950, Jackson made her Carnegie Hall debut. In 1952 she embarked on her first European tour. She signed with Columbia Records in 1954 and in the same year she had her own weekly TV show in Chicago. With

MAHALIA JACKSON

13/11/00

Mr Benedict
requires information
on Samual Coldridge
    Taylor

(musician)

He will phone back about
12:30pm

the heavy promotion that Columbia Records afforded, Jackson gained a large white following and became a celebrity. Her new status alienated many of her black fans, however, who accused her of selling out. In 1958 she performed at the Newport Jazz Festival.

Jackson's biggest hits include "Precious Lord," "If You See My Savior," "What Could I Do," "How I Got Over," "He's Got the Whole World in His Hands," "His Eye Is on the Sparrow" and "Search Me, Lord." Jackson also appeared in the films *St. Louis Blues* (1958), *Imitation of Life* (1959), *Jazz on a Summer's Day* (1960) and *The Best Man* (1964).

She invested her earnings well. She had real-estate holding nationwide. There were also Mahalia Jackson beauty products and chicken dinners.

Mahalia Jackson died of heart disease on January 27, 1972.

1931: Blues vocalist and pianist Detroit Junior is born Emery Williams, Jr., in Haynes, Arkansas.

Detroit Junior is a consummate Chicago blues club player who blends humor with the blues. His best-known recordings, "Money Tree" (1960) and "Call My Job" (1965), are considered classics. His best LP is 1971's *Chicago Urban Blues*.

1951: William "Bootsy" Collins, the funk era's most famous bass player, is born in Cincinnati.

Collins played with James Brown's band from 1969 to 1971. In 1972 he joined the Parliament/Funkadelic crew.

Collins then fronted a crew called Bootsy's Rubber Band, whose members were Phelps Collins, Frank Waddy, Joel Johnson, Mudbone Cooper and P-Nut Johnson. During his stage act Collins appeared as his funky alter ego, Bootzilla. He was known for his outrageous glasses and other attire.

The Rubber Band had a string of soul hits, including "Stretchin' Out" (1976), "I'd Rather Be with You" (1976), "Psychoticbumpschool" (1976), "The Pinocchio Theory" (1977), "Bootzilla" (1978), "Hollywood Squares" (1978), "Jam Fan" (1979) and "Body Slam" (1982).

OCTOBER 27

1945: Singer Melba Moore is born in New York City.

Moore, who had appeared in such Broadway productions as *Hair*, *Purlie* and *Timbuktu*, recorded several successful albums in the 1980s, including *The Other Side of the Rainbow*, *Never Say Never*, *Read My Lips* and *A Lot of Love*, from which were culled the hit singles "Love's Comin' at Ya" (1982), "Keepin' My Lover Satisfied" (1984) and "Falling," which was one of the 20 best-selling black singles of 1987.

Besides being a hot vocalist and dynamic stage personality, Melba Moore had a hand in writing material for and producing her albums. She won a Tony for her portrayal of Lutiebelle in *Purlie*.

OCTOBER 28

1962: The Contours' "Do You Love Me" is the number 1 R&B chart hit and one of the best-selling singles of the year.

The Contours were lead singer Billy Gordon; bass Hubert Johnson; guitarists Hugh Davis, Joe Billingslea, Sylvester Potts and Billy Hoggs; and future Temptation Dennis Edwards. Their other hits include "Shake Sherry" (1963), "Can You Jerk Like Me" (1965) and "First I Look at the Purse" (1965). "Do You Love Me" was written and produced by Mr. Motown himself, Berry Gordy, Jr.

OCTOBER 29

1902: The Dinwiddie Quartet puts the first black music on record.

The quartet, from Dinwiddie County, Virginia, traveled to Camden, New Jersey, and recorded five spirituals and a pop tune for the Victor Talking Machine Company. The discs were released in December on Victor's Monarch label.

OCTOBER 30

1930: Jazz trumpeter Clifford Brown is born in Wilmington, Delaware.

Brown got his first trumpet from his father at the age of 15. He studied trumpet, piano, jazz harmony and theory. By

the age of 18 he was playing in Philadelphia with Miles Davis, Max Roach and Fats Navarro. Brown studied at Maryland State University but was sidelined for two years after a car wreck.

In 1952 he played with an R&B group, and in 1953 he played with Tadd Dameron and Lionel Hampton. He was also with Art Blakey's group briefly, in 1954. In mid-1954 he teamed up with Roach to form the Clifford Brown–Max Roach Quintet, considered one of jazz's finest groups. It included pianist Richie Powell, bassist George Morrow and, at times, saxophonist Sonny Stitt, Harold Land and Sonny Rollins.

On June 26, 1956, Clifford Brown, Richie Powell and Powell's wife were killed in a car crash. Though his career was brief, Brown left a legacy of excellent recordings. Among them are *Clifford Brown in Pairs*, *Clifford Brown and Max Roach, Inc.*, *Study in Brown*, *The Clifford Brown Jam Sessions*, *Clifford Brown with Strings* and *Brown–Roach at Basin Street*.

1939: Singer, songwriter and producer Eddie Holland is born in Detroit.

Holland formed a phenomenally successful Motown production trio with his brother Brian and Lamont Dozier. Eddie Holland was also a moderately successful Motown recording artist. His biggest hit was "Jamie," in 1962. His other hits include "Just Ain't Enough Love" (1964) and "Candy to Me" (1964).

After leaving Motown, Holland-Dozier-Holland created the Invictus/Hot Wax label.

1954: The sweet doo-wop group Otis Williams and the Charms make their chart debut with "Hearts of Stone."

The Charms were Richard Parker, Donald Peak, Joe Penn and Rolland Bradley. Their biggest hits were "Ling, Ting, Tong" (1955), "Two Hearts" (1955), "Ivory Tower" (1956) and "United" (1957). The group was from Cincinnati.

OCTOBER 31

1896: Blues singer, gospel singer and actress Ethel Waters is born in Chester, Pennsylvania.

Waters sang in church choirs as a child. She went to work in vaudeville after winning an amateur contest at a local theater and played the northern vaudeville circuit under the name Sweet Mama Stringbean.

She moved to New York in 1917 and soon became a headline act. In 1921 and 1922 she recorded for the Black Swan label and toured with the Black Swan Troubadors, led by Fletcher Henderson.

In the 1920s and 1930s Waters appeared in such shows as *Africana*, *Black Bottom Revue*, *Rhapsody in Black*, *The Black Birds*, *As Thousands Cheer* and *Heatwave*. She also toured Europe and recorded with Duke Ellington, Benny Goodman and the Dorsey Brothers. From 1935 to 1939 she toured in her own musical revue. In 1939 Ethel Waters scored a big success with her dramatic role in the play *Mamba's Daughter*. She appeared in the films *Rufus Jones for President* (1933), *Gift of Gab* (1934), *Bubbling Over* (1942), *Cairo* (1942), *Cabin in the Sky* (1943), *Pinky* (1949), *A Member of the Wedding* (1952) and *The Sound and the Fury* (1959). Waters was nominated for an Academy Award for best supporting actress in 1949 for her role in *Pinky*. She also appeared in the stage versions of *Cabin in the Sky* and *A Member of the Wedding*. Her work in TV included "Route 66," "The Ed Sullivan Show," "Matinee Theater," "The Tennessee Ernie Ford Show," "Daniel Boone," "The Dick Cavett Show," "The Mike Douglas Show" and "The Tonight Show."

Waters experienced many "firsts" in her career. She was the first black female singer to appear on radio (1922), the first black woman to star in a commercial network radio show (1933), the first black woman to star on Broadway in a dramatic show (1939) and the first black singer to appear on TV (1939). Her autobiography is titled *His Eye Is on the Sparrow* and was published in 1951.

In 1964 Waters suffered a mild heart attack while appearing at the Pasadena Playhouse, but she returned to work shortly afterward. Ethel Waters died on September 1, 1979, in Los Angeles.

1902: Vocalist and pianist Julia Lee is born in Boonville, Missouri.

Lee joined her father's band at the age of four and worked from 1920 to 1933 in her brother George E. Lee's band. At the height of her popularity she performed for President Harry S. Truman in the White House.

Lee was noted for her risqué style and her double-entendre lyrics. With her band, the Boyfriends, she had several top R&B hits, including "Gotta Gimme Watcha Got" (1946), "I'll Get Along Somehow" (1947), "Scratch and Grab It" (1947), "King Size Papa" (1948), "That's What I Like" (1948), "Tell Me Daddy" (1948), "I Didn't Like It the First Time" (1949) and "You Ain't Got It No More" (1949).

Julia Lee died of a heart attack on December 8, 1958.

1902: Tenor saxophonist Jean-Baptiste "Illinois" Jacquet, one of the major molders of the honking, bar-walking R&B sax style so popular in the late 1940s and early 1950s, is born in Broussard, Louisiana.

Jacquet grew up in Houston and worked with Milt Larkin's band in 1939 and 1940. In 1949 he joined the new Lionel Hampton band. It was with Hampton that Jacquet made his mark. His 64-bar solo on the original recording of "Flying Home" is considered one of jazz's great solo masterpieces. After he left Hampton he worked in the bands of Cab Calloway and Count Basie.

In the mid-1940s Jacquet formed his own band. In the early and mid-1950s his "Texas tenor" sax style made him an in-demand leader for the orchestra that backed the R&B package show. In 1952 he had an R&B chart hit with "Port of Rico."

Throughout the 1960s and 1970s Jacquet worked with trios. In 1984 he formed his legendary big band.

In the 1990s Jacquet is very much in vogue. He was the subject of a film documentary, *Texas Tenor*, and he played at the inaugural gala of President Bill Clinton. His best LPs are *Flying Home*, *Sing's the Thing* and *Genius at Work*.

1953: The Drifters make their chart debut with "Money Honey."

The original Drifters, a smooth doo-wop group, were formed in 1953 and consisted of lead singer Clyde McPhatter, Gerhart Thrasher, Andrew Thrasher and Bill Pinkney. With McPhatter singing lead, they racked up hits with "Such a Night" (1954), "Honey Love" (1954), "Big Bam" (1954), "White Christmas" (1954), "Whatcha Gonna Do" (1955), "Adorable" (1955), "Steamboat" (1955), "Ruby Baby" (1956) and "Fools Fall in Love" (1957).

In 1954 Clyde McPhatter was drafted. Luckily, the group had recorded plenty of McPhatter-led material. When McPhatter was discharged from the Army he went solo.

The Drifters continued with various changes until 1958, when manager George Treadwell disbanded the group. Then, in 1959, Treadwell took a singing group called the Five Crowns and renamed them the Drifters. When this crew stepped into the studio to record, on March 6, 1959, it consisted of lead singer Ben E. King, Charlie Thomas, Dock Green and Elsbeary Hobbs. Their vocals were slick and pop: the background music was light rhythm and strings. Their first hit was a smash, "There Goes My Baby." King sang lead on the song and on such follow-ups as "Dance with Me" (1959), "This Magic Moment" (1960), "Save the Last Dance for Me" (1960) and "I Count the Tears" (1961) before going solo.

THE DRIFTERS

The next few Drifters hits—"Some Kind of Wonderful" (1961), "Sweets for My Sweet" (1961), "Up on the Roof" (1962) and "On Broadway" (1963)—featured lead vocals by Rudy Lewis. Johnny Moore, who had sung briefly with the old Drifters in 1957, came back to do lead vocals on "Under the Boardwalk" (1964), "Saturday Night at the Movies" (1964) and "At the Club" (1965).

The Drifters have appeared in almost as many courtrooms as rock 'n' roll shows. The name is in constant dispute, and the matter has been in litigation for the past 20 years. It seems that anybody who ever sang with the group or even thought about singing with the group has organized his own group of Drifters. At one point there were almost a dozen Drifters groups appearing in the U.S. and England. The owners of the name have spent a lot of time tracking down bogus Drifters and suing them.

NOVEMBER 1

1898: Beulah "Sippie" Wallace, one of the classic blues singers of the 1920s and 1930s, is born in Houston.

Wallace began her career working in tent shows and on the theater circuit. In the 1920s she recorded with King Oliver and Louis Armstrong. In 1929 she settled in Detroit. Based there, she worked the blues clubs and festival circuit, as well as touring abroad, until the 1970s.

In her heyday, Wallace was billed as the Texas Nightingale. Her best-known recordings include "Suitcase Blues," "I'm a Mighty Tight Woman" and "Caledonia Blues." The best collection of her work is *Sippie Wallace, 1923–1929.* She was a major influence on Bonnie Raitt, currently a popular blues performer.

1926: Jazz saxophonist Lou Donaldson is born in Badin, North Carolina.

Donaldson moved to New York in the early 1950s and recorded with Milt Jackson, Thelonious Monk, Art Blakey and Charles Mingus. In the mid-1950s he formed his own group and has been working ever since. Because of his affinity for R&B, Donaldson was lumped into the "soul jazz" category in the '60s. His best LPs include *Blues Walk, Alligator Boogaloo, The Natural Soul* and *Back Street.*

NOVEMBER 2

1937: Cadillacs lead singer Earl "Speedo" Carroll is born in New York City.

The Cadillacs, originally called the Carnations, were formed in 1953 by Carroll, Laverne Drake, Robert Phillips and Gus Willingham in Harlem. In 1954 they added Jim Clark to the group and acquired Esther Navarro as their manager and musical arranger. Navarro landed the group a recording contract, and she changed their name to the Cadillacs.

In June 1954 the Cadillacs released a doo-wop classic, "Gloria." Follow-ups include "Zoom" (1956), "Woe Is Me" (1956), "Rudolph the Red-Nosed Reindeer" (1956), "My Girlfriend" (1957) and "Peek-a-Boo" (1958). In 1958 Carroll left the Cadillacs and joined the Coasters.

NOVEMBER 3

1978: "One Nation Under a Groove," by Funkadelic, is the number 1 black chart single, and one of George Clinton's biggest hits. It sold over a million copies and sat at the top of the black singles chart for six weeks.

Much of the Parliament/Funkadelic sound was created by guitarist Eddie Hazel, bassist William "Bootsy" Collins and keyboardist Bernie Worrell. At one point the lineup also included former James Brown sidemen Maceo Parker and Fred Wesley.

NOVEMBER 4

1961: Ray Charles's classic "Hit the Road, Jack" is the number 1 R&B single. It was written especially for Charles by Percy Mayfield and hit number 1 on both the pop and R&B charts.

NOVEMBER 5

1931: Vocalist, guitarist, pianist, songwriter, arranger, record producer and bandleader Ike Turner is born in Clarksdale, Mississippi.

While still in school, Turner formed a band called the Kings of Rhythm, which featured saxophonists Jackie Brenston and Raymond Hill. Turner was the consummate hustler. On a given night, the Kings of Rhythm might play pop tunes at white clubs and then go across the tracks and play R&B at black after-hours joints. Turner also earned several hundred extra dollars a week working as a talent scout for Los Angeles–based Modern Records. He also worked as a session guitarist in Memphis, backing

the likes of B. B. King, Howlin' Wolf and Johnny Ace.

In 1951 Turner and crew recorded a song called "Rocker 88" for Sun Records. Through a strange turn of events, the hit record's label read Jackie Brenston and His Delta Cats.

In 1956, while playing in east St. Louis, Turner met a singer named Anna Mae Bullock, who became the vocalist for the Kings of Rhythm. In 1958 she and Turner were married. It is a matter of some speculation when Bullock first used the name Tina Turner. The most frequent version of the story is that the name came from Sun Records owner Juggy Murray in 1960, with the release of "A Fool in Love." Turner had written the song for another singer, but they had an argument and he had his wife record it. The song was a smash, and Turner organized an exciting stage show, the Ike and Tina Turner Revue, which toured coast to coast and around the world and featured Tina, the Ikettes and the Kings of Rhythm.

The team of Ike and Tina Turner flourished until the mid-1970s. Their stormy marriage is a matter of public record. Tina Turner left in 1974, and they were divorced in 1976. While Tina Turner soared to superstardom, Ike Turner became involved in a maze of legal hassles, including arrests for drug possession and income-tax evasion, and he spent time in prison.

1956: Nat "King" Cole becomes the first black entertainer to host his own weekly TV variety show.

"The Nat 'King' Cole Show" debuted on Monday night at 7:30 on NBC. Initially the show was only 15 minutes long but was expanded to half an hour in July 1957.

Musically, the show was superb. It featured such guest stars as Count Basie, Mahalia Jackson, Pearl Bailey, Billy Eckstine, Sammy Davis, Jr., the Mills

Brothers, Cab Calloway, Ella Fitzgerald, Peggy Lee, Tony Bennett and Harry Belafonte. It lasted until December 17, 1957. In 1990 the Public Broadcasting System began rerunning the show.

NOVEMBER 6

1937: The Jive Five's lead singer, Eugene Pitt, is born in Brooklyn.

The other Jive Five members were Jerome Hanna, Billy Prophet, Richard Harris and Norman Johnson. Their biggest hits included "My True Story" (1961), "Never, Never" (1961), "What Time Is It?" (1962), "I'm a Happy Man" (1965) and "Sugar" (1968). Eugene Pitt was one of the best lead singers of the doo-wop era.

NOVEMBER 7

1938: Singer Dee (Delecta) Clark is born in Blythesville, Arkansas.

Clark moved to Chicago in 1941. As a teenager, he belonged to a recording group called the Hambone Kids, with Sammy McGrier and Ronny Strong. They recorded the popular "Hambone Hambone" ditty in the early 1950s. In the mid-1950s Clark was a member of a singing group that at one time or another was called the Goldentones, the Kool Gents and the Delegates.

In 1957 Clark went solo. His first hit was "Nobody But You" (1958). He followed up with "Just Keep It Up" (1959), "Hey Little Girl" (1959), "How About That" (1960), "Your Friends" (1961), "Raindrops" (1961) and "'I'm Going Back to School" (1962).

Dee Clark died of a heart attack on December 7, 1990.

1987: Rapper Kool Moe Dee, whose given name is Mohandas DeWese, makes his chart debut.

Kool Moe Dee was one of the most popular rap stars of the late 1980s. His best-selling singles include "Go See the Doctor" (1987), "How Ya Like Me Now" (1987), "Wild Wild West" (1988) and "I Go to Work" (1989). His best-selling LPs are *Kool Moe Dee*, *How Ya Like Me Now*, *Knowledge Is King* and *African Heritage*.

In the early 1980s he belonged to a rap crew called the Treacherous Three, who appeared in the film *Beat Street*.

NOVEMBER 8

1913: Blues shouter Arnold "Gatemouth" Moore is born in Topeka.

Moore's biggest hit was "I Ain't Mad at You, Pretty Baby," in 1945. In 1947 Gatemouth Moore gave up the blues and became an ordained minister in the Church of God in Christ.

1947: Singer Minnie Riperton is born in Chicago.

From 1967 to 1970 Riperton was lead singer of the R&B-rock group Rotary Connection. In 1973 she was part of Stevie Wonder's backup group, Wonderlove. In 1975 she had a number 1 pop hit with her million-selling single, "Loving You."

Minnie Riperton died of cancer on July 12, 1979.

MINNIE RIPERTON

NOVEMBER 9

1985: The Winans, the first family of black gospel music in the late 1980s and early 1990s, make their singles chart debut.

The gospel quartet comprising brothers Michael, Ronald, Marvin and Carvin Winans has had such top-selling gospel LPs as *Decisions*, *Tomorrow*, *Live at Carnegie Hall*, *Brotherly Love*, *Return* and *Let My People Go*. The group won a Grammy and a Stellar Gospel Music Award in 1986 and another Grammy in 1988. Almost all the Winans are award-winning gospel singers. Brother and sister Bebe and Cece Winans have won many awards for their LPs. Daniel Winans won a Grammy in 1989 for his album *Let Brotherly Love Continue*. Vickie Winans had a top-selling record, "Be Encouraged," and Mom and Pop Winans released their LP *For the Rest of My Life* in 1992.

NOVEMBER 10

1929: Blues singer and harmonica player George "Mojo" Buford is born in Hernando, Mississippi.

Buford's grandfather was a preacher, and Buford got his start singing in the church choir. He moved to Chicago in 1953. Throughout the 1960s and 1970s he played harp with Muddy Waters and his band. Mojo Buford's best LPs are *State of the Harp* and *Mojo Buford's Blues Summit*.

1939: Jazz flutist Hubert Laws is born in Houston.

Laws got his first professional gig at the age of 15, with the Jazz Crusaders, where he remained until 1960. During the '60s he played with Mongo Santamaria, Sergio Mendes, Lena Horne, Benny Golson and Clark Terry.

Equally at home in classical music, he played with the Metropolitan Opera Orchestra from 1968 to 1973 and was also with the New York Philharmonic.

In the mid-1970s he formed his own group, which played a combination of jazz, fusion and what might be called jazz adaptations of classical music.

Hubert Laws's best LPs include *Afro Classic*, *The Rite of Spring*, *Romeo and Juliet*, *Crying Song* and *I Love My Daddy*.

1956: The Dells make their chart debut with "Oh, What a Night," the signature song of the Chicago-based group. The song went to number 4 on the R&B charts in 1956. In 1969 the group rerecorded it, and it went to number 1 on the soul charts and to number 10 on the pop charts.

The Dells—lead singer Johnny Funches, tenor Marvin Junior, tenor Verne Allison, baritone Mickey McGill and bass Chuck Barksdale—are one of the longest-lasting of all the R&B singing groups. They were formed back in the early 1950s doo-wop days at Thornton Township High School, in Harvey, Illinois. They were originally called the El Rays and recorded for the Chess label in 1953.

After their initial success, the Dells suffered a dry spell until the 1960s, when they left Chess and began hitting the charts with such tunes as "There Is" (1968), "Stay in My Corner" (1968), "Always Together" (1968), "I Can Sing a Rainbow/Love Is Blue" (1969), "Open Up My Heart" (1970), "The Love We Had" (1971), "Give Your Baby a Standing Ovation" (1973), "My Pretendings Are Over" (1973), "I Miss You" (1973), "Slow Motion" (1976) and "I Touched a Dream" (1980).

Johnny Funches left in 1970 and was replaced by ex-Flamingo John Carter.

NOVEMBER 11

1920: Singer Annisteen Allen is born Ernestine Allen in Champaign, Illinois.

From 1946 to 1951 Allen was a vocalist with the popular Lucky Millinder Band. She provided the vocals on such Millinder hits as "I'll Never Be Free" (12951) and "I'm Waiting Just for You" (1951). In 1953 she hit the R&B Top 10 with "Baby, I'm Doin' It." Her other hits include "There's Good Blues Tonight" (1946) and "Fujiyama Mama" (1955).

1929: LaVern Baker, one of the most popular female R&B singers of the early rock 'n' roll era, is born Delores Williams in Chicago.

Baker made her singing debut at the age of 12. By the age of 17 she was billed as Little Miss Sharecropper and singing in Chicago night spots. In 1952 and 1953 she sang with the Todd Rhodes orchestra. Her biggest hits include "Tweedlee Dee" (1955), "Bop-Ting-A-Ling" (1955), "That's All I Need" (1955), "Play It Fair" (1955), "Still" (1956), "I Can't Love You Enough" (1956), "Jim Dandy" (1956), "Jim Dandy Got Married" (1957), "I Cried a Tear" (1958), "I Waited Too Long" (1959) and "See See Rider" (1962). In the mid-1960s she recorded a series of popular duets with Jackie Wilson.

NOVEMBER 12

1906: Bukka White, a master of the Delta blues, is born Booker T. Washington White in Houston, Mississippi.

White began singing the blues and playing piano in barrelhouses around St. Louis in the early 1920s. He recorded for Victor, Vocalion and Okeh Records in the 1930s. He was also a professional boxer and a professional baseball player in the Negro Leagues. White served time in Parchman Farm Prison at one point, for assault. His most important recordings came in the late 1930s. His classic songs include "Parchman Farm," "Aberdeen Mississippi Blues," "Fixin' to Die" and "Panama Limited."

After World War II White settled in Memphis and moonlighted as a musician. In 1962 "Fixin' to Die" became a favorite of such folk artists as Bob Dylan and Buffy Sainte-Marie, which caused a renewal of interest in White's music. He began recording again and toured the folk festival and coffeehouse circuits. His best recordings can be found on such collections as *Aberdeen Mississippi Blues, 1937–1940* and *The Complete Sessions, 1930–1940.*

Bukka White died on February 26, 1977.

BUKKA WHITE

1911: Jazz trumpeter Wilbur Dorsey "Buck" Clayton is born in Parsons, Kansas.

Clayton spent his early professional career working with Laverne Floyd and Charlie Echols. At the age of 21 he toured China for two years, leading his own band. In California he was the bandleader at the West Coast Cotton Club.

In 1936 he joined Count Basie's band in Kansas City. Clayton remained with Basie until being called up for military service, in 1943. He spent his service years in military bands. When he got out of the service, in 1946, he joined the "Jazz at the Philharmonic" show.

In 1948 he was with Jimmy Rushing's band, and in the '50s he co-led a popular quintet with pianist Joe Bushkin and recorded *The Buck Clayton Jam Sessions.* In 1959 he recorded the LP *Songs for Swingers.* In the '60s and '70s Buck Clayton spent a lot of time touring England and Europe and concentrated on teaching and arranging.

1944: Organist Booker T. Jones is born in Memphis.

Jones earned a degree in music from Indiana University. In the glory days of Stax Records, Booker T. and the MGs (the MG stands for Memphis Group) were more than just another hit-making instrumental group. They were the nucleus of the Stax house bands that backed up artists like Otis Redding, Carla Thomas, Wilson Pickett and Eddie Floyd. The group was made up of Jones on organ, Steve Cropper on guitar, Donald "Duck" Dunn on bass and Al Jackson, Jr., on drums. The group's biggest hits included "Green Onions" (1962), "Bootleg" (1965), "Hip Hug Her" (1967), "Groovin'" (1967), "Soul Limbo" (1968) and "Time Is Tight" (1969).

Booker T. and the MGs broke up in 1969, and Jones became a record producer. He produced such artists as Willie Nelson, Rita Coolidge, Earl Klugh and Bill Withers. Steve Cropper and Duck Dunn joined John Belushi and Dan Aykroyd in the Blues Brothers Band. Al Jackson was murdered in 1975.

NOVEMBER 13

1894: Pianist, composer and bandleader Bennie Moten, probably best known as the man who gave

Count Basie his first big break, is born in Kansas City.

Moten started out with a trio, playing Dixieland jazz. He recorded for the Okeh label in 1923 and built a following around Kansas City. In the pre-Basie days the three most important bands in Kansas City belonged to Moten, George E. Lee and Walter Page.

By the early 1930s Moten's outfit included Basie, Ben Webster and Lester Young. Look for an LP called *The Complete Bennie Moten*, and you'll see where Count Basie got his swing.

Bennie Moten died at the height of his popularity, on April 2, 1935.

1913: Singer Louisa "Blue Lu" Barker is born in New Orleans.

Barker's best-known hit is a late-1940s risqué piece called "Don't You Make Me High." Her other hits included "Lu's Blues" and "A Little Bird Told Me." She often performed with the Fly Cats, the band of her husband, Danny Barker.

1940: Singer Jeanette "Baby" Washington is born in Bamburg, South Carolina.

In the 1980s Washington recorded with Parlet, one of George Clinton's off-shoot groups. Baby Washington's biggest R&B and pop hits included "The Time" (1959), "The Bells" (1959), "Nobody Cares" (1961), "That's How Heartaches Are Made" (1963), "Leave Me Alone" (1963) and "Only Those in Love" (1965).

NOVEMBER 14

1934: Pianist and composer Ellis Marsalis, father of Wynton, Branford and Delfeayo Marsalis, is born in New Orleans.

Marsalis earned his music degree from Dillard University and played in the band of jazz trumpeter Al Hirt. After his gig with Hirt, Marsalis became an instructor at the New Orleans Center for the Creative Arts, a multidisciplinary arts high school whose alumni include Wynton and Branford Marsalis and Harry Connick, Jr. Ellis Marsalis's current LP is *Heart of Gold*.

1936: Blues harmonica player Carey Bell is born in Mason, Mississippi.

Bell moved to Chicago in 1956 and worked clubs in the bands of Eddie Taylor, Earl Hooker and John Lee Hooker. Later on he was with Muddy Waters, Willie Dixon, Hound Dog Taylor and Jimmy Dawkins. Bell often performs with his sons, guitarist Lurrie Bell and bassist Carey Bell, Jr. Carey Bell's best LPs include *Carey Bell's Blues Harp*, *Everybody Wants to Win*, *Goin' on Main Street* and *Blues Harp*.

NOVEMBER 15

1933: Clyde McPhatter is born in Durham, North Carolina.

McPhatter began as a gospel singer. In 1950 he joined the R&B group Billy Ward and the Dominoes, as lead singer. In the early '50s the Dominoes had such big R&B hits as "Do Something for Me," "Sixty-Minute Man" and "Have Mercy, Baby." In 1953 McPhatter left the Dominoes to form his own group, the Drifters.

The Drifters were an immediate success, scoring number 1 R&B hits with "Money Honey," "Honey Love" and "Adorable." In 1954 McPhatter was drafted and spent the next couple of years entertaining the troops. When he got out of the U.S. Army, in 1956, he went solo.

McPhatter ran up a string of best-selling R&B and pop hits: "Seven Days" (1956), "Treasure of Love" (1956), "Without Love" (1957), "Just to Hold My Hand" (1957), "Long Lonely Nights" (1957), "Come What May" (1958), "A Lover's Question" (1958), "Lovey Dovey" (1959), "Ta Ta" (1960) and "Lover Please" (1962). When his career began to fade, McPhatter battled alcohol and drug addiction.

Clyde McPhatter died on June 13, 1971, in New York City. He was inducted into the Rock 'n' Roll Hall of Fame in 1987.

1937: Singer Little Willie John is born in Cullendale, Arkansas. Various sources list his given name as either William Edgar John or William John Woods.

Little Willie John was raised in Detroit. He stood just slightly over five feet tall. In the early 1950s he sang with the bands of Paul Williams, Duke Ellington and Count Basie. He began recording in 1953 for a small label called Prize Records. In 1955 he signed with King Records and began hitting the R&B charts, with such hits as "All Around the World" (also known as "Grits Ain't Groceries," 1955), "Need Your Love So Bad" (1956), "Home at Last" (1956), "Fever" (1956), "Letter from My Darling" (1956), "Talk to Me, Talk to Me" (1958), "Heartbreak" (1960), "Sleep" (1960) and "Take My Love" (1961).

In May 1966 Little Willie John was convicted of manslaughter for stabbing a man to death in a fight in Seattle. He was sent to Washington State Penitentiary, where he died of pneumonia on May 26, 1968.

1969: The Jackson Five make their chart debut with "I Want You Back."

The Jackson Five were brothers Jackie, Tito, Jermaine, Marlon and lead singer Michael Jackson. They were managed by their father.

Joe Jackson put the group together in 1966 in Gary, Indiana, to play local clubs. They were discovered by Diana Ross and signed to Motown Records.

The Jackson Five had enormous success immediately. Their first four singles—"I Want You Back," "ABC," "The Love You Save" and "I'll Be There"—all hit the number 1 spot on the pop charts. Their next two, "Mama's Pearl" and "Never Can Say Goodbye," went to number 2.

The Jackson Five toured to consistently sold-out concert venues, appeared on "The Ed Sullivan Show" and even had their own cartoon show. Their hits continued, with such singles as "Sugar Daddy" (1971) and "Dancing Machine" (1974). Changes came in the mid-1970s. Michael Jackson began to record solo, and in 1976 Jermaine Jackson left the group. He was replaced by another brother, Randy. By 1975 the group was known as the Jacksons. They had a pair of platinum-selling singles, "Enjoy Yourself" (1976) and "Shake Your Body Down" (1979). They also left Motown and signed with CBS Records. Michael was completely a solo act by 1979. Jermaine stayed with Motown and released the LPs *Let's Get Serious* and *I Like Your Style* in the 1980s. Then he too left Motown, for Arista Records, where he scored with singles "Dynamite" and " I Think It's Love." Sisters LaToya, Rebbie and Janet Jackson also began to release LPs (Janet was the most successful), and Marlon embarked on a solo career.

In 1984, at the height of Michael Jackson's worldwide fame, the Jacksons undertook a tour for their *Victory* LP. Even Michael decided to join the tour. Before the show played a singe date, there was controversy over the $20-plus-and-up tickets, which were sold via a national lottery system. There were squabbles about who would actually promote the show, with bidding wars among promoters offering and guaranteeing the Jacksons up to $45 million. Such varied figures as boxing promoter Don King, New England Patriots owner Chuck Sullivan and political activist Reverend Al Sharpton got involved. When the shows finally played, the tour's security measures made the Secret Service look like an amateur operation.

NOVEMBER 16

1873: Composer William Christopher "W. C." Handy is born in Florence, Alabama.

Handy was originally a cornetist with the Bessemer Brass Band. In 1893 he took a vocal quartet to Chicago, and in 1896 he became musical director for the Mahara Minstrels. He taught at Huntsville Agricultural and Mechanical College and led a band.

Handy was the first to put the essence of jazz and blues down on paper. His most famous compositions are "Memphis Blues," which he wrote in 1912, and his masterpiece, "St. Louis Blues," which he wrote in 1914. Other great Handy tunes include "Yellow Dog Blues," "Beale Street Blues," "Ole Miss Rag" and "Hesitating Blues."

In 1917 Handy took a band to New York to record his compositions. In 1918 he teamed up with Harry Pace to form a music publishing company.

Handy went blind in the early 1920s. From then on he worked mostly as a composer, but he did a brief tour with Jelly Roll Morton's band. In the 1930s he toured with Clarence Davis's band, and in 1936 he led his own band at the Apollo Theater. In 1938 a concert celebrating Handy's 65th birthday was held at Carnegie Hall.

In 1943 Handy was severely injured when he fell onto the tracks of the New York City subway. He spent the rest of his life as a semi-invalid. He died on March 28, 1958.

W. C. Handy's autobiography, *Father of the Blues*, was published in 1941. In 1958 the biographical film *St. Louis Blues*, starring Nat "King" Cole, was released. In 1960 a statue of Handy was erected in Memphis, and in 1969 a W. C. Handy commemorative postage stamp was issued in the U.S.

W. C. HANDY

1901: Songwriter and arranger Jesse Stone is born in Atcheson, Kansas.

In the 1920s Stone was a bandleader. In 1927 Jesse Stone and His Blue Serenaders cut a song called "Starvation Blues" for Okeh Records. In the 1930s he played the Cotton Club with Duke Ellington's troupe. He wrote jokes and songs for comedians Pigmeat Markham and Dusty Fletcher and wrote musical arrangements for acts at the Apollo Theater.

In the late 1930s Stone was an arranger for Chick Webb's band. One of Webb's trumpet players wanted to sing and put together his own band. He asked Stone to write him some arrangements, and Stone did. The trumpet player's name was Louis Jordan.

In 1942 Stone wrote the Benny Goodman hit "Idaho" and the song "Sorghum Switch" for Doc Wheeler. In the late 1940s Stone joined the staff of newly created Atlantic Records as a writer and arranger. At Atlantic he wrote such hits as "Money Honey" for the Drifters, "It Should Have Been Me" for Ray Charles and "Good Lovin'" and "Your Cash Ain't Nothin' But Trash" for the Clovers. Under the name Charles E. Calhoun he also crafted Big Joe Turner's classic hits "Shake, Rattle and Roll" and "Flip, Flop and Fly" and wrote the R&B classic "Smack Dab in the Middle."

1931: Blues guitarist Hubert Sumlin is born in Greenwood, Mississippi.

Sumlin learned guitar at the age of 11. From 1955 to 1976 he was lead guitarist for blues legend Howlin' Wolf. After Wolf's death Sumlin embarked on his own recording career. His best LPs are *Hubert Sumlin's Blues Party* and *Heart and Soul*. Hubert Sumlin is also a regular performer on the blues club circuit.

1933: Singer Garnet Minns is born in Ashland, West Virginia.

Garnet Minns sang with the gospel groups the Evening Stars and the Harmonizing Four in the 1950s. In the 1960s Garnet Minns and the Enchanters had top R&B chart hits with "Cry Baby" (1963), "Baby, Don't You Weep"(1963) and "A Quiet Place" (1964).

NOVEMBER 17

1895: Vaudeville star Katie Crippen is born in Philadelphia.

In the 1920s Crippen starred in such shows as *Shuffle Along Jr.*, *Fidgety Feet* and *The Shuffling Sextet Revue*. She recorded for the Black Swan label and performed as Kate Crippen and Her Kids and as Crippen and Brown.

Katie Crippen died of cancer on November 25, 1929, in New York City.

1936: Jazz trumpeter Don Cherry is born in Oklahoma City.

Cherry took up the trumpet in junior high school. In 1956 he joined Ornette Coleman's group. Cherry stayed with Coleman until 1961, recording on Coleman's important "free jazz" LPs.

He played with John Coltrane and Sonny Rollins before becoming a founding member of the New York Contemporary Five, which included Archie Shepp. He toured Europe with Albert Ayler.

In the late 1960s Cherry shuttled among the U.S., Europe, Asia and Africa before settling in Sweden, in 1970, where he worked on children's radio and TV programs.

Cherry has spent much time studying various ethnic musics and rhythms and was involved in a series of concerts with the Organic Music Theater. In 1976 he recorded the LP *Old and New Dreams*, and in 1980 he recorded the LP *Playing*. Cherry received a grant from the National Endowment for the Arts in 1982 for his project of introducing black schoolchildren to the music of such jazz performers as Thelonious Monk and Charlie Parker.

In the early '90s Don Cherry's daughter, Nenah Cherry, hit the pop charts with her hip-hop/rock tune "Buffalo Stance."

1936: Singer and songwriter Hank Ballard is born in Detroit.

Ballard and the Midnighters were one of the most successful R&B and rock 'n' roll groups of the 1950s. They had 20 R&B and pop chart hits, but they are best remembered for their slightly suggestive 1954 songs "Work with Me Annie" and "Annie Had a Baby." Ballard wrote most of the group's hits, but his best-known song is the one that spawned America's greatest dance craze—"The Twist." When Ballard recorded the song, in early 1959, it barely squeaked into the Top 40. A year later, performed by Chubby Checker, "The Twist" was a monster hit.

The story of Hank Ballard and the Midnighters began in 1952, when Henry Booth, Charles Sutton, Lawson Smith and Sonny Woods formed a singing group called the Royals. In 1953 Ballard joined, replacing Smith, and became lead singer. In 1954 the Royals hit the top of the R&B charts, with the song "Get It."

The group's record label, Federal, decided to change the group's name so that fans wouldn't confuse the Royals with the popular group the Five Royales. Thus they became the Midnighters. Their string of hits included "Sexy Ways" (1954), "Annie's Aunt Fannie" (1954), "It's Love" (1955) and "Baby" (1955).

The late '50s brought a dry spell. They changed their billing to Hank Ballard and the Midnighters, signed with King Records and returned to the charts in 1959, with "Teardrops on Your Letter" ("The Twist" was the B side of that record). They followed up with a series of Top 10 R&B and pop hits: "Fingerpoppin' Time" (1960), "Let's Go, Let's Go, Let's Go" (1960), "The Hoochi Coochi Coo" (1961), "The Continental Walk" (1961), "The Float" (1961), "The Switch-A-Roo" (1961) and "Nothing But Good" (1961).

The original group broke up in 1965. Hank Ballard later reorganized the Midnighters and worked in James Brown's show.

1971: Marvin Gaye's "Inner City Blues" is the number 1 black chart single, one of three Gaye hits that dealt with crime, drugs, civil rights, poverty and the ecology. The other two were "What's Going On" and "Mercy, Mercy Me (the Ecology)." All three were culled from Marvin Gaye's million-selling LP *What's Going On*.

1896: Gospel singer and music publisher Sallie Martin is born in Atlanta.

Martin and the Reverend Thomas Dorsey established the foundation for black gospel music as we know it today. They made gospel music a very lucrative business by establishing its first music-publishing outlet and creating its tour circuit. Martin met Dorsey when she joined his Ebenezer Baptist Church choir, in 1932, and became lead singer for his group. The Dorsey-Martin partnership ended in 1940. (Later, Martin teamed up with Kenneth Morris to found the Martin and Morris Publishing Company, which specialized in selling sheet music to churches.)

Martin then formed the Sallie Martin Singers, one of whom was the young Ruth Jones, who later changed her name to Dinah Washington. The Sallie Martin Singers became the first successful all-female gospel group.

In 1946 Martin teamed up with the choir of the St. Paul Baptist Church of Los Angeles for the world's first gospel-music television broadcast. Martin's biggest hit recording was "Just a Closer Walk with Thee." In the mid-1950s she disbanded the Sallie Martin Singers. In the mid-1980s, at the age of 90, Sallie Martin was still active in gospel music.

1904: Coleman Hawkins, jazz's first great tenor saxophonist, is born in St. Joseph, Missouri. (Some sources list 1901 as the year of his birth.)

Hawkins, who also played piano and cello, took up the sax at the age of nine. At 11 he was playing in the school band, and by 16 he was playing professionally with bands around Kansas City.

In 1921 he was signed by blues singer Mamie Smith to join her band, the Jazz Hounds. He played with Smith until 1923.

He spent from 1924 to 1934 as a member of Fletcher Henderson's orchestra. In 1934 Hawkins left for a tour of Europe and remained there until 1939. He then returned to the U.S. and formed his own 16-piece big band, playing such venues as the Apollo Theater and the Savoy Ballroom.

In February 1941 Hawkins disbanded his group and formed a sextet, in which he could better showcase his solo talent. In 1944 he recorded the classic "Body and Soul." In 1945 his group appeared in the film *The Crimson Canary*. In 1946 Hawkins took part in the first "Jazz at the Philharmonic" tour.

In the late '40s and early '50s Hawkins was again touring Europe. In 1962 he recorded with Duke Ellington on the LP *Duke Ellington Meets Coleman Hawkins*. Some of his best collections are *The Chocolate Dandies, 1940 and 1943*; *The Genius of Coleman Hawkins*; *Coleman Hawkins Encounters Ben Webster*; and *Body and Soul*.

Coleman Hawkins died on May 19, 1969, in New York City.

1909: Pianist and arranger Lloyd Glenn is born in San Antonio, Texas.

Glenn moved to California, where he became a popular R&B session musician, working in the bands of Kid Ory and Big Joe Turner. He began recording as a solo artist in 1947. His best-remembered R&B hits include "Blue Shadows" (1950), "Low Society Blues" (1950), "Old-Time Shuffle Blues" (1950), "Chica Boo" (1951) and "It Moves Me" (1953).

Lloyd Glenn died of a heart attack on May 23, 1985.

1948: Jazz drummer and keyboardist Alphonse Mouzon is born in Charleston, South Carolina.

Mouzon's career has carried him through several types of music. He worked with Chubby Checker in 1965. In 1969 he was in the orchestra of the Broadway show *Promises, Promises*. In 1970 and 1971 he was with Roy Ayers, and in 1971 and 1972 he was a member of Weather Report. He then played with McCoy Tyner and spent the mid-1970s with Larry Coryell's Eleventh Hour. He also worked with Roberta Flack and Stevie Wonder. In the early 1980s Mouzon had jazz-fusion hits with "The Lady in Red" (1982) and "Our Love Is Hot" (1984). Alphonse Mouzon's LPs include *By All Means*, *Early Spring*, *Love Fantasy* and *Morning Sun*.

NOVEMBER 22

1971: "The Theme from *Shaft*," by Isaac Hayes, is the number 1 pop single.

Shaft was one of the most successful examples of an early-1970s genre of film that has been dubbed "blaxploitation." These films were expressly marketed to black audiences. The hero was always black and the bad guy was always "the

Man." In the end the hero always stuck it to the Man. *Shaft* starred Richard Roundtree as a New York private eye who was always up to his ears in sex and violence. Roundtree starred in two sequels, *Shaft's Big Score* and *Shaft in Africa*, as well as in a "Shaft" TV series. Blaxploitation films' top female star was Pam Grier.

NOVEMBER 23

1931: Jazz and pop vocalist Gloria Lynne, one of the top nightclub singers of the 1960s, is born in New York City.

Gloria Lynne's single hits include "Impossible" (1961), "You Don't Have to Be a Tower of Strength" (1961), "I Wish You Love" (1964), "I Should Care" (1964), "Be Anything" (1964), "Don't Take Your Love from Me" (1964) and "Watermelon Man" (1965).

1939: Singer Betty Everett, the top female vocalist on the Vee Jay Records roster in the 1960s, is born in Greenwood, Mississippi.

Everett began singing in church choirs at the age of 14. She moved to Chicago in 1957 and was discovered by bluesman Magic Sam. She signed with a predominantly blues-oriented label, Cobra Records, and had several Chicago-area hits before signing with Vee Jay, in 1963.

Her biggest hits were "You're No Good" (1963), "The Shoop-Shoop Song (It's in His Kiss)" (1964) and a pair of duets with Jerry Butler, "Let It Be Me" and "Smile," both in 1964.

NOVEMBER 24

1868: Pianist and composer Scott Joplin, popularly called the king of ragtime, is born in Texarkana, Texas.

Joplin taught himself to play the piano. At age 11 he began taking lessons. In his teens he settled in St. Louis and lived there from 1885 until 1893. He began playing cabarets and saloons. In 1894 he formed a group called the Texas Medley Quartet, based in Sedalia, Missouri. That year Joplin also played the World's Fair in Chicago.

In 1895 Joplin sold his first compositions, "Please Say You Will" and "Picture

of Her Face." He also enrolled in George Smith College, to learn how to write down the ragtime rhythms that he heard. He continued writing, and his rags became hits in the houses of Sedalia's red-light district.

In 1899 Joplin composed "Maple Leaf Rag." It sold 75,000 copies of sheet music in its first year. He soon followed up with another hit, "The Swipsey Cakewalk." Over the next three years Joplin also wrote two ragtime operas, *The Ragtime Dance* (actually a ballet) and *The Guest of Honor*. Other successful rags were "Easy Winners" and "The Entertainer." The 1973 film *The Sting* used "The Entertainer" as its theme, and this caused a renewal of interest in his work.

In the early 1900s Joplin contracted syphilis. By 1910 he was almost unable to talk or play the piano. In 1916 he was admitted to Wards Island Hospital. He died on April 1, 1917. Perhaps the best collection of Joplin's original work is an LP called *Ragtime King: Piano-Roll Solos Performed by Scott Joplin*.

NOVEMBER 25

1897: Stride pianist Willie "The Lion" Smith is born William Henry Joseph Bonaparte Bertholoff in Goshen, New York.

Smith was one of the jazz world's larger-than-life characters. In his heyday he dressed flashily and carried a cane, and when he entered a club to play, he roared, "The Lion is here" before settling down at the keyboard.

Smith played the organ before switching to piano. Between 1912 and 1916 he played dives and joints in Harlem and Atlantic City. He joined the U.S. Army in 1916, saw action in France (he supposedly got his nickname from spending 33 days nonstop on the front lines) and played in a military band before being discharged, in 1919. He then went back to playing clubs in New York. In the early '20s he became a sought-after player for recording sessions and accompanied Mamie Smith on her historic recording of "Crazy Blues."

In 1922 and 1923 Smith toured with a revue called *Holiday in Dixieland*. He formed his own band to play clubs and theaters and appeared in the Broadway play *The Four Walls*.

In the '30s Smith recorded such pieces as "Morning Air" and "Echoes of Spring" and played every place in New York from the Onyx Club to the Apollo Theater.

Smith continued to appear at clubs throughout the '40s. He toured Europe in 1949. In the '50s, '60s and '70s he played clubs and festivals and toured Europe and Canada many times.

Willie Smith died on April 18, 1973, in New York City.

1914: Blues vocalist and guitarist Eddie Boyd is born in Stovall, Mississippi.

Boyd moved to Chicago in 1941. He worked with Memphis Slim, Sonny Boy Williamson and Muddy Waters. He became a session player for RCA Records in 1947.

In the early 1950s Boyd had R&B chart hits with "Five Long Years" (1952), "Twenty-Four Hours" (1953) and "Third Degree" (1953). In the 1960s he moved to France and in 1971 he settled permanently in Finland.

1928: Vocalist Etta Jones is born in Aiken, South Carolina.

Jones is equally at home with blues, pop or jazz. In the late '40s and early '50s she was the featured vocalist with the Earl "Fatha" Hines band. In 1960 she had the R&B and pop hit single "Don't Go to Strangers."

Jones has recorded many LPs. Among her best are *Don't Go to Strangers*, *Fine and Mellow*, *If You Could See Me Now*, *Sugar* and *Save Your Love for Me*. Etta Jones appears almost weekly at New York's popular Blue Note Jazz Club.

1931: Jazz cornetist Nat Adderley, younger brother of saxman Julian "Cannonball" Adderley, is born in Tampa, Florida.

Nat Adderley played with Lionel Hampton from 1954 to 1958 and was with Cannonball Adderley's group from 1959 to 1975. He also composed the jazz hits "The Work Song" and "Jive Samba." Nat Adderley's LPs include *Blue Autumn*, *Branching Out*, *That's Nat* and *On the Move*.

1966: Singer Stacy Lattisaw is born in Washington, D.C.

Lattisaw recorded her first LP at the age of 12. She had single hits with "Dynamite" (1980), "Let Me Be Your Angel" (1980), "Love on a Two-Way Street" (1981), "Don't Throw It All Away" (1982), "Nail It to the Wall" (1986) and "Every Drop of Your Love" (1988). She also recorded several hit duets with Johnny Gill.

NOVEMBER 26

1939: Rock 'n' roll legend Tina Turner is born Anna Mae Bullock in Nutbush, Tennessee. Turner is also an R&B legend, a show-business legend and perhaps the hardest-working woman in show business.

Turner spent her childhood living with a variety of relatives, until her 15th birthday, when she moved to St. Louis to live with her mother. There she met a young guitarist, songwriter and bandleader named Ike Turner. Turner and his Kings of Rhythm were the hottest band in the area, able to play in both black clubs and white. Turner began singing with Ike's group and eventually married him.

Ike and Tina Turner hit the charts in 1960, with a wailing rocker, "A Fool in Love." The song took them from southern clubs to "American Bandstand."

With the vibrant Tina Turner out front, the Ike and Tina Turner Revue, featuring the Ikettes and the Kings of Rhythm, became the world's most exciting R&B road show, touring nonstop throughout the '60s and early '70s. They turned out a string of hits: "I Idolize You" (1960), "It's Gonna Work Out Fine" (1961), "River Deep, Mountain High" (produced by Phil Spector, 1966), "Bold Soul Sister" (1969), "Come Together" (1970) and their Grammy-winning version of Creedence Clearwater Revival's "Proud Mary" (1971).

But while life onstage was thrilling, Ike and Tina's offstage relationship was deteriorating. There were reports that Ike was physically and mentally abusing Tina. Finally, in 1974, they parted company, professionally and otherwise.

Tina then embarked on a solo career. She kept busy by playing nightclubs but could not find the right recording formula. Her breakthrough came in 1983,

when her version of Al Green's "Let's Stay Together" rocketed up the British charts and clicked in New York City dance clubs.

Turner's LP *Private Dancer* was released in May 1984. The second single from the LP, "What's Love Got to Do with It," gave Turner her first number 1 American single. *Rolling Stone* critics named it the best single of 1984. Turner also won two American Music Awards and took three Grammy awards. "What's Love Got to Do with It" was named song of the year. The LP sold over 10 million copies and made Turner a superstar.

With Ike, Tina Turner had appeared in such concert films as *Soul to Soul* and the Rolling Stones' *Gimme Shelter*, and she had portrayed the Acid Queen in the film version of the Who's rock opera, *Tommy*. In 1985 she costarred with Mel Gibson in the film *Mad Max: Beyond Thunderdome*. Her recording of the film's theme, "We Don't Need Another Hero," landed in the Top 5 worldwide. Tina also joined 40 other superstars on the USA for Africa *We Are the World* LP, and she performed a notorious duet with Mick Jagger at the Live Aid concert.

Tina Turner's year-long *Private Dancer* tour encompassed more than 200 dates. She also starred in a trio of HBO specials, one filmed before 80,000 people in Brazil at carnival time. Her 1986 LP *Break Every Rule* continued to yield hit singles, including "Typical Male," "Two People" and "What You Get Is What You See."

TINA TURNER

NOVEMBER 27

1961: The Crystals, one of producer Phil Spector's "wall of sound" groups, make their chart debut with "There's No Other (Like My Baby)."

The Crystals were Barbara Alston, Lala Brooks, Dee Dee Kennibrew, Mary Thomas and Patricia Wright. They came from Brooklyn. Their biggest hits included "Uptown" (1962), "He's a Rebel" (1962), "He's Sure the Boy I Love" (1963), "Da Doo Ron Ron" (1963) and "Then He Kissed Me" (1963).

On "He's a Rebel" and "He's Sure the Boy I Love" Phil Spector used Darlene Love as lead vocalist. Love was lead singer of the Blossoms and was also with Spector's group Bob B. Soxx and the Blue Jeans. In 1963 Darlene Love had a trio of pop hits produced by Spector: "The Boy I'm Gonna Marry," "Wait Till My Bobby Comes Home" and "A Fine Fine Boy." Love starred in the off-Broadway show *Leader of the Pack* and appears as Danny Glover's wife in the popular *Lethal Weapon* film series.

1942: James Marshall "Jimi" Hendrix, the most famous guitarist in rock history, is born in Seattle.

After a stint in the service, Hendrix began his career as a studio musician and backup player for such noted R&B acts as B. B. King, Ike and Tina Turner, Solomon Burke, Jackie Wilson, Little Richard, the Isley Brothers, Wilson Pickett and King Curtis.

He formed his own band, Jimmy James and the Blue Flames, and settled in New York, where he was discovered in a club by Rolling Stones guitarist Keith Richards and ex-Animals bassist Chas Chandler, who had become a talent manager. Chandler took Hendrix to England. There they put together the Jimi Hendrix Experience in 1966, with Noel Redding on bass and Mitch Mitchell on drums.

Hendrix signed with Polydor Records. His first single, "Hey Joe," was a smash in England in 1967. His first U.S. chart single, later in 1967, was "Purple Haze."

Hendrix released a series of best-selling LPs: *Are You Experienced* (1967), *Axis Bold As Love* (1967), *Smash Hits* (1968) and *Electric Lady Land* (1968). He also had hit singles with "Foxy Lady" (1967), "All Along the Watchtower" (1968) and "Crosstown Traffic" (1968).

In August 1969 Hendrix headlined the Woodstock festival. His performances at Woodstock and at the 1967 Monterey Pop Festival were captured on film. He also starred in the concert film *Rainbow Bridge*.

In late 1969 Hendrix disbanded the Experience and formed the Band of Gypsies, with bassist Billy Cox and drummer Buddy Miles. Their LP was released in 1970. Also in that year Hendrix played to over a quarter of a million people at the Isle of Wight Festival.

Hendrix was noted for his psychedelic blues style and for his onstage theatrics, which included playing the guitar behind his neck, playing it with his teeth, smashing it into the stage, setting it on fire and experimenting with all types of sound distortions. He was also known for his rock 'n' roll lifestyle. On September 18, 1970, the lifestyle caught up with him, and he died of a heroin overdose.

JIMI HENDRIX

NOVEMBER 28

1929: Motown Records founder Berry Gordy, Jr., is born in Detroit.

Gordy was one of seven children. He was an amateur boxer and had begun to get interested in the music business when he was drafted into the U.S. Army.

After being discharged, Gordy met Jackie Wilson and began writing songs, including Wilson's first hit, "Reet Petite." Wilson also cut several other Gordy tunes: "That's Why (I Love You So)," "I'll Be Satisfied" and "To Be Loved."

Gordy began producing records for Marv Johnson and Smokey Robinson and the Miracles, for such labels as United Artists and Chess. In late 1958 he borrowed $800 to start his own label, Motown Records. Motown's first hit came in August 1959, with the single "Money," by Barrett Strong.

Gordy developed Motown not only as a record company but also as a viable publishing and personal-management company. In the early '60s he developed the Motortown Revue, a stage show that featured only Motown artists.

Motown grew to be one of the world's largest black-owned businesses. In the 1970s Motown branched out into the film industry. Gordy directed the 1975 film *Mahogany*, starring Diana Ross, and acted as executive producer for the films *Lady Sings the Blues* and *Bingo Long*.

Berry Gordy, Jr., sold Motown Records in the 1980s.

NOVEMBER 29

1915: Composer and arranger Billy Strayhorn is born in Dayton, Ohio.

Strayhorn spent his early years in Hillsboro, North Carolina, and attended high school in Pittsburgh, Pennsylvania. He studied music and in 1938 submitted some of his work to Duke Ellington, who liked the material and signed Strayhorn to compose and arrange for his orchestra.

Strayhorn rarely appeared with the band in public, but he collaborated with Ellington for 28 years on such hits as "Take the 'A' Train," "Lush Life," "Blood Count," "Rain Check" and "Johnny Come Lately."

Billy Strayhorn died on May 31, 1967, in New York City.

NOVEMBER 30

1909: Blues singer and guitarist Robert Nighthawk is born in Helena, Arkansas.

Nighthawk started playing the blues in the 1920s around Memphis. In the 1930s he worked with John Lee Hooker and Jimmie Rodgers. In the mid-1930s he was a carnival musician and recorded under the name Robert Lee McCoy. He settled in Chicago around 1937 and recorded for the Blue Bird and Decca labels before returning to the Memphis area, where he worked on several radio shows. He took his name from his 1937 recording "Prowling Nighthawk."

Nighthawk returned to Chicago in the early 1950s. For the rest of his career he shuttled back and forth between Chicago and the Deep South. His best LPs are *Bricks in My Pillow*, *Robert Lee McCoy: The Complete Recordings* and *Live on Maxwell Street*.

Robert Nighthawk died on November 5, 1967, in Helena, Arkansas.

1915: Bluesman Walter Brown "Brownie" McGhee is born in Knoxville, Tennessee.

McGhee learned the guitar from his father at the age of seven. In the late 1920s he dropped out of school and began playing in carnivals, medicine shows and minstrel shows around Tennessee.

He met Sonny Terry in 1939. The team moved to New York and worked with such artists as Paul Robeson, Josh White, Leadbelly, Pete Seeger and Woody Guthrie. In 1940 they began recording for the Okeh label.

In the early 1940s McGhee and Terry operated the Home of the Blues Music School and performed on the Office of War Information radio broadcasts. In 1946 they appeared in the "Blues at Midnight" concert at New York's Town Hall. In 1947 they recorded the soundtrack for the film *The Roosevelt Story*. Later in their careers they worked on the soundtracks for the films *A Face in the Crowd*, *Buck and the Preacher*, *Book of Numbers* and *Leadbelly*.

McGhee and Terry recorded prolifically and toured the U.S. and Europe. They appeared in such theatrical productions as *Simply Heaven* and *Cat on a Hot Tin Roof* and in the films *The Roots of American Music: Country and Urban Blues*; *Blues Under the Skin*; *Out of the Blacks, Into the Blues*; and *Sincerely, the Blues*. Some of their best LPs are *Climbin' Up*, *Brownie McGhee and Sonny Terry Sing* and *I Couldn't Believe My Eyes*. Brownie McGhee's brother, Stick McGhee, recorded the R&B classic "Drinking Wine, Spo-Dee-O-Dee."

1944: Singer Luther Ingram is born in Jackson, Tennessee.

Ingram's biggest hits include "Ain't That Loving You" (1970), "If Loving You Is Wrong (I Don't Want to Be Right)" (1972), "I'll Be Your Shelter" (1972) and "Do You Love Somebody" (1978).

1964: Bandleader Don Redman dies.

Redman was born in West Virginia in July 1900. He studied music at the Chicago and Boston Music Conservatories. In 1923 he joined Fletcher Henderson's orchestra.

Redman was best known as the leader, from 1927 to 1931, of a swing band called McKinney's Cotton Pickers. When the Cotton Pickers disbanded, Redman formed the Don Redman Orchestra, one of the most popular black dance bands in the New York area during the 1930s.

In the mid-1940s Redman became a top big-band arranger. He arranged Tommy Dorsey's big hit "Deep Purple" and did charts for Count Basie, Harry James and the NBC studio band. In 1951 Don Redman became musical director for Pearl Bailey.

DECEMBER 1

1934: Singer Billy Paul is born Paul Williams in Philadelphia.

Paul attended the West Philadelphia Music Academy and began singing on the radio at the age of 12. He began recording in 1952. It took him twenty years to get a hit single. In 1972 he hit number 1 on both the soul and pop charts, with a million-selling single called "Me and Mrs. Jones." Billy Paul's other chart hits include "Am I Black Enough for You" (1973), "Thank You for Saving My Life" (1973) and "Let's Make a Baby" (1976).

1935: Lou Rawls is born in Chicago.

Rawls grew up in Chicago and sang with such gospel groups as the Teenage Kings of Harmony, the Holy Wonders, the Chosen Gospel Singers, the Pilgrim Travelers, the Highway Q.C.s and the Soul Stirrers. After a stint in the U.S. Army he moved to Los Angeles and began doing pop music.

In 1961 he signed with Capitol Records. In 1962 he sang backup for his old Soul Stirrers comrade, Sam Cooke, on "Bring It On Home." Then Rawls began hitting the pop singles charts, with songs like "Love Is a Hurting Thing" (1966), "Dead-End Street" (1967), "Your Good Thing Is About to Come to an End" (1969) and "A Natural Man" (1971), from the LPs *Lou Rawls Live* and *Lou Rawls: Soulin'*. Many of his songs featured extended "raps."

In the mid-1970s Rawls signed with Gamble and Huff's Philadelphia International Records. He had a million-selling single in 1976 with "You'll Never Find Another Love Like Mine." In 1977 he won a Grammy for his LP *Unmistakably Lou*. His other Philadelphia International hits include "Groovy People" (1976), "See You When I Get There" (1977), "Lady Love" (1977) and "Let Me Be Good to You"

(1979). His later LPs include *Love All Your Blues Away* and *At Last*.

For more than 10 years Lou Rawls has hosted the annual United Negro College Fund Parade of Stars Telethon. He has also been a spokesman for Anheuser-Busch, Inc.

DECEMBER 2

1930: Jazz pianist Wynton Kelly is born in Brooklyn.

Kelly began in R&B, playing live and recording with Hal Singer, "Cleanhead" Vinson, Eddie "Lockjaw" Davis and Roy Abrams. He cut his first jazz LP for Blue Note Records at the age of 19.

In 1951 and 1952 he worked with Dinah Washington, Dizzy Gillespie and Lester Young. After a stint in the service, Kelly rejoined Dinah Washington, in 1955. In 1957 he played in Gillespie's big band and was also in Charles Mingus's group.

Kelly led his own trio for a couple of years, before joining Miles Davis in 1959. He remained with Davis until 1963 and then formed a new trio, with Paul Chambers and Jimmy Cobb. The Wynton Kelly Trio was featured in a series of recordings, accompanying guitarist Wes Montgomery. The trio also backed Cannonball Adderley and Hank Mobley. Kelly's best LPs include *Kelly Blue, Blues on Purpose, Someday My Prince Will Come* and *The Last Trio Session*.

Wynton Kelly died on April 12, 1971.

DECEMBER 3

1961: The Marvelettes' "Please, Mr. Postman" is the number 1 R&B single and the first Motown record to hit number 1 on the pop charts.

"Please, Mr. Postman" was a slow mover. It was released on September 4. On November 13 it hit the top spot on the R&B charts and remained there for seven weeks. On December 11 it became the number 1 pop single. It

stayed at the top for only one week and was replaced by the Tokens' doo-wop rendition of an old African hymn, "The Lion Sleeps Tonight."

DECEMBER 4

1915: Pianist Eddie Heywood, Jr., is born in Atlanta.

Heywood's father played piano, trumpet and sax. He was musical director for the vaudeville team of Butter Beans and Susie. He also led the house band at Atlanta's 81 Theater. Eddie Jr. got his start playing piano in his father's band.

The Eddie Heywood Sextet was the hottest band to play at New York's famed Cafe Society in the mid-1940s. The band also recorded classic sides with such artists as Billie Holiday, Ella Fitzgerald, the Andrews Sisters and Bing Crosby and had a big hit with a version of "Begin the Beguine."

In 1947 Heywood developed arthritic paralysis of the hands and had to stop performing. In the early '50s he began composing. He wrote such songs as "Land of Dreams," "Soft Summer Breeze" and "Canadian Sunset" (from which the opening riff of Mary Wells's hit "My Guy" is taken). By the '70s Heywood's hands had improved, and he played at the 1974 Newport Jazz Festival.

1927: Duke Ellington opens at the Cotton Club.

The Cotton Club, in Harlem, opened in the fall of 1923. An elegant speakeasy, owned by gangsters, it had a "whites only" admission policy. A bottle of champagne went for $30, and a fifth of bootleg Scotch might cost almost $18.

The Cotton Club featured only the best in black entertainment. Besides Ellington, other top black stars who performed at the Cotton Club included Lena Horne, Cab Calloway, Louis Armstrong, Ella Fitzgerald and Ethel Waters.

The Cotton Club closed on June 10, 1940.

1899: Blues harmonica player Sonny Boy Williamson is born Aleck Ford in Glendora, Mississippi.

Williamson often used the name Alex "Rice" Miller. He began playing guitar and harmonica at the age of five. In the early 1920s he used the name Little Boy Blue and sang and played in juke joints around Mississippi and Arkansas. He often worked as a one-man band.

In the 1930s he played Nashville's Grand Ole Opry and worked with such bluesmen as Elmore James and Robert Johnson. In the late '30s he worked with Howlin' Wolf and Robert "Junior" Lockwood.

In 1941 he assumed the name Sonny Boy Williamson and became a regular performer on the King Biscuit–sponsored radio program from Helena, Arkansas. He remained with the show until 1945. He also appeared with Elmore James on the Talaho Syrup radio show from Yazoo, Mississippi, and with Howlin' Wolf on the Hadacol show from West Memphis, Arkansas.

Sonny Boy Williamson began recording in 1947. He first hit the R&B charts in 1951, with "Eyesight to the Blind." His hits included "Nine Below Zero" (1952), "Mighty Long Time" (1952), "Keep It to Yourself" (1956) and "Don't Start Me Talkin'" (1958).

In the late 1950s he moved his base of operations from the Deep South to Chicago. In the early '60s he toured Europe. In 1964 he recorded with the British rock group Brian Auger and the Trinity.

Williamson's best LPs include *Down and Out Blues*, *The Real Folk Blues* (Chess 1503), *The Best of Sonny Boy Williamson*, and his boxed set, *The Chess Years*.

Sonny Boy Williamson died on May 25, 1965, in Helena, Arkansas.

1931: The Reverend James Cleveland is born in Chicago.

Cleveland grew up on Chicago's South Side. He began his career at Pilgrim Baptist Church and earned a reputation as a freelance choir director.

In 1949 he moved to Detroit, where the Reverend C. L. Franklin hired him as choir director at new Bethel Baptist Church. While there he taught Franklin's daughter, Aretha, how to sing gospel music. Years later he produced her Grammy-winning LP *Amazing Grace*.

In the early 1950s Cleveland sang and played piano with the Gospelaires. In the mid-1950s he joined the famed Caravans.

He began recording as a solo artist in 1960, for Savoy Records. His first big hit was *Peace Be Still*, which sold over 800,000 copies, unheard of for a black gospel LP. Other best-selling gospel LPs include *Lord Hold My Hand*, *Live at Carnegie Hall*, *His Name Is Wonderful*, *He Shall Feed His Flock*, *99½ Won't Do* and *Having Church*.

Cleveland was credited with writing and arranging over 400 gospel songs, including "Everything Will Be All Right," "The Love of God," "I'll Do His Will" and "Lord Help Me to Hold Out." He founded the Gospel Music Workshop of America and the Cornerstone Institutional Baptist Church of Los Angeles. He was the first gospel performer to receive a star on Hollywood's Walk of Fame.

The Reverend James Cleveland died on February 9, 1991.

THE REVEREND JAMES CLEVELAND

1935: Little Richard is born Richard Wayne Penniman in Macon, Georgia.

Little Richard is rock 'n' roll's original wildman. With his screaming vocals, keyboard-rattling piano style, outrageous makeup, gaudy costumes and jewelry and his ultra-extroverted personality, Little Richard is one of the genre's all-time flamboyant performers.

Little Richard grew up in Macon, one of 12 children. His parents ran a nightclub called the Tip In Inn. He spent his youth singing in gospel choirs. At 15 he started singing with the B. Brown Orchestra and later worked with Sugarfoot Sam's minstrel show. In 1951 Little Richard won a talent contest and a contract with RCA Records.

In 1953 he moved to Houston and worked with a group called the Tempo Toppers, who recorded for the Peacock label.

He met Lloyd Price in 1955. Price sent a demo of Little Richard's music to his own label, Specialty Records, and Little Richard was signed to a recording contract.

He hit the R&B charts in November 1955, with "Tutti Frutti," which became a pop hit as well. He followed up with such wild rockers as "Long Tall Sally" (1956), "Slippin' and Slidin' " (1956), "Rip It Up" (1956), "Ready Teddy" (1956), "She's Got It" (1956), "The Girl Can't Help It" (1956), "Lucille" (1957), "Jenny, Jenny" (1957), "Keep a-Knockin' " (1957) and "Good Golly, Miss Molly" (1958). He also appeared in such rock 'n' roll films as *The Girl Can't Help It*, *Don't Knock the Rock* and *Mister Rock 'n' Roll*. In 1957, in the middle of a sold-out tour, Little Richard quit rock 'n' roll to become a preacher. The following year he became an ordained minister in the Seventh Day Adventist Church, and he earned a degree in theology in 1959.

From 1959 to 1962 Little Richard recorded gospel music. In 1962 he returned to rock 'n' roll. He toured England and performed with several up-and-coming groups, including the Beatles and the Rolling Stones. In 1964 he signed with Vee Jay Records and rerecorded his best-known songs. Later on he recorded for the Okeh, Modern and Reprise labels.

In 1976, after the death of his brother, Little Richard returned to being an evangelist. In the 1980s he appeared in the films *Down and Out in Beverly Hills* and *Twins*. He was inducted into the Rock 'n' Roll Hall of Fame in 1986. In 1993 he was given a lifetime-achievement Grammy.

DECEMBER 6

1989: "Blame It on the Rain," by Milli Vanilli, is the number 1 pop single.

In 1989 there was no hotter act in pop music than the German-based duo known as Milli Vanilli (Rob Pilatus and Fab Morvan). The act had been created by record producer Frank Farian. Milli Vanilli's first single, "Girl You Know It's True," sold over two million copies. The next two, "Baby Don't Forget My Number" and "Girl I'm Gonna Miss You," were also million-sellers. Their fourth single, "Blame It on the Rain," sold another two million copies, and Milli Vanilli won the 1989 Grammy for best new artist.

Then the roof fell in. It was discovered that neither Pilatus nor Morvan had sung on these monster hits. The vocals had been recorded by studio singers Charles Shaw, John Davis and Brad Howe. Milli Vanilli was stripped of the Grammy, and the duo's record company offered refunds.

DECEMBER 7

1974: "Kung Fu Fighting," by Carl Douglas, hits number 1 on the pop charts.

Douglas was born in Jamaica and raised in California. He went to college in England. He sold a million copies of this ode to the Far East adventure films that, spawned by the success of Bruce Lee, were the cinematic rage in the early and mid-1970s.

DECEMBER 8

1925: Actor, singer and dancer Sammy Davis, Jr., is born in New York City.

Davis's career began when he was five and joined his dad and uncle in a club-and-vaudeville act called the Will Masten Trio. He remained with the act until 1948, when he began a solo act—singing, dancing and doing impressions. He signed with Decca Records in 1954. On November 19 of that year he lost his left eye in a car wreck in Las Vegas.

Davis had hit records such as "Something's Gotta Give" (1955), "Love Me or Leave Me" (1955), "That Old Black Magic" (1955), "What Kind of Fool Am I" (1962), "The Shelter of Your Arms" (1963) and his 1972 million-seller, "The Candy Man." He starred in the films *Oceans 11*, *Pepe*, *Sergeants Three*, *Convicts Four*, *Johnny Cool*, *Robin and the Seven Hoods*, *Sweet Charity*, *Salt and Pepper* and *A Man Called Adam*. He also appeared on Broadway, in shows like *Mr. Wonderful*, *Lucasta*, *Porgy and Bess* and *Golden Boy*. His television credits include "The Mod Squad," "The Name of the Game," "Laugh-In," "The Ed Sullivan Show," "The Lucy Show" and "All in the Family."

Sammy Davis, Jr., died of throat cancer on May 15, 1990.

SAMMY DAVIS, JR.

1925: Jazz organist Jimmy Smith is born in Norristown, Pennsylvania.

Smith won an amateur contest at the age of nine. He studied bass and piano and switched to organ while playing with the R&B group of Dan Gardner, from 1952 to 1955.

He formed his own trio in 1956 and began recording for Blue Note Records. In 1960 he switched to the Verve label.

Smith's LPs include *The Cat*, *Back at the Chicken Shack*, *Off the Top*, *The Sermon* and *The Organ Grinder Swing*.

1939: Vocalist Jerry Butler is born in Sunflower, Mississippi.

Butler grew up in Chicago. He and boyhood pal Curtis Mayfield sang with the Mother Jubilee Gospel Singers and later with a pop group called the Quail. In 1957 Butler and Mayfield joined the Roosters, who later became the Impressions. In 1958 Butler and the Impressions had a Top 10 soul and pop hit, with "For Your Precious Love," featuring Butler on lead vocals. On the strength of that recording, Butler became a solo artist in late 1958.

Butler, called the Iceman because he's so cool and suave in appearance, persona and vocal delivery, has placed over 50 singles on the pop and R&B charts. His greatest hits include "He Will Break Your Heart" (1960), "Find Yourself Another Girl" (1961), "I'm a-Tellin' You" (1961), "Moon River" (1962), "Make It Easy on Yourself" (1962), "Need to Belong" (1963), "I Stand Accused" (1964), "Let It Be Me (with Betty Everett, 1964), "I Dig You Baby" (1967), "Never Give You Up" (1968), "Hey Western Union Man" (1968), "Only the Strong Survive" (1969), "Moody Woman" (1969), "What's the Use of Breaking Up" (1969), "If It's Real What I Feel" (1971), "Ain't Understanding Mellow" (1971), "Close to You" (with Brenda Lee Eager, 1972), "One-Night Affair" (1972) and "I Wanna Do It to You" (1977).

DECEMBER 9

1932: Singer Jessie Hill is born in New Orleans.

Hill sang and played piano and drums with Huey "Piano" Smith and the Clowns. In 1958 he went solo, and in 1960 he hit the top of the charts with a classic chunk of funk, "Ooh Poo Pah Doo."

1932: Jazz trumpeter Donald Byrd is born in Detroit.

Byrd was educated at Wayne State University and at the Manhattan School of Music. He received his Ph.D. from Columbia University.

Byrd came to notice in the mid-1950s as a member of Art Blakey's Jazz Messengers. In 1958 he formed his own group and played jazz festivals throughout Europe.

Byrd has split his time between the worlds of jazz and education. In the 1960s he spent a good deal of time studying and teaching at jazz clinics and at New York City's Music and Art High School. In the early 1970s Donald Byrd became chairman of the Black Music Department at Howard University, in Washington, D.C. While teaching at Howard he formed the Blackbyrds, who have had such chart hits as "Walking in Rhythm" (1975) and "Happy Music" (1976). His 1973 LP *Blackbyrd* was a best-seller in both the soul and jazz markets.

Donald Byrd's other hit LPs include *Byrd in Hand, Free Form, Harlem Blues, Fuego* and *At the Half Mate Cafe.*

1934: Blues harp master Junior Wells is born Amos Wells in Memphis.

Wells learned the harmonica as a child and played on the streets for tips. He moved to Chicago in 1946 and, together with Louis and Dave Myers, formed a group called the Little Boys and worked in a club called the C&T Lounge. In 1948 they renamed the group the Three Aces.

In 1949 Wells replaced Little Walter in Muddy Waters's band. When he got out of the service, in 1955, he returned to the Waters band and then reorganized the Three Aces.

Wells first worked with Buddy Guy in 1958. The duo recorded for the Chess label. In 1965 Wells recorded his classic blues LP *Hoodoo Man Blues*, and in 1974 Wells and Guy recorded the live LP *Drinkin' TNT & Smokin' Dynamite.*

Junior Wells has worked not only the blues club circuit but also the top folk, jazz and blues festivals since the 1960s. His best LP collections include *Southside Blues Jam, Messin' with the Kid* and *Blues Hit Big Town.*

DECEMBER 10

1913: Jazz trumpeter Ray Nance is born in Chicago.

Duke Ellington called Nance "Floorshow" because, along with being a first-rate trumpet player, Nance was a violinist, singer, dancer and comedian. Nance joined Ellington's band in November 1940, replacing Cootie

Williams. He supplied the vocals on the Ellington hit "A Slip of the Lip." In 1944 Nance left Ellington to lead his own group but returned in 1945 and remained until 1963.

Ray Nance died on January 28, 1976.

1926: Guitar Slim is born Eddie Jones in Greenwood, Mississippi.

Guitar Slim began his career in the late 1940s, in a trio with Huey "Piano" Smith. He had only one hit, a million-selling blues classic called "The Things I Used to Do," early in 1954. The record went to number 1 on the R&B charts and to the Top 20 on the pop charts. It featured the work of a young pianist named Ray Charles. Guitar Slim's best work can be heard on such LPs as *The Things I Used to Do* and *Red Cadillacs and Crazy Chicks.*

Guitar Slim died of pneumonia on February 7, 1959.

1967: Singer Otis Redding is killed in a plane crash.

Plane crashes have claimed many other musicians as well, including rockers Buddy Holly, Richie Valens and the Big Bopper, rock group Lynyrd Skynyrd, country star Patsy Cline and singer and songwriter Jim Croce.

It was early Sunday morning, and Redding had just finished a concert in Madison, Wisconsin, and was bound for Cleveland. Four miles into the trip the plane plunged into Lake Monona.

Also on board the ill-fated flight were four members of the Barkays, a group that had hit the top of the charts with the instrumental "Soul Finger" and was on tour with Redding. Those killed were guitarist Jimmy King, organist Ronnie Caldwell, drummer Carl Cunningham and saxophonist Phalon Jones. Trumpeter Ben Cauley and bassist James Alexander were not on the plane.

Nearly 5,000 people attended the funeral of Otis Redding.

DECEMBER 11

1926: Blues singer Willie Mae "Big Mama" Thornton is born in Montgomery, Alabama.

Thornton's mother was a singer, and Willie Mae began singing as a small child. In 1939 she won first prize in an

amateur contest in Montgomery. In 1941, after her mother died, she toured with a group called Sammy Green's Hot Harlem Revue, working as a singer, dancer and comedian. In 1948 she settled in Houston and began working such local clubs as the Bronze Peacock.

Thornton first recorded for a small label, E&W, in 1951. Later that year she joined the Johnny Otis show and signed with Peacock Records. It was Johnny Otis's orchestra that backed her on the recording session for "Hound Dog," a song later made famous by Elvis Presley. Her own version of the song hit number 1 on the R&B charts in early 1953.

In 1952 Thornton played the Apollo Theater and worked with such top R&B acts as Roy Milton, Joe Liggins, Johnny Ace, Junior Parker and Clarence "Gatemouth" Brown. Throughout the '50s she worked primarily the black club and package-show circuits. In the early 1960s she worked mostly on the West Coast, and in 1964 she performed at the Monterey Jazz Festival. In 1967 she was a performer in the "Spirituals to Swing" concert at Carnegie Hall.

Janis Joplin's late 1960s recording of Thornton's "Ball and Chain" caused a renewal of interest in Thornton. She began to appear at the largest blues and jazz festivals and on TV shows, including "Midnight Special." In 1971 she recorded the soundtrack for the film *Vanishing Point*. Among Thornton's hit LPs are *The Original Hound Dog, Big Mama Thornton, Ball and Chain* and *In Europe.*

Big Mama Thornton died on July 25, 1984, in Los Angeles.

1938: Jazz pianist McCoy Tyner is born in Philadelphia.

At the age of 15 Tyner was leading his own jazz group and gigging around Philadelphia. In 1959 he joined the Jazztet, a group led by Art Farmer and Benny Golson. He was with John Coltrane from 1960 to 1965, and in 1966 he formed his own trio and began recording for the Blue Note label. His LP *The Real McCoy* is considered one of the best jazz albums of the late '60s.

In 1972 Tyner's album *Sahara* was voted record of the year in the *Down Beat* magazine critics' poll. In 1973 he recorded the live LP *Enlightenment at the Montreux Jazz Festival*. The LP also won the Montreux Diamond Prize as album of the year.

McCoy Tyner has recorded more than three dozen albums in all, including *Uptown/Downtown*, *Fly with the Wind*, *Passion Dance* and *Night of Ballads and Blues*.

1964: Soul legend Sam Cooke is shot to death in Los Angeles.

Cooke was killed by a shot from a .22-caliber pistol wielded by the woman who managed the motel where he was staying when an argument broke out. The manager claimed that Cooke was about to attack her, and that she fired in self-defense. The shooting was ruled a justifiable homicide.

DECEMBER 12

1918: Blues and jazz vocalist Joe Williams is born in Cordele, Georgia.

Williams moved to Chicago in 1922. At the age of 15 he contracted tuberculosis, and his left lung collapsed.

He began singing around Chicago at weddings and funerals. In 1935 he was with a gospel group called the Jubilee Boys. Also in the mid-1930s he joined Jimmy Moone's orchestra as a singer, performing in Chicago nightclubs. In 1939 and 1940 he toured with the Les Hite Dance Band.

In 1941 Williams worked with Coleman Hawkins. In 1943 he was with Lionel Hampton's band. In 1946 and 1947 he sang with Andy Kirk's orchestra. He made his first records with the Kirk outfit. He then went on to work with the bands of Albert Ammons, Pete Johnson, Red Sanders and Hot Lips Page.

In 1952 Williams had a huge R&B hit, "Every Day I Have the Blues," backed by the King Kolax Orchestra. In 1954 he became a regular vocalist with Count Basie's orchestra. He remained with Basie until 1960, and then he went solo.

Williams appeared on every top TV variety show and in the films *Cinderfella* and *The Moonshine War*. His best LPs include *Basie Swings*, *Joe Williams Sings: Every Day I Have the Blues*, *Nothing But the Blues*, *Chains of Love* and *Every Night*.

Joe Williams won the *Down Beat* critics' poll as best male singer for five consecutive years, starting in 1974.

1928: Bluesman Lonesome Sundown is born Cornelius Green in Donaldsonville, Louisiana.

Sundown began his career as guitarist with zydeco king Clifton Chenier's band. In the 1950s he recorded for the Excello label. His best-known singles were "My Home Is a Prison" and "Lonesome Lonely Blues." His best LP was titled simply *Lonesome Sundown*. In the mid-1960s he gave up the blues for religion, but in the 1970s he returned to record the LP *Been Gone Too Long*, with Phillip Walker.

1940: Dionne Warwick is born in East Orange, New Jersey.

Warwick grew up in a gospel family. Her mother was manager of the famous Drinkard Singers, a church choir that gave Warwick her first musical experience. She later former her own gospel trio, the Gospelaires, and earned a scholarship to Hart College of Music.

In 1960 she met composer Burt Bacharach while doing backup vocals on a Drifters song, "Mexican Divorce." She began cutting demos for Bacharach and his partner, Hal David, and the three wound up with a contract at Scepter Records.

In December 1962 "Don't Make Me Over" became a Top 10 hit, the first of a long list of smashes for the writing-producing-singing collaboration. Others were "Anyone Who Had a Heart," "Walk On By," "A House Is Not a Home," "Message to Michael," "Alfie," "Theme from *Valley of the Dolls*" and "Do You Know the Way to San Jose," for which Warwick won a Grammy. By 1966 she had sold 12 million records and appeared on many of the major TV variety shows.

Warwick spent much of the 1970s with Warner Brothers Records before signing with Arista, in 1979. Her first LP for that company, *Dionne*, sold well over a million copies, and she became the first woman to win simultaneous Grammy awards in both the pop and R&B categories.

In the 1980s such hit LPs as *Heartbreaker*, *No Night So Long*, *Hot*

Live and Otherwise, *Friends in Love* and *Reservations for Two* kept her on the LP and singles charts throughout the decade. She was given a star on Hollywood's Walk of Fame and developed and launched her own line of "Dionne" perfumes. In 1986 the single "That's What Friends Are For" featured Warwick, Gladys Knight, Stevie Wonder and Elton John. It won a Grammy for best performance by a duo or group and one for best song (the writers were Burt Bacharach and Carol Bayer Sager). All proceeds from the single and a video of the recording session benefited the American Foundation for AIDS Research (AmFAR). The record was number 1 on *Billboard*'s Top 100 chart for four weeks and raised more than a million dollars for AmFAR.

DIONNE WARWICK

1959: Singer and drummer Sheila E. is born in San Francisco.

Sheila E. has been making music all her life. Raised in Oakland, she is one of four children of legendary Bay Area percussionist Pete Escovedo. At the age of five she was playing conga drums and performing live with her dad and her uncle Coke. At 10 she began taking violin lessons. Before she stopped, five years later, she had been offered three music scholarships. By that time she was on the road, playing congas and singing with her father's group, Azteca.

She also began playing with producer and musician George Duke. That creative collaboration lasted three years. She toured extensively with Duke and cut two LPs with her father. Her session career also blossomed as she worked in the recording studio with artists like Con Funk Shun, Herbie Hancock, Lionel Richie, Jeffrey Osborne, Diana Ross and Marvin Gaye.

She met Prince, with whom she performed on the smash *Purple Rain* soundtrack. Thanks to Prince, she was signed as a solo artist to Warner Brothers Records in 1983. She also joined Prince as both an opening act and a member of his stage band on his record-breaking *Purple Rain* Tour.

The Glamorous Life, written, performed and produced by Sheila E., was released in the spring of 1984 and earned popular and critical acclaim. The title track was a hit single. The LP was a multiple-Grammy nominee.

In 1985 *Romance 1600*, a musical-fantasy LP, gave her another hit single, with "Love Bizarre." This success gave her a spot as opening act for Lionel Richie on his world tour.

She released her third album, *Sheila E.*, early in 1987, the same year that brought her most stunning performance as a musician, in Prince's 1987 concert film *Sign o' the Times*.

DECEMBER 13

1895: Jazz drummer William Alexander "Sonny" Greer is born in Long Branch, New Jersey.

Greer and Duke Ellington played their first gig together on March 20, 1920. Greer remained with Ellington until 1951.

After leaving Ellington, Greer worked with the groups of Johnny Hodges, Red Allen and others. Besides being Ellington's greatest drummer, Greer was also one of the jazz world's all-time great characters, a consummate hipster and jive talker.

Sonny Greer's work can be found on any classic Ellington piece from the 1930s or 1940s. He died on March 23, 1982.

1981: Comedian Dewey "Pigmeat" Markham dies of a stroke in the Bronx.

Markham was born in Durham, North Carolina, in 1904. He started out working carnivals and medicine shows as a dancer and comic. In the mid-1920s he moved to New York and began working in vaudeville, often with partner and straight man George Wilshire.

Markham was a favorite at the Apollo Theater. He did monologues, but his best work was in comedy sketches. His most outstanding character was the flamboyant Judge Pigmeat, who upon entering the courtroom would shout, "The Judge is high as a Georgia pine…everybody gonna do some time." In the late 1960s, when the hit TV show "Laugh-In" popularized the phrase "Here come da Judge," the reference was to that phrase's originator, Pigmeat Markham.

Other great skits included "Have You Seen My Wife," "Go Ahead and Sing," "7 x 13 = 28" and a hilarious version of Dusty Fletcher's "Open the Door, Richard." He recorded 16 comedy LPs, including *The Trial at the Party; Open the Door, Richard;* and *Save Your Soul, Baby,* for Chess Records. He also invented the 1940s dance style called "truckin'." In the late '60s Pigmeat Markham appeared on "Laugh-In" and other TV shows, and he recorded a single called "Here Comes the Judge," which hit the Top 20.

DECEMBER 14

1902: Singer Viola Wells is born in Newark, New Jersey.

Wells, known as Miss Rhapsody, was a popular nightclub and show performer in the 1930s and 1940s. She starred in shows like the *Dixie to Harlem Revue* and worked with the bands of Bunny Berrigan, Bill Doggett, Benny Carter, Art Tatum and Erskine Hawkins. She retired from music in the 1960s but returned in the 1970s, performing both jazz and gospel music.

Viola Wells died on December 22, 1984.

1917: Vocalist and pianist Martha Davis is born in Wichita, Kansas.

Davis was called "queen of the ivories" in the late 1940s. She had hot jukebox hits like "Little White Lies" (1948), "Don't Burn the Candle at Both Ends" (1948) and "Daddy O" (1948). She frequently worked with Louis Jordan.

1930: Clark Terry, a distinctive stylist on both trumpet and flugelhorn, is born in St. Louis.

Terry played in Lionel Hampton's band and then worked in the bands of Charlie Barnet (1947–1948), Count Basie (1948–1951), Duke Ellington (1951–1959) and Quincy Jones (1959–1960). He was a staff musician at NBC and co-led a quartet with trombonist Bob Brookmeyer. Terry is also noted for his scatting vocal style, which he calls "the mumbles." Some of Clark Terry's best LPs are *Yes the Blues, The Happy Horns of Clark Terry, Serenade to a Bus Seat* and *The Oscar Peterson Trio with Clark Terry.*

DECEMBER 15

1903: Blues guitarist Tampa Red is born Hudson Whittaker in Smithville, Georgia.

Tampa Red began recording in 1928 and continued until 1953. Some sources say that he recorded about 335 songs on 78 records. Some of his best-known songs are "It's Tight Like That," "Kingfish Blues," "Better Let My Gal Alone," "Mean and Evil Woman," "Mercy Mama Blues," and "You Missed a Good Man." They can be found on such LPs as *The Guitar Wizard, It's Tight Like That* and *Keep Jumping.*

Tampa Red played a unique style of bottleneck guitar that was influenced by Hawaiian guitarists he had heard. When not recording on his own, he was in demand as an accompanist and recorded with such well-known blues singers as Georgia Tom Dorsey, Ma Rainey and Memphis Minnie. Throughout most of his career Tampa Red played mostly small blues clubs. He was one of the few noted bluesmen who did not participate in the blues revival of the 1960s.

Tampa Red retired in 1974 and died on March 19, 1981.

1933: Singer Jesse Belvin is born in Texarkana, Arkansas.

Belvin moved to Los Angeles in 1939. At the age of seven he began singing in his mother's church choir. At 16 he joined Big Jay McNeely's band.

He did the vocals on McNeely's "All That Wine Is Gone" (1950).

In early 1953 Belvin and Marvin Phillips, billed as Jesse and Marvin, had the R&B hit "Dream Girl." In 1954, while in the U.S. Army, Belvin wrote the R&B classic "Earth Angel" for the Penguins. In 1956 Belvin had a great R&B hit single with the romantic ballad "Good Night, My Love," which became famed deejay Alan Freed's closing theme song. It got Belvin a contract with RCA Records. Belvin's biggest hit on RCA came in 1959 with the song "Guess Who," which his wife, JoAnn, had written.

On February 6, 1960, Jesse and JoAnn Belvin were killed in a car wreck.

DECEMBER 16

1978: Chuck Brown and the soul Searchers make their chart debut with "Bustin' Loose."

Chuck Brown and the Soul Searchers are known as the godfathers of Go Go music, a form of heavily funk-laden dance music that developed in the black clubs around Washington, D.C., and Baltimore. Other well-known Go Go bands include Trouble Funk, Experience Unlimited (better known as E.U.) and Rare Essence.

Go Go came into the limelight in 1987. It was an integral part of the film *Good to Go*, which starred Art Garfunkel and was the subject of the concert documentary film *Go Go Live*. E.U. hit the Top 5 on the black singles chart in early 1988 with "Da Butt," a dance smash from the soundtrack of the Spike Lee film *School Daze*.

"Bustin' Loose" became a number 1 black chart single and sold over a million copies.

DECEMBER 17

1910: Sy Oliver, one of the best-known and most prolific arrangers in the history of jazz and popular music, is born in Battle Creek, Michigan.

Oliver grew up in a musical household. He could read music by the age of four or five. In his late teens he played trumpet in the bands of Cliff Barnet, Zack Whyte and Alphonso Trent.

In 1933 he joined Jimmie Lunceford's band as trumpeter and staff arranger and did the charts for such classics as "Dinah," "Ain't She Sweet" and "T'aint What You Do." His arrangements rivaled those of Duke Ellington.

In 1939 Oliver became staff arranger for Tommy Dorsey's band. He arranged Dorsey's hit "Sunny Side of the Street."

Oliver formed his own band in 1946 but gave it up to became a freelance arranger for record companies. He arranged and produced highly successful albums for Frank Sinatra, Ella Fitzgerald, Sammy Davis, Jr., and Louis Armstrong. In the late 1960s Sy Oliver returned to bandleading.

1939: Organist James Booker is born in New Orleans.

Booker worked in the backup band of singer Dee Clark and was a session player for Duke/Peacock Records. His big R&B hit was the instrumental "Gonzo," in 1960.

James Booker died on November 8, 1983.

1939: Temptations co–lead singer Eddie Kendricks is born in Union Springs, Alabama.

Kendricks joined the Temptations when they were still known as the Primes. His falsetto can be heard on such Temptations hits as "Get Ready," "The Way You Do the Things You Do" and "Just My Imagination."

Kendricks went solo in 1971 and scored his first big hit, a number 1 pop and soul chart hit called "Keep On Truckin', Part 1." His other solo hits included "Boogie Down" (1973), "Son of Sagittarius" (1974), "Shoeshine Boy" (1975) and "He's a Friend" (1976). In 1982 Kendricks returned to the Temptations for a short reunion tour. In the mid-1980s he teamed up with David Ruffin and Daryl Hall and John Oates for a series of recordings and concerts.

Eddie Kendricks died of lung cancer on October 5, 1992, in Birmingham, Alabama.

DECEMBER 18

1897: Bandleader, pianist, composer and arranger Fletcher Henderson, whose orchestra in the

1920s laid the foundation for 1930s-style swing, is born in Cuthbert, Georgia.

Henderson began playing piano at the age of six. He earned a degree in chemistry from Atlanta University College and in 1920 moved to New York to do postgraduate work. Instead, he took a job as a song demonstrator for the Pace-Handy Music Company.

In 1921 Henderson became recording manager for the first black-owned record company, Black Swan Records. In the fall of 1921 he organized his first band, to accompany Black Swan's biggest star, Ethel Waters, on tour. The show was billed as Ethel Waters's Black Swan Troubadours and was on the road until the summer of 1922.

In 1923 Henderson organized a band under his own name and began playing at the Club Alabam. In 1924 the band moved to the famed Roseland Ballroom and stayed for five years.

During Henderson's Roseland stint his orchestra became American's most popular black dance band. For black musicians, a job with Henderson was a gig to die for. Among the many greats who played in the band during this period were Louis Armstrong, Coleman Hawkins, Rex Stewart, Buster Bailey, Don Redman, Benny Carter and Bennie Moten. The Henderson orchestra featured superb arrangements, but Henderson was not a strict disciplinarian, and things often were less tight than they should have been. Henderson's orchestra finished at Roseland in 1929 and then played various ballrooms and clubs for the next decade.

In 1939 Henderson joined Benny Goodman as arranger. In 1941 he reorganized his big band and played venues like the Apollo Theater. Throughout the 1940s he reorganized and disbanded his orchestra several times. In the late '40s he worked again with Ethel Waters.

On December 21, 1950, he suffered a stroke and was partially paralyzed. He was never able to play piano again, but he continued to do arrangements for bands like those of Teddy Hill and Will Bradley.

There are several LP and CD collections of Henderson's recorded music: *The Crown*

King of Swing; Fletcher Henderson's Orchestra, 1923–1927, 1927–1931; and *Hocus Pocus, 1927–1936.*

Fletcher Henderson died on December 28, 1952.

1914: Blues guitarist Pee Wee Crayton is born Connie Curtis Crayton in Rockdale, Texas.

Crayton was a protégé and friend of guitarist T-Bone Walker. He moved to California in 1935. He formed his own band in 1945 and also played in the bands of such R&B singers as Jimmy Witherspoon and Ivory Joe Hunter. Crayton is usually categorized as a Texas blues guitarist, but he actually made his mark in the genre of West Coast blues.

In 1948 and 1949 Crayton had R&B chart hits with "Blues After Hours," "Texas Hop" and "I Love You So." In the 1950s he worked with the Red Callender band and toured with several R&B package shows. For most of the 1960s he was out of the music business. In the early 1970s he worked with Johnny Otis.

Pee Wee Crayton died of a heart attack on June 25, 1985.

1917: Saxophonist and band-leader Eddie "Cleanhead" Vinson is born in Houston.

Vinson began his career in the early 1930s, with the Texas-based bands of Chester Boone, Milt Larkin and Floyd Ray. In 1942 he joined Cootie Williams's band as singer and saxophonist. In 1945

EDDIE "CLEANHEAD" VINSON

he formed his own 16-piece band but later cut it to half that size. His 1947 band included a young saxophonist named John Coltrane.

As a composer, Vinson wrote such pieces as "Tune Up," which was recorded by Miles Davis. In the late 1940s Vinson had R&B chart hits with "Old Maid Boogie" (1947), "Kidney Stew Blues" (1947) and "Somebody Done Stole My Cherry Red" (1949).

1933: Bluesman Lonnie Brooks, whose fast, electrifying guitar style has earned him the nickname Louisiana Lightnin', is born in Dubuisson, Louisiana.

Brooks didn't take up the guitar seriously until he was in his 20s. He got his first professional job with the band of zydeco superstar Clifton Chenier. He then began playing clubs and fraternity parties under the nickname Guitar Junior. He had a regional rock 'n' roll hit called "Family Rules."

In 1959, while touring with Sam Cooke, he landed in Chicago and began playing the clubs under his own name, since there was already another Guitar Junior in Chicago.

In 1969 Brooks released his first LP, *Broke and Hungry.* Since then he has released such high-voltage blues albums as *Bayou Lightning, Blues Deluxe, Hot Shot* and *Wound Up Tight. Blues Deluxe* was nominated for a Grammy.

Lonnie Brooks is extremely popular in Europe, where he tours constantly and headlines large blues festivals.

DECEMBER 19

1918: Professor Longhair is born Henry Roeland "Roy" Byrd in Bogalusa, Louisiana.

He moved to New Orleans as an infant. As a child, he used to tap dance and "hambone" for tips at Rampart and Bourbon Streets. His first instrument was the guitar, but he picked up piano by hanging out in local dives and watching barrelhouse pianists like Drive-'Em-Down Toots Washington and Sullivan Rock, who taught him the basics. Soon he was playing in clubs and theaters.

His first professional job was in a joint called the Cotton Club, with Champion

Jack Dupree. In the late 1930s he accompanied harp player Sonny Boy (Alex "Rice" Miller) Williamson.

He joined the Civilian Conservation Corps but in 1940 was not drafted into the U.S. Army because of a bad knee. In 1942, however, he was inducted anyway. When he got out of the service, in 1944, he started cooking and playing piano in a place called Hicks Barbecue Pit. In the late 1940s he played clubs, and in 1949 he cut his first record. In 1950 he hit number 5 on the national R&B charts, with the song "Baldhead." He signed with Atlantic and released such records as "Mardi Gras in New Orleans," "Professor Longhair Blues" and "Walk Your Blues Away."

In 1953 he released his New Orleans classic, "Tipitina." In the mid-1950s Professor Longhair suffered a stroke but was playing again by 1955.

As a pianist, Professor Longhair is credited with having been the first to weave together all the different strains of New Orleans blues, jazz, Dixieland, R&B, Cajun, Tex-Mex and rhumba into the cohesive form that is so well known today. He was a guru to many New Orleans musicians. His piano style influenced such well-known Crescent City artists as Fats Domino, Allen Toussaint, Huey "Piano" Smith and Dr. John.

In 1971 Professor Longhair was the uncontested hit of the New Orleans Jazz Festival, which brought him international attention and bookings into events like the Montreux Jazz Festival. In the 1970s he played the top blues clubs and festivals.

Professor Longhair died on January 30, 1980, in New Orleans, right before the release of his LP *Crawfish Fiesta.* Other great Professor Longhair LPs include *Rock 'n' Roll Gumbo; House Party, New Orleans Style;* and *Mardi Gras in New Orleans.*

1941: Earth, Wind and Fire leader Maurice White is born in Memphis.

The story of Earth, Wind and Fire is basically the story of Maurice White. White began singing gospel at the age of four. When he was 10 he was playing in a band with Booker T. (of the MGs) Jones. When he was 15 he and his family moved to Chicago, and he studied at the Chicago Conservatory of Music.

In 1963 White signed on as staff recording drummer for Chess Records. He played behind such greats as Billy Stewart, John Lee Hooker, Muddy Waters, Howlin' Wolf and Ramsey Lewis.

After several years as drummer for the Ramsey Lewis Trio, White decided to form his own band. In 1970 his group, the Salty Peppers, released a single on Capitol Records and moved to Los Angeles. In 1971 the group's name was changed to Earth, Wind and Fire, and the group was signed to Columbia Records. Earth, Wind and Fire consisted of vocalists White and Philip Bailey, with Verdine White on saxophone; Andrew Woolfolk on horns; Roland Bautista, Al McKay and Johnny Graham on guitars; Larry Dunn on keyboards; and Ralph Johnson and Fred White on drums and percussion. Maurice White also played drums and saxophone. In 1973 their *Head to the Sky* album went gold. In 1974 *Open Your Eyes* became their first platinum success. Earth, Wind and Fire had a banner year in 1975. *That's the Way of the World* sold double platinum, and the gold single "Shining Star" earned the group its first Grammy.

Maurice White quickly became one of the country's hottest producers. Besides Earth, Wind and Fire, he produced gold and platinum records for such diverse artists Barbra Streisand, Deneice Williams, Jennifer Holliday, Ramsey Lewis and the Emotions.

Earth, Wind and Fire continued to turn out hits like "September," "Got to Get You into My Life" and "Boogie Wonderland."

In 1979 "After the Love Has Gone" won a Grammy for record of the year. In the '80s Earth, Wind and Fire continued its Grammy-winning ways, with singles like "Let's Groove" and "I Wanna Be with You."

Maurice White disbanded the group in 1983. In 1985 he released his first solo LP, *Maurice White*. Philip Bailey also released several solo LPs, including a gospel album and *Chinese Wall*, which included his smash duet with Phil Collins, "Easy Lover."

In the fall of 1986 White and Bailey began discussing the possibility of reorganizing the band. Most of the members came back, and *Touch the World* was released in late 1987. Earth, Wind and Fire had not lost its touch. The album yielded two number 1 black chart hits, "System of Survival" and "Thinking of You." The band also headlined the Budweiser Superfest Tour in 1988.

A large part of Earth, Wind and Fire's appeal has always been its personal mystique, which includes elements of religion, gospel, astrology and Egyptology.

DECEMBER 20

1957: Singer Anita Baker is born in Memphis.

By the time she was 12 the folks at church were calling Anita Baker "the little lady with the big voice." It was during that time that Baker decided she wanted to become a professional singer, but she didn't tell anybody because such things were not practical, according to her upbringing and her environment. Raised in inner-city Detroit, Baker joined a local rock band called Chapter Eight when she was 18. When the group cut its first LP, she moved to Los Angeles. Chapter Eight and its recording ventures failed, however, and Baker returned to Detroit and found work as a legal secretary.

After two years away from singing, she returned to performing and to Los

ANITA BAKER

Angeles, at the behest of record producer George Duke, in 1982. In 1983 she released an album called *Songstress*, which provided her with two hit singles on the black music charts.

After a series of legal problems, Baker signed with Arista Records. In 1986 she recorded and released her masterpiece, *Rapture*. It was an unexpected success, remaining on the LP charts for two years and yielding top single hits like "Sweet Love," "You Bring Me Joy" and "Caught Up in the Rapture."

Baker's powerful voice shows her years as a gospel singer, but it also reflects her innate emotional capacity and her love of great jazz performers like Sarah Vaughan and Nancy Wilson.

DECEMBER 21

1901: Blues vocalist and pianist Peetie Wheatstraw, billed as the Devil's Son-in-Law and the High Sheriff from Hell, is born William Bunch in Ripley, Tennessee.

Wheatstraw had a knack for writing and recording devilish and erotic blues songs. He recorded over 150 sides between 1930 and 1941. Many of them had the same tune, but his lyrics were always interesting. Some of his best-known songs were "The Devil's Son-in-Law," "Suicide Blues," "Doin' the Best I Can" and "Banana Man."

Peetie Wheatstraw was at the peak of his popularity in December 1941, when his car was hit by a train at a railroad crossing in East St. Louis, Illinois. He was killed instantly.

1942: Singer Carla Thomas, daughter of Rufus Thomas, is born in Memphis.

During the 1960s Carla Thomas was Stax Records' number 1 female vocalist. Her biggest hits include "Gee Whiz" (1961), "I'll Bring It Home to You" (1962), "I've Got No Time to Lose" (1964), "B-A-B-Y" (1966) and "I Like What You're Doing to Me" (1969).

In 1967 she teamed up with Otis Redding to record the best-selling LP *King and Queen*. From that LP came a trio of hit singles: "Tramp," "Knock on Wood" and "Lovey Dovey."

Carla Thomas remained with Stax Records until the company folded, in 1976.

1943: Singer Gwen McCrae is born in Pensacola, Florida.

McCrae had a number 1 soul and disco hit in 1975 with the tune "Rockin' Chair." Her other hits include "For Your Love" (1973), "Love Insurance" (1975) and "Funky Sensation" (1981).

She married singer George McCrae, who later became her manager.

1953: Singer Betty Wright is born in Miami.

Wright started out in her family's gospel group, the Echoes of Joy. In 1971 she had a million-selling single, "The Cleanup Woman." Betty Wright's other soul chart hits include "Babysitter" (1972), "Let Me Be Your Lovemaker" (1973), "Where Is the Love" (1975), "Tonight Is the Night" (1978) and "No Pain, No Gain" (1988).

DECEMBER 22

1919: Singer Lil Green is born in Mississippi.

Green dropped out of school and became a singing waitress in clubs around Chicago. In 1940 she recorded with bluesman Big Bill Broonzy and later worked with the orchestras of Tiny Bradshaw and Luis Russell. She hit the R&B charts with songs like "Romance in the Dark" (1941), "Knockin' Myself Out" (1941), "Why Don't You Do Right" (1941), "Let's Be Friends" (1942) and "Keep Your Hands on Your Heart" (1942). Because her career was so short, she is one of the hidden treasures of 1940s R&B.

Lil Green died of pneumonia on April 14, 1954, in Chicago.

DECEMBER 23

1935: Singer Little Esther Phillips (later Esther Phillips) is born Esther Mae Jones in Galveston, Texas.

Phillips was the youngest female singer to have a number 1 hit on the R&B charts. She accomplished that feat early in 1950, with a tune called "Double-Crossing Blues."

Phillips moved to Los Angeles in 1940. There she sang in the sanctified church and in local amateur shows. In 1949 she won first place in a contest at the Barrelhouse nightclub. As a result, she joined the Johnny Otis Rhythm and Blues Caravan Show and began recording with the Otis orchestra.

Phillips had several other R&B hits in the early '50s, several recorded with the Otis band's chief male vocalist, Mel Walker: "Mistrustin' Blues" (1950), "Misery" (1950), "Cupid's Boogie" (1950), "Deceivin' Blues" (1950), "Wedding Boogie" (1950), "Faraway Blues" (1950) and "Ring-a-Ding Doo" (1952). Phillips toured with Johnny Otis until 1954. Then she moved back to Texas and did little in terms of a musical career.

In 1962 she signed with a label called Lenox Records and produced a Top 10 R&B and pop single, "Release Me." She was also battling drug addiction, which constantly interrupted her career.

Some of her later single hits were "And I Love Him" (1965), "I've Never Found a Man" (1972) and the disco-flavored "What a Difference a Day Makes" (1975). She worked both blues and jazz clubs from coast to coast and appeared on many TV shows. *Rolling Stone* magazine named her best blues singer in 1974, and she received an NAACP Image Award in 1975.

Esther Phillips died of liver and kidney failure on August 7, 1984.

1935: Alto saxophonist Frank Morgan is born in Minnesota.

Morgan's *A Lovesome Thing* was critically acclaimed as one of 1991's best jazz LPs. Other LPs include *You Must Believe in Spring*, *Bebop Lives*, *Reflections* and *Major Changes*.

Morgan is unknown to most current jazz fans because he spent most of the early '50s to the early '80s in San Quentin Prison after being convicted of drug possession.

DECEMBER 24

1954: Johnny Ace fatally shoots himself in Houston.

Ace was appearing in a big R&B show on Christmas Eve at the City Auditorium on Louisiana Street. He had just left the stage and was playing with a .22 pistol in his dressing room. Some reports say that he was playing Russian Roulette, others that he was just fooling around with the gun to impress a woman. In any case, he put a round into the chamber, spun it, pointed it at his head and pulled the trigger.

Johnny Ace died on Christmas morning in a Houston hospital.

1920: Songwriter and bandleader Dave Bartholomew is born in Edgard, Louisiana.

Bartholomew acted as producer and arranger and played trumpet on most of Fats Domino's biggest hits. He also co-wrote such Domino classics as "The Fat Man," "Ain't That a Shame," "Walkin' to New Orleans," "Let the Four Winds Blow," "I'm Walkin'," "I Wanna Walk You Home," "I'm in Love Again" and "Blue Monday." In addition he wrote Elvis Presley's hit "One Night" and produced the Lloyd Price classic "Lawdy Miss Clawdy," as well as records for Frankie Ford, Smiley Lewis, Chris Kenner and Robert Parker.

1924: Singer Lee Dorsey is born in New Orleans.

Dorsey grew up in Portland, Oregon, and in the 1950s boxed professionally under the name Kid Chocolate. He had a string of New Orleans–produced R&B and pop hits in the 1960s. The biggest were "Ya Ya" (1961), "Ride Your Pony" (1965), "Get Out of My Life, Woman" (1966), "Working in a Coal Mine" (1966) and "Holy Cow" (1966).

Lee Dorsey died of emphysema on December 1, 1986.

DECEMBER 25

1907: Cab Calloway—vocalist, bandleader, drummer, sax player and "His Hi-De-Ho-Highness of Jive"—is born Cabell Calloway in Rochester, New York.

Calloway was raised in Baltimore. Later he moved to Chicago. He began singing in a local Methodist church choir. His parents wanted him to become a lawyer, but his sister Blanche, also a performer, got him a job in a musical show, *Plantation Days*, at the Loop Theater. Calloway later worked as master of ceremonies at the Sunset Cafe and toured with Blanche.

In 1929 he took over leadership of an 11-piece band, the Alabamians. Calloway and the band moved from Chicago to New York, but their relationship was brief. Calloway joined the company of a show called *Hot Chocolates*, and in 1930 he went to the Savoy Ballroom as frontman for a band called the Missourians. In February 1931 the band was renamed the Cab Calloway Orchestra and joined Duke Ellington's group at the Cotton Club.

On March 3, 1931, Calloway recorded his signature song, "Minnie the Moocher," which became a national hit and made Calloway a hot prospect. Over the next few years the Cab Calloway Orchestra spent 40 to 50 weeks a year on the road, and Calloway's "hi-de-ho" greeting became a national catch phrase. He had such hits as "Saint James Infirmary," "You Rascal You," "Between the Devil and the Deep Blue Sea" and "The Lady with the Fan."

Calloway and his crew toured England and Europe in 1934. In the late '30s and early '40s they were constantly among the 10 highest-earning bands in the U.S. Over the years, players in Calloway's band included Jonah Jones, Dizzy Gillespie, Cozy Cole, Chu Berry and Ben Webster. In 1948 Calloway disbanded the group and began working with a sextet.

From 1952 to 1954 Calloway played the role of Sportin' Life in *Porgy and Bess*. In the mid-1960s he toured with the Harlem Globetrotters. He also spent three years in the all-black production of *Hello, Dolly*, which starred Pearl Bailey. In the '70s he was in the Broadway show *Bubblin' Brown Sugar*.

Cab Calloway has appeared in many films, including *The Big Broadcast*, *International House*, *Stormy Weather*, *St. Louis Blues* and *The Blues Brothers*. He also acted as a consultant for the 1985 film *The Cotton Club*.

1929: Singer and songwriter Chris Kenner is born in Kenner, Louisiana.

Kenner is best known for his 1961 Top 10 soul and pop hit "I Like It Like That." He was also a very successful songwriter. He wrote and recorded the original versions of such well-known

songs as "Something You Got" and "Land of 1000 Dances."

Chris Kenner died of a heart attack on January 25, 1977.

1944: Jazz pianist and organist Don Pullen is born in Roanoke, Virginia.

Pullen grew up in a musical family, surrounded by blues, gospel and R&B. In college he discovered jazz, especially the works of Ornette Coleman and Eric Dolphy. He moved to New York in the early 1960s and, after playing in club organ trios, became involved in the avant-garde jazz scene, playing with Albert Ayler and others.

He made his recording debut in 1964, with Giuseppe Logan. He also worked as half of a duo with Milford Graves. He played with Nina Simone in 1970 and 1971, briefly with Art Blakey in 1974 and with Charles Mingus from 1973 to 1975.

Pullen then teamed up with saxophonist George Adams to form the Don Pullen–George Adams Quartet. The group remained intact for 10 years and recorded 10 LPs before disbanding, at which point Pullen went solo.

Don Pullen's best LPs include *Kele Mou Bana*, *New Beginnings* and *Random Thoughts*.

DECEMBER 26

1940: Producer and songwriter Phil Spector is born in the Bronx.

Spector is generally seen as a rock 'n' roll producer. Nevertheless, apart from the "blue-eyed soul" Righteous Brothers, all of Spector's biggest acts were black. He wrote and produced all the hits by the Ronettes, the Crystals, Bob B. Soxx and the Blue Jeans and Darlene Love. Spector also coproduced Ben E. King's classic "Spanish Harlem," and that's Phil Spector laying down the "chnng-chnng" signature guitar riff on the Drifters' hit "On Broadway."

DECEMBER 27

1929: Bluesman Matt "Guitar" Murphy is born in Sunflower County, Mississippi.

Murphy began his career in Memphis and was a member of Howlin'

Wolf's band. He was also a member of the Blue Flames, which recorded for the Sun label and included Junior Parker. Murphy worked as a session man on records by Parker and Bobby "Blue" Bland. In 1991 he released his first solo LP, *Way Down South*.

DECEMBER 28

1903: Jazz pianist Earl "Fatha" Hines is born in Duquesne, Pennsylvania.

Hines grew up in Pittsburgh, where his early inspiration came from the revues written by Noble Sissle and Eubie Blake. By the age of 21 Hines was leading his own band at the Entertainers Club in Chicago. In 1927 he was musical director for Louis Armstrong's Stompers. He first recorded in 1928.

Hines invented a piano technique known as "trumpet style," based on the trumpet stylings of Louis Armstrong. In December 1928 Hines put together a big band and opened at Chicago's Grand Terrace Ballroom. The group played there for the next 10 years. At various times, sidemen in the band included Charlie Parker, Dizzy Gillespie, Ray Nance and Jonah Jones. Vocalists included Herb Jeffries, Billy Eckstine and Sarah Vaughan. Gillespie is commonly credited with founding bebop in the 1940s, but the roots of bebop can be heard a decade earlier, in the music of Earl "Fatha" Hines.

In 1942 Hines had an R&B hit with a version of "Stormy Monday Blues," with vocals by Eckstine. In 1943 the group included an all-woman string section. Hines briefly fronted Duke Ellington's band in 1944, when Ellington was ill. In 1947 Hines broke up his big band, and in 1948 he joined Louis Armstrong's All Stars. He stayed until 1951.

Hines then formed a smaller band, playing mostly in California and Europe during the late 1950s and early 1960s. He also toured Russia and Japan. In 1966 he was elected to *Down Beat* magazine's Jazz Hall of Fame.

Some record catalogues list over 50 LPs by Hines. To catch him in his prime, try *The Fatha Jumps*, *Fatha Blows Best* and *Earl Hines Plays Duke Ellington*.

EARL "FATHA" HINES

Earl "Fatha" Hines died on April 22, 1983.

1910: Singer Billy Williams is born in Waco, Texas.

From 1930 to 1950 Williams was lead singer for the Charioteers, who were regulars on the "Kraft Music Hall" radio program with Bing Crosby and had the 1949 R&B hit "A Kiss and a Rose." In 1950 Williams formed his own quartet and was a semiregular on the 1950s TV variety series "Your Show of Shows," which starred Sid Caesar. Williams had a monster R&B and pop single in 1957, "I'm Gonna Sit Right Down and Write Myself a Letter."

In the early 1960s, because of complications from diabetes, Williams lost his voice. He settled in Chicago and was active as a social worker for the rest of his life.

Billy Williams died on October 17, 1972.

1915: Singer and guitarist Roebuck "Pop" Staples is born in Winona, Mississippi.

Staples became a blues guitarist while he was still a teenager. In 1935 he joined the gospel group the Golden Trumpets. He moved to Chicago in 1936 and played for five years with the gospel group the Trumpet Jubilees.

In 1951 he formed the Staple Singers, composed of himself, his son Pervis and his daughters Yvonne, Cleotha and Mavis. In 1956 the Staple

Singers had a huge gospel hit with "Uncloudy Day."

The Staple Singers signed with Stax Records in 1968, and in 1970 they began a run of soul and pop single hits, including "Heavy Makes You Happy" (1970), "Respect Yourself" (1971), "I'll Take You There" (1972), "This World" (1972), "If You're Ready" (1973), "Touch a Hand, Make a Friend" (1974), "City in the Sky" (1974) and "Let's Do It Again" (1975). On most of their hits Mavis Staples handled the lead vocals. Pervis Staples left the group in 1971.

1921: Vocalist, songwriter, talent scout, record producer, nightclub owner and stage-show producer Johnny Otis is born John Veliotes in Vallejo, California.

Otis began his career playing piano, drums and vibes in Harlan Leonard's band. In 1945 he formed his own band, and in 1948 he opened the Barrelhouse nightclub in Los Angeles. Amateur night at the Barrelhouse provided a showcase for much young talent.

Otis also worked as a talent scout for King Records. He is credited with discovering such top R&B talent as Etta James, T-Bone Walker, Charles Brown, Lowell Fulson, the Robins, Little Esther Phillips, Jackie Wilson, Little Willie John, Big Mama Thornton and Hank Ballard.

Otis's band was basically the house band for Don Robey's Duke and Peacock labels in their early days. He took the band and the newly discovered talent on the road, in a show called *The Johnny Otis Rhythm and Blues Caravan*.

In the early 1950s Otis and his band had a string of R&B hits featuring vocals by Phillips and Walker. These included "Double-Crossing Blues" (1950), "Dreamin' Blues" (1950), "Faraway Blues" (1950), "Rockin' Blues" (1950), "Gee Baby" (1951), "All Night Long" (1951), "Sunset to Dawn" (1952) and "Call Operator 210" (1952). In 1957 Johnny Otis hit the Top 10 on both the R&B and pop charts, with a serious rocker called "Willie and the Hand Jive."

DECEMBER 29

1962: The Supremes—Diana Ross, Mary Wilson and Florence Ballard—make their chart debut with "Let Me Go the Right Way."

While still in high school, the Supremes were called the Primettes and were a sister act to a male group called the Primes (later known as the Temptations). On January 15, 1961, the group had been signed to Motown Records and renamed the Supremes. Their first two records (the other was "When the Love Light Starts Shining Through His Eyes," in 1963) barely made the pop charts and never hit the Top 20 on the R&B charts.

In 1964, working with the writer-producer team of Holland-Dozier-Holland, the Supremes caught fire. They scored 10 number 1 hits and appeared on "The Ed Sullivan Show" 20 times. Their biggest hits of the period included "Where Did Our Love Go" (1964), "Baby Love" (1964), "Come See About Me" (1965), "Stop in the Name of Love" (1965), "Back in My Arms Again" (1965), "Nothing But Heartaches" (1965), "I Hear a Symphony" (1965), "My World Is Empty Without You" (1966), "Love Is Like an Itching in My Heart" (1966), "You Can't Hurry Love" (1966), "You Keep Me Hanging On" (1966) and "Love Is Here and Now You're Gone" (1967).

In 1967 the Supremes underwent changes. Several books have indicated that all was not always love and kisses among Ross, Wilson and Ballard. The group's name officially became Diana Ross and the Supremes, and Florence Ballard left. She was replaced by Cindy Birdsong, formerly of Patti Labelle and the Blue Belles. They continued to hit the top of the charts, with tunes like "Reflections" (1967), "Love Child" (1968), "I'm Living in Shame" (1969) and "Someday We'll Be Together" (1969).

Diana Ross went solo in 1969 and was replaced by Jean Terrell. The Supremes, without Ross, continued to have a measure of recording success. Their later hits included "Up the Ladder to the Roof" (1970), "Stoned Love" (1970), "Nathan Jones" (1971) and "Floy Joy" (1972). The group continued into the late 1970s with a varying membership, including Lynda Lawrence,

Scherrie Payne and Susaye Green. Florence Ballard died of a heart attack on February 22, 1976.

DECEMBER 30

1928: BoDiddley is born Otha Ellas Bates McDaniels in McComb, Mississippi.

BoDiddley got his nickname as a mischievous child. He moved to Chicago in 1934, where he studied violin and played in a Baptist church orchestra. He taught himself to play guitar and as a teenager formed his first band, the Langley Avenue Jive Cats. In the late 1940s and early 1950s BoDiddley played parties and clubs around Chicago. He was also a boxer.

In 1954 he signed with Chess-Checker Records. In 1955 he hit the number 1 spot on the R&B charts with his classic "BoDiddley." He followed it up with such hits as "Diddley Daddy" (1955), "I'm a Man" (1955), "Bring It to Jerome" (1955), "Pretty Thing" (1955), "Who Do You Love" (1956), "Hey BoDiddley" (1957), "Say Man" (1959), "You Can't Judge a Book by the Cover" (1962) and "BoDiddley Is a Gunslinger" (1963).

BoDiddley also became a top concert attraction. He was backed by a band that featured his half-sister, the Duchess, on guitar and included bassist Jerome Green. He appeared on "The Ed Sullivan Show," played the black theater circuit and toured with Alan Freed's rock 'n' roll show. BoDiddley has also appeared in the films *The TNT Show* and *Let the Good Times Roll*.

1950: The Five Blind Boys of Mississippi hit the R&B charts, with "Our Father." The song went to number 10.

The group came out of the Piney Woods School for the Blind, near Jackson, Mississippi. It featured lead singer Archie Brownlee, the greatest of the gospel screamers. The other four members were Lloyd Woodard, Joseph Ford, Isaiah Patterson and Lawrence Abrams.

The five began performing in 1944, as the Jackson Harmoneers. By 1946 the group consisted of Brownlee, Abrams, Woodard, Percell Perkins and J. T. Clinkscales. In 1946 they began recording for the Excelsior label and changed their name.

The Five Blind Boys of Mississippi signed with Peacock Records in 1950. They remained with Peacock until the 1960s, recording 27 singles and five LPs for the label. They were one of gospel music's top attractions.

On February 8, 1960, Archie Brownlee died of pneumonia. He was replaced by Roscoe Robinson. Lloyd Woodard died in the 1970s. Lawrence Abrams died in 1982. The group is not to be confused with the Five Blind Boys of Alabama, which featured lead singer Clarence Fountain, a gospel group formed in the mid-1940s at the Talladyce Institute for the Deaf and Blind, by Velma Taylor.

DECEMBER 31

1908: Jazz trumpeter Jonah Jones is born in Louisville.

Jones's career began in the 1920s. He played in the bands of Horace Henderson, Jimmie Lunceford, Lil Armstrong, Stuff Smith, Benny Carter and Fletcher Henderson.

Jones was a great showman and a great trumpet player. He was with the Cab Calloway Orchestra from 1941 to 1952.

In the 1950s and 1960s he had such hit LPs as *Muted Jazz*, *I Dig Chicks*, *Jumpin' with Jonah* and *Jonah Jones at the Embers*. On most of his LPs he both sang and played trumpet.

1930: Folksinger Odetta is born in Birmingham, Alabama.

Odetta began her career on the West Coast in the late 1940s. In the early 1950s she performed at San Francisco's "hungry i" nightclub. In the late '50s she worked the coffeehouse circuit and played the Newport Folk Festival.

Odetta has appeared on numerous TV shows, including dramas, variety and talk shows. She also had a part in the TV movie *The Autobiography of Miss Jane Pittman*. Other film credits include *The Last Time I Saw Paris* and *Sanctuary*.

Odetta's best LPs are *Movin' It On*, *The Essential Odetta* and *Odetta and the Blues*.

ODETTA

1948: Singer Donna Summer, the queen of disco and the only superstar of the genre, is born Adrian Donna Gaines in Boston.

Summer dropped out of high school to join a band that played small clubs around Boston. After moving to New York, she got a part in an overseas production of *Hair* and moved to Germany. She had roles in several more musical productions and then began recording with producer and writer Giorgio Moroder.

Starting in 1975, with her erotic ballad "Love to Love You, Baby," Summer kept the disco floors hopping with such million-selling hits as "Last Dance," "Macarthur Park," "Heaven Knows," "Hot Stuff," "Bad Girls" and "Dim All the Lights." Initially released in Europe, "Love to Love You, Baby" was picked up by a U.S. record company, which led to long-term contracts with Casablanca Records for both Summer and Moroder.

Anderson, Robert, and Gail North. *Gospel Music Encyclopedia*. New York: Sterling, 1979.

Aylesworth, Thomas G., and John S. Bowman. *The World Almanac Who's Who of Film*. New York: World Almanac, 1987.

Bergman, Billy. *Hot Sauces*. Dorset, England: Blandford Press, 1985.

Bird, Christiane. *The Jazz and Blues Lovers Guide to the U.S.* Reading, Mass.: Addison-Wesley, 1991.

Brooks, Tim, and Earle Marsh. *The Complete Directory of Prime Time Network TV Shows 1946–Present*. New York: Ballantine Books, 1979.

Brown, James, and Bruce Tucker. *James Brown, The Godfather of Soul*. New York: Macmillan, 1986.

Carr, Ian, Digby Fairweather, and Brian Priestly. *Jazz: The Essential Companion*. New York: Prentice-Hall, 1988.

Case, Brian, and Stan Britt. *The Harmony Illustrated Encyclopedia of Jazz*. New York: Harmony Books, 1986.

The Celebrity Who's Who. New York: World Almanac, 1986.

Chilton, John. *Who's Who of Jazz*. Philadelphia, Pa.: Chilton Book Company, 1978.

Clifford, Mike. *The Harmony Illustrated Encyclopedia of Rock*. New York: Harmony Books, 1988.

Dixon, Willie, and Don Snowden. *I Am the Blues*. New York: Da Capo Press, 1989.

Fox, Ted. *Showtime at the Apollo*. New York: Holt, Rinehart & Winston, 1983.

Foxx, Redd, and Norma Miller. *The Redd Foxx Encyclopedia of Black Humor*. Pasadena, Calif.: Ward Ritchie Press, 1977.

Govenar, Alan. *Meeting the Blues*. Dallas: Taylor, 1988.

Gregory, Hugh. *Soul Music A–Z*. London: Blandford Press, 1991.

Gribin, Anthony J., and Matthew M. Schiff. *Doo Wop*. Iola, Wisc.: Krause Publishers, 1992.

Hager, Steven. *Hip Hop*. New York: St. Martin's Press, 1984.

Hannusch, Jeff. *I Hear You Knockin'*. Ville Platte, La.: Swallow Publishers, 1985.

Harris, Sheldon. *Blues Who's Who*. New York: Da Capo Press, 1979.

Harris, Steve. *Jazz on Compact Discs*. New York: Harmony Books, 1987.

Haskins, Jim. *The Cotton Club*. New York: Random House, 1977.

Hayes, Cedric J. *A Discography of Gospel Records 1937–1971*. Denmark: Karl Emil Knudsen Publishers, 1973.

Heilbut, Anthony. *The Gospel Sound*. New York: Limelight Editions, 1985.

Herzhaft, Gerard. *Encyclopedia of the Blues*. Fayetteville: University of Arkansas Press, 1992.

James Brown—Star Time Booklet. Polygram Records, 1991.

Larson, Rebecca. *Paul Robeson: Hero Before His Time*. New York: F. W. Watts, 1989.

Mansfield, Cary E., and Patti Drosins. *Hitsville USA: Motown 1959–1971*. Los Angeles: Motown Record Corporation, 1992.

Marsh, Dave. *The Heart of Rock and Soul*. Markham, Ontario: Penguin Books Canada, 1989.

Muirhead, Bert. *The Record Producers File*. Dorset, England: Blandford Press, 1984.

Nelson, Havelock, and Michael A. Gonzalez. *Bring the Noise*. New York: Harmony Books, 1991.

Nite, Norm N. *Rock On*. New York: Thomas Y. Crowell Company, 1974.

Nite, Norm N. *Rock On Volume II*. New York: Thomas Y. Crowell Company, 1978.

Palmer, Robert. *Deep Blues*. New York: Penguin Books, 1981.

Pavlow, Big Al. *The R&B Book*. Providence, R.I.: Music House Publishers, 1983.

Poling, James. *Esquire's World of Jazz*. New York: Esquire, 1962.

Pruter, Robert. *Chicago Soul*. Chicago: University of Illinois Press, 1992.

Roxon, Lillian. *Lillian Roxon's Rock Encyclopedia*. New York: Workman, 1969.

Sales, Grover. *Jazz—America's Classical Music*. New York: Prentice-Hall, 1984.

Scott, Frank. *The Downhome Guide to the Blues*. Pennington, N.J.: A Cappella Press, 1991.

Shaw, Arnold. *Honkers and Shouters*. New York: Collier Books, 1978.

Shipton, Alyn. *Life and Times of Fats Waller*. New York: Universe Books, 1988.

Singleton, Raymona Gordy. *Berry, Me and Motown*. Chicago: Contemporary Books, 1990.

Tosches, Nick. *Unsung Heroes of Rock 'N' Roll*. New York: Harmony Books, 1984.

Truitt, Evelyn M. *Who Was Who on Screen*. New York: R. R. Bowker Company, 1984.

Turner, Tina, and Kurt Loder. *I, Tina*. New York: Avon Books, 1986.

Walker, Leo. *The Big Band Almanac*. New York: Da Capo Press, 1978.

Warner, Jay. *The Billboard Book of American Singing Groups*. New York: Billboard Books, 1992.

Whitburn, Joel. *Billboard Book of Top 40 Albums*. New York: Billboard Publications, 1987.

Whitburn, Joel. *Top Country Singles 1944–1988*. Menomonee Falls, Wisc.: Record Research, 1989.

Whitburn, Joel. *Top Pop Singles 1955–1990*. Menomonee Falls, Wisc.: Record Research, 1991.

Whitburn, Joel. *Top R&B Singles 1942–1988*. Menomonee Falls, Wisc.: Record Research, 1988.

White, Adam. *The Billboard Book of Gold and Platinum Records*. New York: Billboard Books, 1990.

White, Charles. *The Life and Times of Little Richard*. New York: Pocket Books, 1984.

Davis, Clarence, 136
Davis, Clifton, **119**
Davis, Clive, 42
Davis, Eddie "Lockjaw," **32,** 88, 142
Davis, Hugh, 129
Davis, James B., 112
Davis, John, 144
Davis, Kay, 57
Davis, Marlena, 78
Davis, Martha, **147**
Davis, Miles, 6, 12, 17, 20, 31, 36, 54, 58, 60, 64, **67,** 74, 84, 86, 93, 99, 101, 103, 105, 106, 109, **116,** *116,* 122, 129, 142, 149
Davis, Rev. Gary, **57**
Davis, Sammy, Jr., 16, 97, 98, 132, **144,** *144,* 148
Davis, Steve, 113
Davis, Theresa, 79
Davis, Thomas Maxwell, **9**
Davis, Tyrone, **60**
Dawkins, Jimmy "Fast Fingers," 97, **127,** 135
Day, Morris, 72, **96**
Deacons, 82
DeBarge, 71
DeBarge, Bobby, 71
DeBarge, Bunny, 71
DeBarge, Chico, 71
DeBarge, Eldra "El," **71**
DeBarge, James, 71
DeBarge, Mark, 71
DeBarge, Randy, 71
Dee, Kool Moe (Mohandas DeWese), 61, **133**
Dee, Mercy. *See* Walton, Mercy Dee
Deele, 95
DeFranco, Buddy, 122
DeJohnette, Jack, **93**
DeKnight, Rene, 15
Delegates, 133
Delite, Derrick, 31
Dells, **133–34**
Dell Vikings, **38,** 87
Del-Phis, 87
Delphonics, 10, 41
Delta Big Four, 98
Delta Rhythm Boys, **15,** 72
Demps, Larry, 62
Denby, Al, 103
Denby, Junior, 92
Dennis, Bernardo, 81
Denton, Sandy "Pepa," 41
DeSanto, Sugar Pie (Marsema Umpeylia Balinton), **124,** 128
Detroit Junior (Emery Williams, Jr.), **128**
Detroit Red. *See* Perryman, Rufus "Speckled Red"
DeVoe, Ronald, 21
Dewalt, Autry, II. *See* Walker, Junior
Diana Ross and the Supremes. *See* Supremes
Dickey, Gwen, 121
Dillard, Moses, 52
Dillard, Varetta, 20, 73
Dinwiddie Quartet, **129**
Dixie Cups, **75,** *75*
Dixie Hummingbirds, **112**
Dixie Nightingales, 10
Dixie Stompers, 17
Dixie Syncopators, 62
Dixon, Eugene. *See* Chandler, Gene
Dixon, Floyd, **23**
Dixon, Heather, 103
Dixon, Henry, 116
Dixon, Willie, **17,** 48, **81,** 104, 116, 119, 135
Dizzy Gillespie's Revival Big Band, 15
D.J. Jazzy Jeff (Jeff Towners), **66**
DMC (Darryl McDaniels), **66**
Doctor Feelgood, 127
Dodds, Baby, 125
Dodds, Charles, 62
Dodds, Johnny, 125
Doggett, William Ballard, 12, **27,** 93, 126, 147
Dolphy, Eric Allen, 7, 60, **76–77,** *77,* 152

Domino, Antoine "Fats," **3,** 9, 17, 24, **30,** *30,* 82, 149, 151
Dominoes. *See* Billy Ward and the Dominoes
Donald, Leo Edward. *See* Darnell, Larry
Donaldson, Lou, **132**
Don and Dewey, 76
Don Ellis Big Band, 8
Don Pullen–George Adams Quartet, 152
Don Redman Orchestra, 141
Dorham, Kenny, 54, 122
Dorsey, Clarence, 69
Dorsey, Georgia Tom, 147
Dorsey, Lee, 9, **151**
Dorsey, Rev. Thomas A., 11, 17, 76, **81,** 128, 137
Dorsey, Tommy, 61, 92, 141, 148
Dorsey Brothers, 130
Douglas, Carl, **144**
Douglas, Lizzie. *See* Memphis Minnie
Douglas, Tommy, 101
Doulphin, Edward, 24
Dow, Gary, 127
Downing, Big Al, **6**
Doyle, Daniel, 56
Dozier, Lamont, **75,** 129
Drake, Laverne, 132
Dramatics, **62**
Drayton, William. *See* Flavor-Flav
Dr. Dre, 91
Drifters, 5, 73, 111, 115, **130–31,** *130,* 135, 136, 146, 152
Drinkard Singers, 146
Dr. John, 149
Duchess, 154
Duhe, Lawrence, 62
Dukays, 83
Duke, George, **8,** 35, 64, 80, 147, 150
Duke, Robin, 47
Duke Ellington and His Washingtonians, 56
Duke Ellington Orchestra, **26–27,** 35, 57
Dunbar, Sly, 125
Duncan, Adolph, 73
Duncan, Cleve, **88**
Dunn, Donald "Duck," 134
Dunn, Freddie, 121
Dunn, James, 41
Dunn, Larry, 150
Duponts, 6
Dupree, William Thomas "Champion Jack," **83,** 127, 149
Duran Duran, 76
Durham, Eddie, 71
Dylan, Bob, 134
Dyson, Ronnie, **71**

Eager, Brenda Lee, 144
Eaglin, Snooks, **11**
Earle, Diane. *See* Ross, Diana
Early, Delloreese Patricia. *See* Reese, Della
Earth, Wind and Fire, 62, 79, 119, **149–50**
"Easier Said Than Done," by the Essex, **87**
Easton, Amos. *See* Bumble Bee Slim
Easton, Sheena, 72, 95
Eaton, Cleveland, 68
Echoes of Joy, 151
Echols, Charlie, 134
Eckstine, William Clarence "Billy," 6, 19, 31, 43, 52, 67, **84,** 101, 122, 126, 132, 152
Eclipse, 44
Eddie Cole's Solid Swingers, 38
Eddie Heywood Sextet, 142
Eddie Randall's Blue Devils, 67
Eddie Williams and the Brown Buddies, 23, 29
Edison, Harry "Sweets," 98, **121**
Edmonds, Kenneth. *See* Baby Face
Edwards and Edwards, 87
Edwards, Bernard, 112
Edwards, David "Honey Boy," **79**
Edwards, Dennis, 20, 63, 129

Edwards, Jody. *See* Butter Beans
Edwards, Raymond, 34
Edwards, Robert "Big Sonny," 84
Edwards, Susie, 87
Edwards, Tommy, **27**
Edwards, William, 82
Ekaya, 120
Eldridge, Roy, 5, 6, **17,** 30, 116, 118, 126
Electric Flag, 104
Eleventh Hour, 138
Ellington, Edward Kennedy "Duke," 23, 26, 35, 54, 55, **56–57,** *57,* 61, 64, 85, 88, 93, 96, 112, 115, 116, 118, 120, 126, 130, 135, 136, 138, 140, 142, 145, 147, 148, 152
Ellington, Mercer, **35,** 49
Ellis, Herb, 95
Elmer Payne and His Ten Royal Americans, 98
El Rays. *See* Dells
Emotions, **79,** 150
Enchanters, 72
Eric Burdon and the Animals, 24, 99
Errico, Gregg, 37
Erskine Hawkins Orchestra, 88
Ervin, Frankie, 29
Escovedo, Pete, 146
Escovedo, Sheila. *See* Sheila E.
Esquires Combo, 69
Essex, **87**
Estes, Sleepy John, 12, **14–15,** 38, 44, 86
E.U. (Experience Unlimited), 148
Evans, Ernest. *See* Checker, Chubby
Evans, Herschel, 84
Evening Stars, 136
Everett, Betty, **138,** 144
Every Hour Blues Boys, 104

Fair, Yvonne, 121, 128
Fairfax, Frank, 126
Fairfield Four, 66, 98
Faith, Hope & Charity, 3
Fakir, Duke, 96
Falcons, 30, 39, 78
Falls, Mildred, 128
Fambrough, Henry, 47
Fame, Georgie, 110
Famous Flames, 21, 59, 96, 128
Farian, Frank, 144
Farley, Jesse, 20
Farmer, Art, 10, 15, 51, **98,** 103, 145
Feaster, Carl, 82
Feaster, Claude, 82
Felder, Ray, 21
Felder, Wilton, 19, **102**
Ferguson, Johnny, 56
Ferguson, Maynard, 75
Fields, Ernie, 118
Fields, Frank, 3
Fields, Vanetta, 8
Fifth Dimension, **59,** *59*
Finch, Richard, 76
Fisher, Carl, 36
Fitzgerald, Ella, 6, 17, **54–55,** *55,* 84, 98, 123, 126, 128, 133, 142, 148
Five Blind Boys, 66
Five Blind Boys of Alabama, 154
Five Blind Boys of Mississippi, **154**
Five Breezes, 81
Five Crowns, 115, 130
Five Gospel Harmonaires, 48
Five Keys, 18, **97**
Five Royales, **14,** 137
Five Satins, **103**
Flack, Roberta, 9, **24,** 25, 52, 118, 138
Flamingos, 11, **28**
Flavor-Flav (William Drayton), 22
Fletcher, Dusty, 136, 147
Floyd, Eddie, 44, **78–79,** 106, 134
Floyd, Laverne, 134
Fly Cats, 135
Flyte Time, 96
Ford, Frankie, 151
Ford, Joseph, 154
Ford, Willie, 62
Forest, Earl, 73
Foster, Frank, 98

Foster, Paul, 20
Fountain, Clarence, 154
Four Arms. *See* Four Tops
Four Boys and a Kazoo. *See* Mills Brothers
Four Gents, 10
Four Jumps of Jive, 81
Four Keys, 55
Four Mitchells, 67
Four Pennies, 53
Four Tops, 75, **96,** *96,* 111
Fowler, Billy, 93
Foxx, Charlie, 107
Foxx, Inez, **107**
Francis, Connie, 97
Frankie Lymon and the Teenagers, 117
Franklin, Aretha, 5, 10, 12, 17, 22, 32, **42,** *42,* 53, 105, 106, 118, 143
Franklin, Elmer, 119
Franklin, Ermant, Jr., 119
Franklin, Melvin, 63
Franklin, Rev. C. L. (Clarence Le Vaughn Franklin), **12,** 42, 143
Freddie Keppard's Original Creole Orchestra, 20
Freddy, Fab Five, 91
Fredericks, Henry Saint Claire. *See* Taj Mahal
Freed, Alan, 22, 78, 84, 89, 128, 148, 154
Freeman, Bobby, 37, **75**
Freeman, Ernie, **96–97**
Freeman, Jim, 103
Fresh Prince (Will Smith), **66**
Frierson, Reyvolda. *See* Lester, Ketty
Frost, Frank, **52**
Fuller, Blind Boy, 57, 127
Fuller, Johnny, **53,** 73
Full Gospel Tabernacle, 51
Fulsom, Lowell. *See* Fulson, Lowell
Fulson, Lowell, 9, 24, **45,** 95, 106, 114, 153
Funches, Johnny, 133, 134
Funkadelic, 47, 87, 88, 129, **132**
Fuqua, Charlie, 127
Fuqua, Harvey, 25, 46, **88,** 89
Furious Five, 3, 61
Futuretimes, 12

Gaillard, Slim (Bulee Gaillard), **3–4,** 112
Gaines, Adrian Donna. *See* Summer, Donna
Gaines, Charlie, 84
Gaines, Grady, **64**
Gaines, Otha Lee, 15
Gaines, Walter, 116
Gainey, Earl, 56
Galloway, Charlie, 105
Galloway, William, 99
Gamble, Kenny, 39, 84, 91, 107
Gant, Cecil, **47**
Gap Band, **35–36**
Gardner, Carl, 45
Gardner, Dan, 144
Garfunkel, Art, 148
Garland, Hank, 41
Garland, Red, 67
Garner, Erroll, **3,** 34, **75,** 122
Garner, Henry, 121
Garnes, Sherman, 117
Garnet Minns and the Enchanters, 136
Gary Kings, 50
Gaston, Henry, 56
Gathers, Helen, 103
Gaye, Marvin, 38, 42, **46–47,** *47,* 60, 89, 105, 116, **137,** 147
Gaynor, Gloria, **105–6**
Gayten, Paul, **17**
George, Barbara, **97**
George, Langston, 68
Georgia Bill. *See* McTell, Blind Willie
Georgia Tom. *See* Dorsey, Rev. Thomas A.
Gerry Mulligan Quartet, 112
Gershwin, George, 55
Getz, Stan, 36, 54, 74, 80, 103, 126
Giants of Jazz, 121, 122
Gibson, Mel, 139
Gilbeau, Phil, 69